Battles of the Red River War

Battles of the RED RIVER WAR

ARCHEOLOGICAL PERSPECTIVES ON THE INDIAN CAMPAIGN OF 1874

J. Brett Cruse

With Contributions by
Martha Doty Freeman and Douglas D. Scott

Foreword by
Robert M. Utley

TEXAS A&M UNIVERSITY PRESS *College Station*

Second printing, 2017

This paper meets the requirements of ANSI/NISO Z39.48-1992
(Permanence of Paper).
Manufactured in China
♾

Unless noted otherwise, photos and illustrations are courtesy of the Texas Historical Commission. The material in this book is based upon work assisted in part by a grant from the Department of the Interior, National Park Service. Any opinions, findings, and conclusions or recommendations expressed in this material are those of the authors and do not necessarily reflect the views of the Department of the Interior.

Library of Congress Cataloging-in-Publication Data

Cruse, J. Brett, 1960–
Battles of the Red River War : archeological perspectives on the Indian campaign of 1874 / J. Brett Cruse ; with contributions by Martha Doty Freeman and Douglas D. Scott ; foreword by Robert M. Utley.—1st ed.
p. cm.
Includes bibliographical references and index.
ISBN-13: 978-1-60344-027-1 (cloth : alk. paper)
ISBN-10: 1-60344-027-5 (cloth : alk. paper)
ISBN-13: 978-1-62349-152-9 (flex)
1. Red River War, 1874–1875. 2. Indians of North America—Southern Plains—Antiquities. 3. Excavations (Archaeology)—Red River Valley (Tex.–La.) 4. Excavations (Archaeology)—Texas—Palo Duro Canyon. 5. Red River Valley (Tex.–La.)—Antiquities. 6. Palo Duro Canyon (Tex.)—Antiquities. 7. Southern Plains—Antiquities. I. Title.
E83.875.C78 2008
976.4'21—dc22

2007039365

Contents

List of Illustrations

Figure

List of Tables

Table

Foreword

Robert M. Utley

The cause of history is rarely better served than by the union of historian and historical archeologist. Historians mine documentary archives. Archeologists mine outdoor archives—the tangible remains in the earth that complement the documentary record. Archeological findings can add missing content to the documents, confirm or dispute them, clarify obscurities, tell their own story. Documents can give critical meaning to archeological remains, help identify specimens, account for their distribution, and give directions to the sites themselves.

So fruitful is the collaboration of the two disciplines that it ought to happen far more than it does. J. Brett Cruse's *Battles of the Red River War: Archeological Perspectives on the Indian Campaign of 1874* is an extraordinary demonstration of the process and value of such collaboration. It is also the best model I have seen for the harmonious and productive cooperation of experts in the two disciplines. The Texas Historical Commission has performed a notable service in bringing it to print.

The Red River War of 1874–75, which ranged across western Oklahoma into the Texas Panhandle, was a landmark event in relations between the United States and the Indian tribes of the Southern Plains—Kiowa, Comanche, Cheyenne, and Arapaho. Modern generations more attuned to Indians as victims than as barriers to the westward movement of whites have judged the war harshly. Whatever the moral dimension, however, the Red River War ended for all time hostilities with these tribes and confined them to reservations. No longer would Kansas settlers live in terror of lethal raids. For the first time in half a century, the Texas frontier would no longer endure the ravages of Comanche war parties sweeping south into Mexico. However historians and the public care to judge the Indian wars of the West in general and the Red River War in particular, an accurate rendition of what actually happened on the ground is a crucial element of history and part of the basis for informed conclusions.

As a historian and veteran of archival research myself, I was stunned by the archival quest of historian Martha Doty Freeman. An abundance of official documents had been available on microfilm long before this project was conceived. Historians had tended to regard this compilation as nearly complete. Skeptical, Martha Freeman hit the National Archives in Washington with determination, persistence, an understanding of both military structure and archival filing systems, a growing knowledge of where documents should be and where more might be found, and a keen instinct for unlikely places where relevant documents might have come to rest. Her achievement brought to the fieldwork a treasure of documentary sources and a personal knowledge of events that contributed enormously to the success of the project.

J. Brett Cruse brought to the fieldwork distinguished professionalism, commitment to the potential of archival and archeological collaboration, experience in the methods of excavation and survey, powers of deduction from the documentary and archeological record, management skills in mobilizing and directing volunteer fieldworkers, and persistence in the face of funding challenges. Despite the refusal of some landowners to grant access, he probed the major battle sites and added greatly to the overall record of the war.

In this book Cruse sets forth the history and findings of the project. The detailed account of how historical and archeological specialists worked together, year by year, and site by site, is a valuable blueprint for others contemplating such a union of disciplines. Recovered artifact collections consisted largely of expended cartridges and fired bullets. With these finds plotted on maps, battle lines could be visualized in terms described in the documents. In at least one important instance, fighting did not occur where historians had always assumed but at another site, identified by substantial remains.

The technology of firearms and ammunition identification has now reached a level of sophistication that permits an expended bullet to be matched with the particular weapon that fired it. This analysis was performed by Douglas D. Scott of the National Park Service's Midwest Archeological Center, whose proficiency grew out of similar archeological work at the Little Bighorn Battlefield in the 1980s. One conclusion drawn from his work on the Red River War specimens is that the Indians possessed fewer modern firearms than previously believed.

The results of the Red River War project are twofold. First, we now know much more about the major battles of the war than before, and thus more about the war itself. Second, we have a splendid model for demonstrating and charting the course of collaboration between historians and historical archeologists.

Those are results well worth the money and effort. All involved, including the leadership of the Texas Historical Commission, deserve the plaudits of the professions that deal with the past and the interested public as well.

■ Acknowledgments

The successful completion of this project involved many individuals, most of whom gave their time, resources, and knowledge without thought of any compensation. To everyone who participated I owe a debt of gratitude that I can never fully repay. I wish to thank everyone who has helped with the project, and I apologize if I inadvertently overlooked anyone.

When the concept for the Red River War Battle Sites Project was being developed in 1997, the late Curtis Tunnell, then executive director of the Texas Historical Commission (THC), was very supportive and gave me the necessary flexibility to rearrange my schedule and work priorities so that I could direct the overall project. Current executive director Larry Oaks has been just as supportive, as have the commissioners of the THC. Other personnel at the THC who assisted with various phases of the project include Jim Bruseth, Patricia Mercado-Allinger, and Dan Potter. Maureen Brown and Pam Folds cleaned and sorted the artifacts, and Roland Pantermuehl created most of the graphic illustrations.

Funding for the project came from the generosity of Harold and Joyce Courson, the American Battlefields Protection Program of the National Park Service, the Abell-Hanger Foundation, the Amarillo Area Foundation, the David and Nona Payne Foundation, the C. J. and Syble Fowlston Trust, the Summerlee Foundation, the M. K. Brown Foundation, the Amos N. Molyneaux Trust, the Josephine Anderson Trust, the Summerfield G. Roberts Foundation, and the Helen Irwin Littauer Educational Trust. To each of these individuals and institutions I offer my sincerest thanks and gratitude for your generous support.

Several individuals deserve recognition for their expertise, generosity, and persuasive encouragement in various phases of the project. First among these is Neil Mangum, former superintendent of the Little Bighorn Battlefield National Monument, for being the driving force that got the project off the ground. His enthusiastic interest in the Indian wars of the West and dogged persuasion to have the Red River War battle sites investigated were the catalysts that convinced the THC to undertake the project. Douglas D. Scott of the Midwestern Archeological Center conducted the firearms analysis of the recovered cartridges and bullets from the various battle sites and also provided expertise in identifying other recovered artifacts. Jay Blaine shared his incredible knowledge of metal artifacts and assisted with the identification of some of the recovered items. David Jackson also assisted with the identification of some of the firearms-related artifacts. Bob Rea, archeologist with Fort Supply Historic Site, freely shared his knowledge of the Southern Plains Indian wars, assisted with the fieldwork, and provided information on important documents and archival resources. Kent Hicks, regional archeologist with the Texas Parks and Wildlife Department, and Mike Lloyd, former resource manager at Palo Duro Canyon State Park, provided logistical support and assisted with the fieldwork at the Battle of Palo Duro Canyon site in Palo Duro Canyon State Park. John Sipes freely shared his amazing knowledge of the Southern Cheyenne and the other Native American tribes that participated in the war. J. C. Fowler of Silverton, Texas, allowed me the opportunity to examine and catalog his collections from the Battle of Red River site. Paul Long provided information about

Maj. William R. Price and the 8th Cavalry. Jack Melton assisted with the identification of the Hotchkiss artillery shell fragments.

The property owners of the various sites and their families were very cooperative and hospitable to us during the months that we were in the field, even though we were a constant imposition on them. These kind folks include Hugh Bailey, John Lee Bell, Anna Brown, Craig Cobb, Billy and Rank Cogdell, Charles Crownover, Toney and Francis Dickey, Andrew Eubank, Billy Finsterwald, Billy Joe Fulton, James and Yvonne Franklin, Evelyn Harrison, Paul Hathaway, David Hefley, Jack and Bernice Hefley, Keith Horn, Thurman Horn, Verne Lohberger, Louis Mason, Kent McLaughlin, Grant Meek, Skip Morgan, Jim Nicholson, J. D. Paris, William Ridgway, Cornelia Ritchie, Nancy Shelton, Joe Shelton, Clinton and Maurita Stribling, Joe VanZandt, Glen Bill Walker, Pat Walker, Rodney Weatherly, and Harold Wilson. The project could not have been completed without the cooperation and interest shown by each of these fine people.

The project succeeded in no small part through the hard work, dedication, and cooperation of the field crew. The crew members were Lee Allen (second season), Luis Alvarado (first and second seasons), Steve Baird (first season), Alvin Lynn (first and second seasons), Randy Vance (second season), and Rusty Winn (second season). These individuals did a fantastic job under some very trying conditions. Many were the days when temperatures in the field exceeded 100 degrees, and it seemed a rattlesnake lurked behind every rock or under every bush, but these hardy individuals never complained and were always ready to check "just one more hill." It is certain that, without Alvin Lynn and his skill at figuring out just where we needed to search, the project would have been much more difficult to complete. Thank you, Alvin.

I also extend my most sincere thanks and appreciation to the individuals who volunteered to assist with the fieldwork. Each of them was enthusiastic and dedicated, and I hope they enjoyed the experience as much as I did:

Kelly Baker	Meg Indeck
Brian Barrett	Dick Irvine
James Briscoe	Richard Mackie
Vanessa Buzzard	Marvin Marshall
Linda Cecil	Stephanie Modlin
Robert Cecil	Ronald McDaniel
Shawn Coleman	Janna Montgomery
Jerry Denson	Max Montgomery
Leon Fillingim	Rolla Shaller
John Forister	Len Slesick
John Gadberry	Henry Thomason
Charles Haecker	Millie Vanover
Layne Hedrick	Bill Webb
Kent Hicks	Joe Wheeley
Bobbie Hill	Ed Wiley
Jeff Indeck	Gerald Wright

I offer a special thanks to the Panhandle-Plains Historical Museum in Canyon, Texas, for its overall support of the project and to several key personnel there for their assistance: Walt Davis, Jeff Indeck, Lisa Jackson, Rolla Shaller, and Millie Vanover all assisted with various aspects of the project—from working with us in the field, to locating and copying obscure documents from the museum's archives, to taking photographs of artifacts from the museum's collections. Also, Betty Bustos, archivist at the museum, graciously helped us find many of the photographic images that appear in this book.

I cannot express in an adequate way how grateful I am to my wife Meg for her support during this project. When the fieldwork began in April 1998, Meg was working full time, she was pregnant with our second child Samuel, and our oldest child Zachary was in kindergarten. I was in the field until October of that year and Samuel was born in November. I returned to the field in May 1999 and was there for six more months. How Meg put up with and endured all that she did during that time I will never know. What I do know is that she never stopped supporting or encouraging me to do whatever was necessary to make the project a success. For that, I am eternally grateful.

Finally, I express my deepest heartfelt gratitude for my mother, Lawana. I grew up in Turkey, Texas, a small town in the Panhandle, and when the fieldwork portion of this project was taking place at various locations around the Panhandle I had several opportunities to visit with Mom and to stay with her at Turkey. At each visit she would sit patiently and listen as I told her about our investigations at the latest battle site and how our work was providing important new details about the events of the Red River War. During my last visit with my mother, after I had finished rambling about our latest discoveries, Mom nodded her head and then said, "Brett, you have to write a book about what you are doing. People need to know about this."

We completed the fieldwork portion of the project in May 2003. Three months later my mother was killed in a car accident. Though she will never see this book, I know that she would be thrilled and very proud that I followed her advice. It is to her memory that I dedicate this book.

J. Brett Cruse

Battles of the Red River War

1

Introduction

The decade after 1865 was a period of great transition for the United States. The nation had experienced and narrowly survived a bitter civil war and many of its citizens were now seeking new beginnings in the West. As a result, a massive migration of easterners moved toward the Pacific Ocean and straight into conflict with the various Native American tribes that occupied the Great Plains—that vast middle one-third of the continental United States that stretches from Canada to Texas. Though conflicts between Anglos and Indians had occurred in the past, neither side was prepared for the scale and intensity of the battles that would be waged over the next twenty-five years. For the most part, the majority of the battles would be fought on the Great Plains, which was the homeland of numerous Indian tribes. As the number of settlers encroaching on their homelands increased, so too did the number of Indian attacks on wagon trains, miners, and buffalo hunters. White settlers demanded that the U. S. Army be mobilized to protect them, a demand that could not be ignored since westward expansion was being actively encouraged by the government.

As federal troops moved onto the Plains, they built forts and established reservations for the Indians. It soon became the army's duty to not only put the Indians on the reservations but also ensure that they remained there. But the concept of reservations was totally alien and unacceptable to the free-roaming Plains Indians and, as they saw it, their only recourse was to fight. With the end of the Civil War in 1865, the U.S. Army began operations against the Sioux on the Northern Plains and over the next two and one-half decades would continue to pursue and engage the various tribes of the Great Plains in what would come to be known as the Plains Indian Wars, which culminated in 1890 with the Sioux massacre at Wounded Knee, Dakota Territory. With the end of these wars came the end of the traditional nomadic lifestyle of the Plains Indians as the West was colonized by white settlers.

On the Southern Plains, during the summer of 1874 the U.S. Army launched a major offensive against the Indians in an effort to remove them permanently from the region and force them onto reservations that had been established in western Indian Territory, now western Oklahoma. The army's offensive against the Southern Cheyenne, Arapaho, Kiowa, and Comanche tribes was officially referred to as the Indian Campaign of 1874, but it is better known today as the Red River War. Fought largely on and near the headwaters of the Red River in the Texas Panhandle, the Red River War resulted in the defeat of the Southern Plains Indians and their removal from their homelands on the buffalo plains.

Previous Research

The Red River War was, without question, one of the most significant events in the history of the state of Texas and the western expansion of the United States. Yet it has received relatively little attention from historians and researchers of military history and, until now, no investigation by professional archeologists. Of the books that have been written on the Red River War, James L. Haley's (1976) *The Buffalo War: The History of the Red River Indian Uprising of 1874* is the most comprehensive and thoroughly researched. This book is an excellent study of the events leading up to the war, and it provides good overviews of the major battles. Specific chapters in William H. Leckie's (1963) *The Military Conquest of the Southern Plains* give general overviews of the war, as does Frederick Rathjen's (1973) *The Texas Panhandle Frontier* and Robert M. Utley's (1973) *Frontier Regulars: The United States Army and the Indian, 1866–1891.*

Other books have focused on specific aspects of the Red River War. For example, William Y. Chalfant's (1997) *Cheyennes at Dark Water Creek: The Last Fight of the Red River War* examines the events that led to the Battle of Sappa Creek, which was the last engagement of the war that took place in Kansas, in April 1875, between a band of Cheyennes and a company of the 6th Cavalry. In *The Moccasin Speaks: Living as Captives of the Dog Soldier Warriors* (1998), Arlene F. Jauken relates the story of how sisters Catherine, Sophia, Julia, and Adelaide (Addie) German (also spelled Germain or Germaine) were taken captive by Southern Cheyennes after their father, mother, and other siblings were killed by the Cheyennes and how the sisters were later rescued by army forces during the Red River War. Charles M. Neal's (2002) *Valor across the Lone Star* provides excellent summaries of the engagements fought in frontier Texas, including those of the Red River War, where soldiers earned Congressional Medals of Honor.

Still other books are autobiographies and biographies of some of the soldiers, scouts, and civilians who saw action in the war. These include *Personal Recollections and Observations of General Nelson A. Miles* (1896), Virginia W. Johnson's (1962) *The Unregimented General: A Biography of Nelson A. Miles,* Robert Wooster's (1993) *Nelson A. Miles and the Twilight of the Frontier Army,* Robert G. Carter's (1935, 1961) *On the Border with Mackenzie,* Ernest Wallace's (1964, 1993) *Ranald S. Mackenzie on the Texas Frontier,* Michael D. Pierce's (1993) *The Most Promising Young Officer: A Life of Ranald Slidell Mackenzie,* Robert H. Steinbach's (1989) *A Long March: The Lives of Frank and Alice Baldwin,* Olive K. Dixon's (1927) *Life of "Billy" Dixon,* and J. T. Marshall's (edited by Lonnie J. White, 1971) *The Miles Expedition of 1874–1875: An Eyewitness Account of the Red River War.*

Two books by Wilbur S. Nye, *Carbine and Lance: The Story of Old Fort Sill* (1937) and *Bad Medicine and Good* (1962), attempt to relate accounts of the war from the perspective of the Native Americans who participated in some of the battles. Finally, two journals have published collections of army records related to the Red River War. These are "Ranald S. Mackenzie's Official Correspondence Relating to Texas, 1873–1879," *Museum Journal* 10 (1968), edited by Ernest Wallace, and "The Indian Campaign on the Staked Plains, 1874–1875: Military Correspondence from War Department Adjutant General's Office, File 2815-1874," *Panhandle-Plains Historical Review* 34–35 (1961–62), compiled and edited by Joe F. Taylor.

Although all of these works are by and large good resources and generally reliable, the Red River War lacks a definitive and comprehensive history. The general histories of the war rely largely on personal letters and diaries of army soldiers along with military accounts that often are riddled with large gaps in their sequence of events, sometimes raising more questions than they answer. For the most part, these general histories have not attempted to record or use Native American accounts or oral histories of the events. As a result, these histories reflect, to a large extent, the army's perspectives and biases of the reasons for the war, its attitudes toward the Indians, and how the battles unfolded and were fought. In addition, some authors have misinterpreted or misunderstood certain statements in the military records, resulting in inaccurate or incorrect placement of some locations and events.

The purpose of the present study of the Red River War is not to fill all the gaps or correct all the shortcomings of the previous studies. Nor is it to provide a definitive and all-encompassing history of the war. Rather, the primary focus of this book is the archeological investigations conducted between 1998 and 2003 by the Texas Historical Commission at six of the Red River War battle sites. One purpose is to demonstrate how archeology can supplement the historical documents and provide a level of detail that is not always available in the historical records.

None of the previous scholarly studies of the Red River War has enjoyed the benefits that archeology can provide to complement the historical documents. Historical records and documents, especially firsthand accounts, are critical to understanding what happened at a particular time and place, but so too are the artifacts left behind. The archeological record contains historical clues in the form of physical remains, including artifacts, and their contextual relationships. The distributions and spatial associations of various types of artifacts can relate a great deal about what happened at a site.

Because human behavior is patterned, the artifacts at a site, which are the residue of that behavior, are also patterned and reflect details of that behavior. It is through the careful retrieval and analysis of artifacts that archeology can either corroborate the historical accounts or bring into question certain aspects of the historical documents and can aid in overcoming the biases that are often contained in the documents. In the case of battlefields, an example is the archeological investigations conducted at the Little Bighorn battle site in Montana. At this famous battle, archeological investigations showed that, though some of the traditional views of the battle were accurate, others were not. In addition, by discovering and accurately plotting the cartridges and bullets at the battle site the investigators were able to reconstruct the various tactical positions of the combatants through time and space.[1]

The Red River War Battle Sites Project

In 1998, a year before the 125th anniversary of the Red River War, the Archeology Division of the Texas Historical Commission recognized the historical significance of the occasion and initiated the Red River War Battle Sites Project. The primary goals of the project were twofold: (1) to locate precisely and document through archeological means some of the more significant battle sites of the Red River War, to assess their conditions, and to see what additional information the artifacts at the battle sites could provide to supplement the historical records and documents; and (2) to conduct a more thorough search of the unpublished historical documents that relate to the war than had been accomplished in the past.

Though there were as many as twenty battles and smaller skirmishes during the Red River War, most historians generally recognize seven battles as being the most significant (fig. 1.1). These are, in chronological order, Colonel Miles's battle on Red River, the Battle of Lyman's Wagon Train, the Buffalo Wallow fight, Major Price's battle at Sweetwater Creek, Colonel Mackenzie's battle in Palo Duro Canyon, Lieutenant Farnsworth's engagement on Round Timber Creek, and Lieutenant Baldwin's battle on McClellan Creek. Not all of these engagements were significant for their tactical importance to the outcome of the war. The Buffalo Wallow battle, for example, which was militarily insignificant, was nonetheless widely publicized at the time as a heroic engagement, and it has subsequently come to be viewed as an important event in the development of local lore and a source of regional pride.[2] Though the four soldiers and two scouts who were in the battle were surrounded by an overwhelming force of Indians, five of the six white men survived and all six were awarded Congressional Medals of Honor, a feat unparalleled in U.S. military history.

With the aid of a modest grant from the National Park Service's American Battlefields Protection Program (ABPP), the Red River War Battle Sites Project began in May 1998. The project initially attempted to locate four of the better-known battle sites precisely through archeological means and to document and record the sites. The four battles, all of which took place on what is now privately owned property, are the Battle of Red River (also known as the First Battle of Palo Duro Canyon)[3] in present Armstrong and Briscoe counties, the Battle of Lyman's Wagon Train (also referred to as the Battle of the Upper Washita) in present Hemphill County, the Battle of Buffalo Wallow also in Hemphill County, and the Battle of Palo Duro Canyon (also known as the Second Battle of Palo Duro Canyon) in Armstrong County. Unfortunately, we were not able to persuade the owners of the Battle of Palo Duro Canyon site to grant us access to the site, and it was necessarily dropped from the project.

The field investigations showed that, for the most part, the battle sites retained excellent integrity and had the potential to yield significant new information regarding combatant positions and movements at the battles, as well as information on weapon types and the number of weapons represented at the battles. During this initial phase of the project, which was conducted from May through September 1998, we completed the investigations at two of the targeted sites and estimated that approximately 40 percent of the Battle of Red River site had been investigated.

The project continued in 1999, with support again coming from the ABPP as well as several foundations and a private individual. The goals during this season were to complete the investigations at the Battle of Red River site and to attempt to locate and document the Battle of Sweetwater Creek (Price's engagement), which was believed to have taken place in the northwestern portion of present Wheeler County, Texas. During this season we also attempted to gain access to the Battle of McClellan Creek site (Baldwin's battle) in Gray County but were not granted access to the site from the landowner. Our fieldwork in 1999 was conducted from June through October and was successful in completing the investigations started the previous summer at the Battle of Red River site and in locating and documenting the Battle of Sweetwater Creek site. In addition, we identified a probable Cheyenne village site near the mouth of Tule Canyon that appears to have been one of the villages the army was attempting to capture during the Battle of Red River. This is apparently also where Colonel Nelson Miles temporarily established his headquarters camp after the battle.

With the completion of the 1999 field season, four battle sites had been investigated and more than 3,100 battle-related artifacts recovered. At this point in the project it was decided that no additional fieldwork would be undertaken until the artifacts from the 1998 and 1999 field seasons could be cleaned, cataloged, conserved, and analyzed and the necessary reports to our project donors completed. These tasks were accomplished during 2000 and 2001. In the meantime, historian and consultant Martha Doty Freeman was hired to conduct searches for previously unpublished Red River War battle-related historical documents at the National Archives in Washington, D.C., and other repositories. During her search in 2001, Freeman found several documents and maps that shed new light on the location of Lt. Henry J. Farnsworth's engagement (termed by us the Battle of Round Timber Creek) with Chief Grey Beard's band

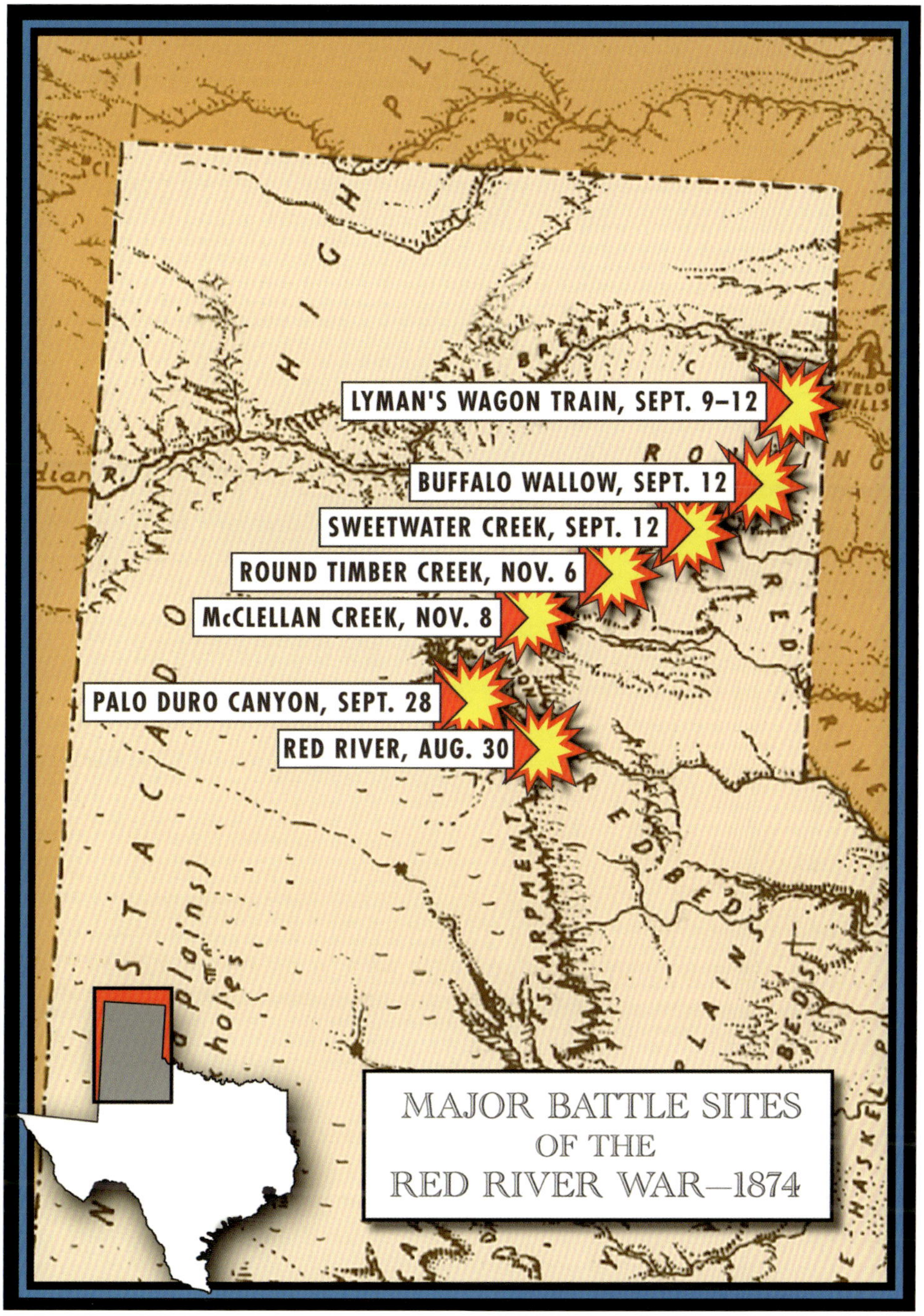

Fig. 1.1. Though there were as many as twenty battles and smaller skirmishes during the Red River War, seven battles are generally viewed by most historians as most significant. Illustration by Roland Pantermuehl

of Southern Cheyenne near the North Fork of the Red River in present Gray County. With this newly found information we began to make plans to locate and investigate the Battle of Round Timber Creek site, but additional funding would first have to be secured before the fieldwork could take place. A grant proposal was written and again submitted to the ABPP as well as to the David D. and Nona S. Payne Foundation to support the proposed investigations. The Payne Foundation approved funding in October 2002. With funding for the fieldwork in place, the investigations at the Battle of Round Timber Creek site were conducted in April and May 2003. These investigations were successful in locating and documenting not only the battle site proper but also Grey Beard's village where the Battle of Round Timber Creek actually started.

During the fall of 2002, personnel with the Texas Parks and Wildlife Department (TPWD) made plans to conduct a metal detector survey of portions of Palo Duro Canyon State Park in Randall and Armstrong counties as part of their resource management plan for the park. The purpose of the survey was to determine how much, if any, of the Battle of Palo Duro Canyon site fell within the park boundaries. The Battle of Palo Duro Canyon is arguably the most significant battle of the Red River War, and many historians have viewed it as the event that marked the turning point in the war for the U.S. Army. At the battle, Col. Ranald S. Mackenzie surprised, attacked, and destroyed the winter stores and horses of several Cheyenne, Comanche, and Kiowa bands that had taken refuge in the canyon. After these devastating losses, many of the Indians returned to the reservations.

It has long been known that most of the Battle of Palo Duro Canyon took place outside park boundaries on privately owned property, which we had unsuccessfully tried to gain access to in 1998. Over the years since the park was first established, park employees and park visitors alike had found artifacts within the state park that were probably associated with the battle. In addition, historical documents indicate that the battle extended up the canyon some 4 miles from its point of origin near the mouth of Cita Canyon. If the documents are accurate, this would place the final events of the battle well within the park. At the request of TPWD, I directed the metal detector survey, which was completed in November 2002, with a crew of TPWD park personnel and local volunteers. Though only a few days were allotted for the survey, sufficient numbers of battle-related artifacts were recovered to demonstrate that the Battle of Palo Duro Canyon did in fact extend into the park. A clearer picture of the later stages of the battle emerged as a result of the investigations.[4]

With the conclusion of fieldwork in May 2003, the Red River War Battle Sites Project had successfully located and documented portions of six of the better-known battle sites of the war. Additional Red River War battles and skirmishes await field identification and documentation. These and other Red River War–related sites and locations are discussed in more detail in chapter 12.

Research Objectives

The research objectives for the Red River War Battle Sites Project were devised on the basis of archeological remains at each of the battle sites. Though the Red River War battles were, as a group, part of the larger Plains Indian Wars and, as such, have similar characteristics, each site is unique. Some of the battles were running engagements that covered long distances, with the army and Indian combatants roughly equal in number. Examples of such engagements are the Battle of Red River and the Battle of Sweetwater Creek, in which the army was in pursuit of retreating Indians. Other battles such as Buffalo Wallow and Lyman's Wagon Train were stationary, with the army forces apparently greatly outnumbered by Indian forces. In the Battle of Palo Duro Canyon the army surprised and attacked Cheyenne, Comanche, and Kiowa villagers who had taken refuge in the canyon, and the element of surprise worked significantly in the army's favor. In the Battle of Round Timber Creek a small group of soldiers on a scouting expedition apparently rode into what they believed was an abandoned Indian village, where they were ambushed by a larger force of Cheyenne warriors. This engagement also turned into a long running battle, but this time the Indians were in pursuit of the retreating cavalry.

The available historical documents relating to the Red River War provided some direction to our overall research orientation for the project. Historical documents are, however, often incomplete and biased in their presentation of events. Archeological investigation is based on the tenet that a behavioral relationship exists between historical events and the physical remains of those events. By identifying and analyzing the physical artifacts in their historical contexts, we can better understand cultural behaviors on the battle sites. The research objectives were designed to examine these behaviors.

Chronology of Events at the Battle Sites

The primary objective for each battle site was to establish the chronology of the events, which entailed tracing the deployments of the army and Indian combatants during the battles. To accomplish this objective we recorded the precise location of each battle-related artifact in order to trace combatant movements and to assess battle developments. This level of documentation provided a means for observing variations in artifact patterns, densities, and associations. By analyzing the artifact types and patterns across the battle sites and comparing these patterns with the historical documents, we could establish the chronology of battle events and their locations on the battle sites.

Army and Indian Military Tactics

In addition to establishing the chronology of events, we also wanted to examine the military tactics used by both the army and the Indians and to see how those tactics were expressed and preserved in the archeological record. Prior to and during the Civil War, the U.S. Army had precise deployment tactics for infantry and cavalry units. These tactics had their roots in Europe and were refined during the Civil War, when the opposing Union and Confederate forces were trained and equipped in similar fashion. How did these tactics change after the Civil War as the army now faced a military foe whose tactics were unlike any it had previously encountered—those of the comparatively unstructured, individually based Plains Indians?

The Indians likewise were now facing a foe that was superior in weapons, supplies, and manpower. Even though numerous engagements between the Southern Plains Indians and whites had occurred prior to 1874, the Indians now found themselves in a situation significantly different from previous encounters. For many years, Indian warriors had been able to make long-distance raids against the Anglo settlers to the east and southeast and against the Mexicans to the south and southwest and then return to the relative safety of their villages on the plains. Even when the army sent troops in pursuit of the Indians, it was usually to "teach a lesson" to a particular Indian group or band and not to subjugate every Indian who occupied the Southern Plains. That changed in 1874 when the army sent troops onto the Southern Plains from virtually every direction with the intention of forcibly and permanently removing all Indians. How did the Indians respond militarily to this sudden onslaught in their homeland and against their villages? Did they rely on their traditional military tactics, or did they adopt new tactics to meet this challenge?

Armaments and Weapon Types

One of the most important battle site objectives is to determine the types of armaments used. The weapons the troopers were using in 1874 are well documented in army records and ordnance returns. Much less is known about the types and numbers of firearms the Indians had. During the project, firearm types were identified through modern firearms identification analysis. These procedures were used to determine ammunition calibers and to examine distinguishing marks on bullets and cartridge cases. Cartridges that have been fired and then ejected have distinguishing marks, such as those left by the weapon's firing pin and extractor. Firing pin marks are indicative of firearm type and are unique for each individual firearm. By comparing these marks on the recovered cartridge cases from each site, we can ascertain a minimum number of firearms per weapon type for each of the battle sites. Those cartridges not associated with the army, according to official army records and ordnance returns, can be assumed to be from Indian firearms.

Military Records

Another objective of our investigations was to ascertain the accuracy and degree of bias of the army records that pertain to the Red River War battle sites. Many of the records make reference to specific types of weapons being used by Indians along with statements about how well armed the Indians were. In addition, the records often provide specific statements about the number of Indians involved in the battles. Are these statements supported by the archeological evidence?

2

Historical Overview: The Southern Plains Indians

The Indian tribes that occupied the Southern Plains in 1874—the Comanche, Kiowa, Southern Cheyenne, and Southern Arapaho—each considered the region as their homeland, though none of them was native to the area.[1] All the tribes were relatively recent emigrants who had been in the region for less than two hundred years, the Comanche arriving first in the early 1700s, the Kiowa in the late 1700s, and the Cheyenne and Arapaho around 1835. The Kiowa and Comanche were pushed onto the Southern Plains by enemy tribes to the north. Though early hostilities existed between the Kiowas and Comanches, they became allies around 1790.[2]

Offshoots of their main tribes on the Northern Plains, the Southern Cheyenne and Arapaho migrated south to take advantage of the trading benefits to be had along the Arkansas River. Though retaining strong identifications and relationships with their northern peoples, these groups took on their own distinct identities. In 1840, they formed an alliance with the Comanche and Kiowa. This Southern Plains "confederation" helped to establish a prolific trade in horses, guns, furs, and European and American manufactured goods among themselves, the Americans, and the New Mexican Comanchero traders.[3]

The Southern Plains Indians, like virtually all nomadic Indian groups who occupied the Great Plains, were almost wholly dependent on the buffalo for their day-to-day survival (fig. 2.1). The buffalo were plentiful, roaming the Great Plains in herds of millions, and they provided the Indians with more than just food. The tribes made use of every part of the buffalo to the extent that it supplied an incredible proportion of their basic needs, providing clothing, tools, shelter, fuel, and food. In short, the buffalo was the heart of the Plains Indian culture. During the spring and summer when buffalo were plentiful, the Indians consumed large quantities of fresh buffalo meat. During the fall, the meat was dried and stored for consumption in the leaner winter months. From the hides of the shaggy animals the Indians fashioned clothing and covers for the tepees they lived in. They made rope from the hair of the buffalo and made bowstrings from its tendons. Bones of the buffalo were fashioned into tools, hooves were rendered into glue, and bladders were dried and used as canteens. Virtually no part of the buffalo went unused. So dependent were the Indians on the buffalo that it is easy to understand why they revered the animal as a sacred and life-sustaining entity. The Indians believed that, if the buffalo were to some day disappear, they would likewise cease to exist.

Another animal the Plains Indians depended on was the horse. It was the acquisition of horses, in fact, that largely contributed to the Plains Indians making the

Fig. 2.1. Comanche Indians hunt buffalo in George Catlin's *Comanche Indians Chasing Buffalo with Lances and Bows.* Buffalo were essential to the survival of the Southern Plains Indians, for food, clothing, and shelter, and were bestowed enormous religious significance as well. Courtesy Smithsonian American Art Museum, Gift of Mrs. Joseph Harrison Jr.

transition from semisedentary gardeners and gatherers living on the fringes of the Great Plains to nomadic buffalo hunters living in the interior of the plains. In the 1600s, the Spanish settlements in Mexico provided the first horses to the Indians in the Southwest and the Southern Plains. The Pueblo revolt of 1680 greatly increased the availability of horses. By 1700, the horse had spread through the Apaches to the Comanches and Kiowas and west of the Rockies up to the Shoshones. By 1750, the tribes on the Northern Plains all had horses, and by 1770 the diffusion of the horse on the Great Plains was complete.[4]

The horse soon became an integral part of Plains Indian culture, permeating every aspect of the Indians' lives. Hunting, trade, leisure, and war all came to revolve around the horse. With the horse, the Plains Indians became highly mobile, following the great buffalo herds and hunting and killing them with greater efficiency, ease, and success than they had been able to on foot. On horseback, the Plains Indians had a distinct advantage over weaker tribes, and they became formidable warriors. The horse allowed the Plains Indians to make long-range raids not only against their traditional tribal enemies but also against more recent aggressors the Indians viewed as encroachers on their territory. For the Southern Plains Indians, the encroachment was from the Mexicans to the south and southwest and from the Texans to the south and east.

Raids against Mexican and Texan settlements became a means by which young warriors could prove their worth and achieve prestige. The spoils of the raids provided the Southern Plains Indians with horses, mules, slaves, and other plunder, which could be traded to the Comancheros of Santa Fe and Taos in exchange for a wide range of items including guns, ammunition, pots, beads, and foodstuffs. It was because of the acquisition of the horse that raiding, and all the atrocities that usually accompanied it, quickly became firmly assimilated into the Southern Plains Indians' overall cultural scheme. In short, the advent of the horse transformed the Plains Indians and heralded an age of prosperity for them. In fact, the horse became a measure of wealth, providing material evidence of a warrior's prestige.[5]

Events Leading to the Red River War

Prior to the outbreak of the Red River War in 1874, a long history of conflict had developed between the Southern Plains Indians and the whites who pushed incessantly to claim the western frontier. By the end of the 1830s, the domain of the Southern Plains Indians had been rapidly reduced by Texas colonization from the south and American advancement from the east. Beginning in the 1850s, government policy in the West was to confine Indian tribes to reservations, thereby opening vast tracts to white settlement. During this same time, new military posts were being established all across the Southern Plains. These included Forts Mann and Atkinson on the Santa Fe Trail; Fort Arbuckle just north of the Arbuckle Mountains in Indian Territory; and Forts Belknap, Phantom Hill, Chadbourne, and Camp Cooper across north-central Texas. The military posts in Texas were established not only to provide some level of protection to American settlers moving west but also to protect northern Mexico from Indian movements and raids south out of Texas.

When the Civil War began, many of the troops who once provided some measure of protection for westward-bound settlers were withdrawn from the frontier to fight back east. This left the frontier largely unprotected, and the Southern Plains Indians took full advantage. In 1864, Comanches and Kiowas made numerous attacks along the Santa Fe Trail of western Kansas and eastern Colorado Territory. Also in 1864, a large force of Comanche and Kiowa raiders struck the settlements along the valley of Elm Creek a few miles above Fort Belknap in Texas.[6] As the raids in Texas continued with ever-increasing frequency, the frontier settlement line in Texas was driven eastward as the Indians threw greater effort into their attempts to reclaim territory they saw as rightfully theirs. In response to the increased raiding, the settlers who remained on the frontier "forted up" in more concentrated locations for protection. Indian activities viewed by the Anglo settlers as "depredations" continued to increase, as did the pleas from the settlers for Congress to do something to control the Indians.

Congress, confronted with a nation weary of war and eager to cut military expenditures, looked for a permanent and bloodless end to the chaos by creating the Indian Peace Commission in 1867, charged with resolving the problems by negotiation. During the week of October 21–28, 1867, the commission held a conference with the Southern Plains tribes on Medicine Lodge Creek, about 85 miles south of Fort Larned, Kansas. The goal of the conference was to establish a comprehensive treaty with the Southern Plains tribes that would end the hostilities and ensure a lasting peace. Though the whites wanted peace, they made it clear that there could be no real bargaining. In fact, the terms offered by the whites were an ultimatum. If the Indians agreed, they would get presents and annuities; if they did not, there would be a renewed war that the commission representatives threatened would destroy the tribes.[7]

According to the terms of the treaty, the Indians were to live on reservations established in Indian Territory in what is now western Oklahoma (fig. 2.2). The reservation in the southwest was for the Comanches and Kiowas, the ones to the north were for the Cheyennes and Arapahos. The tribes were to be given rifles and ammunition for hunting and seeds and instruction in farming. They would be taught how to build houses and furnished schools and a doctor. Annuity goods would be provided for thirty years. In return, the tribes had to cease all warfare against the whites and not interfere with the roads, railroads, and forts that would be constructed in their country. Significantly, the treaty went on to state that the Indian tribes "yet reserve the right to hunt on any lands south of the Arkansas River so long as the buffalo may range thereon in such numbers as to justify the chase." The Indians understandably took this to mean that they could continue to hunt buffalo in all the area south of the Arkansas River, including southern Kansas, Oklahoma, and Texas. The Indian Peace Commission representatives, however, failed to point out to the Indians that the U.S. government did not have legal authority to represent the State of Texas as owner of the lands in the Texas Panhandle. They could not give anyone the right to hunt in the Panhandle, for this was state-owned land, not federal land. Only the Texas legislature could have set aside the Panhandle for hunting by the Indians, and they had not done so.[8]

At the end of the conference, the Indians signed the Medicine Lodge Treaty, but it was destined for failure. Though many of the Indians voluntarily moved to the

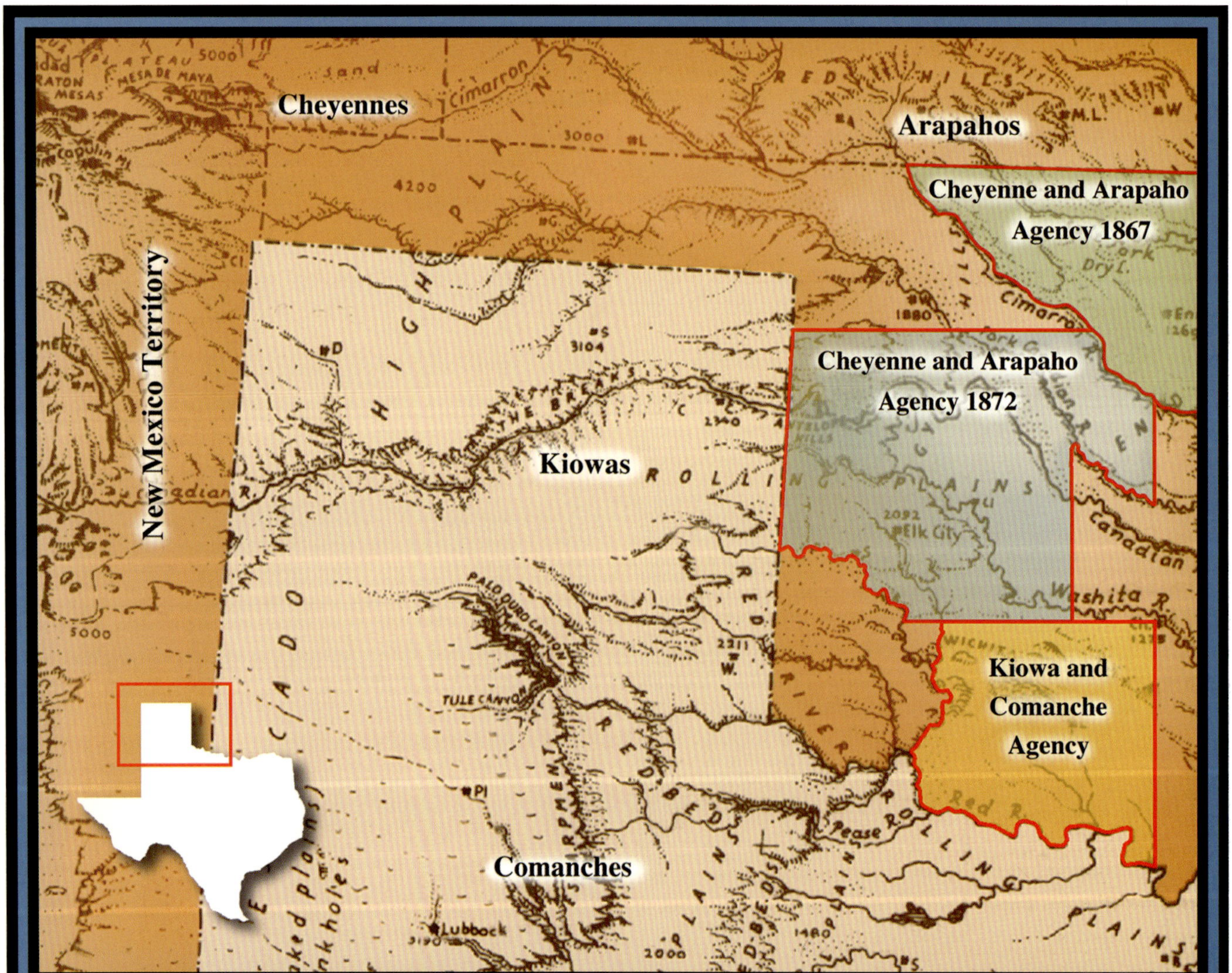

Fig. 2.2. According to the terms of the Medicine Lodge Treaty, the Southern Plains tribes were to live on reservations established in western Indian Territory. Illustration by Roland Pantermuehl

reservations and tried to live by the terms of the treaty, they found it almost impossible to do so because the U.S. government did not live up to its commitment to furnish them adequate food and supplies. The Indians were accustomed to subsisting largely on fresh meat, but they were issued only limited supplies of salt pork and cornmeal. The government had planned to furnish seeds and tools to the Indians for three years, and the rations had been intended as supplementary to the foods the Indians were supposed to produce themselves. But the Indians had no interest in learning to farm, and they were hostile to the idea of taking up any kind of labor except hunting. In general, neither the goods nor the projected life at the reservations were attractive to the Indians, and they immediately began to drift back to the plains. Within a year, the majority of the reservation Indians had gone back to hunting on the plains, paying no attention to their imposed boundaries.[9]

Early in 1869, President Grant was persuaded by leaders from several religious faiths to institute a program to "manage" the Indians that was known as the "Peace Policy." The religious leaders believed that a policy of kindness and gentleness would persuade the Indians to settle down on the reservations and to adopt the white man's way of life. With the adoption of the Peace Policy, Quakers assumed control of the South Plains reservations. The Quakers and their policy of peace did influence some of the Indians, but most were not persuaded, perhaps in large part because of the government's failure to live up to its agreements to furnish sufficient food and supplies for the reservations. As a result, Indian raids continued across the Southern Plains and, in the end, the policy was a failure.

Three years after the Medicine Lodge Treaty went into effect, a series of events took place that brought the uprising of the Southern Plains Indians to a head and sealed their fate. In the fall of 1871, a young New Englander named Josiah Wright Mooar came west and founded the business of hunting buffalo for hides. Within a matter of months, buffalo hides were in such demand by eastern tanners that hundreds of hide hunters rushed to the plains to take part in the suddenly lucrative business.[10] Railroads penetrated deep into the buffalo range at numerous points and were carrying away buffalo hides by the thousands to eastern markets. Dodge City, in southwestern Kansas, became the center of the trade (fig. 2.3). In 1873 alone, the three rail lines serving Dodge City carried away more than 750,000 hides, and for the three years 1872–74 an incredible 4,373,730 buffalo were killed. And that figure was for the rail exports alone; other sources added at least a million more to the total.[11]

The Southern Plains Indians found the wanton slaughter of the northern buffalo herds disdainful, but they made no concerted effort to stop it, since the commercial hunters were confined to lands north of the Arkansas River. Under the terms of the Medicine Lodge Treaty, land south of the Arkansas River was considered Indian hunting grounds, and the hide hunters respected the boundary, at least in the early years of the treaty. Only after the northern Kansas buffalo were gone did the hunters venture south of the Arkansas River into Indian hunting grounds. The buffalo hunters slaughtered the buffalo by the thousands and in one season's kill obliterated the southern Kansas herds on which the Cheyenne and Arapaho subsisted. By 1873, the buffalo hunters were making continuous raids on the herds south of the Arkansas River. The Indians, now fighting within their own territory, became less and less capable of fending off the ever-increasing tide of buffalo poachers.[12]

The army was supposed to be patrolling the Kansas-Indian Territory boundary to see that nobody crossed, but it chose to look the other way. Gen. Philip Sheridan wanted to reduce the buffalo population quickly and to terminate the Indian's hunting rights. Sheridan left no doubt that he wanted the buffalo exterminated when, in 1881, the federal government was considering protecting what was left of the herds.

Fig. 2.3. During the 1870s, buffalo were slaughtered by the millions for their hides, which were shipped to tanners in the East. The buffalo hides stacked here are at Charles Rath's firm in Dodge City, Kansas. Courtesy Panhandle-Plains Historical Museum, Canyon, Texas

He vigorously opposed such action. "If I could learn that every buffalo in the northern herd were killed I would be glad," the general wrote his superiors. "The destruction of this herd would do more to keep Indians quiet than anything else that could happen. Since the destruction of the southern herd, which formerly roamed from Texas to the Platte, the Indians in that section have given us no trouble."[13]

By 1873, the buffalo hunters had decimated the buffalo herds as far south as the Canadian River in the Texas Panhandle. This meant that the Indians had lost control over what had been the territory given them at Medicine Lodge, and they began to panic over the juggernaut of buffalo hunters who were rapidly destroying their very means of survival. With no major retaliation yet inflicted by the Indians, the buffalo hunters began to make plans for the 1874 hunt on the Canadian. By now it was obvious to the hunters, and to the Indians, that the army had no intention of stopping the former from crossing into Indian territories. As far as the Indians were concerned, all the buffalo south of the Arkansas River were theirs. With the buffalo hunters having already devastated the herds north of the Canadian, the heat for revenge among the Indians was high. The presence of white hunters among the last herds of buffalo on the Southern Plains would likely touch off a war with the Indians, but the buffalo hunters were apparently willing to risk it.

In the spring of 1874, the buffalo hunters who had waited out the winter in Dodge City decided it was time to move south in force. The general feeling among the hunters was that, if they all went south together, the Indians would be less likely to attack them. To accommodate the hide men and ease the supply problem, one of the Kansas robe and meat traders, A. C. "Charlie" Myers, agreed to pack up his entire business, move south with the hunters, and open a supply store and market center for their hides in the Texas Panhandle. Myers established his trading post, Adobe Walls, on the Canadian River in present Hutchinson County. He built a stockade, corral, and storehouse and was soon followed by Charles Rath, who set up business in a sod house. Tom O'Keafe established a blacksmith shop, and James Hanrahan opened a saloon.[14]

The sudden swarm of white hunters into the Panhandle buffalo range could hardly have had any other effect than to infuriate the Indians, who demonstrated their objections with swift clarity. Two hunters, Dave Dudley and Tommy Wallace, apparently were caught asleep in a camp on Chicken Creek. Their companion, Joe Plummer, away at the time of the attack, returned to find his associates killed, scalped, and otherwise mutilated, and Dudley's corpse pinned to the ground by a wooden stake driven through the abdomen. In the camp of Anderson Moore on the Salt Fork of the Red River, an Englishman, John Jones, and a German known as "Blue Billy" were killed. Both Plummer and Moore got away to bring word of the tragedies back to Adobe Walls.[15]

By late spring of 1874, the situation with the Indians was on the verge of exploding. Among the Indians there was talk of war and killing, and of driving the white man from the land. During the spring of 1874, a leader and prophet for the Indians emerged in the person of Isatai, of the Kwahada band of Comanches (fig. 2.4). Isatai claimed that he could bring the dead back to life and that he was immune to the bullets of the white man. He also claimed that he could vomit forth at will wagonloads of cartridges. Isatai's medicine was viewed as being very strong, and he was doing his best to incite a war against the whites. Because the majority of the Indians now saw themselves as being in a desperate situation, with the only alternative to starvation being war, it took little persuasion by Isatai to convince the Indian leaders that they must strike back at the whites. Thus the Indians formed a plan to attack and destroy the new settlement of buffalo hunters at Adobe Walls.[16]

In the early morning hours of June 27, 1874, some two hundred Indians, led by Isatai and a young Kwahada Comanche chief named Quanah (fig. 2.5), attacked the Adobe Walls post, which was occupied by one woman and twenty-eight men, two of whom were Billy Dixon and Bat Masterson.[17] The Indians planned to catch the whites by surprise and simply overpower them. What the Indians did not count on, however, was the skillful marksmanship of the hunters and the long-range accuracy of the hunters' .50-caliber Sharps rifles. Not only did the hunters manage to repel the Indians, they killed several of them.[18] So surprised were the Indians by their own lack of success that they began to fall back and by the afternoon had almost completely withdrawn and were firing only sporadically. For all their effort and all their losses, the Indians had killed only three of the hunters. For the Indians, the tactical purpose in attacking Adobe Walls was to kill white hunters. Their broader purpose was to halt the slaughter of the buffalo herds. They had failed on both counts.

Word of the attack on Adobe Walls spread quickly over the buffalo range, and panic spread just as quickly among the buffalo hunters. The Adobe Walls merchants quickly loaded their inventories and returned to Dodge City, with many of the hunters following them. Their fear of the Indians did not last long, however, and within a few months most of the hunters were again killing large numbers of buffalo on the Texas plains.

As conditions continued to worsen on the reservations, many of the Indians who were still there now left to join the renegade bands who had returned to Texas. As the buffalo hunt proceeded, the Indians' frustration escalated, and marauding bands periodically fell upon isolated hunting parties. The increasing realization that their access to ancestral lands was diminishing encouraged many of the Indians to strike at

Fig. 2.4. Isatai (seated to the right) is shown here with members of his family. He became known as a prophet of the Comanches in 1874. Courtesy Panhandle-Plains Historical Museum, Canyon, Texas

the whites. The realization that the buffalo, their main source of survival, was quickly disappearing forced them to fight. After Adobe Walls, the Indians spread out over the plains of Texas for one final grasp at the old ways of life. For them, this ultimately brought military retaliation, defeat, and confinement to the hated reservations.

Overview of the War

After the attack on Adobe Walls, the U.S. Army made plans to subdue the Southern Plains tribes permanently. Known by historians as the Red River War, the primary objective of the army's Indian Campaign of 1874 was the removal of the Indian groups from the Southern Plains, thereby opening the region to Anglo-American settlement. General Sheridan (fig. 2.6) later characterized the military operations as "not only comprehensive, but . . . the most successful of any Indian Campaign in this country

◀ Fig. 2.5. Comanche chief Quanah led the attack on Adobe Walls and was the last of the Southern Plains Indians to surrender to the U.S. Army, in 1875. After his surrender he adopted his mother's maiden name, Parker.

▲ Fig. 2.6. Gen. Philip H. Sheridan was instrumental in devising the army's offensive campaign against the Southern Plains Indians. Courtesy Panhandle-Plains Historical Museum, Canyon, Texas

since its settlement by the whites."[19] Sheridan and Gen. William T. Sherman laid the basis for an offensive campaign against the Indians in early July 1874, and Secretary of War William Belknap approved it on July 20. The new policy called for enrollment and protection of innocent and friendly Indians at their reservations and pursuit and destruction of hostile Indians without regard for reservation or departmental boundaries.[20]

From a military point of view, the campaign against the Indians was masterfully planned and executed. The offensive would utilize five military columns—two from the Department of the Missouri and three from the Department of Texas. The columns were to converge generally on the area of the Texas Panhandle and specifically on the upper tributaries of the Red River where the Indians were believed to be (fig. 2.7). The strategy aimed at full encirclement of the region, thereby eliminating virtually all gaps through which the Indians might escape. From the Department of the Missouri came columns from Fort Dodge and Fort Union. Col. (Bvt. Maj. Gen.)[21] Nelson A. Miles was the overall field commander of the columns from the Department of the Missouri. Colonel Miles departed from Fort Dodge, Kansas, and moved southward with eight companies of the 6th Cavalry and four companies of the 5th Infantry (table 2.1) toward the Washita River and the headwaters of the Red River in the Texas Panhandle. Maj. (Bvt. Brig. Gen.) William R. Price commanded the second column from the Department of the Missouri and led four companies of the 8th Cavalry eastward across the Panhandle from Forts Union and Bascom, New Mexico. From the Department of Texas came Lt. Col. (Bvt. Maj. Gen.) John W. Davidson, who marched westward from Fort Sill in Indian Territory with eight companies of the 10th Cavalry and two companies of the 11 Infantry. Lt. Col. (Bvt. Brig. Gen.) George P. Buell moved northwest from Fort Griffin, Texas, with seven companies of the 9th Cavalry, two of the 10th Cavalry, and two companies of the 11 Infantry. Col. (Bvt. Maj. Gen.) Ranald S. Mackenzie commanded the third column from the Department of Texas. Mackenzie led eight companies of the 4th Cavalry and five companies of the 10th and 11th Infantries northward from Fort Concho, Texas. In total, some three thousand soldiers and scouts participated in the campaign, which called for the converging columns to maintain a continuous offensive until a decisive defeat had been inflicted on the Indians.[22]

Over the course of the next ten months, the army would engage the Indians in battles and skirmishes across the Texas Panhandle. The Indians could claim victories in only a few of the encounters. For the most part, they were simply outnumbered and overpowered by the well-armed and well-supplied U.S. Army. The Indians were refugees in their own land; the buffalo were already hunted out in most of the war zone, depriving them of meat and hides and rendering them helpless when the swift army attacks destroyed their camps and winter stores. The military campaign known to history as the Red River War officially ended in June 1875 when Quanah, who just a year earlier had led the attack on Adobe Walls, now led his band of Kwahada Comanches into Fort Sill and surrendered.[23] By then the majority of the members of the tribes had long since become prisoners of the U.S. Army.

Aftermath of the War

As the various tribes surrendered and made their way to Fort Sill, they were met there by army troops who seized their firearms and other weapons. The more influential chiefs were separated from their tribes and isolated in the post guardhouse; the other Indians were held in Fort Sill's unfinished icehouse until their fate was decided. The Indians who were considered the most "incorrigible" were held in irons. The remaining Indians who had not been accused of any particular crime were released into the custody of the "friendly" chiefs of their respective tribes.[24]

The question of what to do with the Indian ringleaders was answered when the army decided that they should be removed from their families and the rest of the reservation Indians and sent east to be imprisoned at Fort Marion, Florida. It should be noted that none of the Indians was ever given a trial or convicted of any crime. Lt. Richard Pratt, who accompanied the Indian prisoners to Fort Marion and oversaw them there, wrote: "All against whom good evidence of having committed crime could be found were taken out, and charges were alleged with a view to legal action. Another class, composed of those who were notoriously guilty of crime, but against whom no good evidence could be brought, and also of those who were notoriously insubordinate and stirrers up of bad feeling, was selected to be sent east for confinement at some fort. Not many of the first class could be found. . . . When the time came to send them east, for some reason the first class accompanied the second, and all were sent. . . . they arrived on the 21st of May, 1875."[25] As Pratt makes clear, the Indians were imprisoned as suspects, not as convicts; they were never tried before a military tribunal.

Seventy-two Indians were sent to Fort Marion (appendix A): thirty-three Cheyennes, twenty-seven Kiowas, nine Comanches, two Arapahos, and one Caddo.[26] Among the Cheyennes were Grey Beard, Heap of Birds, Bear Shield, Minimic, and Medicine Water and his wife Mochi, the only woman to be sent to Florida. On the

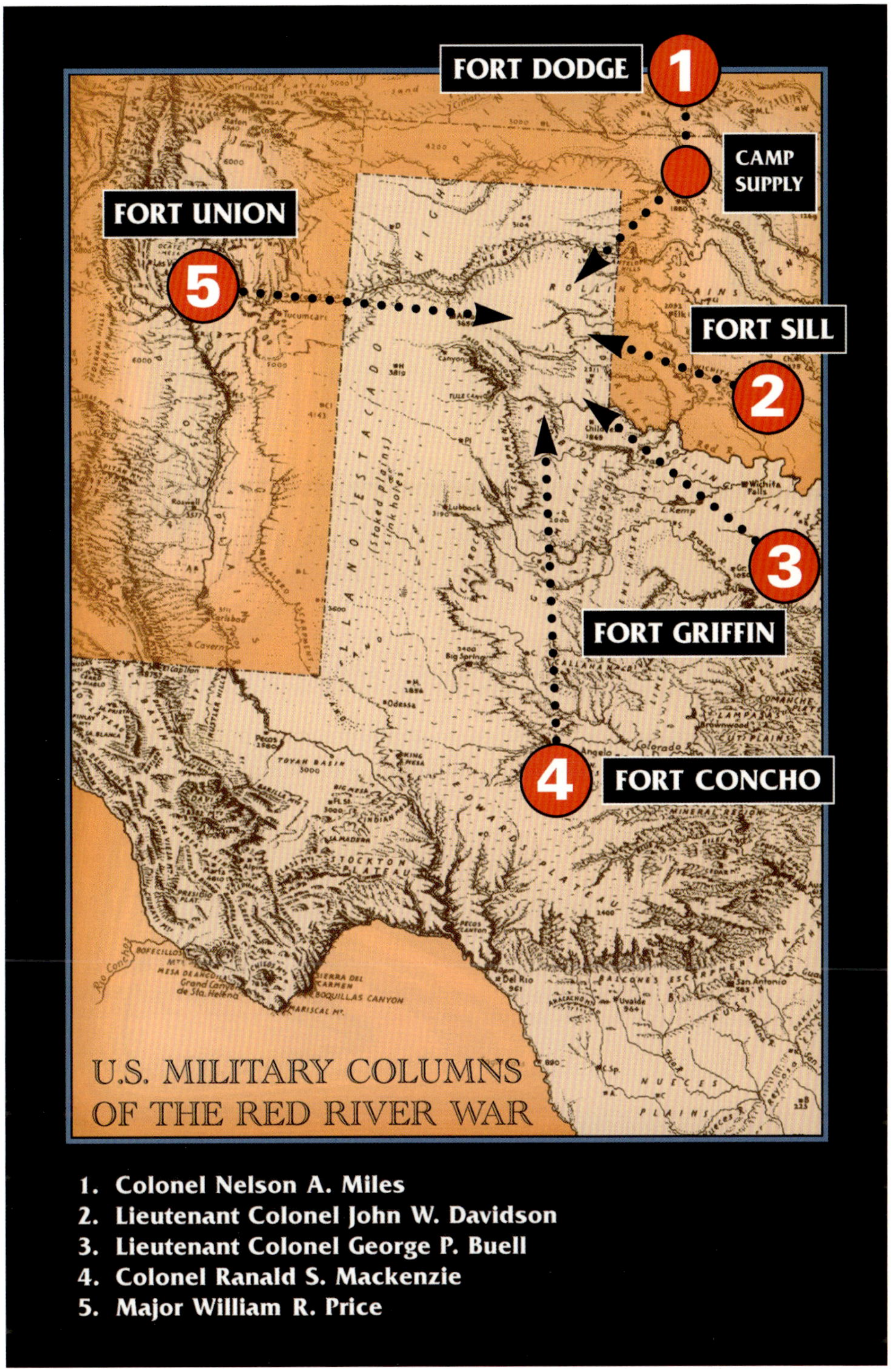

Fig. 2.7. The army's strategic plan called for five military columns to encircle and converge upon the Indians. Illustration by Roland Pantermuehl

train ride to Florida, Grey Beard tried to escape and was shot and killed by the guards. Another of the Cheyennes, Lean Bear, reportedly stabbed himself and two of the guards while en route to Fort Marion on May 19, 1875. He was left at Nashville but was later transported to Fort Marion, where he died on July 24, 1875.[27] The Kiowas who were sent included Lone Wolf, Mamanti, White Horse, Woman's Heart, and Bird Chief, a lesser-known medicine man. Mamanti died there, apparently of pneumonia,

Table 2.1. Cavalry and Infantry Companies of the Red River War Campaign

Column Commander	*Calvary: Companies*	*Infantry: Companies*
Col. Nelson A. Miles	6th: A, D, F, G, H, I, L, M	5th: C, D, E, I
Lt. Col. John W. Davidson	10th: B, C, D, E, F, H, K, L	11th: C, E
Lt. Col. George P. Buell	9th: A, D, E, F, K; 10th: A	11th: A, F
Col. Ranald S. Mackenzie	4th: A, D, E, F, H, I, K, L	10th: A, C, I, K; 11th: H
Maj. William R. Price	8th: C, H, K, L	

on July 29, 1875. Satanta was not sent to Florida but instead to a prison in Huntsville, Texas, where he committed suicide by jumping from a second story window on October 11, 1878.[28]

Most notable among the nine Comanches sent to Fort Marion was Black Horse, second chief of the Kwahadas. The Arapahos selected were Packer and White Bear. The one Caddo was Hu-wah-nee, who was charged with the murder of E. B. Osborne during the uprising at the Wichita Agency on August 22, 1874. The Indian prisoners were held at Fort Marion until 1878, when most of them were returned to their respective reservations in Oklahoma, though several remained in the East where they attended schools such as the Carlisle Indian Industrial School established by Lieutenant Pratt in Pennsylvania.

With the end of the war, Anglo farmers and ranchers moved in quickly to claim the territory that just a few short years before was that of the free-roaming Indians. Cattlemen and farmers soon made their claim to the entire region. Roads and rails were built across the area, further enabling Anglo-American settlement.

3

Field and Laboratory Methods

Prior to the initiation of fieldwork, we attempted to develop a survey strategy that would allow maximum examination of large areas of the terrain in the least amount of time. However, because each battle site was unique, it was somewhat difficult to develop a single survey strategy that would be efficient for use at each site. At the site of the Battle of Lyman's Wagon Train, for example, the general site location was known prior to our investigations; it was recorded in the State of Texas archeological site files by the Panhandle-Plains Historical Museum in 1971, when it was assigned the trinomial 41HH11. At that time, however, no subsurface archeological investigations were conducted and the boundaries of the site were not determined. Thus, archeological investigations were needed to confirm the site location and determine its extent.

The Battle of Buffalo Wallow site was somewhat more problematic. In 1927, the Panhandle-Plains Historical Society erected a granite marker at a location in Hemphill County where they believed the battle had taken place. They based their placement of the marker primarily on oral interviews with Mrs. Olive Dixon, the wife of Billy Dixon, a scout for the U.S. Army and participant at the battle. No archeological investigations had ever been conducted at the site, however, to confirm the battle location.

The battles sites of Red River, Sweetwater Creek, and Round Timber Creek were also problematic. Their precise locations had not been determined, and no information had been identified that would aid in determining them. We used the available military maps and documents of the campaign to identify general areas in Armstrong, Wheeler, and Gray counties, respectively, that seemed to match the areas described in the military documents, but it was not clear from the documents precisely where the battles had taken place. Clearly, on-the-ground archeological surveys, potentially over large areas, would be needed to locate these sites precisely.

The location of the Battle of Palo Duro Canyon has been known for many years, but the full extent of the battle within the canyon has never been determined. The question, then, was how much, if any, of the battle site was within the boundaries of Palo Duro Canyon State Park. Some of the military reports of the battle indicate that the Indians were pursued some 4 miles up the canyon. If true, then some of the battle would have taken place within what is now the state park, and the only way to determine if that was indeed the case was to conduct an archeological survey over that area of the park that would have been part of the battle site in an effort to find and identify any battle-related artifacts.

Faced with the need to examine large areas in order to locate precisely and establish boundaries for most of the sites, and assuming that most of the artifacts associated with the battles would be metallic (e.g., copper cartridges and lead bullets), we elected to use metal detectors in our surveys of the battle sites. The use of metal detectors proved to be most effective given the time and financial constraints of the project.

Field Methods

The archeological methods used during the investigations were similar to those that have been used effectively at other battle sites.[1] The approach included several steps. First, the archeological team, equipped with metal detectors, systematically scanned the study area for metal artifacts (fig. 3.1). The metal detector team was aligned at approximate 10 m (33-foot) intervals, though deviation in spacing was unavoidable in rough terrain. The daily composition of the detector crew ranged from four to six operators. The team proceeded in line, using a sweeping motion to examine the ground. Each operator covered a sweep of 1.5–2 m (4.9–6.6 feet), depending on individual height and technique. When the metal detectors indicated the presence of a metal object on the surface or buried, that place was marked with a surveyor's pin flag. The metal object was then excavated and left in place. If the artifact appeared to be related to the battle, it was assigned a unique identification number. This number was written on the pin flag, and the flag was left in place so the artifact could be recorded (fig. 3.2). Each artifact was then mapped in place and collected.

At the Lyman Wagon Train and Buffalo Wallow sites, a total station electronic distance measurer was used to record the precise location of each artifact along with topographic readings. At the other battle sites we chose not to use a total station to record and map artifact locations because these battle sites covered large areas that were often in very rough terrain and thickly covered with vegetation. At these sites we believed it would be more cost effective and time efficient to map the artifacts using a global positioning system (GPS) receiver that could be operated by one person

▶ Fig. 3.1. The archeological team uses metal detectors to find battle-related artifacts.

▲ Fig. 3.2. A pin flag marks the location of and identifies an Indian-associated rifle cartridge case.

(fig. 3.3). The GPS used was a Trimble Pro XRS GPS data logger receiver with real-time differential correction accurate to less than 1 m.

After the location data for the artifacts had been collected, digital elevation model map files from the U.S. Geological Survey's website (www.cr.usgs.gov) were downloaded and imported into the SURFER software-mapping program to create topographic maps of the individual battle sites. The total station and GPS data were then also imported into the SURFER program and overlaid onto the topographic maps to produce precise maps showing the position of each battle-related artifact.

Various brands of metal detectors were used during the survey. Volunteers furnished their own machines, and this contributed to the variety. One of the primary reasons for using a variety of metal detectors was to avoid the phenomenon known as detector cross talk. Metal detectors that run at the same frequency may interfere with each other when used at close proximity, which results in poor detector performance. The metal discrimination settings for each detector were set to identify all types of metal.

Prior to the initiation of fieldwork, we attempted to identify and interview local people and area landowners who might have information concerning the locations of the battle sites. This proved largely unsuccessful; only a single landowner had any knowledge of a battle site on his property. The landowners of the properties where the other battle sites were eventually identified were unaware of their presence.

Fig. 3.3. The recording crew utilizes a GPS receiver to map each artifact precisely.

Laboratory Methods

The methods used in cleaning and cataloging the artifacts were standard laboratory procedures for metal artifacts from archeological contexts. Essentially the methods consisted of washing the dirt and mud from each artifact and determining which items would need additional cleaning or conservation. All of the cartridges recovered from the investigations were treated in diluted glycolic acid to remove oxides that had built up on them during the years they were in the ground. All of the iron artifacts, as well as some of the cartridges, were subjected to electrolytic reduction treatment to remove oxides and to stop the corrosion of the metal. After the artifacts were cleaned, they were bagged in clear plastic bags along with an acid-free paper tag marked with the project name, the artifact type, and provenience information. The artifacts were then identified, sorted, and analyzed.

The identification, sorting, and analysis consisted of dividing the artifacts into classes of similar objects and then subsorting the artifacts into further identifiable discrete types. For example, the cartridge cases were placed together and then subsorted into their respective types, such as .45/70-caliber Springfield cases or .44-caliber Henry rimfire cartridge cases. Some artifacts were sorted into even more discrete levels if warranted. For example, the .44-caliber Henry cases were sorted into the following categories: long and short cases; head stamped and not head stamped; and single firing pin marks, double firing pin marks, and multiple firing pin marks. Sorting and identification of the cartridges were undertaken by Douglas D. Scott of the National Park Service's Midwest Archeological Center, who compared the cartridges with type collections and with standard reference materials. The other artifacts were identified and analyzed by personnel at the Texas Historical Commission.

Once the analysis of the artifacts was completed and the necessary items conserved, the artifacts were returned to the individual landowners or to curatorial facilities chosen by the landowners. The project records remain on file at the Texas Historical Commission in Austin.

Analysis of Cartridges and Bullets, by Douglas D. Scott

Most of the artifacts recovered from the battle sites were cartridges, cartridge cases, and bullets, which through their class and individual characteristics had the potential to reveal the most information about the battles. The comparative study of ammunition components is known as firearms identification analysis. Firearm characteristics on cartridge cases are firing pin and extractor marks; on bullets they are land-and-groove marks. These characteristics allow determination of the type of firearm (i.e., model or brand) in which a given case or bullet was fired. This then allows determination of the number of different types of firearms in use at a particular battle. Further, individual weapons can be identified by comparing the unique firearm identification characteristics. For example, the number of individual Spencer carbines or Henry repeating rifles represented in the archeological collection can be demonstrated. This capability is important because, coupled with precise artifact locations, identical individual characteristics can be used to trace the movements of individual weapons across the field of battle. With this information, patterns of movement can be established and the battle sequence can be more precisely interpreted.

The means to this analytical end require some explanation. When a weapon is fired, the firing pin strikes the primer contained in the cartridge, leaving a distinctive imprint on the cartridge case head. The primer (fig. 3.4) ignites the powder, thus forcing the bullet down the barrel. The rifling in the barrel imprints the lands and grooves on the bullet in mirror image, and the extractor imprints the spent case as it is extracted from the firearm's chamber. These imprints are called class and individual characteristics. Microscopic examination of a class characteristic allows determination of the weapon type. This is important because many types of ammunition can

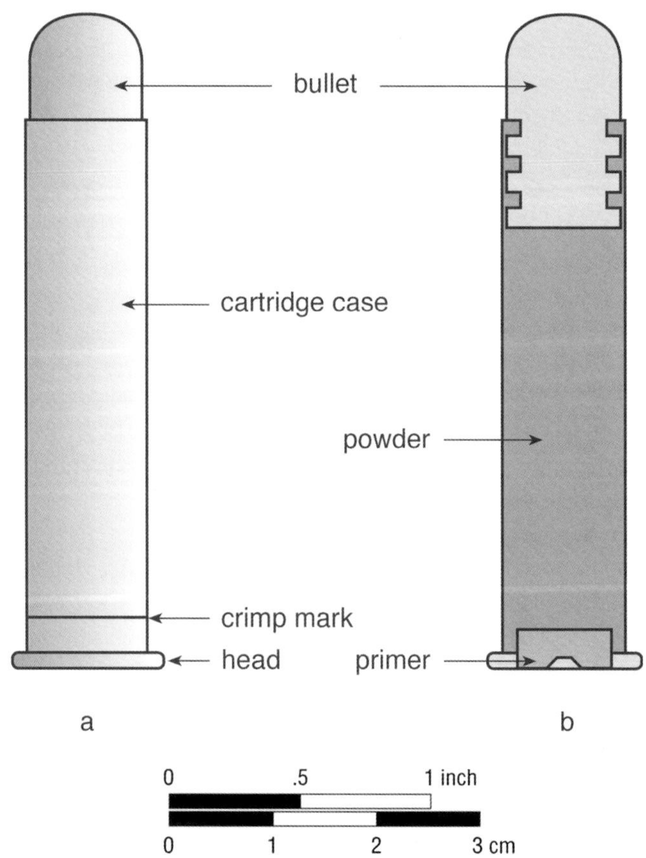

Fig. 3.4. Components of a .45/70 cartridge: a, exterior; b, interior. Illustration by Roland Pantermuehl

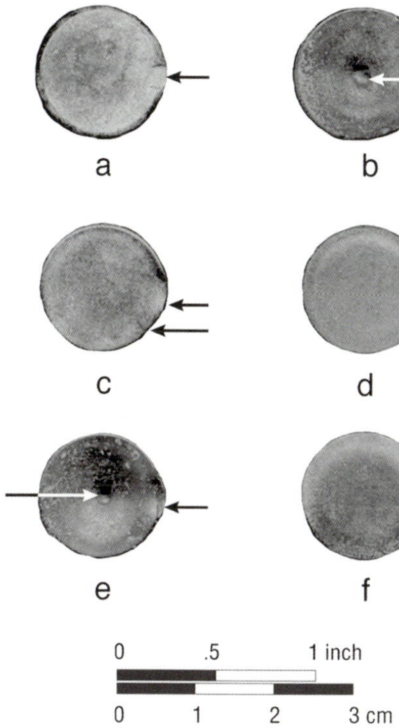

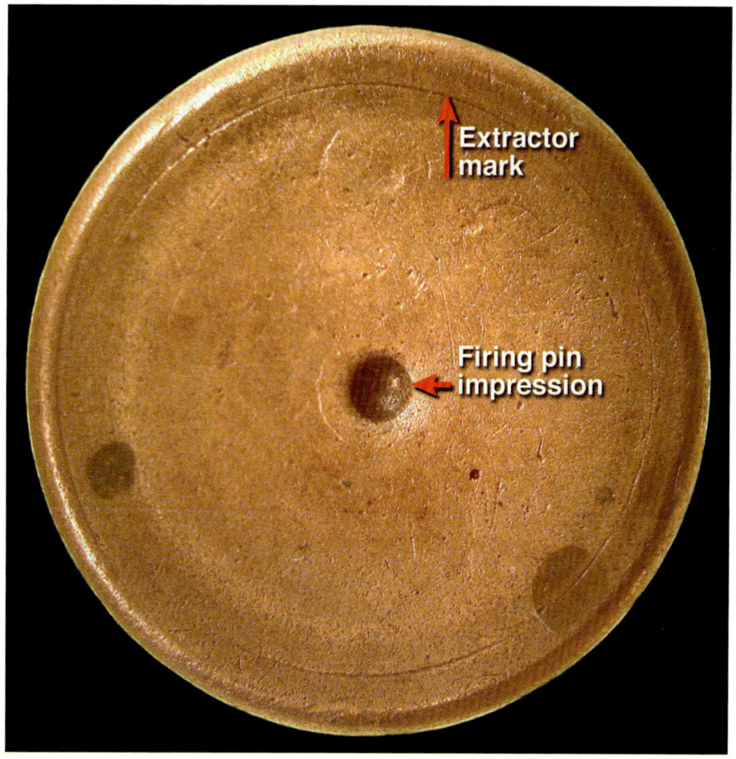

◀ Fig. 3.5. Firing pin marks on cartridges aid the identification of individual weapons: a, Spencer cartridge with a Ballard block type firing pin imprint; b, .50/70 cartridge struck with a Sharps firing pin; c, Spencer cartridge that has been struck twice; d, Spencer cartridge with a Jocelyn firing pin imprint; e, Spencer cartridge that was initially struck by a Sharps firing pin but was fired in a Spencer; f, standard Spencer firing pin imprint.

▲ Fig. 3.6. Microscopic examination of cartridge cases reveals the type of firing pin that struck the cartridge. Here the microscopic view of the head of a .50/70 cartridge shows the firing pin impression and extractor mark made by a Ward-Burton carbine.

be fired in a variety of firearms. By way of example, the .44-caliber Henry cartridge could be fired not only in the Henry repeating rifle (for which the Henry cartridge was designed) but also in the Model 1866 Winchester, the .44 rimfire Colt pistol, and the .44 rimfire Remington revolver. The firing pin of each weapon type is distinctive, and it is thus possible to identify the weapon type in which a given .44 Henry cartridge was fired.

Police agencies have long used the investigative technique of firearms identification as an aid in solving crimes. They commonly compare bullets and cartridge cases to identify weapon types.[2] Police are routinely successful in matching bullets and cartridge cases to a crime weapon simply by demonstrating that the firing pin, extractor marks, or land-and-groove marks could have been made only by a certain weapon. Even if the weapons used in crimes are not recovered, police can say with certainty, on the basis of the class and individual characteristics found on the bullets and cartridge cases, that specific types and numbers of weapons were used.

Macroscopically, firing pins and their characteristics often appear identical from weapon to weapon within a single type. However, minute variations, unique to each firing pin, allow the identification of individual weapons (fig. 3.5). Such variations are visible only through a microscope (fig. 3.6). These unique variations are caused by variable tolerances in tooling machinery and by wear to the cutting surfaces used in the manufacture of a firearm. The individual characteristics left on most ammunition components from the Red River War battle sites are amenable to firearms identification procedures, even after more than 125 years in the ground. In essence, these marks are metallic fingerprints.

Extractor characteristics are also valuable metallic fingerprints. A fired cartridge case is removed or ejected from a firearm by a mechanical device called an extractor. Just like the firing pin, the extractor leaves its imprint on the case (fig. 3.7). An extractor installed in a weapon of a given type, a Spencer rifle or carbine, for example, leaves

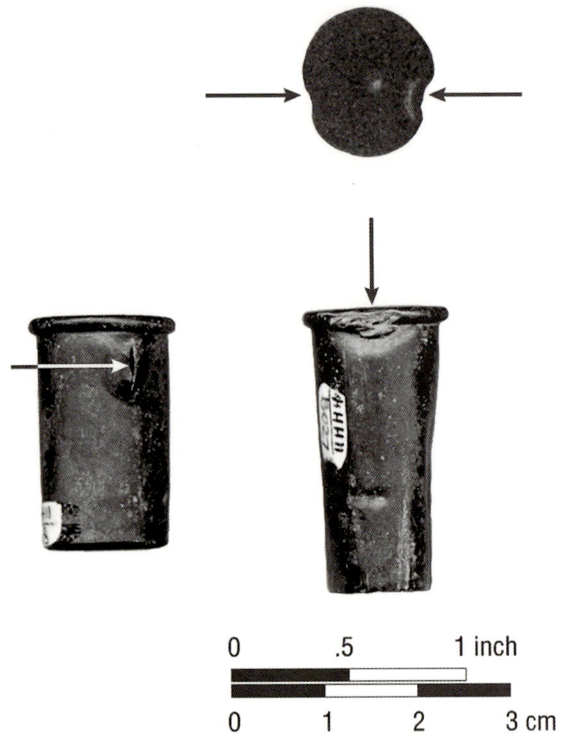

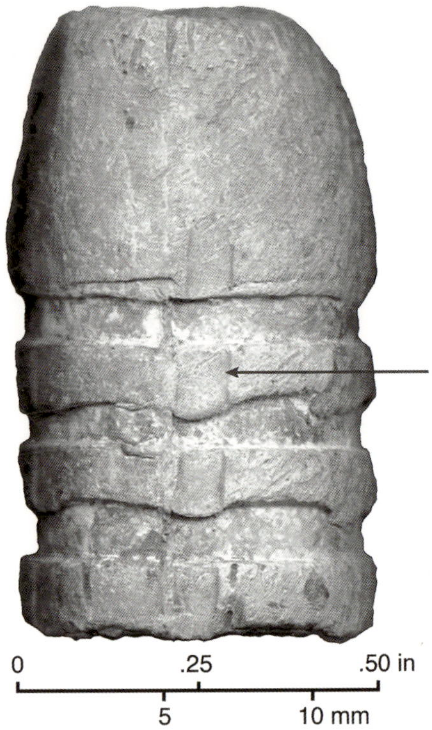

▲ Fig. 3.7. Extractor marks on cartridges can help identify the type of weapon that fired the cartridge. When an extractor becomes worn or is fouled, it can damage the cartridge: top, .50/70 cartridge with extractor marks from a Gatling gun; bottom, Spencer cartridges with damage caused by the firearm's extractor.

▶ Fig. 3.8. The land-and-groove marks on bullets can be used to determine the type of weapon from which they were fired. In this case, the .50-caliber bullet was fired from a Sharps rifle.

a characteristic mark that is peculiar to that extractor type; that is, the extractor characteristic on casings fired from the Spencer carbine is different from signatures left by other weapon types. Furthermore, and again like firing pins, each individual extractor has unique traits that distinguish it from all other extractors of the same type. Given these extractor characteristics, it is possible to identify individual weapons within each type by microscopic examination. The ability to read extractor characteristics provides strong corroborating data when used in conjunction with analyses of the individual characteristics of firing pins, for both appear together on most cartridge cases.

Bullets, of course, are also important in firearms identification. The barrel of a rifled gun has a series of lands and grooves that impart a spin to the bullet as it travels down the barrel. This spin gives the bullet greater aerodynamic stability and accuracy in its trajectory. The bullet is lead, whereas the barrel is steel. Since the bullet fits tightly in the barrel, the barrel leaves its land-and-groove impressions in reverse on the softer lead bullet (fig. 3.8). As with a firing pin, each barrel manufactured for a certain weapon type has individually recognizable characteristics. The land-and-groove characteristics left on the bullets can be used to determine weapon type and individual weapons within a type.

The comparison microscope is critical to the analysis of ammunition. Simply, the microscope is constructed so that a bridge joins two separate microscope tubes with prisms mounted over the tubes. Two separate images are transmitted to the center of the bridge, where another set of prisms transmits the images to central eyepieces. The eyepieces are divided so that each image appears on one-half of the eyepieces. Movable stages allow the objects under scrutiny to be manipulated so that they can be directly compared for class and individual characteristics (see, e.g., figs. D.5, H.3, H.4).

The cartridges, cartridge cases, and bullets from each of the Red River War battle sites were analyzed using these firearms identification procedures.

4

Historiography and Archival Research

MARTHA DOTY FREEMAN

The focus of the archival research for the project was on those aspects of the Red River War that had taken place in Texas; the task was to collect documents that contained information about the locations of battle sites, camp sites, trails, and other aspects of material culture that might be useful to archeologists in the field. By the summer of 2000, when research for the project began, some eighty years' worth of articles and books by historians about the Red River War had already been published. However, since historians nearly always miss some archival resources, and because archives are "fluid," with new materials frequently being added to holdings, it seemed likely that some records and materials had been missed by previous researchers.

A cursory look at earlier studies suggested this was indeed the case. Particularly puzzling was the apparent dearth of manuscript maps from the campaign. Only one study had reproduced a map that illustrated military routes in Texas during the war. Even if previous researchers and historians had not been particularly interested in the same topics that archeologists were, it seemed logical that they would have reproduced such maps if they had found them. Or perhaps they would have referred to them in their discussions of tactics, terrain, and locations of important battles and skirmishes. Thus the question: if maps made in the field or shortly after the campaign were not represented in the known archival record, what else might have been missed? To begin to answer this question it seemed logical to start the search with several commonly used record groups at the National Archives and to expand the search to other archives if new data could not be located there.

Historiography and Previous Research

Participants in the Red River War were the original chroniclers of the conflict, and they wrote diaries describing events during 1874–75 as well as memoirs that were published, sometimes posthumously. Frank T. Baldwin, Charles A. P. Hatfield, Ranald S. Mackenzie, and Thompson McFadden kept diaries and letterbooks.[1] Nelson A. Miles's *Personal Recollections and Observations* was published in 1896 and included two chapters in which he analyzed the causes of the war and briefly described the 1874 battles of August 30 (Red River), September 9–12 (Lyman's Wagon Train, Buffalo Wallow, and Sweetwater Creek), September 28 (Palo Duro Canyon), and November 8 (Baldwin's attack on Grey Beard's village).[2] Scout Billy Dixon published his memoirs in 1914, and Alice Baldwin published the memoirs of her late husband,

Frank D. Baldwin, in 1929.[3] Robert G. Carter, who served with Mackenzie, authored two volumes in 1926 and 1935; J. T. Marshall's eyewitness account of the war was not published until 1971.[4]

Academic, noncombatant interest in chronicling the history of the Red River War dates to the 1920s and 1930s when scholars such as H. H. Richardson, J. Evetts Haley, Wilbur S. Nye, and Carl C. Rister wrote articles and chapters in books about the campaign.[5] They quoted from documents in the National Archives, Library of Congress, and Fort Sill, and they acknowledged the help of people associated with the Panhandle-Plains Historical Society. One of the members of the latter organization, Ernest Archambeau, was its president when it acquired a copy of microfilm from the National Archives that recorded images of what was believed to be the bulk of government documents pertaining to the campaign. These documents were part of the Adjutant General's Office (AGO) File 2815, and the Society made copies of them from the National Archives microfilm. Joe Taylor, a professor at Amarillo College, then organized, transcribed, and annotated the documents, and he published them in the *Panhandle-Plains Historical Review* in 1961 with a map that depicted various military routes. Taylor remarked at the time that AGO File 2815 was not the only record describing the events of the war, since many of the actual participants had written memoirs. But he believed, correctly, that File 2815 was a "major" set of records, most of which had not appeared in print previously.[6]

Taylor's work was particularly useful because it published a large collection of documents that historians of the conflict had recognized as important, and a collection that had been used even before 1961. One of those historians was Nye, who claimed to have seen File 2815 in 1935, when it was still housed in the old War, State, and Navy Building in Washington, D.C. When Nye published *Plains Indian Raiders,* he alleged that the file "contained all the records, including maps, of the campaign of 1874–75," an intriguing statement in light of a dearth of cartographic resources in the file by the time Taylor used it twenty-five years later.[7] The idea that a single file contained all the records of any historical event also seemed more hyperbolic than accurate.

After 1961, historians such as James Haley, Paul A. Hutton, William H. Leckie, Michael D. Pierce, Robert Utley, and Robert Wooster either used File 2815 at the National Archives or referred to Taylor's work and supplemented it with collections in the Library of Congress, which was a repository for the papers of officers who had been involved in the war. Leckie, for example, included two chapters about the Red River War in his book *The Military Conquest of the Southern Plains,* which placed the conflict in the broader context of the Euro-American conquest of the Southern Plains. Beginning his discussion of Indian-white relations in the 1820s, Leckie described events in Texas and north of the Arkansas River as well as the inevitable requests from citizens for protection. In response to those requests, the federal government initiated treaties, constructed military posts between 1848 and the Civil War, and established an Indian reserve and an agency on the Upper Brazos River in Texas. The Civil War was accompanied by a retreat eastward of the lines of settlement and numerous engagements that culminated in the 1864 Sand Creek massacre in Colorado Territory. The massacre ignited an Indian war from the Red River to the Northern Plains that did not end until late 1865 with a treaty that gave the Comanches and Kiowas a reservation that included the Texas Panhandle and Indian Territory west of longitude 98 degrees west.

Pressures from the immigration and settlement of whites were continuous, however, and by the late 1860s the Southern Plains were the last home for the Indians. Conflict continued, both between citizens and Indians and between Indians and military personnel stationed at forts from Duncan on the Rio Grande to McPherson in

Nebraska; the consequences were significant military campaigns in 1868–69 and concentration of numerous Indian bands at the Fort Sill and Camp Supply agencies. Peace was short lived, however, as raiding groups of Kiowas and Comanches struck well into the Texas settlements. Col. Ranald Mackenzie campaigned extensively throughout the Llano Estacado and Rolling Plains areas of Texas beginning in 1871, and he initiated a decisive battle at a Comanche village on September 29, 1872.[8] Indian-white relations were further agitated by the slaughter of buffalo and invasion of the Texas Panhandle by hunters following the last of the herds. By the summer of 1874, the stage was set for a comprehensive military campaign against the Indians.

Leckie related the events of the ensuing Red River War, describing the development of plans for the campaign, organization of the multicolumn structure, the battles of August 30, September 9–12, and September 28 as well as numerous skirmishes, and the aftermath of the campaign. He briefly mentioned Lt. Henry J. Farnsworth's battle of November 6, 1874, but he erroneously stated that Farnsworth departed from Camp Supply, that the battle occurred on McClellan Creek, and that one soldier rather than two was killed during the battle.[9]

In 1973, Robert M. Utley published *Frontier Regulars: The United States Army and the Indian, 1866–1891*. Utley relied heavily on printed original sources and monographs supplemented by manuscript sources at the Library of Congress and official records in the National Archives (Record Groups 75, 94, 98, and 107) to describe the history of relations between Indians and the army after the Civil War. His brief chapter about the Red River War reflected this reliance on published sources, including Taylor's publication and the papers of William T. Sherman. Utley provided an overview of the war, touching on key battles (though failing to mention Lieutenant Farnsworth's battle of November 6) and describing hardships imposed by severe weather and the lack of adequate supplies in the field. He characterized the prosecution of the war as largely uncoordinated, being run by General Augur of the Department of Texas and General Pope commanding the Department of the Missouri "without much coordination between them or guidance from above." He saved his harshest criticism for Nelson A. Miles, whom he described as "temperamental," fearful that problems with supplies would deny him opportunities to "reap the glory" in competition with Mackenzie, and furious because of Pope's supervision.[10]

Several historians went beyond the commonly used sources listed in other works—most notably Paul A. Hutton and Robert Wooster, who returned to the National Archives to find additional documents in the Bureau of Indian Affairs and a variety of other record groups including those in Record Group 393 (the Department of the Missouri). Wooster, in particular, added to the general scholarship by using the Miles collection, but he also erroneously placed Farnsworth's encounter with Grey Beard on McClellan Creek.[11]

James Haley also probed deeper, using records at the Oklahoma Historical Society and other repositories to write the first full-length treatment of the Red River War fifteen years after Taylor's work appeared in print. He followed up on Nye's reference to files at Fort Sill but found that very few of those documents remained at the fort. He noted, mysteriously, that the material had been transferred "beyond his reach." More important, Haley concluded that, beyond Taylor's 1961 transcription of AGO File 2815, "very little military correspondence from the period had been edited and published." He hoped that "the rest of this tremendous mass of letters and documents [would] . . . one day be similarly ordered and brought to print."[12]

Haley did not specify what all that "mass" was, but the idea that it existed, together with the puzzling absence of maps, daily logs, journals, and other records that were usual products of military expeditions, seemed enough to justify an assumption that additional records might exist that could assist in the search for sites associated with the Red River War.

Understanding the Military Structure

Successful searches for apparently missing or "unmined" records often are a function of serendipity and luck, but they always benefit from an understanding of bureaucratic structure and organization. For example, the Adjutant General's Office in Washington, D.C., was the chief administrative and record keeping agency of the U.S. Army. Under the direction of the secretary of war, the adjutant general had custody of War Department correspondence from officers in the field, various military divisions and departments, and other sources.

In some cases, related documents pertaining to particular subjects such as the Red River War were consolidated into single files. These consolidated files vary in size and often are used by historians because they are thought to provide the best opportunity for obtaining a view of all levels of the army's participation in a given situation. The Adjutant General's Office was the final referral point for reports and correspondence, and its files usually contained material from all command levels. The AGO files eventually were transferred to the National Archives, where they were microfilmed. This, then, was the origin of the AGO File 2815 that was published by Joe Taylor.

The Adjutant General's Office was a repository for a vast array of War Department records. In addition, the War Department had divided the United States into various geographic divisions, each of which became a repository for records. The military division that was pertinent to the study of the Red River War was the Division of the Missouri, which was headquartered in Chicago and embraced an area that included the states of Minnesota, Illinois, Iowa, Kansas, Missouri, and Texas as well as Indian Territory and the territories of Montana, Dakota, Utah, Nebraska, Colorado, and New Mexico. The primary business of the Division of the Missouri was Indians, but a subtext was Euro-American settlement and the development of industries such as railroading, the harvesting of wildlife, and the development of agriculture, all of which put settlers on a collision course with Native Americans.

The Division of the Missouri was divided into four departments. From north to south these were the Department of Dakota, Department of the Platte, Department of the Missouri, and Department of Texas. Each department had its own headquarters. The two most relevant to the Red River War were the Department of the Missouri, headquartered at Fort Leavenworth, Kansas, and the Department of Texas, headquartered in San Antonio.

Within each department were numerous districts, subdistricts, forts, posts, and camps; records pertaining to the Red River War were generated at all levels within the organization. Theoretically, records generated in the field, or copies of them, were passed through the hierarchy. They eventually landed in department headquarters in San Antonio or Fort Leavenworth, then were forwarded to division headquarters in Chicago and finally to the Adjutant General's Office in Washington.

But people and records are not always predictable. People sometimes become attached to records, particularly those that have some transcendent or personal meaning. In the nineteenth century particularly, officers frequently considered what are now identified as official records to be personal property—hence the depositing of military records in the Library of Congress, the Pennsylvania Historical Society, the Center for American History in Austin, and numerous other archives rather than exclusively in the National Archives where "proper channels" would be expected to place them. What became clear during the search for Red River War documents was that records occasionally got sidetracked or recalled because someone wished to use them for a purpose other than the reason they were created. In such cases, documents that reentered the system did not necessarily end up where the official structure suggested they might be filed. Instead, they sometimes remained with division, department, post, or even camp files.

In 2000, most of the files that had remained in the possession of government agencies were in the National Archives in various record groups, some of which held obvious appeal for archeologists interested in the material culture of military campaigns or the field identification of sites. Record Group 92, for example, included the records of the Office of the Quartermaster General, always an important function during a military campaign. Record Group 94 (Records of the Adjutant General's Office) was the location of File 2815, but it also included a miscellaneous series of nineteen feet of files that had journals, inspection reports, correspondence, maps, printed materials, and photographs. Record Group 393 (Records of United States Army Continental Commands) seemed to offer enormous potential to the Red River War study. This record group held the records of military divisions that had been established to handle problems requiring an effort beyond the capacity of one department, the Plains warfare of the late nineteenth century being one example of such an effort. Record Group 393 also encompassed reports from headquarters and individual officers, special collections of records concerning Indian relations, records of special field expeditions, correspondence of the Division of the Missouri that paralleled and sometimes duplicated correspondence found in Record Group 94, records of the Departments of the Missouri and Texas, records generated by Nelson Miles, letters and telegrams reporting operations in the field, and records from specific military installations.

Research Effort for This Project

The various relevant record groups are enormous, and the project promised to be complex. Given that Joe Taylor had published the contents of the Adjutant General Office's file about the Red River War, it seemed logical to create an abstract of each piece of correspondence in the file, arranged in chronological order, to avoid duplication of his effort during the search for new documents in other files. An initial trip to the National Archives involved what may best be described as a shotgun approach, in which materials from every record group that seemed to have even the remotest possibility of containing pertinent documents were requested. Among these were Record Group 393, which included letters sent by the Military Division of the Missouri, letters sent by the Department of the Missouri, and special orders concerning the expedition. In addition, there were letters and telegrams received at division headquarters and reports of scouts and expeditions. Moving down the military hierarchy, correspondence collected at posts from which troops had moved or points to which they had returned after being in the field was examined. These posts included Forts Leavenworth, Sill, Griffin, Richardson, and Concho and Camp Supply. One of the most remarkable documents found during this effort was the original handwritten plea for help by Capt. Wyllys Lyman on September 10, 1874, as his supply train was surrounded and under siege by Indians. A copy of this famous document had been forwarded up the chain of command, but the original, written in pencil on a small piece of white paper with an amazingly steady hand, had remained with a small set of records at Camp Supply.

Because it seemed likely that some pertinent records were imbedded in letters sent by units that participated in the war, Record Group 391 (Records of United States Regular Army Mobile Units) and Record Group 77 (Records of the Office of the Chief of Engineers) were examined with the hope that field data generated by engineers who accompanied the expedition might be found. A visit to the Cartographic Branch of the National Archives, which holds maps generated by engineers, yielded several campaign maps that had been extracted from files in the Old Military Branch.

This initial effort turned up many hundreds of pages of documents that were not a part of AGO File 2815. The discovery of so many "new" old records was gratifying, but the initial search had failed to find maps other than the few at the Cartographic Branch. At that point, the example of the Lyman note, which had appeared in an unusual place, led to speculation that records of the Division of the Missouri also contained a consolidated file that was equivalent to AGO consolidated File 2815. Initial inquiries brought the response, first, that it was unlikely that any such records had not been forwarded to the Adjutant General's Office and, second, that some division records had been destroyed in one of the Chicago fires. However, another query to an archivist with long experience in the Old Military Branch resulted in a visit to the stacks and the identification of two boxes marked "Indian Territory Expedition (Red River War), May 1874–Apr. 1875." The boxes contained more than a thousand pages of manuscript material and numerous manuscript maps.

Transcription of this division-level special file revealed, again, hundreds of records that were not duplicated in AGO File 2815. But it seemed that numerous others were still missing, for hints of their existence appeared throughout the new records. For example, Gen. C. C. Augur, Department of Texas, had instructed Col. Ranald Mackenzie on August 28 to "have maps made of the Country passed over. . . . These should be accompanied with description of the route and adjacent Country."[13] In Nelson Miles's three-volume set of letters, endorsements, and special orders from field headquarters there was a note in a letter to the assistant adjutant general at Fort Leavenworth that Miles had, "during the various movements of the different columns of this command, taken particular pains to have careful itineraries preserved, and notes taken by competent men, that I will order to report to the Chief Engineer's Office at the close of operations."[14] So, what had happened to these records?

Repeated queries to reference archivists at the Old Military Branch, and even to the archivist who had revealed the existence of the "new" consolidated file, yielded no additional information. But the official reports and correspondence of Miles, who had repeatedly stated his displeasure with Maj. William Redwood Price and his intention to bring court-martial proceedings against him, suggested another source of information. Because trials often are a source of revealing testimony, it seemed logical to examine the original record of Price's court-martial. This document, which included more than eight hundred pages of detailed testimony about troop movements, also included original maps from the expedition that had been used to support charges against the officer.

The existence of field maps in a court-martial record, rather than in AGO, division, or department records where they should have been, raised another set of interesting questions and answered, in part, the earlier question raised by Miles's references to the records of the expedition. In addition, data imbedded within the trial record documented the existence of comprehensive records and chronicled what had become of them, up to a point. At the end of 1874 or early in 1875, Colonel Miles had instructed 2nd Lt. J. W. Pope, 5th Infantry, to turn over all itineraries, tracings, and notes of the expedition to Lieutenant Anderson of the 6th Cavalry at Camp Supply. The transfer was made in February 1875, and Anderson then sent the records to 1st Lt. E. H. Ruffner, engineer at department headquarters, Fort Leavenworth.[15] Ruffner, who used the records to compile a master map of the territory covered by the expedition, said of the expedition that "through its many movements and on account of the attention given by its Commanding Officer to the subject of the notes covering 3460 miles [this expedition has] left a record of new material which has no equal in the files of this Department since I have been here, and I do not find its superior in any Records that I am familiar with here or elsewhere."[16]

Major Price came to trial at Fort Lyon, Colorado, in the summer of 1875, at which time he requested that certain records of the Red River expedition be sent to him so that he could prepare a defense. The materials were forwarded to Fort Lyon, where the judge advocate took possession of them and stated that the notebooks of the marches of the 8th Cavalry Battalion contained "the original field notes in pencil of some of the important marches of the accused (Price) already in evidence."[17] Some of the map materials appear to have been retained in the court-martial file, but other materials were not in the file. Furthermore, testimony by Price's fellow officers suggested that some of them retained their records. 1st Lt. G. W. Baird, for example, still had official order and letter book volumes in his quarters at Fort Lyon as well as a diagram and notes of Price's march from Oasis Creek. 1st Lt. Frank D. Baldwin had made a written report of "the affair of November 8, 1874," but it was in a trunk that had been lost. Lt. Col. John W. Davidson mentioned at Price's trial that he had various records from the expedition. 1st Lt. H. R. Brinkerhoff stated that his original retained papers and returns pertaining to commissary and quartermaster duties were at his station at Fort Wingate, New Mexico, and he thought the records of the 8th Cavalry headquarters were in the possession of Price. Capt. Charles A. Hartwell stated that he had other 8th Cavalry records.[18]

There were no further hints in the court-martial record or in the records of the Division of the Missouri about the disposition of the expedition records that had not been made a permanent part of the court file. What could have happened to them? Was it possible that the request for evidence at Price's trial had interrupted the normal sequence of events? In other words, was it possible that documents that should have been forwarded from department headquarters at Fort Leavenworth to division headquarters at Chicago and then to the Adjutant General's Office never made it out of Fort Leavenworth? After all, Lyman's original note had been retained in the records of a small, short-lived camp.

The records of the Department of the Missouri did, indeed, contain one more bonanza. There were fourteen boxes for the period of the Red River War, and the first one contained a bundle of documents with the notation "Papers in the case of Major W. R. Price, 8th Cavalry."[19] There were numerous maps and reports by officers in the field that were not replicated elsewhere. There was Price's eleven-page report detailing his movements and actions in October 1874, Farnsworth's description of his fight in early November, and Baldwin's six-page report of his movements about the same time.[20] One of the most interesting documents was a map drawn under the supervision of 1st Lt. G. W. Baird, adjutant to Col. Nelson Miles.[21] The map (fig. 4.1) depicts camps on the Washita and Canadian rivers; trails made by Lyman, Howe, Price, and Biddle; and the scene of Lyman's fight. Distances between each point were precisely measured by odometer under Baird's direction. The number of notes on the map that pertained to Price strongly suggests that the map was intended to support Miles's court-martial case against him. Perhaps unwittingly, Miles also had left an unusually accurate graphic record of several sites associated with the Red River War.

Contributions

Although the focus of the research effort between 2000 and 2002 was on the identification of cartographic and textual records that would assist archeological fieldwork, the project also yielded other benefits. Previously unused documents, for example,

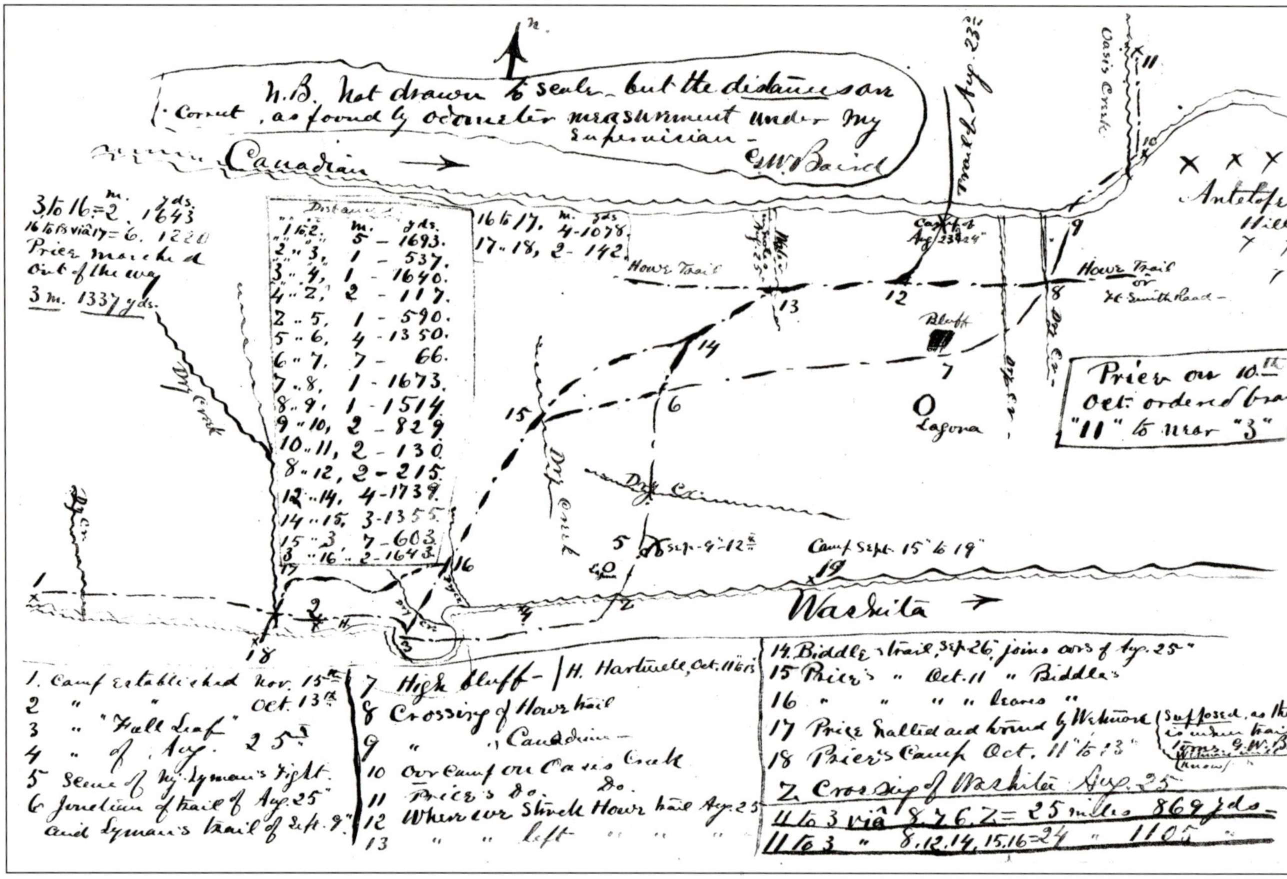

Fig. 4.1. This hand-drawn map by Lt. George W. Baird shows precise distances between several Red River War–related sites as recorded by wagon odometer. Record Group 393, Part I, Entry 2601, Box No. 41, National Archives.

have the potential to contribute new or more in-depth understanding of the parameters and details of the 1874–75 campaign while correcting or modifying widely held ideas about the war.

On the most basic level, some documents provide information that modifies the campaign narrative. Miles's official report about his movements and operations between August 26 and September 1, 1874, was reproduced in Taylor and has been cited by historians frequently. In the interim, however, Miles twice corrected his report, changing some details and adding others. He noted, for example, that his command moved out on the morning of August 26 rather than in the evening; he deleted a reference to Lieutenant Baldwin's party having been on the Canadian; he clarified the positions of the cavalry, artillery, and infantry during the battle of August 30; he analyzed the reasons for the slight loss of troops, noting that after the initial attack the Indians had fought only cautiously; and he speculated about the role the Gatling and Parrott guns had played in both surprising and terrifying the Indians.[22]

In other cases, documents correct published accounts of particular battles. Descriptions of actions by Colonel Buell between October 9 and 12, 1874, found in Leckie and Haley bear little resemblance to the information transmitted in reports by Buell. Haley, for example, stated that Buell "sacked" a Kiowa camp of seventy-five lodges on October 11 and the next day "put to the torch a village that he claimed numbered 475 tipis, all identified as Kiowas." He then accused Buell of "grossly exaggerat[ing]" the number of Kiowas. Buell's own report from the field, however, stated that on October 12 he had found "a recently deserted camp of some three or four hundred lodges of the Shians [Cheyennes]," and his summary report in February 1875 reiterated that his command had found, but not burned, "a recently deserted Cheyenne Camp of several hundred Lodges" on the twelfth.[23]

Misstatements of fact concerning the tribes involved in actions and the populations of each tribe have been accompanied by assertions by other historians that officers inflated the numbers of the enemy. Although some hyperbole does seem to have occurred, particularly in the opening months of the campaign, correspondence in Record Group 393 demonstrates that Lt. Col. Thomas H. Neill, Brig. Gen. C. C. Augur, Col. Nelson Miles, 1st Lt. R. H. Pratt, and Lt. Col. J. W. Davidson paid particular and increasing attention to the numbers and whereabouts of individual bands. Supplementing data from the Indian Bureau with reports by Indians such as White Horse, a Cheyenne chief, sons of Mow-way, and various unnamed Indians, the military focused on putting numbers to the Cheyennes, Kiowas, Comanches, and Apaches at the Cheyenne and Kiowa agencies and at Fort Sill. They also attempted to identify the whereabouts and numbers of lodges associated with chiefs such as Stone Calf, Lone Wolf, and Grey Beard as they moved toward New Mexico, up on the Llano Estacado, or north to the agencies.[24] Collecting such data informed decisions about troop movements and answered the ever-important question: How close was the campaign to a successful conclusion?

Other documents suggest that, although most historians identified Quakers and Quaker agents as factors in the planning and execution of the war, they did not appreciate the complexity and length of negotiations prior to the campaign. Between May and mid-July 1874, the Interior and War departments communicated continuously to develop mutually acceptable rules of engagement. Those negotiations were mirrored in discussions among Pope, Sheridan, Sherman, and the Indian superintendent in Lawrence, Kansas. The resulting, carefully crafted agreements, which required the army not to attack peaceful Indians at the agencies and to consult with and respect the agent, but also required the Indian agent not to interfere with military movements across department and reservation lines as troops followed hostiles onto the reservation and even to the agencies, were developed only after lengthy and detailed discussions. The resulting agreement provided a framework for action that became increasingly important as the campaign drew to a close and bands of hostile Indians sought to return to their respective agencies.

Another set of documents contradicts the widely held belief that communications in the field were extremely poor, and that delays in correspondence severely hampered the commanders. Voluminous correspondence reveals another story, in which Miles corresponded regularly, frequently, and in great detail, closely directing the actions of all but Mackenzie, to whom he deferred, and receiving responses by courier.[25]

One of the most interesting sets of documents contains information about military and Indian tactics. About the first subject, Maj. William Price highlighted the ways in which the prosecution of the Red River War was different from his previous experience in the field. Commenting on the events leading up to his court-martial on several charges brought by Miles, Price remarked that he knew "nothing about fighting Indians by grand combinations [referring to the coordination of multiple columns] or artillery at long range." Rather, he harkened back to his earlier service in New Mexico, where his experience had taught him "to fight them [the Indians] in their own fashion" wherever he could find them.[26] Indeed, Miles himself stated that the campaign had unfolded in a manner completely unlike what he had anticipated. Plans had called for the expedition to operate between Camp Supply and Fort Sill, detouring to the east or west. The military had predicted that the Indians would react by retreating to their agencies. Instead, they had moved away onto the Llano Estacado, through the canyons of the Red River, and to other remote locations, forcing the columns to move in pursuit some two hundred miles from any of the supply posts,[27] an action that frequently made it necessary to discontinue the pursuit.

For their part, the Indians' generally unpredictable behavior extended to more interesting tactics than an unwillingness to capitulate quickly. After the disastrous encounter between Capt. Wyllys Lyman's wagon train and Kiowa and Comanche warriors on September 9–12, Miles reviewed reports of the battle and then examined the site. He concluded that the Indians had practiced new methods of fighting, citing as evidence the descriptions of the battle and evidence in the field: "I found that the efforts of the Indians to capture the Train, were very determined and persistent; they even adopting modes of civilized warfare, such as, making diversions with mounted force and advancing the main force dismounted, and intrenching to hold the ground they gained. There were at least one hundred (100) rifle-pits within close range of the train." Reiterating a common complaint, Miles further wrote: "I deem it not out of place here, and not exceeding my duty, to call attention to the well known and lamentable fact, that while one branch of the government is, or has been supplying arms and ammunition to these Indians, either directly, or through authorized agents; the Officers and Soldiers of the Army have to give up their lives under the fire of these same weapons in the hand of these ruthless savages."[28]

To date, we have assembled approximately 1,200 transcribed pages of archival records that chronicle the events of the Red River War. The inventory is not, however, complete. We did not copy records concerning Col. Ranald Mackenzie's actions because of the focus of the archeological effort. Numerous records were simple notations of mundane affairs and had little if any bearing on the search for sites associated with the war. More important, a set of records that are the most basic evidence of the expedition are still missing. In the archival record there are sporadic references to "men who have charge of the odometers and notes of marches," to "careful itineraries," to Price's "notes of [his] entire scout," to three notebooks kept by Price, to "enlisted men who had been engaged in taking the notes of the marches of the Indian Territory Expedition," and to an engineer sergeant who was responsible for notes and itineraries.[29] These "meat and potatoes" records chronicling the expedition have yet to surface. Perhaps they were retained by officers who participated in the war. Or, perhaps they are sitting in descendants' attics, waiting to be found and rejoined with the balance of the documentary heritage of the Red River War.

5

Army and Indian Strategies, Tactics, and Weapons

After the Civil War, the U.S. Army turned its attention to the western Indians. Decades of intermittent warfare and broken treaties had left the army with no clear strategic policy to resolve the "Indian problem." But as thousands of emigrants were now moving into the western territories, the army was forced to renew its efforts to deal with the Indians and to aid the "manifest destiny" of the nation to expand to the Pacific Ocean. The army, however, found itself faced with several political, economic, and organizational problems that hampered its efforts to deal effectively with the Indians.

The Civil War had left the government with massive debts, which meant that the army had to conduct combat operations against the Indians with only surplus weapons and equipment. At the same time, Congress was drastically reducing the size of the regular army and assigning a large portion of the troops to help with the reconstruction of the South. The Army Appropriation Act of 1869 reduced the army from 54,000 to about 37,000, and by 1874 the number of enlisted men was further reduced to 25,000. By 1867, only slightly more than 15,400 soldiers were assigned to the whole of the Great Plains. As a result, the army during the Indian wars was completely unable to balance resources with requirements, both because of limited manpower and because of the enormous size of the theater of operations.[1]

Another problem the post–Civil War army faced was the poor quality of its soldier recruits. The frontier army was undertrained, underpaid, and recruited mostly from the country's unskilled poor. Nearly half of the recruits after the Civil War were foreign born and, as a general rule, many of them were illiterate, poor, and had difficulty with the English language. The *New York Sun* charged that the army was composed of "bummers, loafers, and foreign paupers."[2]

In addition, the army also now faced a new kind of adversary in the Plains Indian warrior. Where troops had previously been trained to fight massed armies, they now faced small bands of Indians on horseback who had refined the tactics of guerilla warfare into a fine art. How would the post–Civil War army respond to the problems and challenges of insufficient resources and manpower? Would the commanding officers apply Civil War strategies and tactics to their new foes?

During the time that the United States had been engaged in its civil war, the Indians of the Southern Plains enjoyed a period when they could raid Anglo and Mexican settlements and return to the relative safety of the plains with little fear of retaliation by army troops. However, some of the void left when federal troops went back east was filled by military units composed of citizen volunteers. These units would prove their effectiveness as Indian fighters, as Col. John Chivington and the Colorado volunteers demonstrated at Sand Creek, Colorado, in 1864, and Col. "Kit" Carson and the New Mexico volunteers proved against the Navajos in New Mexico and the Kiowas and Comanches at Adobe Walls in the Texas Panhandle in 1864.

Many of the post–Civil War changes that were affecting the U.S. Army were also affecting the Plains Indians. As more settlers moved west, more towns and settlements sprang up, more railroads were built across the plains to service the towns, more forts were established on the western frontier to protect the settlers, and more buffalo hunters moved onto the plains to systematically and drastically reduce the herds that were the livelihood of the Indians. All these factors combined to put tremendous pressure on the Plains Indian groups as they found themselves being boxed in by ever-increasing encroachments by the whites. How did the Indians respond to these pressures? What tactics did the Indians employ when the army launched its military campaigns against them and their villages? What weapons did the Indians have to fight the U.S. Army?

Post–Civil War Army Strategies and Tactics

For the most part, the army officers who were assigned to duty in the West after the Civil War and the commanders who were given the responsibility of bringing the Indian problem to a successful end did the best they could with the resources and support that were given them. The army adopted new strategies and innovations by altering the way cavalry, infantry, and artillery units fought. Officers quickly learned that tactics employed for fighting a European-trained army would not work against the hit-and-run guerilla movements of the Plains Indians; they learned the value of flexibility, innovation, and the application of practical strategies to whatever the current situation called for.[3]

Some officers and commanders—among them generals William T. Sherman, Philip H. Sheridan, John Pope, and George Crook—did have experience in dealing with and fighting Indians, and that experience was instrumental in the development of Indian policy and strategies for Indian fighting after the Civil War. After the Civil War, General Sherman (fig. 5.1) commanded the large Division of the Missouri. In 1869, he became commanding general, and he dominated the army for the next fourteen years. During these years Sherman was outspoken in his belief that Indian policy should be set by the army and that the various tribes should be placed on reservations and forced to stay there. He believed that Indians had no right to prevent white expansion and that hostile Indians should be severely chastised. He also believed that in order to combat the Indians the military had to launch vigorous offensives against their villages and economic bases. It was Sherman, and the beliefs he held, that became the most important force in molding post–Civil War actions against the Plains Indians.[4]

One of the most important concepts to evolve from this emphasis on the offensive was the use of converging columns. In theory, separate columns composed of cavalry and infantry would strike simultaneously at a central target from different directions, thereby surrounding and entrapping an enemy. In practice, the concept had several weaknesses. The biggest flaw was the inability to coordinate the movements of the columns over large geographic areas. The army's lack of mobility, communications, and logistical support were also problems for the operation. Army field units needed extensive food and equipment support, which required that large supply trains travel with the columns. Supply convoys, however, were slow moving and often had to be sent back for additional supplies, which slowed the column even more. Finally, for converging columns to be effective they had to coordinate their strikes against the enemy, and they relied on the enemy target being of a relatively large size and immobile. Plains Indians, though, were generally highly mobile and usually traveled in relatively small groups. Despite these potential problems, Phil Sheridan used converging columns with success against the Southern Plains Indians during his winter campaign in 1868 and again to launch the Red River War campaign in 1874.[5]

Fig. 5.1. Gen. William T. Sherman commanded the Division of the Missouri after the Civil War. Courtesy Panhandle-Plains Historical Museum, Canyon, Texas

Another strategy developed by Sheridan and endorsed by Sherman was the concept of attacking the Indians at their villages during the winter. During the winter months the Plains Indians typically established somewhat permanent camps near sources of water and wood, where they would remain until spring. The army viewed these winter camps as relatively fixed targets that were susceptible to attack, if they could be located. Attacks launched on these camps could lead to Indian horse herds being eliminated, food and supplies destroyed, and prisoners taken. Sheridan initiated his winter warfare concept on November 23, 1868, when he sent George Armstrong Custer and the 7th Cavalry to attack Chief Black Kettle's village of Cheyenne Indians on the Washita River in western Oklahoma Territory. Custer, using Osage Indians as scouts, found and charged into the unsuspecting village, killing more than one hundred Indians, including women and children. The soldiers killed more than seven hundred Indian horses and destroyed the village and winter stores. Though many considered the attack a massacre, Sheridan and Sherman viewed it as a great success, and the practice of destroying winter camps and starving the Indians into submission would be repeated throughout the Plains Indian Wars. The psychological effect of a successful attack on a village was that the survivors often surrendered.[6]

Another departure from conventional methods adopted during the Indian wars was the use of white frontiersmen and friendly Indians as scouts. Intelligence gathering was of enormous strategic and tactical importance. Knowing enemy troop movements, weapons capabilities, and numbers gave commanders in the field clear advantages. Commanders in the West began to understand that frontiersmen and Indian scouts, utilizing their stalking skills and familiarity with the landscape, could find and report on enemy activities without endangering their own troops. Army officers on the frontier knew exactly which intertribal enmities would benefit their mission, and they began to recruit scouts from among the enemies of the tribes hostile to the United States. On the Southern Plains, for example, they used Osage and Tonkawa Indians to lead expeditions against the Comanches and Kiowas. They also used black freedmen of Seminole-Negro heritage as scouts against several tribes.[7]

The U.S. Army used infantry, cavalry, and artillery units during the Plains Indian Wars. Though the infantry had more personnel and regiments than the cavalry and artillery combined, cavalry units—because of their speed and mobility—were typically employed more often against the Indians. Both cavalry and infantry companies operated in the Red River War, with more than two and a half times as many cavalry (thirty-four) as infantry companies (thirteen). The size of the typical company for both cavalry and infantry was about sixty (though often fewer) enlisted men.

Infantry forces provided mass firepower. They could operate in all weather conditions and in virtually any type of terrain. With their breechloader rifles, infantrymen could engage an enemy up to a thousand yards away. On the plains, however, Indians on fast ponies could easily avoid infantry troops, so infantry units were often given the duty of escorting and providing protection for supply wagons as they carried provisions from the supply depot to the cavalry troops closer to the scene of action.

Cavalry forces could be used in several ways. They could charge through a concentrated enemy force if they were making a surprise attack or if the unit was surrounded. They could provide fire while acting as skirmishers or give cover to retreating men. Often cavalry forces dismounted so that they could hold a position with disciplined

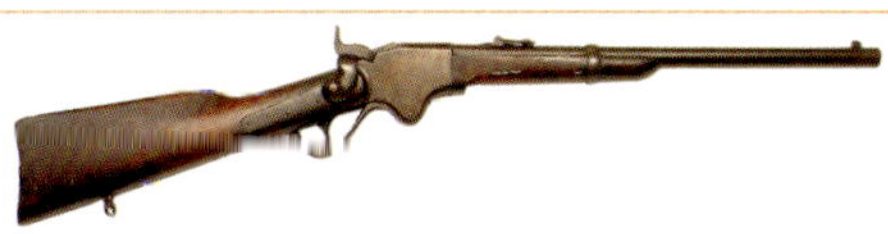

fire or supplement the actions of the infantry. With time, cavalry units learned to adapt to the guerilla style of the Plains Indians. At the end of the Civil War, the cavalry was not trained to meet the Indians horse to horse, but to fight as units. Mass tactics proved useless against the Indians, however, since the warriors would simply swerve away from charges. Massed fire likewise proved ineffective, for the Indians rarely presented a bunched target. Cavalry units learned that by putting sharpshooters—men who could fire at will at the weaving and circling warriors—on their perimeters, they could keep the Indians at a distance and prevent them from attacking their flanks.

One major problem the cavalry contended with throughout the campaigns in the West was the poor endurance of their horses. Even if sufficient grass could be found, which was rare, cavalry horses that were accustomed to subsisting on grain quickly deteriorated under extended exertion. Supplying ample grain to cavalry horses serving in remote areas of the West was extremely difficult, and rare was the campaign that afforded grain in sufficient abundance. Orders by commanding officers to feed only half forage to cavalry horses were common, as were the complaints by cavalry troopers that their horses were worn out and unable to keep up with the Indian ponies. Expressing this sentiment after an engagement with the Cheyenne on McClellan Creek in the Texas Panhandle in 1874, Col. Nelson Miles wrote: "In part of the fight of the 8th, the horses were reeling under the Troopers, and at the last charge of Lieut. Overton's Company, he had not ten men in the front line. This want of food . . . will, if continued, dismount every Cavalry-man. The same difficulty is experienced in regard to the train animals."[8] Col. John Davidson, in his report concerning the failed pursuit of the Indians engaged at McClellan Creek, wrote, "So close was this pursuit that the rear guard of the enemy was engaged by our scouts on the second and third days, but owing to the worn condition of the stock, caused by the absence of forage and the distance previously marched by the command, the pursuit was necessarily abandoned at this point."[9]

The third type of army unit active during the Plains Indian Wars was light artillery, which provided support to infantry and cavalry operations. During these campaigns few artillery units were actually deployed into the field. Instead, infantry and cavalry soldiers manned and operated artillery pieces. Horse-drawn caissons and limbers towed the artillery pieces and carried the ammunition for the guns. The typical artillery pieces were the 3-inch ordnance rifle and field and mountain howitzers, though Gatling guns were also classified as artillery. Although artillery played a relatively minor role in the Plains Indian Wars, during the Red River War Col. Nelson Miles used a 10-pounder Parrott rifle and two .50-caliber Gatling guns during the Battle of Red River on August 30, 1874, and Maj. William R. Price had two mountain howitzers with his 8th Cavalry column, as did Lt. Col. John Davidson with his column from Fort Sill.

When army columns or convoys were moving, they did so in precise formations that stressed the use of advance, flanking, and rear guards to protect the column or convoy. Throughout the Civil War the army had used soldiers to protect the head, flanks, and rear of a column, and they used the same tactics with even greater emphasis during the Plains Indian Wars. Advance guards were used to scout or reconnoiter the area ahead of a column, to cover its movements, and to protect it from an ambush.

If smaller patrols or units were detached from the main column, they often used the same formation to protect their movement. For example, in August 1874, when Colonel Miles was preparing his column to leave Fort Dodge at the beginning of the campaign against the Indians, he sent Lt. Frank Baldwin with a contingent of fifty-three scouts and soldiers ahead of the main column to scout the territory along the exposed

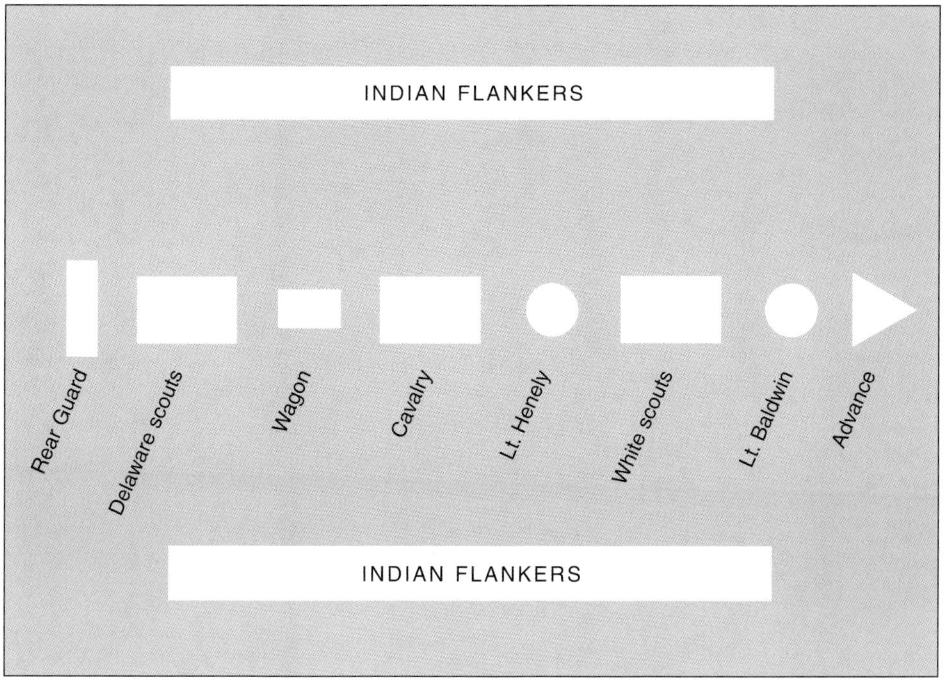

Fig. 5.2. Army units protected a column with advance guards, flankers, and rear guards. Illustration by Roland Pantermuehl

Kansas frontier and southward to Adobe Walls in the Texas Panhandle. Baldwin's party contained white and Delaware Indian scouts and guides, eighteen troopers and Lieutenant Henely of the 6th Cavalry, and one supply wagon. According to Baldwin, the order of his march was that as shown in fig. 5.2, which used advance guards, flankers, and a rear guard to protect the main body of the patrol.[10]

Units were also used to escort supply convoys, which were often difficult to defend. To aid in their defense and if the terrain allowed, convoy trains often traveled two wagons abreast. In this manner the wagons were more concentrated, which facilitated better travel discipline and defense. If the train came under attack, the wagons could quickly form a defensive circle, with the wagons on the right side forming half the circle while those on the left formed the other half. The livestock was placed within the circled wagons, and the troopers likewise took cover within the enclosed circle.

Skirmish drills were the primary tactic used by the army when engaging the enemy. Skirmishers were simply a line of troopers spread about 5 yards or more apart and deployed so as to engage the enemy by firepower. Both mounted and dismounted skirmishing was employed, though dismounted skirmishing was most common. As the company dismounted and deployed, every fourth man remained mounted and was assigned to hold and lead the horses to the rear. Typically each company placed a company reserve position, usually made up of several squads, to its right rear. The reserve position provided protection for the held horses, flanks, and rear and also supported the main line with ammunition or more men.[11]

Skirmish lines were, however, by no means the only tactic used by the army to engage Indians. Sometimes skirmishers made the initial assault while the battalion companies were being deployed. At the Battle of Red River, Colonel Miles used skirmishers initially while the four companies of his 1st Battalion formed a line on the right, the four companies of the 2nd Battalion formed a line on the left, and the three pieces of artillery moved to the center between the two lines. After the battle line was formed, Colonel Miles ordered a general advance while the artillery opened fire. This line formation, made with some six hundred soldiers, was a somewhat unusual formation to use against Indians, especially on a battlefield that was composed of deep canyons and rough terrain. It may have been Colonel Miles's intention to display his forces to demonstrate to the Indians the size of the force they were facing in an attempt to demoralize them and to hasten their retreat from the battlefield and return to the reservations.

Plains Indian Strategies and Tactics

By the late nineteenth century, a long tradition of warfare had developed among the various Plains tribes. The primary reasons for this "tradition of warfare" were economic. As horses spread across the Great Plains in the 1600s and 1700s, there was intense competition among the tribes to acquire them, and horse raiding between the tribes became commonplace. Acquisition of the horse made desirable a new mode of subsistence among the Plains tribes that led to their near total dependence on the buffalo. As a result, competition over desirable hunting grounds likewise led to war. Finally, there was strong competition and conflict among the tribes for European items, particularly guns. As trade networks with Anglos developed, hostilities intensified between tribes who enjoyed direct trade with the whites and those who were forced to deal through intermediaries. Thus it seems that the only method by which Plains societies could survive and prosper was continual warfare.[12]

Unlike the structured and disciplined fighting tactics employed by the U.S. Army, the Plains Indians typically fought not as groups but as individuals whose motives were to gain honor through displays of bravado. Through acts of bravery in warfare a warrior proved his worth to his tribe and achieved prestige. The taking of horses by raiding an enemy's herd became one of the most common ways for a man to display his courage and acquire wealth and prestige. Horse raiding was not, however, the only factor affecting a warrior's rise to prominence. Prestige and honor could also be gained by prowess in battle. The Plains Indian culture was a warrior culture that celebrated the individual, and a great deal of importance and esteem was placed on a warrior's abilities in combat. A warrior's social standing depended on his ability to demonstrate his bravery through war exploits. Perhaps the greatest valor to be had was by counting coup. For the Plains Indians, counting coup referred to deeds of valor or an act of public bravery as would occur in battle. The amount of coup a warrior might earn depended on the specific deed he accomplished. To count coup, a warrior deliberately touched an enemy with his hand or something held in his hand such as a weapon or specially designed "coup stick" without actually harming the enemy. Among most of the Plains tribes, counting coup in this manner was viewed as a greater and more valuable deed than actually killing an enemy.[13]

This system of rewarding individual exploits did not encourage teamwork. Warriors often followed a war chief or leader of a war party only as it suited their inclination. Furthermore, they would often break from a war party or abandon a planned group attack when opportunities for personal distinction presented themselves. Once on the battlefield, the group worked together to gain the greatest advantage over an enemy, though individual acts of bravery and courage were still encouraged and even expected. A warrior fought principally for the honors of war, for revenge or retaliation, for plunder, and for defense of his family and village. This lack of group discipline prevented large numbers of Indians from cooperating throughout long campaigns and, as a result, contributed in no small part to the demise of the Plains Indians in their encounters with the U.S. Army.[14]

Nonetheless, man-for-man the Plains warrior far surpassed the army soldier in every respect of military proficiency. From childhood the Plains Indian male was trained in cunning, stealth, horsemanship, and mastery of the bow and arrow. Plains Indians excelled at guerilla warfare and exploiting the environment for their own advantage and the enemy's disadvantage. They preferred to launch hit-and-run raids or ambushes and to fight on their own terms, when success seemed certain. When faced by a comparable force, Plains warriors would typically flee and scatter in several directions to make pursuit virtually impossible. Only when they were surprised or their village was endangered did they make a concerted stand against an enemy until their families were able to escape.[15]

In combat, they used certain well-established tactics. In attacks against circled wagon trains and smaller groups of soldiers, warriors galloped on horseback in circles around their quarry, drawing closer with each circle while discharging volleys of arrows or bullets. The Southern Plains Indians were particularly skilled horsemen (fig. 5.3). They often used a leather thong to support themselves as they hung alongside their horses opposite the enemy. From this position they leaned under the horse's neck to fire their rifles or discharge arrows. Sgt. Zachariah Woodall described the superb horsemanship abilities of Kiowa warriors at the Battle of Buffalo Wallow in 1874: "At this stage we were eye witness to some of the most magnificent feats of horsemanship that could not be equaled by any like number of men in the world, rising readily from the stirrups while the horses were in rapid motion and standing erect on the backs of their animals while they delivered their fire and then instantly dropping, as if shot, into their stirrups, swinging themselves rapidly under their bellies, in which position they could easily aim and fire."[16]

The circling maneuvers seemed to work well to confuse army soldiers and to prevent them from taking good aim at the Indians, as Capt. J. Lee Humfreville described: "The Indians circled around and around . . . with amazing, dazzling rapidity, necessitating constant movement and vigilance on the part of the troops in every direction, and at every point."[17] Capt. Robert Carter attempted to explain similar Comanche combat tactics:

> Their safety as to casualties urged them to always keep mounted, moving and circling like a swarm of bees and never "bunching." Their tactics under fire is difficult to describe . . . [but a typical one was] . . . in the action with Quanah Parker's band of Qua-ha-da Comanches at the mouth of Cañon Blanco, October 10, 1871, when they assembled their entire force for an open field fight with our command of the 4th Cavalry. Their rapid swing out or rush into a V-shape formation, and then fanning out to the front from these two wings into an irregular line of swirling warriors, all rapidly moving in right and left hand circles, no two Indians coming together, and their quick extensions, while advancing, to the right or left, and as rapidly concentrating or assembling on the center, but without any close bunching, and their falling back in the same manner, sometimes in a fan-shaped or wing formation, all was most puzzling to all of our Civil War veterans who had never witnessed such tactical maneuvers, or such a flexible line of skirmishers; all without any audible commands, but with much screeching and loud yelling.[18]

Another tactic used by Plains Indians when they were facing a mounted foe was for several warriors to break off from the main group in an attempt to draw out and isolate a small number of the enemy, at which point the warriors would rush them to dispatch them in close combat. Yet another tactic was for the warriors initially to evade a pursuing foe, split into two or more groups, and encircle the flanks of the charging enemy. When Indian villagers were being pursued by army troops, Indian

Fig. 5.3. The Southern Plains Indians were skilled horsemen. In George Catlin's *Comanche Feats of Horsemanship,* Comanche men engage in mock warfare and demonstrate their abilities to shoot bows and arrows while hanging on the side of their horses. Courtesy Smithsonian American Art Museum, Gift of Mrs. Joseph Harrison Jr.

warriors often used tactics to slow the troops and provide the villagers more time to make their escape. One such tactic was to attack the troops at night when they were camped and stampede the cavalry horses so the troops would be stranded afoot or have to spend a great deal of valuable time gathering the stampeded animals. Another was to burn the prairie grass behind them to obscure their trail and deny forage for the cavalry horses. Both of these tactics were used with some success by the Indians during the Red River War.

Army Weapons during the Red River War

In 1873, wanting to standardize ammunition and small arms, the U.S. Army adopted the .45-caliber trapdoor Springfield rifle and carbine for use by infantry and cavalry troops, respectively. By the summer of 1874, most infantry and cavalry units had received the new firearms, though some units had not and these units continued to use previously adopted weapons or weapons that had been issued for experimental field trials.

The Model 1873 Springfield rifle (fig. 5.4) had a 32⅝-inch barrel chambered for the new .45/70 cartridge, which contained 70 grains of black powder, and a 405 grain

Fig. 5.4. The .45-caliber Model 1873 Springfield rifle was adopted by the army for use with infantry units in 1873. Courtesy Panhandle-Plains Historical Museum, Canyon, Texas

Fig. 5.5. The .45-caliber Model 1873 Springfield carbine was adopted by the army for use with cavalry units in 1873. This single-shot weapon served the army, with periodic improvements, for the next twenty years. From the collection of Gordon Culwell

bullet that was driven out of the muzzle at a velocity of about 1,350 feet per second. The infantry rifle was accurate to 1,000 yards. The carbine (fig. 5.5) had a 22-inch barrel that also chambered the .45-caliber cartridge, but for mounted cavalry use the cartridge contained only 55 grains of powder to become the .45/55, with a muzzle velocity of just over 1,100 feet per second. The carbine was accurate to 600 yards. There is no difference in the copper cartridge cases or bullet of the two rounds. The only difference between the cartridges was the amount of black powder in the case. To keep the smaller powder volume in the .45/55 cartridge compacted, ordnance personnel developed a wad for the carbine load, and later a cardboard tube liner was used in place of the wad.[19]

The Springfield Armory manufactured just over ten thousand of the new carbines and eighteen thousand new rifles between late 1873 and mid-1874. Initial issues of the carbine were in early 1874, with the bulk of them going to troopers of the 10th Cavalry in Texas. By September 1874, all cavalry regiments except the 5th and the 8th, who were stationed in Arizona and New Mexico, had received the new carbine. These regiments would not receive the new .45-caliber Springfield carbines until 1875.[20] The infantry and cavalry units in the Red River War that did not receive the Model 1873 Springfield continued to rely on a variety of weapons, including the Models 1868 and 1870 Springfield as well as Sharps, Remington, and bolt-action Ward-Burton, all of which were .50-caliber (appendix B).

Also in 1873, the army adopted the Colt Model 1873 single-action revolver (fig. 5.6) as the standard service handgun. The revolver had a 7½-inch barrel, a side-rod ejector, and a fluted six-shot cylinder chambered for a new .45-caliber center-fire cartridge recommended by the ordnance board. The cartridge contained 30 grains of black powder and a 250-grain bullet.[21] The army bought almost thirteen thousand of these six-shooters in 1873–74 and about a thousand each year thereafter until 1891. Like the newly adopted .45 Springfield rifle and carbine, most units received the new Colt revolver by mid-1874, but the units that did not continued to use the .44-caliber Smith & Wesson, the .44-caliber Colt, and the .44-caliber Remington percussion cap.[22]

Although some army commanders regarded artillery as useless in Indian warfare,[23] cannons and Gatling guns were used in several expeditions and engagements during

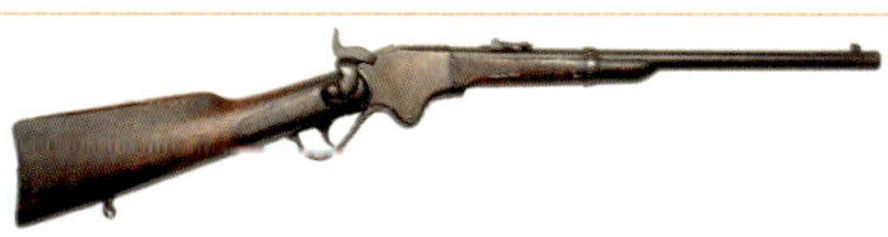

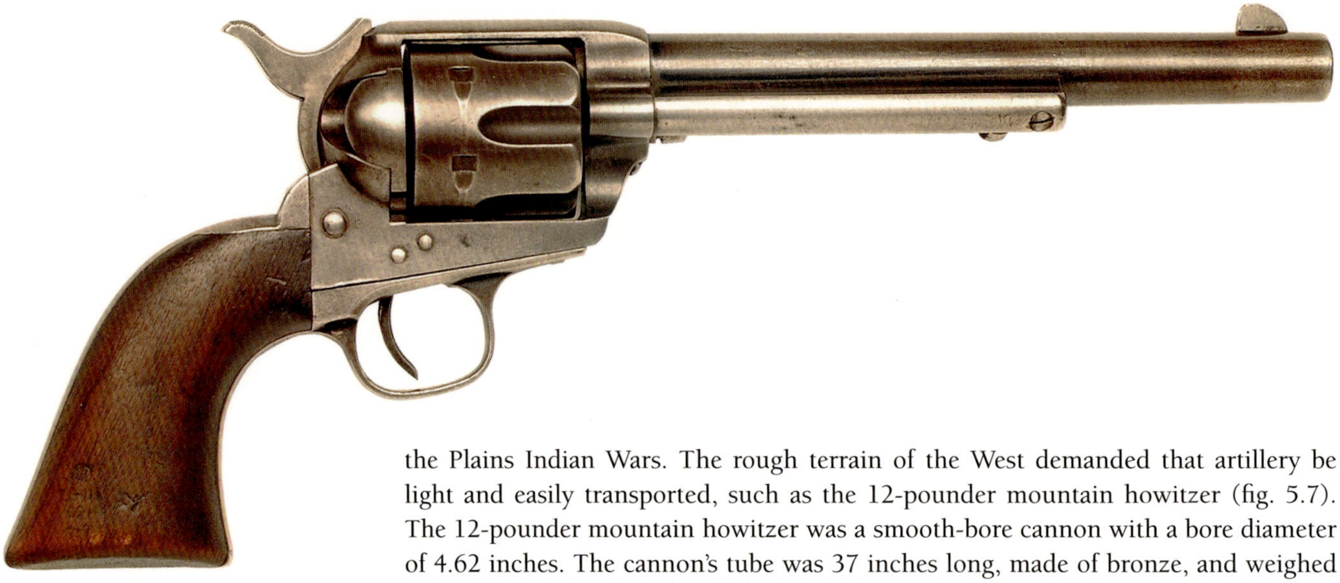

Fig. 5.6. The army adopted the .45-caliber Colt six-shooter as the standard sidearm in 1873. Courtesy Panhandle-Plains Historical Museum, Canyon, Texas

the Plains Indian Wars. The rough terrain of the West demanded that artillery be light and easily transported, such as the 12-pounder mountain howitzer (fig. 5.7). The 12-pounder mountain howitzer was a smooth-bore cannon with a bore diameter of 4.62 inches. The cannon's tube was 37 inches long, made of bronze, and weighed about 220 pounds. The gun was small enough that it could be completely broken down and transported on pack animals if need be, though it was usually pulled by a lone horse or mule. The mountain howitzer had a powder charge of one-half pound and could fire round shot, shell, case-shot, or canister (fig. 5.8).[24]

Round shot was a solid iron projectile that was cast without a powder chamber or fuse hole. Shell, also known as common shell, was a hollow projectile of cast iron containing a bursting charge, which was ignited by means of a fuse. The fuse was usually set so that it would go off in the air above the enemy. Case-shot was similar to shell except that the walls of the projectile were thinner. In both spherical and rifled projectiles, the bursting charge was usually in a thin tin or iron container placed in the center of the internal cavity. The cavity was filled with lead or iron balls in a sulphur or pitch matrix. The small bursting charge of black powder was designed to disperse the case-shot balls in a cone-shaped pattern, similar to the effects of canister but at longer ranges. Canister was a metal cylinder made of tin, iron, or lead with a removable iron top. The cylinder for the 12-pounder howitzer contained forty-eight iron or lead balls arranged in rows with sawdust packed between them. There was an iron plate between the canister balls and the wooden sabot at the bottom. The top edge of the vertical cylinder wall was bent over the iron top plate to help keep the canister contents in place, and the bottom edge was nailed to the wooden sabot. Canister was designed to be used at close range, usually under 350 yards.[25]

Though heavier and less maneuverable than the mountain howitzers, 3-inch ordnance rifles and 10-pounder Parrott rifles also saw action during the Plains Indian Wars. During the closing years of the campaign, the Hotchkiss "mountain gun" became the most popular and effective artillery piece. The 3-inch ordnance rifle (fig. 5.9), sometimes called the 3-inch wrought iron rifle, was used extensively during the Civil War and became a favorite artillery piece among commanders. It was generally considered superior to the 10-pounder Parrott rifle. As the name implies, the 3-inch ordnance rifle had a bore diameter of 3 inches, and the wrought iron tube was 73 inches long and weighed about 820 pounds. The 3-inch ordnance rifle could accurately fire Schenkl and Hotchkiss shells approximately 2,000 yards at 5 degrees elevation, using a 1-pound charge of powder. The Hotchkiss shell was the most common projectile fired from the gun. As with other types of artillery projectiles, several varieties of the Hotchkiss shell were made, including common shells, which were designed to break into many ragged fragments when exploded; case-shot varieties, which contained lead

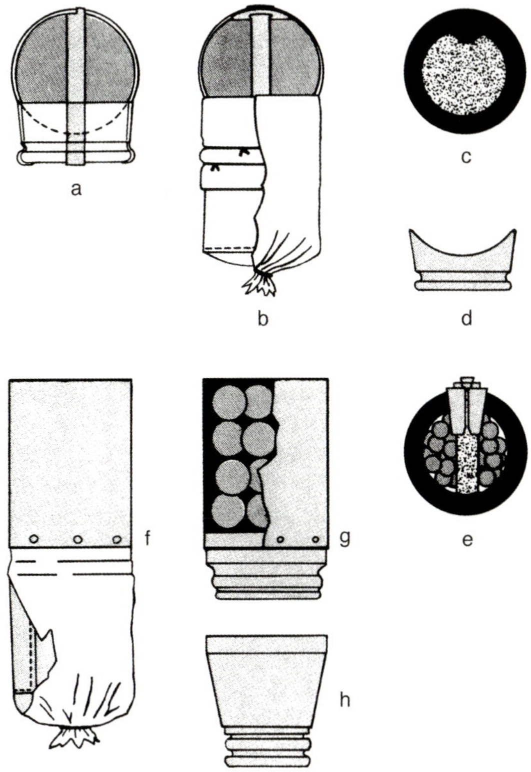

◀ Fig. 5.7. The easily transported 12-pounder mountain howitzer had been a favorite cannon for use on the frontier since the 1840s.

▲ Fig. 5.8. Ammunition for the 12-pounder mountain howitzer: a, round shot attached to the sabot with tin straps; b, shell, complete fixed round; c, cutaway view of common shell; d, sabot for common shell and spherical case; e, cutaway view of spherical case round showing lead ball shrapnel, fuse, and burster; f, canister round, fixed; g, cutaway view of canister showing round shot; h, tapered sabot for howitzer round. Adapted from an illustration in Coggins, *Arms and Equipment of the Civil War*, 67

or iron balls that were propelled outward when the shell exploded; and the solid shot or bolt, which, as the name suggests, was a solid metal projectile.[26]

Parrott rifles were patented in 1861 by Robert P. Parrott. Even though they were not considered the best guns in the service, they were readily available, inexpensive, and accurate. Parrott rifles are distinguished from other artillery guns by the wrought iron reinforcing band around the breech. The 3-inch Parrott rifle (fig. 5.10) had a bore length of 78 inches, a bore diameter of 3 inches, and a weight of 890 pounds. The tube was made of iron, and with a powder charge of 1 pound it could fire a shell approximately 2,000 yards at 5 degrees elevation. The most common ammunition used with the Parrott rifle was shell and case-shot, though solid shot and canister could also be used. Canister, however, was not as accurate or effective when it was fired from rifled guns because the rifling tended to throw the canister into an erratic pattern.[27] Though uncommon, Hotchkiss ammunition could also be fired in the Parrott rifle, as apparently occurred at the Battle of Red River on August 30, 1874 (see chapter 6 and appendix D).

Another artillery piece used during the Red River War was the Gatling gun (fig. 5.11). Richard Jordan Gatling (1818–1903) invented the revolving ten-barreled Gatling gun in 1862. The Gatling gun operates on the principle of reciprocal motion, in which a stationary cam operates the followers, causing separate bolt mechanisms and rifle barrels to rotate around a spindle. There is one bolt/firing pin/extractor assembly for each rifled barrel. As a hand crank turns the mechanism, worm gears pull the firing pin in each bolt to the firing position, a cartridge is dropped into the follower, and the cocked bolt pushes the cartridge into a barrel's chamber, fires it, and extracts the spent round. The cartridge is fired at the three o'clock position (as viewed from the rear) and extracted in the nine o'clock position. The forerunner of the machine gun, the Gatling gun fired 350 rounds of ammunition per minute.[28]

▲ Fig. 5.9. The 3-inch ordnance rifle became a common artillery piece at most frontier posts after the Civil War.

▶ Fig. 5.10. The 10-pounder Parrott rifle was used at the Battle of Red River on August 30, 1874.

The Gatling gun was apparently used only three times in combat prior to the outbreak of the war with Spain in 1898. Gatling guns were fired in combat on two occasions during the Red River War campaign in 1874–75 and once during the Shoshone-Bannock campaign of 1878. Despite reoccurring references to its use by Col. Nelson Miles at the Bear Paw Battle with the Nez Perce in Montana in 1877, one was not used there. Rather, a 1.65-inch Hotchkiss cannon and a 12-pounder Napoleon cannon were employed.[29]

Colonel Miles did use Gatling guns at the Battle of Red River in Texas in 1874, which is the first recorded use of this gun after the Civil War. At this battle, Miles employed two .50-caliber Gatling guns against the Cheyenne (see chapter 6). The second use of the Gatling gun during the Red River War was on April 6, 1875, at the Cheyenne Agency in Indian Territory. At the agency, a Cheyenne warrior was being fitted with shackles in preparation for transport to prison at Fort Marion, Florida, when he suddenly attempted to escape and was shot by troopers of the 5th Infantry. The incident caused panic in the nearby Cheyenne camp, and the Indian villagers took refuge behind a sandy hill near the south bank of the North Fork of the Canadian River, where they dug up a cache of firearms and ammunition. Col. Thomas Neill ordered a Gatling gun be brought up and fired into the Indians' position to flush them out. The next morning, Neill discovered that the Indians had fled to the northwest. The pursuit of the Cheyennes led to the last battle of the Red River War, known as the Battle of Sappa Creek in northwest Kansas.[30]

Even though Colonel Miles used Gatling guns at the opening battle of the Red River War in 1874, he apparently was not satisfied with them as a weapon for fighting Indians. Gatlings "are worthless for Indian fighting," Miles declared to General Sherman in 1876. "The range is no longer than the rifle and the bullets so small that you cannot tell where they strike."[31] Lt. Col. George A. Custer refused to take a Gatling platoon up the Rosebud to the Little Bighorn in 1876, apparently because he believed the guns were too cumbersome and would slow his march.[32]

Indian Weapons

Plains tribes, or those who were soon to become Plains tribes, had been acquiring firearms since the 1700s. These early firearms were flintlocks that had come to the

Indians through raiding and through trade, primarily with French traders along the eastern margins of the plains. By the mid-1800s, Indians on the Southern Plains were also acquiring firearms from New Mexican Comanchero traders.[33] During this time, most firearms in the hands of western Indians were percussion lock muzzle loaders. The percussion lock was an improvement over the earlier flintlocks in that it provided a more reliable and weatherproof means of ignition.

Many of the percussion lock guns were made specifically for trade with Indians. These trade guns were usually either large-caliber smooth-bore guns similar to the military muskets in use at the time or rifles similar to the Kentucky and Plains rifles. The typical trade gun was a .66-caliber smooth-bore with a part octagon, part round, thin-walled barrel. It had a full-length stock with brass butt plates and a large, round trigger guard.[34]

Trade, however, was not the only source of firearms for the Indians. By the 1860s the primary source of Indian-acquired firearms was the U.S. government. Firearms were given to the Indians as partial payments for cession of lands or for promises to keep the peace. Between 1800 and 1850, the government procured eleven thousand rifles specifically for Indian treaty payments. In 1867, when negotiations for the Medicine Lodge Treaty were concluded, the participating Southern Plains Indian signers of the treaty were given percussion revolvers. At Fort Larned, Kansas, Indian agent Edward Wyncoop gave one hundred pistols and eighty muzzle-loading Lancaster rifles together with the necessary powder, lead, and caps to the Arapahos when they assured him that the guns would be used only for hunting.[35] In fact, Indian agents and commissioners to the Comanches, Kiowas, Cheyennes, and Arapahos appear to have given almost unlimited authority to licensed traders to sell guns to any Indians receiving annuities from the government. As a result, the Southern Plains Indians were able to acquire a wide variety of firearms.

Prior to and during the Civil War, there were many innovations and inventions in firearms. Included in these were the development of the Colt revolver, the adoption of

Fig. 5.11. The ten-barreled .50-caliber Gatling gun saw its first use west of the Mississippi River at the Battle of Red River.

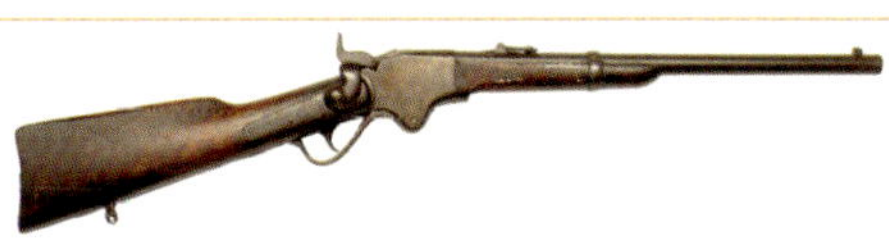

⏶ Fig. 5.12. The Spencer seven-shot carbine was a common Indian firearm during the Red River War. Courtesy Panhandle-Plains Historical Museum, Canyon, Texas

▲ Fig. 5.13. The .44-caliber Winchester Model 1866 was one of the most popular firearms among the Indians. Courtesy Panhandle-Plains Historical Museum, Canyon, Texas

a rifled musket as the standard for army service, the development of the breechloader rifle, and the development of metallic self-contained cartridges. Furthermore, the first repeating rifles, the Spencer and the Henry, were produced during the Civil War. By the mid-1870s more and more Indians had acquired breechloaders and repeaters. The Spencer carbine (fig. 5.12) was introduced in 1863, for use by Union cavalry. It was also produced in civilian models and was a popular weapon that became widely available. The Spencer carbine had an overall length of 39 inches and a weight of 8 pounds 4 ounces. The carbine could fire seven copper rimfire cartridges from a tubular magazine in the end of the butt stock. There were several calibers produced for both military and commercial markets during its production years, though the majority of the Spencer carbines were of .50-caliber and were chambered for the .56-.56 Spencer rimfire cartridge.[36] The earlier rifled musket had proved popular with Michigan cavalry units, although the length was unwieldy for cavalrymen. Prior to the end of the war, the U.S. government purchased nearly ninety-five thousand Spencer carbines, which became popular with mounted troopers in spite of shortcomings: the cartridge, for example, was underpowered, with an effective range of only about 300 yards. After the Civil War the army had a large surplus of Spencer carbines, and they continued to use them until the early 1870s when they were replaced with single-shot .50-caliber Sharps and Springfields. Many of the surplus Spencers were given to "friendly" Indians at the reservations for huntings.[37]

Other repeaters favored by the Indians were the .44-caliber Henry and the Winchester Models 1866 and 1873 (fig. 5.13), each of which was particularly well designed for mounted use. The Henry was a lever-action repeater that carried fifteen rounds in a tubular magazine beneath the barrel. It was manufactured by the New Haven Arms Company, which became the Winchester Repeating Arms Company in 1866. About fourteen thousand Henry rifles were produced between 1860 and 1866. Indians also acquired Sharps, Springfield, Ballard, Remington, and other types of rifles and pistols in various calibers.[38]

Despite the wide variety of firearms in their hands by 1874, firearms had by no means completely replaced the Southern Plains Indians' traditional weapons. The bow and arrow, lance, tomahawk, knife, and shield were still important in the overall Indian arsenal (fig. 5.14). The bow remained one of the most popular of the Indian weapons throughout the conflict with the whites, and it was used in hunting as well as in warfare. The typical bow of the Plains Indians was made of wood, with sinew used for the bowstring. Having been adapted for use on horseback, the bow was usually

42–54 inches long. Though accurate to only about 100 yards, the bow was powerful enough to bring down a buffalo at close range.[39]

As metal became more available, indigenous weapons like the lance, tomahawk, knife, and arrow were all affected. Metal, acquired through trade with whites and Comancheros, rapidly replaced the traditional flint parts of these items. Metal blades were used for spears and lances, and iron or steel arrowheads were traded to the Indians or the Indians learned to make them themselves from scrap pieces of metal. The metal butcher knife served as a utilitarian tool, scalping knife, and weapon in hand-to-hand combat.

Plains Indians used shields more for defense than as weapons. Typically, a shield was 24–30 inches in diameter and constructed from thick buffalo hide that had been dried in the sun. It was padded with hair or feathers and covered with soft buckskin. Though the shield was capable of deflecting an arrow, lance, or low-velocity musket ball, it could not stop the bullets of the more modern firearms that were becoming widespread by the late nineteenth century.[40]

Fig. 5.14. Even though Southern Plains Indians had firearms during the Red River War, traditional weapons remained an integral part of their arsenal. Such weapons included the bow and arrows, lance, knife, and shield like those shown in George Catlin's *His-oo-sán-chees, Little Spaniard, a Warrior.* Courtesy Smithsonian American Art Museum, Gift of Mrs. Joseph Harrison Jr.

6

The War Begins

On July 27, 1874, Col. Nelson A. Miles (fig. 6.1), then only 34 years old, received orders to organize an expedition at Fort Dodge, Kansas, and move south of the Arkansas River to campaign against the Indians. Miles's command would be made up of eight companies of the 6th Cavalry and four companies of his own 5th Infantry. Miles formed the eight companies of cavalry into two battalions, one comprising companies D, F, G, and I, commanded by Maj. Charles Compton, and the other consisting of companies A, H, L, and M, commanded by Maj. James Biddle. Capt. Henry B. Bristol commanded the four companies (C, D, E, I) of the 5th Infantry, and Lt. James Pope of the 5th Infantry commanded a twenty-one-man artillery detachment that included two ten-barreled .50-caliber Gatling guns and a 3-inch 10-pounder Parrott rifle.[1] Crews to man the artillery were drawn from the 5th Infantry.[2]

A contingent of fifty-three scouts also accompanied the expedition. The scouts, commanded by Lt. Frank Baldwin (fig. 6.2) of the 5th Infantry, consisted of one other officer, Lt. Austin Henely of the 6th Cavalry, eighteen troopers of the 6th Cavalry, a signal sergeant, ten white civilians including Adobe Walls veterans Billy Dixon and Bat Masterson, one wagon driver, one servant, and twenty Delaware Indians including Chief Falling Leaf, who was then more than 70 years old.[3]

▶ Fig. 6.1. Col. Nelson A. Miles was the field commander of the troops from the Department of the Missouri. Courtesy Panhandle-Plains Historical Museum, Canyon, Texas

▶▶ Fig. 6.2. Lt. Frank D. Baldwin commanded the scouts under Colonel Miles. Courtesy Panhandle-Plains Historical Museum, Canyon, Texas

In his official report of the campaign, Colonel Miles writes that his command totaled 744 enlisted men and officers and 554 horses.[4] He does not give the number of wagons, ambulances, or other support personnel that accompanied the expedition, but J. T. Marshall, serving in the double capacity of newspaperman for the *Kansas Daily Commonwealth* as well as civilian scout, states, "About one hundred wagons accompany the expedition" and "There will be about 150 citizen employes." Alternately, a report by Lt. Richard H. Pratt notes that Colonel Miles left Camp Supply with sixty-seven wagons and five ambulances, and a correspondent with the *New York Herald* who joined Miles's command at Fort Dodge reports that sixty wagons and five ambulances formed the wagon train.[5]

The Battle of Red River

On August 11, Compton's battalion, with one company of infantry and some of Baldwin's scouts, departed Fort Dodge and took a course slightly south of southwest to scout for hostiles along the exposed Kansas frontier. At the junction of Kiowa Creek and the Beaver River, Compton and Baldwin separated, with Baldwin taking a scouting party of fifty-three men along Palo Duro Creek over to Adobe Walls to rescue the buffalo hunters who remained there.[6] From Adobe Walls, on August 20, Baldwin and his detachment moved down the Canadian about 20 miles to a stream (in present Roberts County, Texas) named Chicken Creek by Baldwin. At Chicken Creek the group came upon two Indians; one escaped, but the other was killed—the first Indian casualty of the Red River War at the hands of the U.S. military.[7]

Meanwhile, Colonel Miles with the remainder of the command left Fort Dodge on August 14 en route to Camp Supply, Indian Territory. From Camp Supply they marched southwest to a point some 12 miles west of the Antelope Hills along the Canadian River in the eastern Texas Panhandle, where they rejoined Baldwin on August 24. The march toward the Texas plains was made in stifling heat, with the summer of 1874 excessively hot and dry. Most of the streams and water holes had dried up early in the summer, and the scarcity of water brought intense suffering to the soldiers. What little water was found was embittered with gypsum, a natural laxative that offered a choice between thirst and dysentery.[8]

Fig. 6.3. Cheyenne chief Iron Shirt may have been the leader of the Cheyennes who fought at the Battle of Red River. He and his followers also participated in the Battle of Palo Duro Canyon on September 28, 1874. Courtesy Research Division of the Oklahoma Historical Society. Photo by Mrs. Gilham, Darlington, Oklahoma Territory, Photo no. 9479.9, Hickox Collection

Miles was delighted with Baldwin's report that he had crossed several Indian trails heading southwest, and he took up the pursuit of the Indians with all haste. At Sweetwater Creek, the scouts discovered a large and fresh Indian trail and a recently abandoned Cheyenne village. A large number of abandoned possessions were found along the trail that lead to the southwest, indicating that the Cheyennes, possibly being led by Chief Iron Shirt (fig. 6.3), had fled in haste.[9] As the soldiers pushed on to the North Fork of the Red River, the trail grew larger as other Indian bands from the north, east, and south joined in the retreat. Baldwin estimated the number of Indians being pursued at three thousand, but this estimate was probably an exaggeration.[10] With the chase growing warm, Miles detached his supply train so he could pursue the Indians with greater speed. He left two companies of troops to protect the supply wagons and pushed forward with his army, now encumbered only by two ambulances, five ammunition wagons, and the artillery. If possible, Miles wanted to deal the Indians a harsh blow and secure a decisive victory early in the campaign.[11]

By the morning of August 30, the army, after traveling over exceedingly rough and broken terrain, emerged from Mulberry Creek[12] and crossed a broad, level plain that ended on the south in a line of low hills that bordered the Llano Estacado in the distance. The trail, now very fresh, led toward the low hills and into a narrow gap between two hills. This gap has historically been assumed to be Wagon Wheel Gap, near the head of Battle Creek in the southern part of present Armstrong County (fig. 6.4). Lieutenant Baldwin and the scouts were approaching the hills from the northeast when seventy-five to one hundred Indians attacked them.[13] The scouts dismounted and, on foot, repulsed the attack while Miles deployed the troops and advanced quickly to assist. The Indians fell back, retreating to a range of high ravine-cut bluffs where the main body of Indians, principally Southern Cheyenne with a few Kiowas and Comanches, had taken position. According to Miles, the Indians occupied the high bluffs in "an irregular line extending five to seven miles, their numbers being estimated at from 400 to 600 warriors." Miles deployed his troops with Biddle's battalion on the left and Compton's on the right and ordered them to advance. The Indians soon abandoned their attack and retreated into a well-chosen battleground—the breaks and ravines of the lower Palo Duro Canyon. For the next five hours, in sweltering heat, a running battle ensued that covered a distance of about 12 miles from the Griffin Hills, down ravines and arroyos, and across the dry bed of the Red River to the mouth of Tule Canyon. By the time they reached the river, the soldiers had grown so thirsty that many of them "resorted to the extreme of opening the veins of their arms and moistening their parched and swollen lips with their own blood."[14]

As the battle continued, the Indian warriors fought a strong rear-guard action among the high bluffs and deep ravines. They made a final stand atop a high bluff on the right bank of the Red River. Miles describes the location as "one of the strongest positions that nature could give them where only two men could advance against them abreast." Capt. Tullius Cicero Tupper led Company G, 6th Cavalry, up the slope with the company bugles blowing. The Indian warriors apparently abandoned their stronghold in panic, putting up little resistance. While the warriors were engaging the army, the Indian families were escaping into Palo Duro Canyon, across the Prairie Dog Town Fork of the Red River, up Tule Canyon, and out onto the high plains of the Llano Estacado. With their retreat, the Indians burned their lodges and anything else they could not carry.[15]

By the time the Battle of Red River was over, only one soldier and one Delaware scout had been wounded, but as many as twenty-five Indian warriors had been killed.[16] The Indian families and other warriors escaped. For Colonel Miles the battle was a barren victory. He was able to destroy several deserted Indian camps in Tule Canyon, but these were of little consequence. Although their material losses were considerable, this fight did not defeat the Indians. Miles had failed to secure a decisive victory in the opening battle of the Red River War, but he did send a strong message to the Southern Plains tribes that the U.S. Army intended to prosecute the war to the fullest.

After the battle, Miles established his camp that night on the south bank of the Red River at one of the burned Indian villages where they found much abandoned Indian property.[17] The next morning the troops climbed out of Tule Canyon and attempted to pursue the Indians, but they soon discovered that the Indian trail had split and branched until it was impossible to follow. Miles was also nearly out of supplies, and if he ran out of food here his campaign would be in great jeopardy. On the other hand, if he withdrew from the area it would leave the Indians in control of that part of the country. Miles made the decision to stay camped in Tule Canyon, and he ordered Capt. Wyllys Lyman to take thirty-six supply wagons back to Camp Supply to restock them with provisions. To guard the train he also sent one company of infantry and several cavalrymen. Miles was counting on the supply train returning before his troops had to resort to slaughtering their horses for food. He intended to wait for Captain Lyman's return and would spend the time planning his next move against the Indians and trying to make contact with the other army columns that were supposed to be operating in the Panhandle.[18]

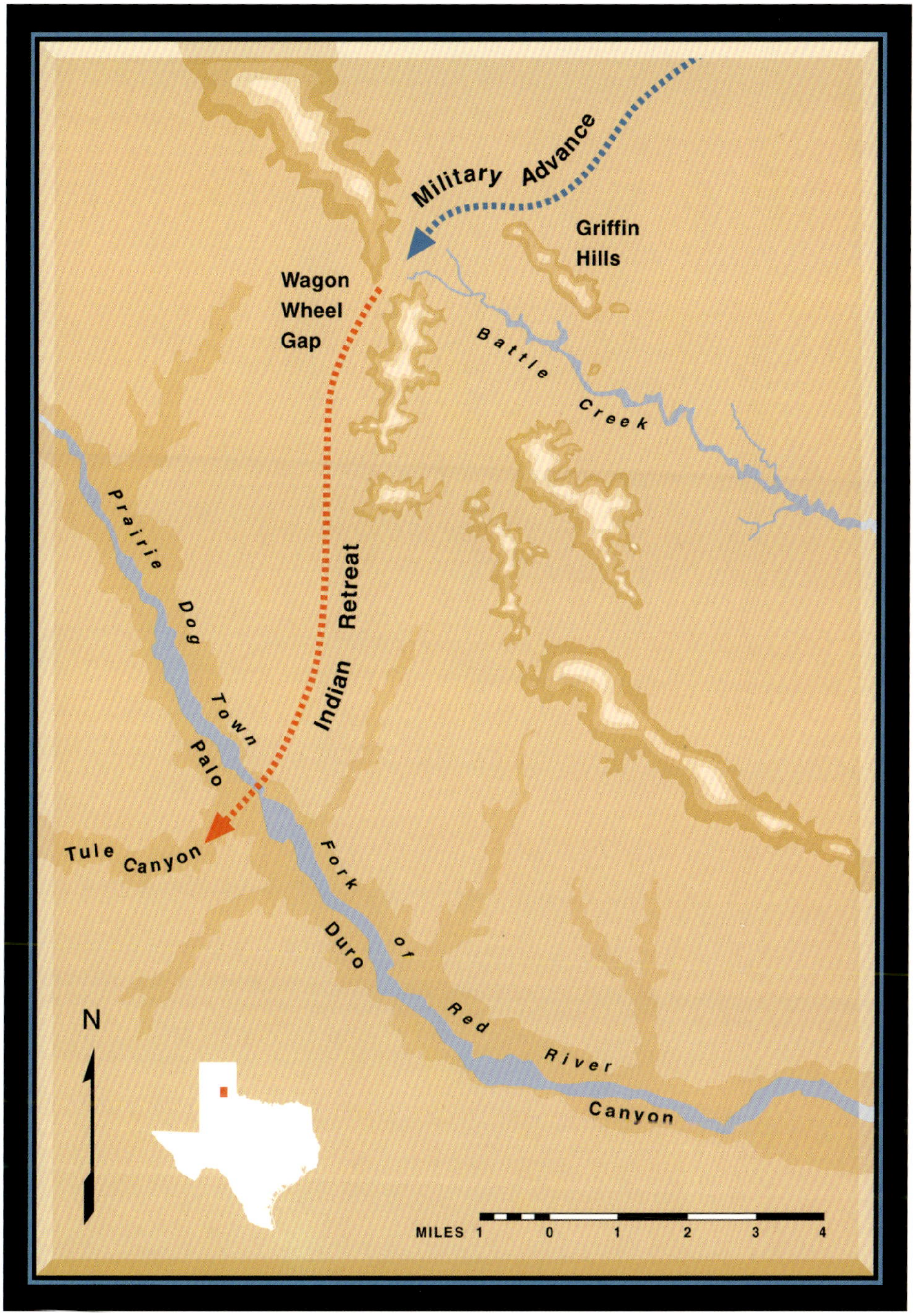

Fig. 6.4. Many researchers have assumed that at the Battle of Red River on August 30, 1874, the army advanced and the Indians retreated through Wagon Wheel Gap. Illustration by Roland Pantermuehl

Current Ownership and Land Use

The site of the Battle of Red River is privately owned. It is recorded in the state archeological site files as Site 41AM10. The battle site is in the southeastern portion of the Texas Panhandle in southern Armstrong and northern Briscoe counties (fig. 6.5). The site area is situated in the lower reaches of Palo Duro Canyon near the mouth of Tule Canyon, where it occupies an area of approximately 34.75 square miles. The Prairie Dog Town Fork of the Red River flows through Palo Duro Canyon, and it is this water source from which the battle site takes its name. The topography of the area is rough and dissected with deep, steep-walled canyons and eroded draws. Elevations range from a low of about 692 m (2,270 feet) above sea level on the bed of the Prairie

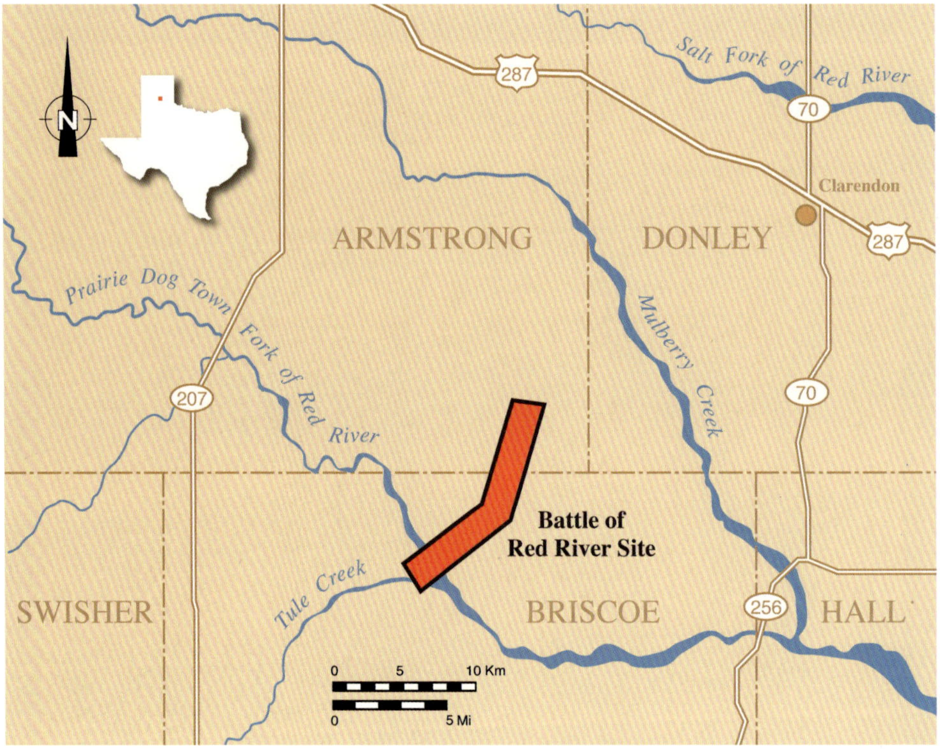

Fig. 6.5. The Battle of Red River took place in present southern Armstrong and northern Briscoe counties, Texas. Illustration by Roland Pantermuehl

Dog Town Fork to more than 884 m (2,900 feet) above sea level at the tops of the ridges and divides between the eroded canyons. The vegetation in the area consists of various grasses, cacti, and thick mesquite and juniper. Today the site area is used exclusively for cattle ranching.

Archeological Investigations and Results

From a historical perspective, the Battle of Red River site is significant. The battle represents the initiation on the Southern Plains of the federal government's policy to rid the plains of Indians so that Anglo-Americans could settle the region. This battle also marked the first time the Gatling gun was used west of the Mississippi River.[19] From an archeological perspective, it was important that the precise location of the site be determined and positively identified. It was our contention that archeological investigations could also corroborate and clarify some of the historical accounts of the battle.

The Battle of Red River site presented some unique problems and challenges that had to be dealt with for the archeological investigations to move forward. The first problem was determining where the battle site was actually located. The available military maps from the campaign showed the general location of the battle (fig. 6.6), but the scales on these maps were insufficient to determine the precise location. It was clear that an on-the-ground reconnaissance would be necessary to find the battle site.

Another challenge the project faced was our insufficient understanding of how large an area the battle site encompassed. From the military documents it was known that the battle was a running engagement that covered a distance of 10–12 miles from its start near the line of low hills to its termination near the mouth of Tule Canyon on the Prairie Dog Town Fork of the Red River.[20] What was not known was how wide an

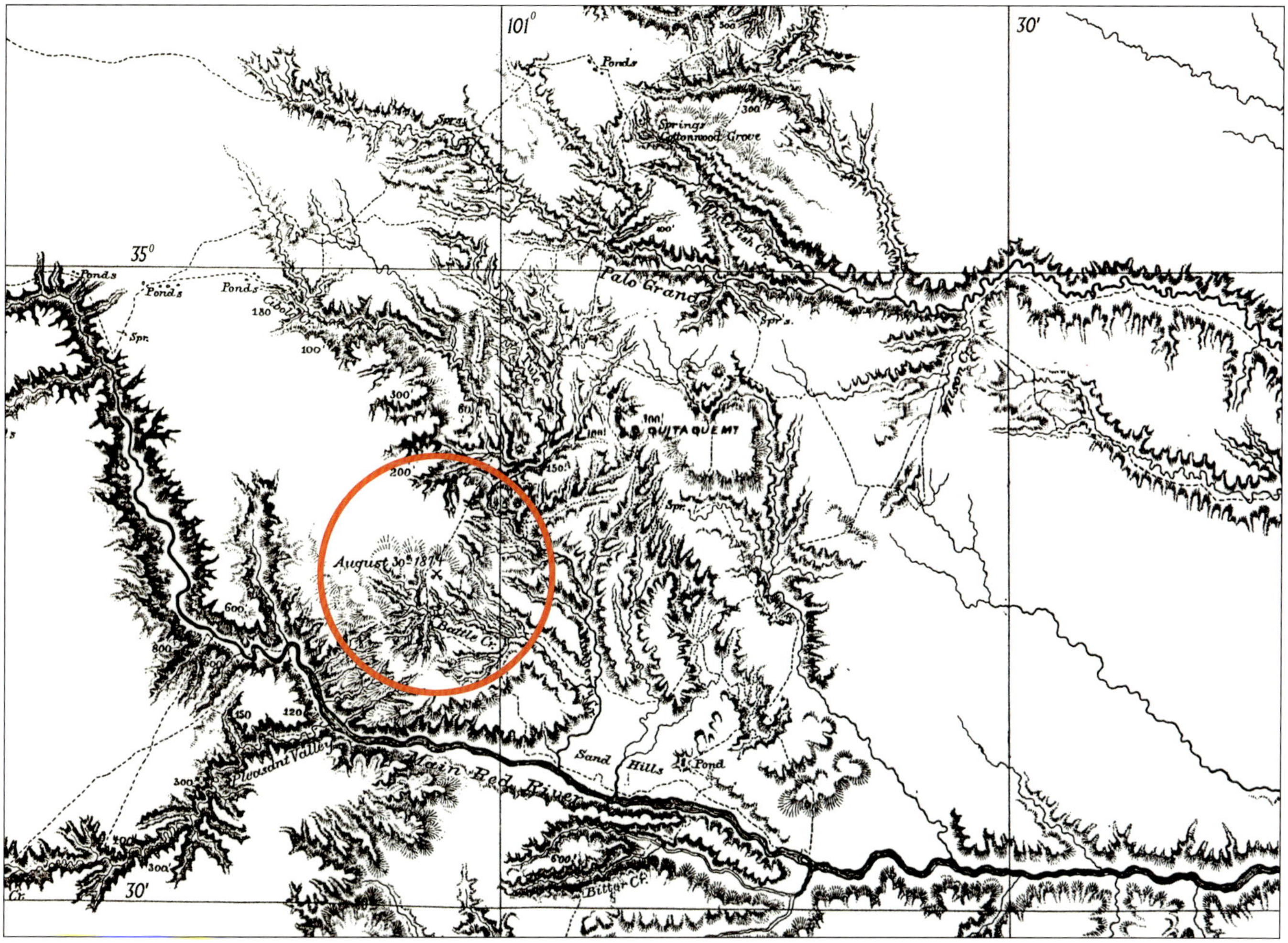

Fig. 6.6. The general location of the Battle of Red River is shown on this military map from the 1874 campaign. Record Group 393, Missouri-1, National Archives

area the battle covered. We believed that minimally the battle would cover an area at least a mile wide, and perhaps more, so we would have to examine, on foot, an area of at least 10 square miles.[21] This task would be formidable even under the best of conditions, and we did not have the best of conditions. The initial phase of fieldwork, for example, was conducted during the summer of 1998—one of the hottest and driest summers on record. Furthermore, the area to be examined was extremely rough, with deep draws and ravines, high bluffs, and thick mesquite and juniper (fig. 6.7). Colonel Miles himself described the area as "the roughest ground that I had until that time seen men fight upon."[22]

Another problem was the unknown archeological integrity of the site. Given that the battle moved quickly over a large area, it was uncertain whether battle-related artifacts would be concentrated sufficiently in certain areas to allow identification of specific battle events or so spread out that interpretation would be impossible. Also not known was whether such large numbers of artifacts had been collected and removed from the site over the years that valid interpretation of the remaining artifacts would be difficult or impossible.

These were our primary challenges as we began the search for the Battle of Red River site. We conducted archeological investigations during the summers of 1998 and 1999. Using the available army documents and various published accounts of the battle, we believed that the area around the Griffin Hills and Wagon Wheel Gap in present southern Armstrong County was probably battle location.[23] The terrain in

Fig. 6.7. This view of the terrain shows what Colonel Miles described as "the roughest ground that I had until that time seen men fight upon."

this area closely matches that described in the accounts and army records. Specifically, the broad, level plain the troops were described as crossing before they reached the line of low hills north of Battle Creek, and the distance from those hills to Palo Duro Canyon and the Red River, seemed to match well with the terrain in this area. In addition, interviews with long-time area ranchers revealed that over the years cartridge cases and several rifle pits had been found in the Griffin Hills.[24] No other engagements were known to have taken place in this vicinity, and we assumed, then, the Griffin Hills to be the low line of hills referred to in the historical accounts. Thus we began our investigations on the west end of the Griffin Hills, which is the end nearest Wagon Wheel Gap.

The Griffin Hills are about 2 miles in length, running in a northwest–southeast direction. The archeological survey team covered about 75 percent of the length of the hills without finding any artifacts. But as they neared the eastern end of the hills, they began to find artifacts of the right period (fig. 6.8), including several clusters of spent rifle cartridges of the types typically used by the Indians at that time, .44-caliber Henrys and Spencer 56/50s. The cartridges were found on the highest points of the Griffin Hills overlooking the broad plain to the north and east, suggesting this as the area where the Indians were concealed just before they attacked Lieutenant Baldwin and the scouts approaching the hills from the northeast.

As the archeological team continued to move across the eastern end of the Griffin Hills and onto the broad plain to the north and east, they found numerous fired and unfired .45/55 or .45/70 cartridges as well as several Gatling gun cartridges. The .45/70 was the standard cartridge issued to the infantry in 1874; the cavalry used the .45/55 cartridge.[25] The distribution of cartridge cases suggests that most of the fighting

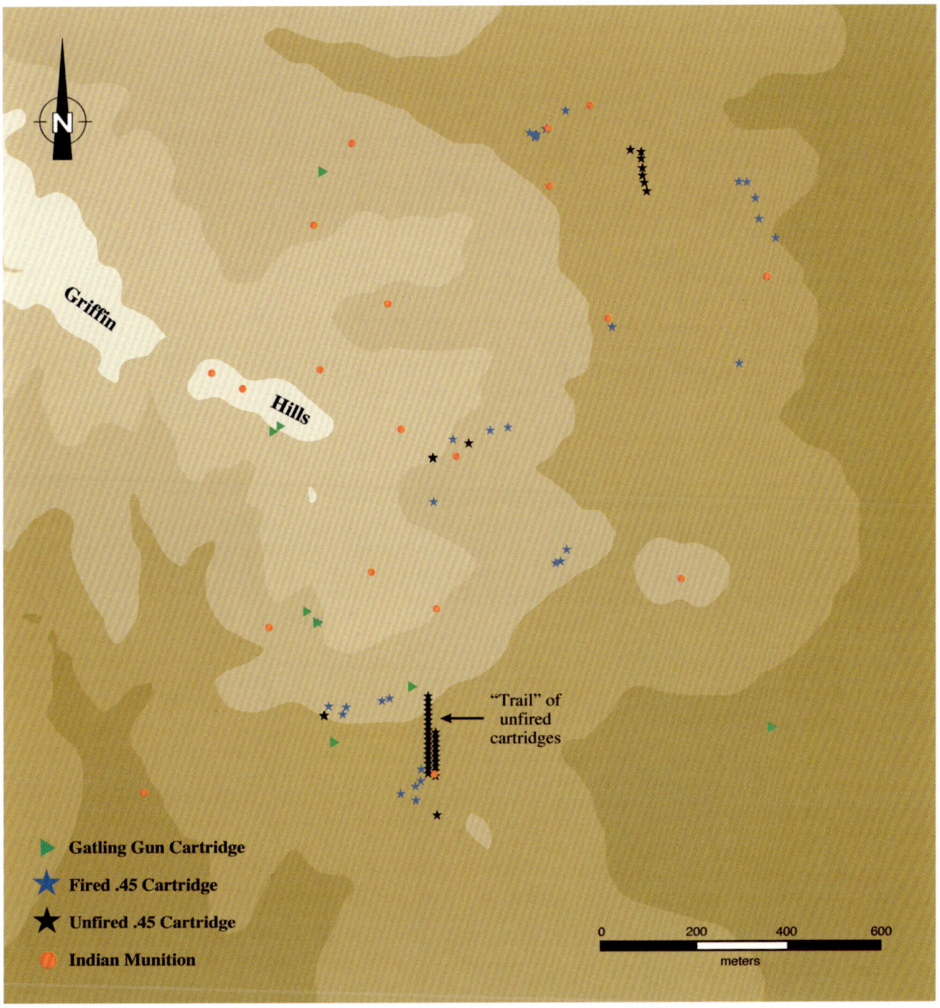

Fig. 6.8. The distribution of artifacts on and near the eastern end of the Griffin Hills confirmed that the Battle of Red River began there. Illustration by Roland Pantermuehl

during the early stages of the battle occurred in the broad plain north and east of the Griffin Hills. Lieutenant Baldwin and scout Thomas McFadden both indicate that the Indians charged down from the hills and attacked the scouts, who were about 2 miles in advance of the rest of the command.[26] The presence of the Gatling gun cartridges indicates that when the artillery reached the Griffin Hills the Gatling guns were set up and fired from there during the early stages of the battle.

Many of the army cartridges were found around shallow depressions, which appear to be the remains of rifle pits. One of the more interesting features encountered was a "trail" of unfired .45/55 or .45/70 rifle cartridges and .45 Colt pistol cartridges (figs. 6.8, 6.9). This line of forty-two unfired cartridges began on the north side of a small hill, crossed over the crest of the hill, and then continued partially down the south side. This intriguing trail of unfired cartridges most likely is where one of the army ammunition wagons, with at least two open ammunition boxes, made its way over the Griffin Hills, bouncing live ammunition out of the wagon, and continued toward the south.

The army artifacts and features found on the eastern end of the Griffin Hills suggest that Colonel Miles and his troops rendezvoused here after the Indians were cleared from the hills by the scouts. For the troops to move toward Wagon Wheel Gap from this position, they would have to make a sharp turn almost due west over some extremely deep ravines and rough terrain, a feat that would be almost impossible for the

Fig. 6.9. A "trail" of unfired .45 Colt and .45 Springfield cartridges marked where the ammunition wagons crossed the Griffin Hills. Illustration by Roland Pantermuehl

now unlimbered artillery. As the archeologists continued the survey of the area around the Griffin Hills, they found an almost continuous line of spent army cartridges and other artifacts extending from the Griffin Hills south toward Battle Creek, not west toward Wagon Wheel Gap. In fact, the archeological investigations have shown that after its start near the east end of the Griffin Hills, the battle moved south to Battle Creek, crossed the creek, then turned back toward the southwest to move through a smaller gap in the hills and continued south toward Tule Canyon. The search in and

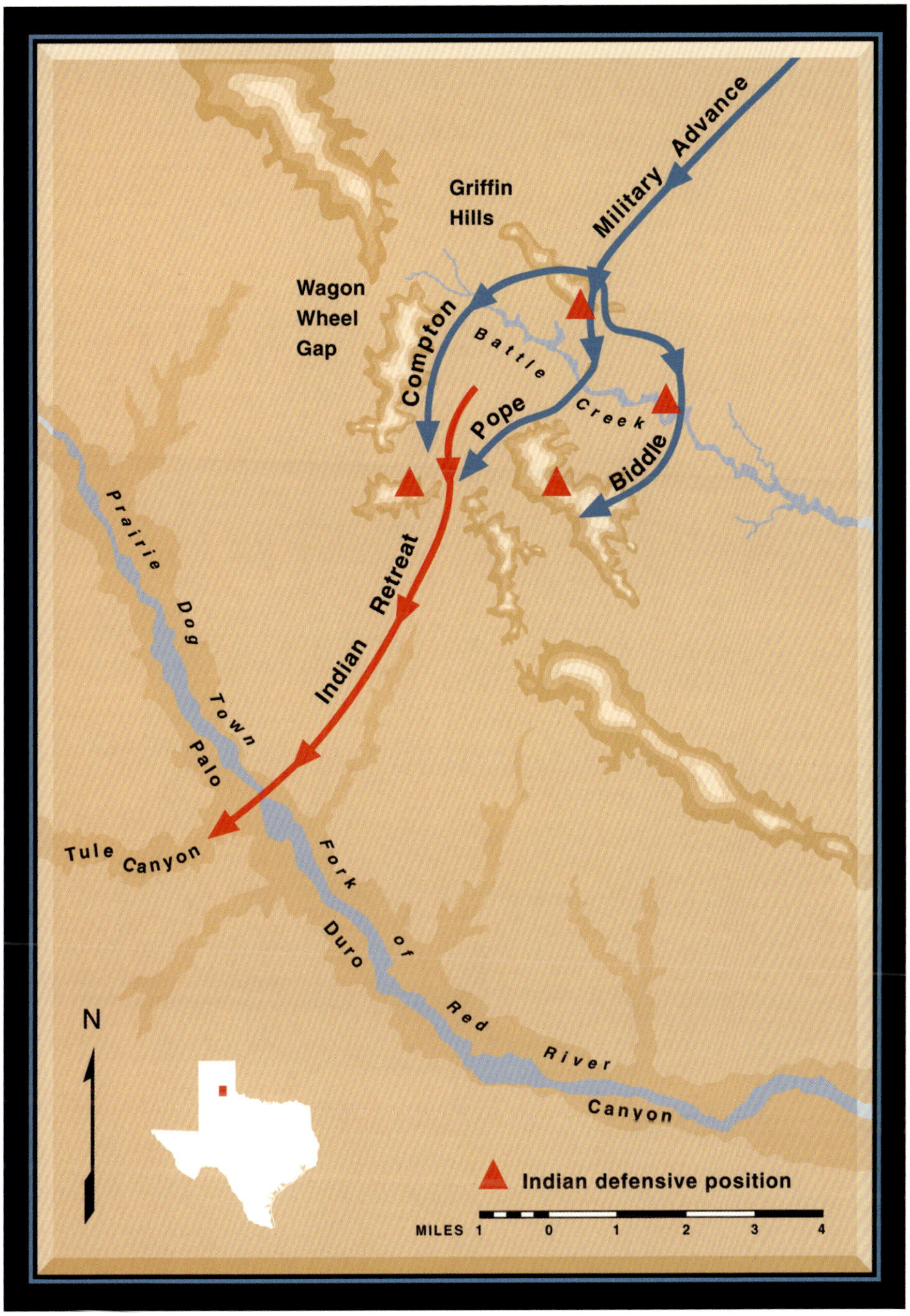

Fig. 6.10. The archeological investigations at the Battle of Red River site identified the actual lines of the army advance and the Indian retreat and showed that Wagon Wheel Gap was not where the battle took place. Illustration by Roland Pantermuehl

around Wagon Wheel Gap failed to produce any artifacts, and it now appears that Wagon Wheel Gap saw no action whatever in the Battle of Red River (fig 6.10).

Colonel Miles, in his report of the battle, offers surprisingly few details about specific events or even how the troops were deployed. He does state that "a skirmishing fire was kept up while our command was deploying: The First Battalion of Cavalry on the right, the Second Battalion on the left, and the pieces of artillery in the center with Captain Ewer's Co. "E" 5th Infantry for support and Captain Lyman held his Co. "I" as a reserve. A general advance was ordered, the artillery opened fire . . . the troops scarcely making a halt, advancing from crest to crest, the Indians retreating take a good position only to be charged out." From the description given by Miles, it is apparent

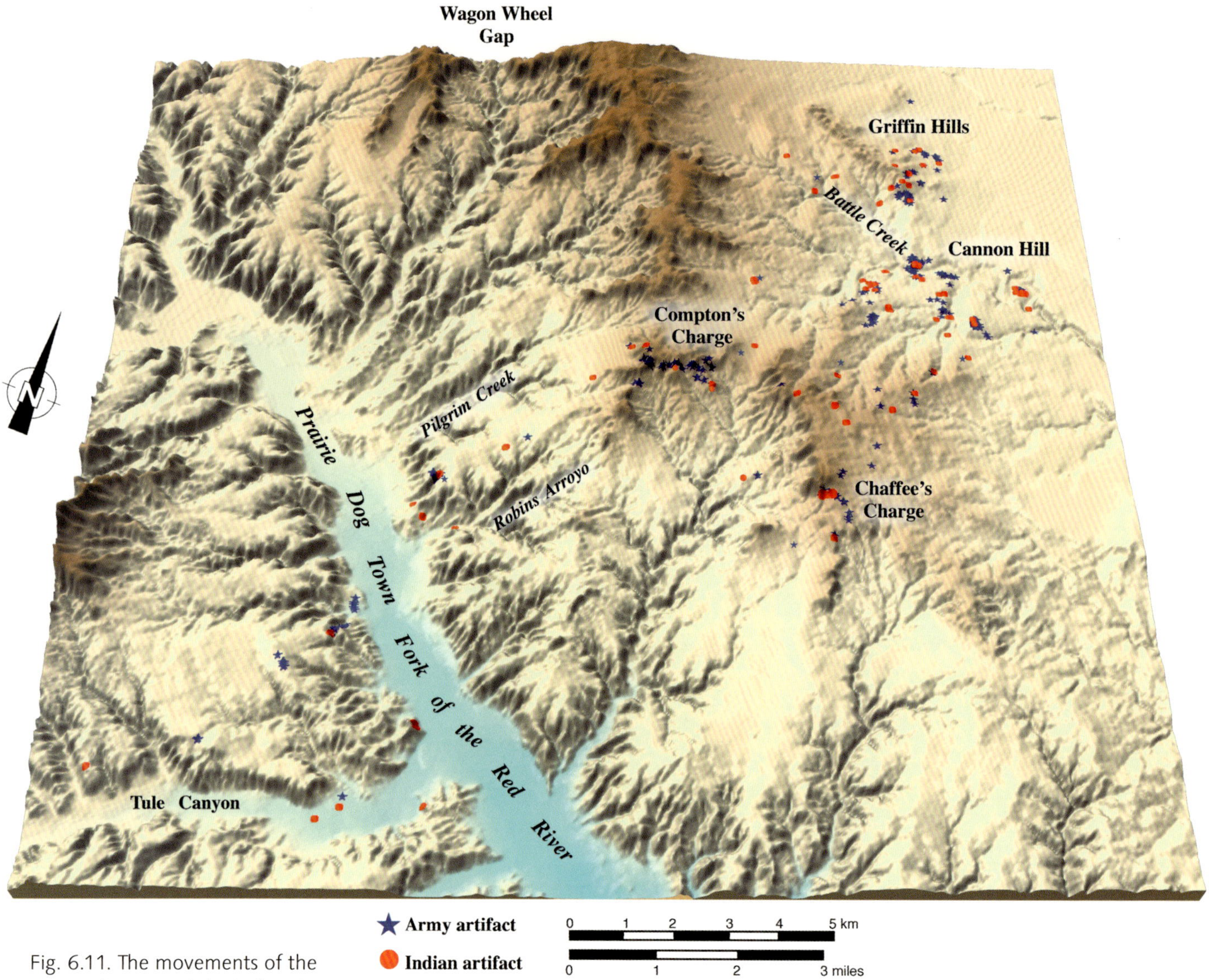

Fig. 6.11. The movements of the army columns and the Indians' retreat during the Battle of Red River are reflected in the distribution of the artifacts at the site. Illustration by Roland Pantermuehl

that the troops were operating in three columns. Maj. Charles Compton commanded the right column or wing, Lt. James Pope was in charge of the center command with the artillery, and the left wing was under the command of Maj. James Biddle. To the left of Major Biddle's column were Lieutenant Baldwin and the scouts, who were apparently operating independently of the other columns, which Baldwin makes clear when he writes, "My entire actions during the day was on my own judgement."[27]

The distribution of army artifacts across the battlefield can be attributed to one of these three military movements. The analysis of these distributions adds to the existing historical database. In fig. 6.11, note the cluster of army cartridges on the hill marked "Compton's Charge." An enlarged view of this area is shown on fig. 6.12. Since Major Compton was commanding the right column, this hill is undoubtedly the one referred to by Miles when he states in his report, "The Indians had taken position opposite the right, occupying a high crest in strong force, a few [artillery] shell were fired at this body, and a splendid cavalry charge was made by the 1st Battalion 6th Cavalry under Major and Lt. Col. Compton . . . up a steep crest of 200 feet and the position carried in fine order."[28] In addition to the army cartridges, the archeological

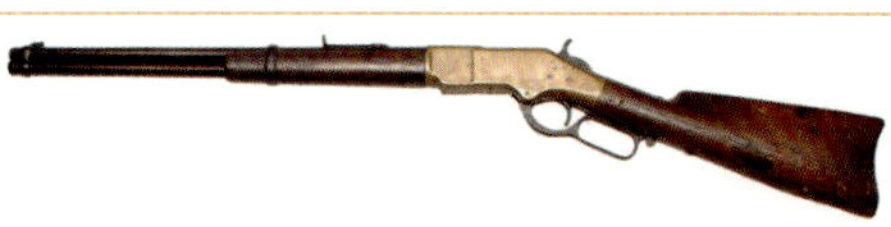

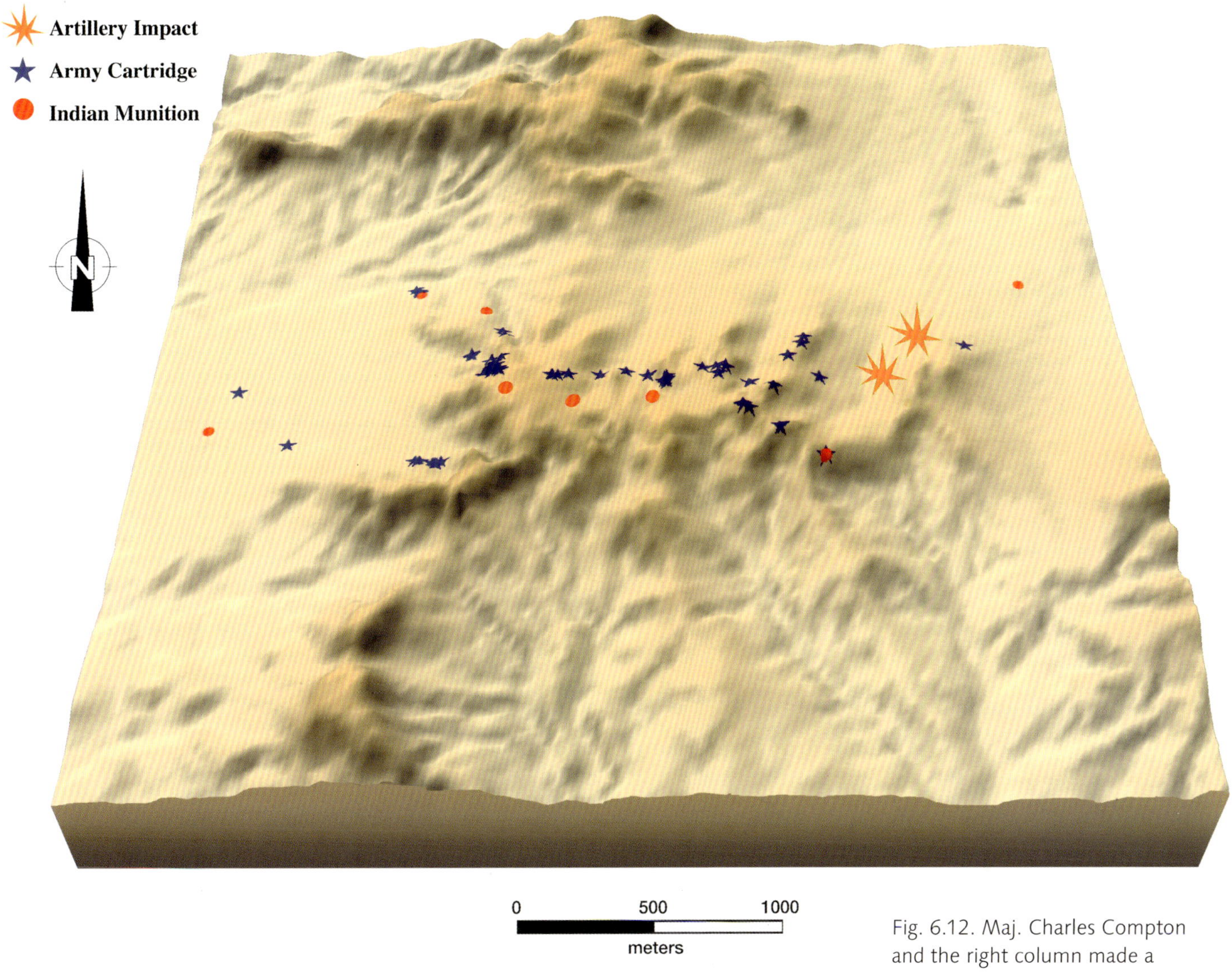

Fig. 6.12. Maj. Charles Compton and the right column made a cavalry charge "up a steep crest of 200 feet and the position [was] carried in fine order." This map shows the distribution of artifacts left from that charge. Illustration by Roland Pantermuehl

investigations also recovered fragments of two exploded Hotchkiss artillery shells near the north base of the hill.

After taking this hill, the right column apparently continued to the Red River and then moved south into Tule Canyon. Lieutenant Baldwin writes that the right column "advanced about 3 miles south of Red River," apparently in pursuit of the Indians.[29] The archeological evidence clearly reflects this movement and indicates that the right column followed the divide between Pilgrim Creek and Robins Arroyo to get to the Red River (see fig. 6.11). The artifacts recovered along the divide suggest that the column stopped on the bluffs that overlook the river, where they may have replenished their ammunition, though little fighting was apparently taking place at this stage of the battle. This is indicated by the fact that of the 131 cartridges recovered from the divide during the investigations, 122 are unfired and apparently were simply lost as the ammunition wagons made their way to the Red River. The majority of the unfired cartridges were recovered from the north-side bluffs above the river. Because the bluffs along this portion of the river are steep, it seems likely that the ammunition wagons were forced to stop here until a way could be found to cross the river. While the wagons were stopped, the troopers probably took the opportunity to reload quickly, carelessly dropping many cartridges, and then continued the pursuit of the

Indians across the river. The ammunition wagons probably followed at a hurried pace once they found their way off the bluffs and crossed the river. This is evident in the archeological record in that the trail of unfired cartridges continued on the south side of the river. In fact, the cartridge trail was found to extend from the south bank of the river approximately 3 miles, where it ended near Tule Canyon. This seems to confirm Baldwin's statement that the right column advanced 3 miles south of Red River. Only a few spent army and Indian cartridges were recovered along the trail, suggesting that the Indians were now in full retreat and firing only sporadically.

As for the movements of the center column and the artillery, it appears that the Gatling guns were unlimbered on the Griffin Hills and fired from there during the early stages of the battle, as evident from the recovery of several Gatling gun cartridges on the eastern end of the hills. There is no evidence that the Parrott rifle was fired from the Griffin Hills, but about a mile south of the Griffin Hills is a low hill (marked "Cannon Hill" in fig. 6.11) that overlooks Battle Creek and a large area of rugged and broken terrain to the south and west. This hill was apparently significant during the battle, for a substantial concentration of army-related cartridges was found here. It also seems that the Parrott rifle was set up and fired here during the early stages of the battle; though no direct evidence was recovered to prove the Parrott rifle was fired from this location, it seems likely since this is the only hill in the immediate area that overlooks the rugged terrain surrounding Battle Creek. This may be substantiated in a narrative written by J. W. McKinley, a soldier under Miles's command:

> The following morning the scouts led out pretty early with the cavalry following after some formality. The cannon was delayed in getting out of Salt Fork breaks [actually Mulberry Creek], but having succeeded to smoother grounds, we heard firing in the distance and an aide from the General brought an order for the cannon to be brought to the front immediately and for the teams to keep up with it if they could. The soldiers of the guard apportioned themselves to the ten wagons mounted and the chase began. We reached Battle Creek in a short time. A fight was in progress some distance to the right but the range was too far to do any hurt. The big cannon was run onto a low mound, unlimbered, and fired perhaps six or eight times.[30]

The area from the Griffin Hills south to this low hill is relatively smooth and could be accessed with wheeled artillery. McKinley's statement that they reached Battle Creek in a short time suggests that the artillery was not encumbered by rough terrain. West or south of this hill, the terrain becomes rugged and would be extremely difficult to maneuver with artillery, though not impossible. In fact, as the battle progressed, the artillery was maneuvered all the way to the Red River and into Tule Canyon.

Other evidence suggesting that this is the hill from which the Parrott rifle was fired can be found in the distribution of the artillery shell impacts identified during the investigations. Though the 10-pounder Parrott rifle could fire a shell 5 miles or more, it is unlikely that it was used at this range during the battle. It seems probable that the Indian warriors were trying to stay just out of range of the army carbines and rifles during most of the battle—or about 1,000–1,200 yards away. If that was the case, then the Parrott rifle would have been elevated between two and three degrees and firing from 1,000–1,300 yards.[31] During the investigations, nine locations were identified where artillery shells had impacted and exploded (fig. 6.13). Six of these impacts were within 1,100–1,850 yards of our "Cannon Hill," and the other three were between 3,200 and 4,600 yards. It seems likely, then, that this hill was an important location during the battle. The position of the 3-inch Parrott rifle on Cannon

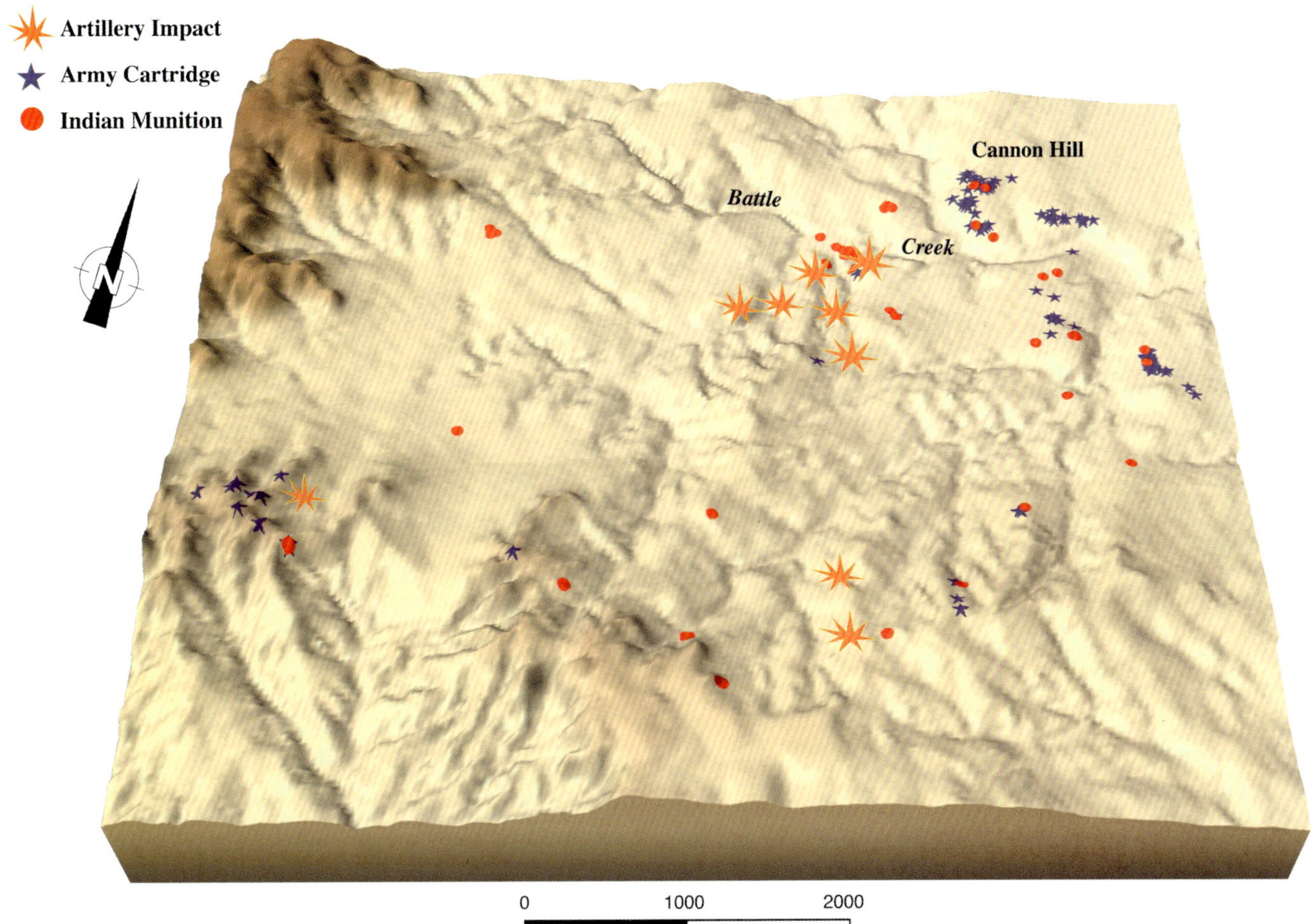

Fig. 6.13. The army's artillery was with the center column. Nine artillery shell impacts were mapped during the archeological investigations at the battle site. Illustration by Roland Pantermuehl

Hill represents part of the central movement of the artillery under Lieutenant Pope's command.

The third column, under Major Biddle's command, was ordered to take the left side of the battlefield, as were Lieutenant Baldwin and the scouts. Baldwin, in his account of the battle, writes: "When Gen. Miles came up I asked for orders and was directed to go to the left, gathering all of my men together and move down about ½ mile in front of and to the left of Col. Biddles battalion, facing to the front and went forward again, crossing Battle Creek under a sharp fire charged forward taking the ridge on the south bank. Here I halted for some little time to wait for the cavalry to move forward as I now had Indians on my right and front."[32]

From Baldwin we learn that he and the scouts were ordered to the left side of the battlefield, where they pushed across Battle Creek and secured a ridge on the south bank and waited for Biddle's cavalry to move up. The archeological investigations identified a ridge south of Battle Creek where an army skirmish line appears to have been established (fig. 6.14). This ridge may be where Baldwin and the scouts moved through on the left side of the battlefield. Baldwin goes on to write: "The red devils had collected a considerable number on a very high and prominent point in our front and Captain Chaffey [*sic*] having moved forward on the right of Biddle but getting considerably in advance, he moved to his left flank down the entire front of the battalion and charged the hill which was covered with Indians, taking it in a most handsome and gallant manner."[33]

N
Army Cartridge
Indian Munition
0
50
100
meters

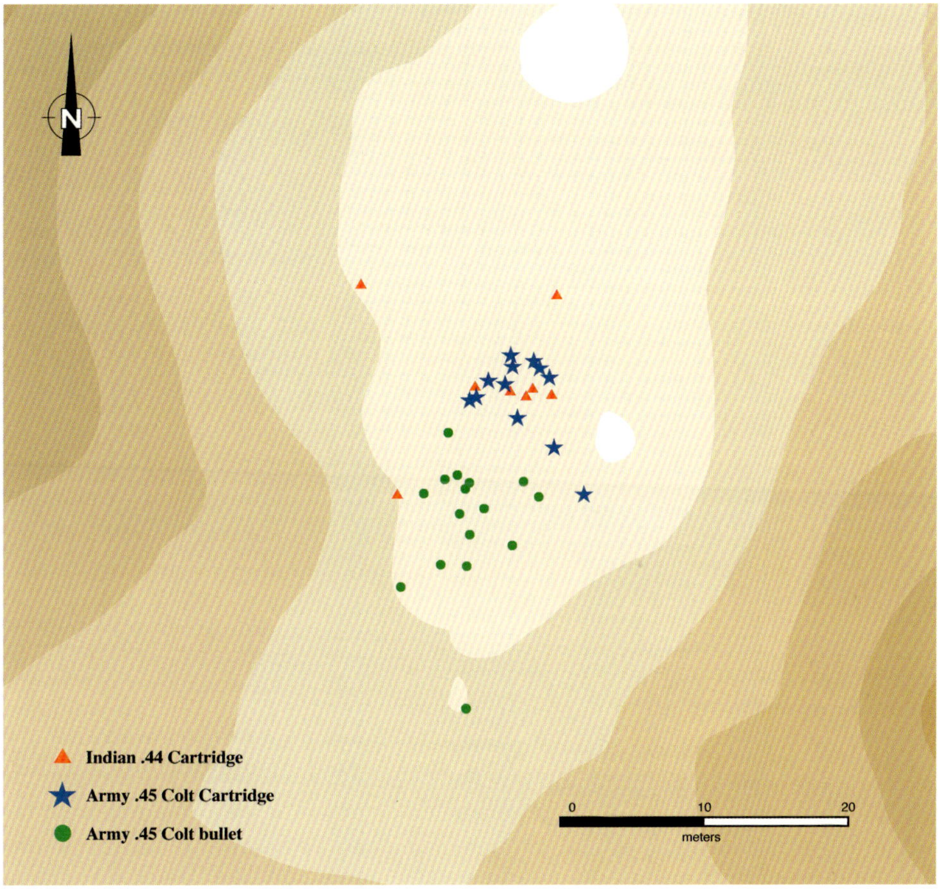

Fig. 6.14 (*facing page*). Lieutenant Baldwin and the scouts crossed Battle Creek and established a skirmish line on a ridge ahead of the left column. This map shows the distribution of cartridge cases on a ridge that probably marks that skirmish line. Illustration by Roland Pantermuehl

Fig. 6.15. Captain Chaffee and I Company were with the left column under Major Biddle's battalion when they made a charge using only their pistols. This map shows the distribution of recovered artifacts associated with that charge. Illustration by Roland Pantermuehl

Of Captain Chaffee's charge Colonel Miles writes, "Capt. Chaffee gallantly led his company ("I" 6th Cavalry) in a charge using only their pistols."[34] During the investigations, army pistol cartridges and bullets along with Indian .44-caliber rifle cartridges were recovered on a prominent hill (fig. 6.15) on what would be the left side of the battlefield. The fact this hill is on the left side of the battlefield, which would be in front of the scouts as described by Lieutenant Baldwin, and produced several pistol cartridges and bullets suggests that the hill is the location of Captain Chaffee's charge and the place where the left column moved through during the battle.

The mapped distribution of the artifacts across the site revealed distinct patterns, giving insights into specific battle events and the movements of army and Indian combatants. Topography was an important factor in how the battle unfolded and, consequently, in where the artifacts were found. The local topography is of high ridges and hills separated by deep canyons. Not unexpectedly, the Indian warriors were utilizing the high ridges and hills as offensive positions to fire at the approaching army and then retreating behind the hills as the army continued to advance. In this manner they were able to spread the army troops out and keep them guessing as to where they would appear next. This tactic worked to delay the army long enough for the Indian families to escape up Tule Canyon and out onto the Llano Estacado. The primary route of the Indian families' escape was clearly marked by the personal items apparently discarded or lost as they made their way to Tule Canyon.

Once the army took a hill, it used that hill to fire down on the retreating Indians. As a result, the majority of military artifacts were found on the higher elevations of the battle site. The distribution of army-related artifacts also corroborates the historical accounts of the battle in that the army apparently did advance across the battlefield in three separate columns, with the right column advancing some 3 miles south of the Red River and entering Tule Canyon.

Indian Village Site (41BI544) in Tule Canyon

After the battle, Colonel Miles established his headquarters camp near the mouth of Tule Canyon at one of the deserted Indian villages, of which there apparently were several in Tule Canyon. Miles's headquarters camp was one of four camps established in the area after the battle. The camp for the cavalry units was established several miles farther up Tule Canyon where there was better water and grass for the horses, the scouts were camped some distance beyond the cavalry, and the main supply camp was some 8 miles back on Battle Creek.[35] During the archeological investigations we identified a location approximately 1,200 m upstream from the mouth of Tule Canyon that we believe is where one of the Indian village sites and Colonel Miles's headquarters were situated (fig. 6.16). At this location, which is recorded as Site 41BI544, we recovered several historic Indian and U.S. Army–related artifacts. Because of time and funding constraints, we did not attempt to find any of the other village sites or army camps during our investigations.

Site 41BI544 occupies an area approximately 500 m by 200 m (547 yards by 219 yards) along the north side of Tule Creek. At the time of the archeological investigations in 1999, the stream terrace on which 41BI544 is situated was thickly covered with mesquite trees, sunflowers, cactus, and various grasses, which severely limited our ability to conduct a thorough metal detector survey of the site. In addition, it appears that over time Tule Creek has cut away significant portions of the terrace, resulting in a contemporary terrace that is substantially narrower than it likely was in 1874. Despite these limitations, we recoverd 181 artifacts—both Indian and army—from the site. For the most part, the artifacts were widely scattered across the site area, so only general statements concerning artifact distributions are possible.

Of the recovered artifacts, fifty-seven are associated with the Indian villagers (fig. 6.17).[36] These include a variety of camp and clothing items such as awls, buckles, buttons, and iron arrowpoints; horse-related items such as rein chains, *coscojos* (jinglers), and tinklers; and several fired .44-caliber rifle cartridges and bullets of various calibers. These items were spread in a linear distribution across the terrace and parallel to Tule Creek. There does not appear to be any discernible patterns in the distribution of these artifacts other than a single cluster found on the extreme western end of the site consisting of six iron arrowpoints, one arrowpoint preform, and several pieces of cut metal debris. These indicate that in this area metal arrowpoints were being manufactured.

The 124 army-associated artifacts recovered at 41BI544 were, like the Indian-associated artifacts, spread across the site in linear fashion (fig. 6.18). Several discernible artifact clusters are evident. Most of these artifacts are small square nails, most likely from boxes used to transport and store rations and supplies. The box nails were primarily found in two clusters near the central and eastern portions of the site. Most of the nails in the clusters were burned, perhaps indicating that the empty supply boxes were used for firewood by the soldiers. Leaded cans were also found in these clusters associated with the box nails. The two clusters of box nails and tin cans may represent mess areas for the soldiers.

The distribution of horse-related artifacts such as horseshoes, horseshoe nails, and picket pins is fairly spread out across the site, though in an area near the east end of the site several of the horseshoes and used horseshoe nails were recovered. This may

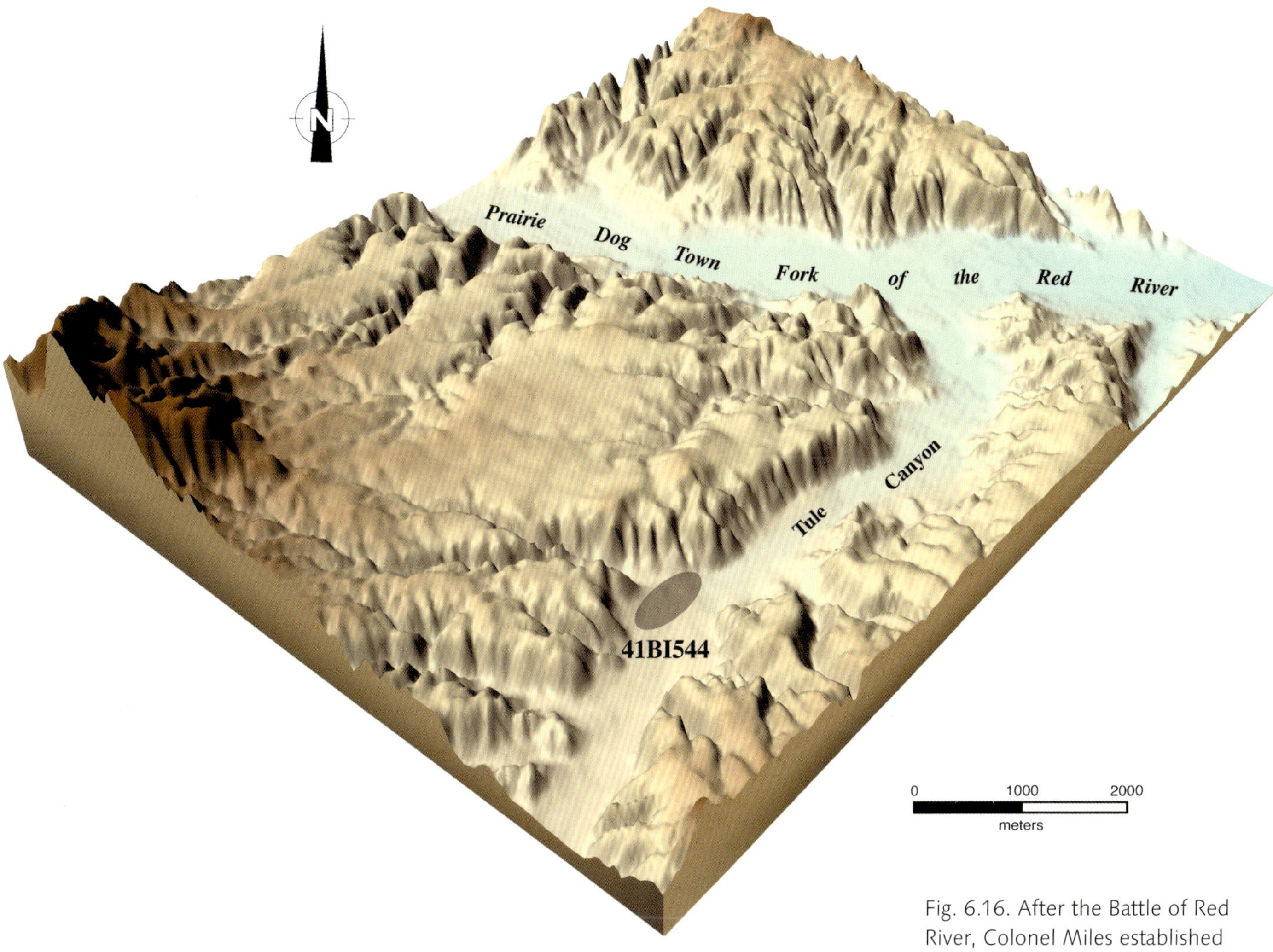

Fig. 6.16. After the Battle of Red River, Colonel Miles established his headquarters at an abandoned Indian village site (Site 41BI544) on Tule Creek. Illustration by Roland Pantermuehl

be an area where reshoeing of some of the horses took place, but the relatively small number of artifacts recovered makes it difficult to say with certainty. A small cluster of unused horseshoe nails was found about 75 m northwest of where the horseshoes and used horseshoe nails were recovered. These may have been lost out of a supply box since they were found near the central cluster of burned box nails and tin cans discussed earlier.

The distribution of unfired .45-caliber cartridges is interesting, but its meaning remains uncertain. Of the unfired .45-caliber cartridges, sixteen are Springfield cartridges and three are Colt pistol cartridges. These unfired rounds were scattered across the length of the site, though there were two clusters, each containing three cartridges, near the west end of the site. From the current level of investigations it is unclear whether these unfired cartridges mark places where individual soldiers were encamped or whether they were simply randomly lost during the nine days the soldiers were there.

Artifacts Recovered

During two seasons of fieldwork at the Battle of Red River site, 1,214 artifacts were recovered. Of these, 1,064 are associated with the U.S. Army and 150 with Indians. At Site 41BI544, 181 artifacts were recovered. Of these, 124 are associated with the army's

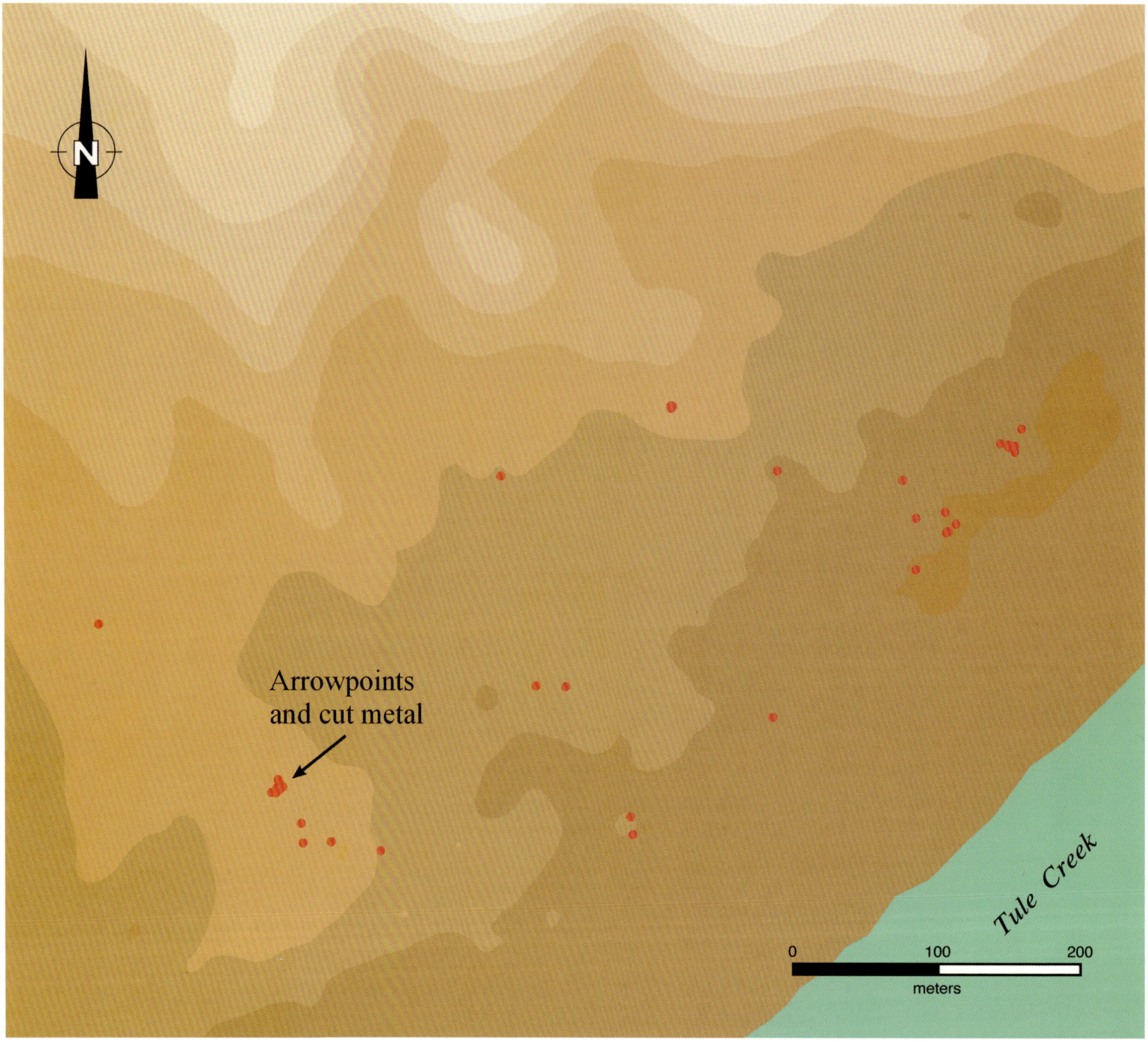

Fig. 6.17. The Indian-associated artifacts at the village site were spread in a linear pattern. Illustration by Roland Pantermuehl

occupation of the site and fifty-seven with the Indian villagers. Table 6.1 summarizes the artifacts from both sites by type and association. The complete listing of the artifacts recovered from the sites and the attendant analyses are included as appendix D. Most of the artifacts are munitions related and include 464 fired and 288 unfired rifle and pistol cartridge cases of various calibers used by the army and the Indians. The fired cases are .44-caliber cases that were fired in Henry rifles or Model 1866 Winchesters, .45-caliber Colt cartridges fired from Model 1873 revolvers, .45-caliber cartridge cases fired in Model 1873 Springfield rifles or carbines, .50-caliber cartridges fired from one or more Gatling guns, and .50- and .56-caliber cartridges fired from Spencer carbines.

Bullets from the various cartridge types were also recovered. Round lead balls, which are typically fired from muzzle loader firearms, make up a surprising 26.7 percent of the total number of bullets recovered from the battle site and indicate that the Indians were relying substantially on obsolete muzzle loaders even as late as 1874.

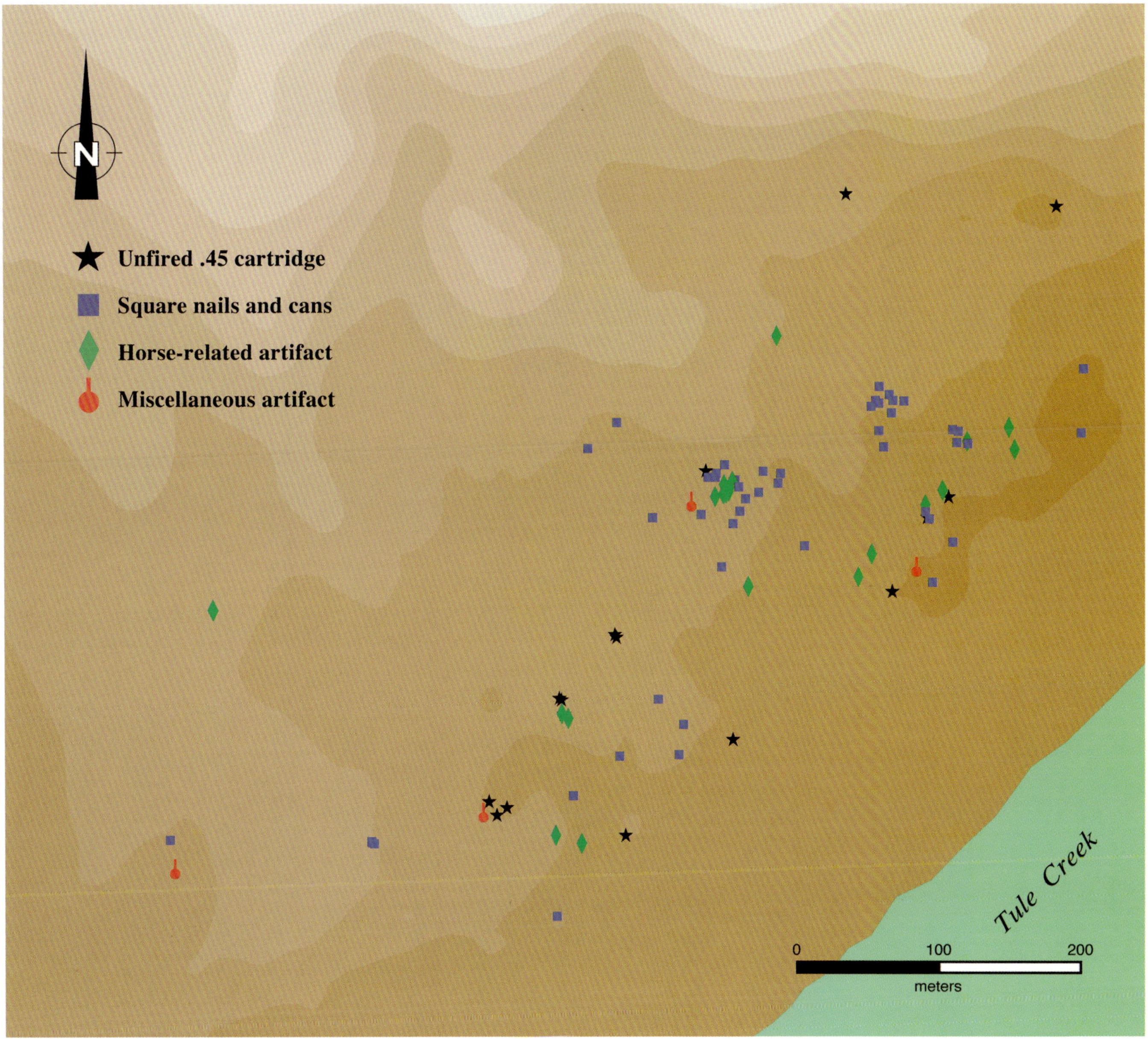

Fig. 6.18. Like the Indian artifacts at Site 41BI544, the army artifacts were spread in a linear pattern, but there were several discernible clusters. Illustration by Roland Pantermuehl

In most instances, the bullets and cartridges can be clearly assigned as either Indian-associated or army-associated. In 1874, the U.S. Army was primarily using the .45-caliber Model 1873 Springfield carbine and rifle and the .45-caliber Model 1873 Colt revolver. The Indians were using a variety of weapons, primarily older model firearms they were able to secure through trade, from illicit gunrunners, or directly from the U.S. Army.

An array of other artifacts were also recovered, including shrapnel from exploded Hotchkiss artillery shells fired from the army's 10-pounder Parrott rifle and metal arrowpoints and other metal tools such as awls, fleshers, and other utensils used by the Indians. Other artifacts not related to munitions include horse tack, horseshoes and horseshoe nails, and personal items such as buttons from army and Indian clothing, harmonica parts, bells, a cavalry spur, and a watch chain. Like the munitions-related artifacts, these other artifacts were assigned to association based on where they were recovered and their copresence with other diagnostic artifacts.

Table 6.1. Artifacts from the Battle of Red River Site and Site 41BI544

	Battle Site		Site 41BI544		
Item	*Army*	*Indian*	*Army*	*Indian*	*Total*
Artifacts Related to Munitions					
.44-caliber cartridge case, fired		24		11	35
.45 Colt cartridge case, fired	16				16
.45 Colt cartridge, unfired	42		3		45
.45-caliber cartridge case, fired	349				349
.45-caliber cartridge, unfired	228		13		241
.50/70 cartridge case, fired	41	2			43
.50/70 cartridge, unfired	1		1		2
56/50 Spencer cartridge case, fired		16			16
56/56 Spencer cartridge case, fired		5			5
.36-caliber Colt bullet				1	1
.40-caliber Sharps bullet		4			4
.44-caliber bullet		17		2	19
.44-caliber ball		2			2
.45 Colt bullet	7				7
.45-caliber bullet	17				17
.50-caliber Sharps bullet		7		2	9
.50-caliber bullet fired in Gatling gun	6				6
.50-caliber ball		19			19
.54-caliber ball		2			2
.61-caliber copper ball				1	1
bullet, unidentified fragment		8		1	9
gun hammer, Colt M1860 revolver				1	1
gun flint				1	1
Hotchkiss shell shrapnel	145				145
rifle barrel, .50-caliber musket		1			1
rifle ramrod, M1868 Springfield		1			1
iron arrowpoints and preforms		8		7	15
Subtotal, munitions	852	116	17	27	1,012
Other Artifacts					
awl		1		4	5
bell		2			2
bore cleaning tip		1		1	2
buckle, miscellaneous	7			1	8
buckle, spur	1				1
button, U.S. Army	1		3		4
button, other	1	6		4	11
can, leaded	6		19		25
canteen top and chain	2				2
cinch ring tongue				1	1
concha		4			4
coscojo		2		3	5
curry comb	1				1
cut iron and brass				9	9
flesher		2			2
harmonica core	3				3
headstall plate or bridge		1			1
horseshoe	29		6		35
horseshoe nail, unused	140		9		149
horseshoe nail, used	14		5		19
kettle bail ear, brass		1		1	2
mule shoe			1		1
nail, box square			60		60

Table 6.1, *continued*

Item	*Battle Site*		*Site 41BI544*		
	Army	*Indian*	*Army*	*Indian*	*Total*
percussion cap container				1	1
picket pin			2		2
pommel ornament, brass			1		1
punch		1			1
rein chain and ring		1		2	3
rivet, brass	1				1
saddle/harness D- or O-ring	4				4
spur, U.S. Cavalry	1				1
tinkler		1		2	3
trace chain	1				1
utensil		11		1	12
watch chain			1		1
Subtotal, other	212	34	107	30	383
Total artifacts	**1,064**	**150**	**124**	**57**	**1,395**

Discussion

Of the 1,214 artifacts recovered, the majority are cartridges and bullets. On the basis of firing pin signatures, at least thirteen different types of firearms were used in the battle, representing a minimum of seventy-one individual weapons (table 6.2). Of the individual weapons identified, fifty-two are associated with the U.S. Army and nineteen with the Indians. This is a ratio of approximately 2.7 army firearms to every Indian firearm. It should be noted that it is likely that many more firearms were used in the battle. The seventy-one individual weapons identified represent the minimum number of firearms based on the cartridge cases and bullets recovered during the investigations, which in all likelihood is a small percentage of the total number of firearm artifacts at the site. The Battle of Red River site is spread over roughly 35 square miles, and we have no way of determining what percentage of the total number of artifacts were recovered from the site during our investigations. Another factor that affected the number of individual weapons identified was the number of heavily oxidized or other problematic cartridge cases (n=133) that could not be analyzed. All of the oxidized cartridges, however, are .45-caliber like those used by the U.S. Army, suggesting that the number of firearms used in the battle by the army was even higher than the 2.7:1 ratio indicated by the analyzed cartridges.

In addition, of the 453 fired cartridges recovered from the battle site, 406 (90 percent) were fired from the army firearms and only forty-seven (10 percent) from Indian-associated firearms. On the basis of these numbers, each of the fifty-two army-associated firearms fired an average of 7.8 cartridges, compared to only 2.5 cartridges fired from each of the nineteen Indian-associated firearms.

There were 744 men in Colonel Miles's command, but one or two companies had been left to escort the detached supply wagons, and at least two companies were held in reserve during the battle and did not actively participate in the engagement. Thus the number of soldiers who potentially fired their weapons during the battle is estimated at about five hundred. Of the fifty-two army-associated firearms identified, two are Gatling guns and the other fifty are firearms used by individual soldiers. Assuming that there were five hundred soldiers who fired their weapons at least once during the

Table 6.2. Firearm Types Used at the Battle of Red River

Firearm Type	*Army-Associated*	*Indian-Associated*	*Total*
.40-caliber Sharps rifle		1	1
.44-caliber Henry or Winchester M1866 rifle		3	3
.44-caliber Remington M1858 revolver		1	1
.44-caliber Sharps rifle		1	1
.45-caliber Colt M1873 revolver	9		9
.45-caliber Springfield rifle or carbine	39		39
.50- and .56-caliber Spencer carbine		9	9
.50-caliber Gatling gun	2		1
.50-caliber Plains rifle or trade gun		1	1
.50-caliber Remington carbine		1	1
.50-caliber Sharps carbine		1	1
.50-caliber Springfield M1868 or 1870 rifle	2		2
.54-caliber Plains rifle or trade gun		1	1
Total	**52**	**19**	**71**

battle, then the fifty individual firearms represent 10 percent of the army firearms. If the nineteen Indian-associated firearms also represent 10 percent of the Indian firearms, then there would have been a projected 190 Indian firearms used at the battle. Colonel Miles estimated that there were four hundred to six hundred Indian warriors. If we accept this as accurate, then approximately 32 percent (if six hundred warriors) to 48 percent (if four hundred warriors) of the Indian combatants had firearms. Of the Indian firearms identified at the site, 63 percent of them (a projected 120 guns) are repeaters such as the Henry and Winchester Models 1866 and Spencer carbines of various calibers.

The cartridge and bullet analysis suggests that either the Indians at the battle were not as well armed as the army accounts seem to indicate or Colonel Miles's estimate of four hundred to six hundred warriors is inflated. Just five days before the battle, Colonel Miles wrote to the adjutant general at Fort Leavenworth, stating, "I am of opinion that the strength of the Indians has been greatly underrated, and that they are well armed with rifles of improved pattern, and provided with abundance of ammunition." After the battle he reported to General Pope, "The Indian trail is still very large; they are holding their families and tribes together; there cannot be less than two thousand (2000) or three thousand (3000) retreating before us."[37] It seems probable that, if there were as many Indians as Colonel Miles estimated and if they were as well armed as he thought, then there would be substantially more Indian-associated weapons represented in the cartridge and bullet analysis.

One factor that may partially explain an underrepresentation of Indian-associated weapons is the Indians' apparent reliance on muzzle loader rifles. Of the fifty bullets recovered that can be attributed to the Indians, twenty-two (44 percent) are .50- or .54-caliber balls from muzzle loaders. Since muzzle loaders did not use cartridges and no percussion caps were recovered from the battlefield, only the fired rifle balls that were recovered from the site can be analyzed. With no firing pin signature to examine, it becomes much more difficult to determine how many rifles fired the balls. Thus, we can only state that a minimum of one 50-caliber and one .54-caliber muzzle loader are represented.

The number of muzzle loader balls recovered from the battle site suggests that the Indians were relying heavily on this type of firearm. The broken .50-caliber muzzle loader rifle barrel that was also recovered from the site is additional evidence that the Indians were using muzzle loaders. Compared to repeating rifles such as the Spencer, Winchester, and Henry, muzzle loaders had a slow firing time. Consequently, these repeating rifles had essentially replaced muzzle loaders by the mid-1860s. By 1874, muzzle loaders would have been obsolete. It is curious that in 1874 an enemy that was armed with a significant number of muzzle loaders would be considered "well armed" by an officer of the U.S. Army.

In defense of Colonel Miles, the archeological evidence clearly shows that the Indians were also using firearms other than muzzle loaders. In fact, repeating rifles account for eleven of the Indian weapons, though these too were older models. For example, the .44-caliber cartridges recovered were fired from a Henry or Winchester Model 1866 rifle, and the majority of the Spencer cartridges recovered were manufactured prior to 1867. This suggests that the Indians were conserving and even curating their cartridges, hardly a practice of a well-armed and well-supplied foe. Nonetheless, the repeater rifles the Indians had were formidable weapons at ranges of 300 yards or less. Other than a few brief encounters involving closer-range firing, however, the bulk of the fighting appears to have been long-range firing as the Indians were retreating. Miles states, for example, that the Indians "fought in a cowardly manner, shooting very wildly and at extreme long range."[38]

Even more significant, it appears that less than half of the Indians were fighting with no firearms at all. In the initial attack by the Indians on the army scouts, Miles notes, one of the army's Delaware scouts was wounded by a spear, and the Indians were "sending a few arrows."[39] These statements suggest that some of the Indian warriors were not armed with firearms of any kind, which is further supported by a statement by Henry W. Taylor, who, upon examining a portion of the battle site just eight years after the battle, observed, "The [Griffin] hills were also covered with Indian arrows, pieces of broken tomahawks, broken bows and bow strings, and pieces of old broken rifles, indicating that a battle was fought there."[40] This statement makes it clear that the Indians were using a variety of native-made weapons in addition to firearms during the battle. The archeological investigations support this conclusion with the recovery of metal arrowpoints from both the battle site and Site 41BI544.

It is not known how many artifacts collectors may have previously removed from the site, but certain patterns seem clear. Either Colonel Miles overestimated the number of Indians at the battle, or the Indians were not as well armed as he believed. On the basis of the archeological evidence, it is likely that there were not as many Indians as Colonel Miles estimated, and that the ones who were there were not well armed, at least not as well as Miles believed they were.

7

The Indians Take the Offensive

During the pursuit of the Indians toward the Prairie Dog Town Fork of the Red River and the battle that occurred there on August 30, Col. Nelson A. Miles had seriously overstretched his supply lines, and provisions for the troops were now dangerously low. Consequently, Miles decided to establish his headquarters on the Red River and send a military escort under the command of Capt. Wyllys Lyman (fig. 7.1) with thirty-six empty supply wagons back toward Camp Supply in Indian Territory to restock the provisions. Miles was unaware that on August 22 a large group of Kiowas and Comanches who had been registered at the Wichita Agency near Anadarko had revolted and fled westward and were now in position to cut him off from his supply route to Camp Supply.

Fig. 7.1. Capt. Wyllys Lyman was in command of the supply train for Colonel Miles. Courtesy Panhandle-Plains Historical Museum, Canyon, Texas

Through a system of couriers, Miles arranged for another caravan to move south from Camp Supply to meet Lyman's wagons. The two trains met at Commission Creek in what is now Ellis County, Oklahoma, and after transferring the supplies to his wagons Lyman and his men started back to rejoin Miles.[1] According to the army records, Lyman's command consisted of thirty-six infantry, twenty cavalry, and thirty-six civilian teamsters, of whom only ten were armed. This would make sixty-six his total of armed men.[2] On the way back, the supply train encountered Lt. Frank Baldwin and three scouts carrying dispatches to Camp Supply. The four men had with them a white Kiowa captive named Tehan, whom they had taken prisoner while skirting Lone Wolf's camp. Thinking that Colonel Miles would be interested in questioning Tehan, Baldwin turned the prisoner over to Captain Lyman before continuing.[3]

The Battle of Lyman's Wagon Train

On September 9, as the Lyman supply train was heading back toward the Red River, some of the Kiowas and Comanches who had recently fled the Wichita Agency and been searching for Tehan came upon the train as it was crossing the divide between the Canadian and Washita rivers. The Indians began firing at the train from long range while a small group ascended the ridge ahead of the wagons, but the defensive maneuvers of the cavalry enabled the train to move 12 miles farther south until it reached a steep ravine about a mile north of the Washita River. The train successfully forded the ravine, but as the wagons approached the river the Indians began to press the attack and Lyman ordered the wagons to form into a protective corral for better defense. The right column of the train formed with the customary bulge to the outside, but the left column, conforming to the terrain, aligned itself nearly parallel to the right, forming a crescent, or D-shaped, enclosure in contrast to the usual circular pattern.[4]

As the wagons were circling, a group of about seventy warriors attacked from the right and rear of the train and almost overran the skirmish lines that had been established by the infantry. The skirmishers held and repulsed the attack, but Sgt. William DeArmond was killed during the assault and Lt. Granville Lewis was severely wounded. One of the teamsters, a man by the name of McCoy, was seriously wounded while carrying ammunition to the troops and died the next day. On September 11 another teamster, James L. Stanford, was wounded and later died at the Camp Supply hospital, on November 27.[5] According to Sgt. George Kitchen, who was at the battle, both Sergeant DeArmond and teamster McCoy were buried inside the confines of the circled wagon train "with brief but impressive ceremony."[6]

When the initial attack by the Indians failed, they retreated to the surrounding ridges and began to lay siege to the wagon train. In his report of the battle, Captain

◀ Fig. 7.2. Kiowa chief Satanta was a noted orator and diplomat. Courtesy Panhandle-Plains Historical Museum, Canyon, Texas

▼ Fig. 7.3. Kiowa chief Big Tree with a traditional bow and fur-trimmed arrow bundle. Courtesy Panhandle-Plains Historical Museum, Canyon, Texas

Fig. 7.4. Scout William F. Schmalsle made a daring ride through the Indians to reach Camp Supply and summon help for Lyman's besieged wagon train. Courtesy Panhandle-Plains Historical Museum, Canyon, Texas

Lyman states: "The enemy had opposite here a parallel ridge at about 400 yards, and beyond, another and higher one running somewhat circularly at about 900 yards. He occupied these lines strongly, and his fire was constant and severe. He had also good positions at 500 yards." Lyman goes on to state that the Indians "were Comanches and Kiowas who had gone on the war path from Wichita Agency. They were about 400 in number, and it is believed they were directed by Lone Wolf." It was later learned that, in addition to Lone Wolf, several other prominent chiefs took part in the battle, including Satanta (fig. 7.2) and Big Tree (Fig 7.3).[7]

With the onset of darkness the fighting fell off, but it was now apparent to Lyman that the Indians intended to continue their siege, and he ordered the men to dig rifle pits around the perimeter of the circled train to afford additional protection. According to Lyman, "The corral [the circled wagon train] on the right, front and rear was protected by a series of pits close upon the wagons, and forage sacks, etc., were used to fortify some of these. . . . Sergeant Singleton, Company A, 6th Cavalry, was severely wounded in the leg on this night at a pit he had charge of, and where he did good service. Next morning Private Buck, Company I, 5th Infantry, was painfully wounded on the head at Sergeant Hay's pit."[8]

The next morning the Indians resumed their fire. By nightfall on September 10, seeing that the situation was desperate, Lyman sent one of the scouts, William F. Schmalsle (fig. 7.4), to Camp Supply to get help. As Schmalsle left the wagon train, he was pursued by some of the Indians, but he managed to evade them by riding his horse into a large herd of buffalo, which caused the herd to stampede. Schmalsle rode his horse to death but arrived at Camp Supply on foot on the morning of September 12.

In the meantime Tehan had slipped away from his captors and returned to his adopted people. He apparently advised the Kiowas to fortify a small waterhole that lay some 400 yards from the wagon train since the soldiers were in need of water. So desperate were the soldiers for water that they "punctured the canned stuffs and drank the liquor. Vinegar, and even urine was drank." The Indians apparently heeded Tehan's advice, because on the night of September 10 several of the soldiers and teamsters made an "unauthorized" attempt to reach the pool but were driven back by a volley from Indian firearms. Lyman writes that thirty Indian rifle pits were later found around the water pool.[9]

The Indians kept up their siege throughout the day of September 11, but on the morning of the twelfth they began to abandon the siege to continue their intended trek southwest toward Palo Duro Canyon. Other soldiers, apparently Major Price and the 8th Cavalry from Fort Union, had been spotted in the near vicinity, and the warriors began to worry for the safety of their nearby families. As the Indians began to drift away from the wagon train, a young half-breed named Botayle decided it was time to prove his worth as a courageous warrior. Botayle mounted his horse, slung himself over on the horse's side, then rode through the entrenched soldiers and army camp and returned to the Indians. As the Indians stood awestruck, Botayle repeated his ride three more times, with the soldiers firing at him during each ride. After the fourth ride through the soldier's line, Botayle returned to the Indians completely unharmed. So amazed were the Indians with Botayle's feat that Chief Poor Buffalo recognized his bravery by giving him a new name: Eadle-tau-hain, which means, "He Would Not Listen."[10]

As the ranks of Indian warriors continued to thin out, the troops finally cleared those remaining away from the waterhole. During the afternoon of the twelfth a cold rainstorm set in and continued through the next day. Even though the command was almost out of supplies (they were depending wholly on the train for rations and

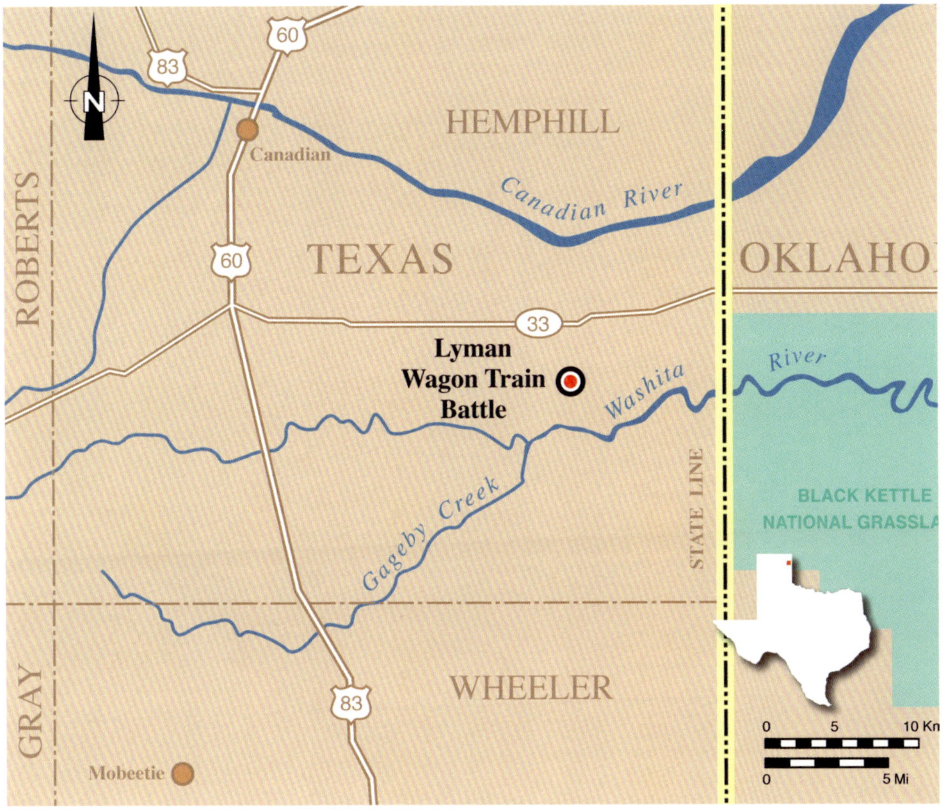

Fig. 7.5. The Battle of Lyman's Wagon Train took place in present southeastern Hemphill County, Texas. Illustration by Roland Pantermuehl

Fig. 7.6. A small granite marker was placed on the battle site by the Hemphill County Historical Commission.

forage), Lyman decided not to move the wagons in the storm. Several of the horses had been injured, twenty-two mules for the wagons had been killed, and the others were "tottering on their feet." Fortunately for the train, in the early morning hours of the fourteenth, Company K, under the command of Lt. Henry Kingsbury, arrived from Camp Supply with medical aid and an ambulance. With the siege broken, Lyman moved out with the wagons and later that morning joined Colonel Miles, who had moved his command north to the Washita River in search of his supply train. On the recommendation of Colonel Miles, thirteen troopers were awarded the Medal of Honor (appendix C) for their bravery in the fight and Lyman was eventually promoted for his performance.[11]

As for the number of Indian casualties during the battle, Lyman states in his official report, "There were thirteen ascertained cases of killed and badly wounded, and, I believe, others." However, in October 1874, the *Army and Navy Journal* published a letter written by Lyman in which he claimed that twenty-seven Indians were killed. In addition, Sergeant Kitchen, one of the Medal of Honor recipients at the battle, stated that "Captain Lyman, about a week after the action, went over the ground and in one ravine counted forty fresh mounds, graves of the Indian slain, but their loss in fatally wounded and disabled must have been much more."[12] Though we will probably never know the precise number of Indian casualties, the number given in Lyman's official report is likely the most accurate.

Current Ownership and Land Use

The Lyman Wagon Train battle site is privately owned land in southeastern Hemphill County (fig. 7.5) in an area which, like the county as a whole, is rural, with farming

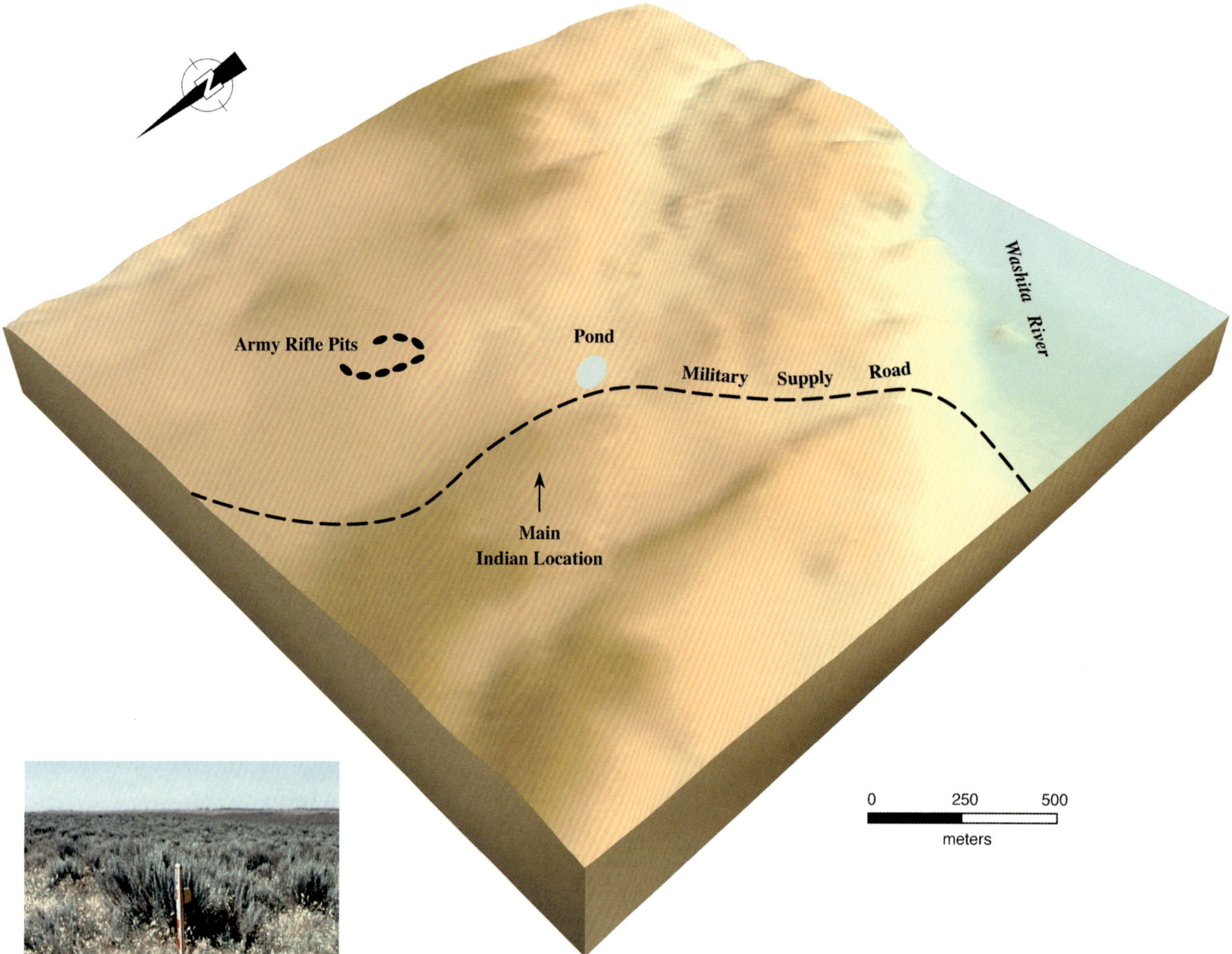

⯭ Fig. 7.7. Oval rifle pits still mark where Captain Lyman's wagon train made its defensive circle. Illustration by Roland Pantermuehl

▲ Fig. 7.8. One of the army rifle pits still visible at the Lyman Wagon Train battle site.

and ranching the primary sources of income. The area is pastureland and has never been cultivated. The soils are sandy loams, and the groundcover is mainly sagebrush and native grasses. The terrain can be characterized as gently rolling with scattered small hills and ridges. The battle site is bounded on the north by a county-maintained dirt road and on the east by an unpaved ranch road. To the west is open pasture, and to the south are the breaks and floodplain of the Washita River. In 1971, the Hemphill County Historical Commission placed a small concrete and granite monument on the north edge of the site to mark the battle (fig. 7.6).

Archeological Investigations and Results

In 1971, personnel of the Panhandle-Plains Historical Museum recorded the location of the Lyman's Wagon Train battle site with the state as Site 41HH11. One of the members of that recording team was Rolla Shaller, now assistant curator of archeology at the museum. In March 1998, Shaller, along with the site property owner, Glenn Bill Walker, accompanied us to the site, where we viewed the monument that had been placed there by the Hemphill County Historical Commission. Walker also

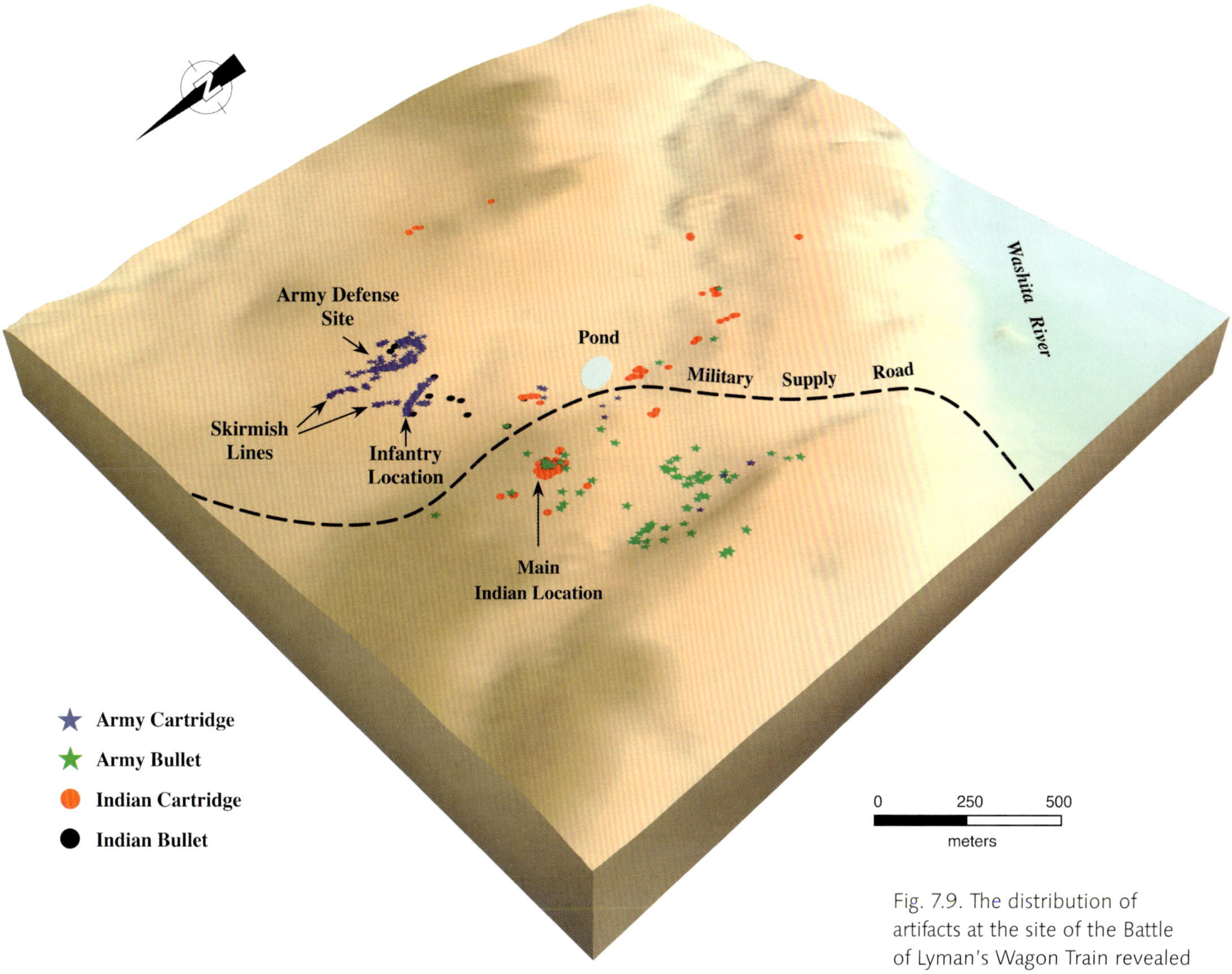

Fig. 7.9. The distribution of artifacts at the site of the Battle of Lyman's Wagon Train revealed clear patterns and locations of specific battle events. The circled wagon train and positions of the Indians during the battle are clearly shown by the mapped artifacts. Illustration by Roland Pantermuehl

showed us the general areas where he had collected cartridges, wagon hardware, an army uniform button, and miscellaneous other items that seemed to be associated with the battle.

The archeological investigations at the site began on May 10, 1998, and were concluded on June 21, 1998. The archeological team initiated a metal detector survey of the areas where Walker had recovered artifacts. Most of the artifacts he had collected were .45-caliber cartridges of the types used by the army at the time of the battle. We also observed several rectangular to oval depressions that we believed were the remains of rifle pits (figs. 7.7, 7.8). Thus, this area of the site was presumed to be where the wagon train had formed its defensive circle.

The artifacts distribution shown by the metal detector survey clearly revealed discreet patterns and locations of specific battle events. The location of the circled wagon train is discernible by a circular pattern of army-related artifacts (fig. 7.9). Most of these artifacts are spent .45/55 or .45/70 cartridge cases, but .50/70 cartridges, wagon hardware, horse tack, and leaded tin cans were also recovered. Many of the .45- and .50-caliber cartridges were found in or around shallow depressions, which are undoubtedly rifle pits that are now mostly filled with blow sand. Most of the leaded tin

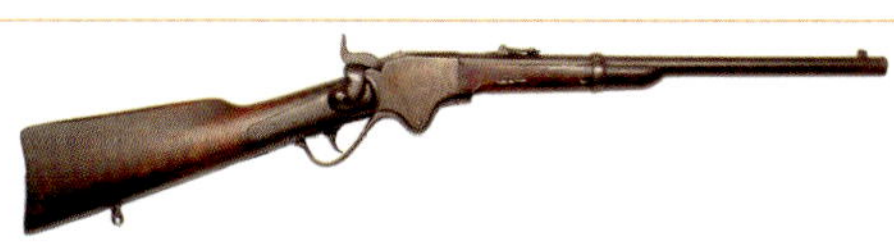

cans, which held the rations and provisions consumed by the army personnel during the battle, were found in or near the rifle pits.

The artifact distribution also provided information on other combatant locations. Just north of the circled wagon train were two distinct lines of spent army cartridges, which most likely mark the skirmish lines established during the initial stages of the battle as the train was forming its defensive circle. The lines are oriented northeast–southwest and would be on the right and rear of the train, since the wagons had now abandoned their trek toward the southwest and turned southeast in an attempt to reach higher ground ahead of the charging Indians. This matches Captain Lyman's description of the actions of the skirmishers when he writes: "They [the Indians] rode within 100 yards. This occurred on the rear where Lieutenant Lewis had charge. He had skilfully handled his skirmishers according to his own judgment up to this time, and when the attack was making he shifted his lines to meet it to the right and rear of the train and opened fire."[13]

Just west of the skirmish lines is a small ridge where numerous .45/55 or .45/70 cartridges were recovered. We found cartridges in fifteen distinct clusters on the east side of and just below the crest of the ridge. This line of army-related cartridges most likely marks the advance of the infantry in their attempt to drive the Indians from the only source of water, a small pond about 400 yards to the southwest. Captain Lyman gives this brief description of the attempt by the army to drive the Indians from the pond: "During the morning of the 12th the enemy was seen to withdraw a part of his force across the Washita River and over the prairie beyond. . . . A light fire, however, continued from small parties until it was decided to skirmish for water. Lieutenant West moved out his mounted men, and Sergeant Mitchell deployed an infantry party of fifteen men. They cleared the ridge beyond the water of Indians."[14] The fifteen clusters of spent cartridge cases on the ridge to the west of the wagon train most likely correspond to the infantry charge to take the water pond.

The main body of Indians were on a ridge about 550 m (601 yards) west of the army defense site, as indicated by the high proportion of Indian cartridges recovered there. These cartridges were primarily Spencer 56/56 cartridge cases and Sharps .50/70 cases, along with a few .44-caliber Winchester cartridge cases. Additional corroboration that most of the Indians were on this ridge is provided by the fact that most of the bullets fired by the army rifles were found behind the ridge to the west of the Indian cartridges and are clearly the result of overshots by the army. Other Indian positions were identified on hilltops to the southwest and south of the army defense site, at distances up to 985 m (1,077 yards) away. About 500 m (547 yards) southeast of the army defense site is a prominent hill where several additional Indian-associated cartridges were recovered. On the basis of the number of cartridges recovered from these other scattered hilltops, it appears that fewer individuals occupied these positions. The distribution of Indian-related artifacts indicates that the Indians were primarily utilizing the more prominent hilltops and ridges to the west, southwest, south, and southeast of the wagon train as defensive locations. To the north and northeast of the army defense site, the terrain levels out and no ridges or hilltops are available for defense. Consequently, the archeological survey did not recover any battle-related artifacts in these directions. On the basis of artifact distributions, the Lyman Wagon Train battle site encompasses about 350 acres.

Colonel Miles's comments on the types of firearms the Indians used and how they adopted "modes of civilized warfare" are interesting. He writes: "On receiving the reports and on an examination of the ground, I found that the efforts of the Indians to capture the Train, were very determined and persistent; they even adopting modes of civilized warfare, such as, making diversions with mounted force and advancing the main force dismounted, and intrenching to hold the ground they gained. There were at least one hundred (100) rifle-pits within close range of the train. They were undoubtedly Kiowas and Comanches who have hitherto been living at the Agencies. They were abundantly furnished with the most improved weapons and ammunition; as their rifle-pits contain shells of the Henry, Spencer, Sharp and needle-gun ammunition."[15]

Some of the Indian-made rifle pits are still visible at the battle site, though most of them are now filled with blow sand. None of the rifle pits was excavated during the archeological investigations.

Artifacts Recovered

A total of 1,176 battle-related artifacts were recovered from the Battle of Lyman's Wagon Train site (table 7.1). The complete listing of the artifacts recovered and the attendant analyses are included as appendix E. Of the recovered artifacts, 892 are associated with the army and 284 with the Indians. Most of the artifacts are cartridges, among them 852 fired and forty-eight unfired cases of various calibers used by the army and Indians. The fired cases are .44-caliber cartridges fired in Henry rifles or Model 1866 Winchesters, .44-caliber cartridges fired from a Colt pistol, .45-caliber cartridge cases fired in the Model 1873 Springfield rifle or carbine, .50-caliber cartridge cases fired in Model 1868 or 1870 Springfield rifles and in Sharps carbines, and .50-, .52-, and .56-caliber cartridge cases fired in Spencer carbines.

Bullets from the various cartridge types were also recovered, as were bullets from .36-, .41-, .44-, and .45-caliber Colt pistols. Rifle balls in .40-, .44-, .50-, and .54-caliber were also recovered. The rifle balls indicate that at least some of the Indians were using obsolete muzzle loaders at the battle.

Other items recovered from the site and associated with the army include a variety of horse tack and equipment, wagon hardware, camp equipment and debris, buttons and personal items, and ration and supply cans. Other than cartridges and bullets, the only recovered artifacts associated with the Indian combatants are one iron arrowpoint and three butcher knives.

Table 7.1. Artifacts from the Battle of Lyman's Wagon Train

Item	*Army*	*Indian*	*Total*
Artifacts Related to Munitions			
.44-caliber cartridge case, fired		16	16
.44-caliber Colt cartridge case, fired		2	2
.45-caliber cartridge case fired in Springfield	515	3	518
.45-caliber cartridge case, unfired	36		36
.50/70-caliber cartridge case fired in Springfield	65	9	74
.50/70-caliber cartridge case fired in Sharps	2	37	39
.50/70-caliber fired cartridge case, gun undetermined	19	11	30
.50/70-caliber cartridge case, unfired	10	1	11
56/56-caliber Spencer cartridge case, fired		133	133
56/56-caliber Spencer cartridge case, unfired		1	1
56/52-caliber Spencer cartridge case, fired		1	1
56/50-caliber Spencer cartridge case, fired		38	38
Spencer cartridge fragment, caliber unknown, fired		1	1
.41-caliber Colt bullet		1	1
.44-caliber bullet		2	2
.45-caliber Colt bullet	1		1
.45-caliber bullet fired in Springfield	51		51

Table 7.1, *continued*

Item	*Army*	*Indian*	*Total*
.50-caliber bullet fired in Springfield	20	4	24
.50-caliber bullet fired in Sharps		6	6
.50-caliber bullet, gun type unknown	2	5	7
bullet fragment, caliber unknown	1		1
.36-caliber Colt ball		1	1
.40-caliber ball		1	1
.44-caliber ball		1	1
.44-caliber Colt ball		2	2
.50-caliber ball		3	3
.54-caliber ball		1	1
iron arrowpoint		1	1
Subtotal, munitions	722	281	1,003
Other Artifacts			
bolt	5		5
boot heel	2		2
brad	1		1
breast chain	3		3
bridle boss, embossed "US"	1		1
buckle, miscellaneous	3		3
button, military	1		1
button, other	1		1
can key	1		1
can lid, not leaded	2		2
can, leaded	13		13
cartridge extractor	1		1
chain link	2		2
cotter pin	1		1
glass	3		3
handle, cookware	1		1
harness chain	1		1
harness hardware, miscellaneous	2		2
horseshoe	2		2
knife		3	3
leather	1		1
mule shoe	8		8
nail, round	3		3
nail, square	78		78
nut	2		2
picket pin	2		2
primer	1		1
screw pin	1		1
screw, wood	9		9
spur	1		1
strap, unidentified	6		6
trigger	1		1
unidentified	5		5
wagon curtain fastener	1		1
wagon plate	2		2
washer	1		1
wire, unidentified	2		2
Subtotal, other	170	3	173
Total artifacts	**892**	**284**	**1,176**

Discussion

The cartridge cases and bullets from the Lyman Wagon Train battle indicate that at least seventeen types of firearms were used in the fight (table 7.2). Among these are Colt revolvers of various calibers, Plains rifles or trade guns, .44-caliber Henry or Winchester Model 1866 rifles or carbines, .45-caliber Springfield rifles or carbines, .50-caliber Springfield Model 1866 rifles, .50-caliber Springfield Model 1868 or 1870 rifles, and Spencer, Sharp, Ballard, and Jocelyn carbines. The number of firearms used in the fight, on the basis of cartridge case and bullet evidence, is at least 122 individual weapons.

A wide variety of firearm types are associated with the Indian combatants at the site. In fact, of the seventeen firearm types represented, fifteen were used by the Indians and represented sixty-four different firearms. Conversely, only five types are associated with the army, representing fifty-eight different firearms. The army personnel were primarily using Model 1873 Springfield .45-caliber rifles and carbines; it appears that the Indians were mostly relying on Spencer carbines and Sharps rifles, and even some early Plains rifles and trade guns.

Although the number of firearms at the site appear to be evenly distributed between the army and Indian combatants, it is important to keep in mind the number of army personnel versus the number of Indian warriors participating in the battle. According to Lieutenant Lewis, Captain Lyman had sixty-six armed men, whereas Lyman estimated the number of Indian warriors to be four hundred. The fifty-eight individual firearms associated with the army represent a firearm-to-man ratio of 0.88 to 1. If Lyman's estimate of the number of Indians is accurate, then the sixty-four firearms associated with the Indians represent a firearm-to-man ratio of only 0.16 to 1.

In his report of the battle, Lyman notes that the Indian fire on them was "constant and severe" and was "so sharp that we had to lie close." He goes on to state

Table 7.2. Firearm Types Used at the Battle of Lyman's Wagon Train

Firearm Type	*Army-Associated*	*Indian-Associated*	*Total*
.36-caliber Colt revolver		1	1
.40-caliber Plains rifle		1	1
.41-caliber Colt revolver		1	1
.44-caliber Ballard		2	2
.44-caliber Colt Open Top revolver		1	1
.44-caliber Henry or Winchester M1866 rifle or carbine		5	5
.44-caliber Plains rifle		1	1
.45-caliber Colt M1873 revolver	1		1
.45-caliber Springfield rifle or carbine	41		41
.50-, .52-, and .56-caliber Spencer carbine		29	29
.50-caliber Plains rifle		1	1
.50-caliber Sharps rifle	1	12	13
.50-caliber Springfield M1866 rifle	3	2	5
.50-caliber Springfield M1868 or 1870 rifle	12	4	16
.54-caliber Plains rifle		1	1
.56-caliber Ballard rifle		1	1
.56-caliber Jocelyn carbine		2	2
Total	58	64	122

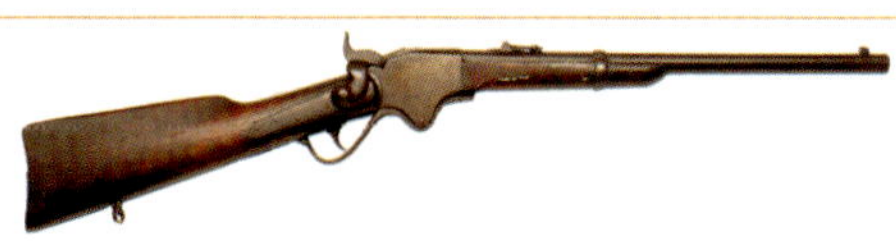

that the Indians "had our own arms and ammunition, caliber .50, as well as Spencer, Sharps, and Henry rifles," and that "they must have expended a great quantity of ammunition."[16] Of the 853 fired cartridge cases recovered, 601 can be attributed to the sixty-six army personnel, with only 252 associated with the estimated four hundred Indians. This works out to an average of about nine cartridges fired by each of the army personnel to less than one cartridge for each of the Indian warriors.

If there were sixty-six armed men in Lyman's command, then the fifty-eight firearms identified as associated with the army combatants represent 88 percent of the army firearms. If the sixty-four Indian-associated firearms also represent 88 percent of the Indian guns, then only seventy-three of the Indians had firearms. Of the identified Indian firearms at the site, 53 percent (a projected thirty-nine guns) are repeaters. If seventy-three Indian guns is an accurate number and if Lyman's estimate of four hundred Indian warriors is accurate, then only 18.3 percent of the Indian combatants had firearms. This seems like an extremely low percentage and suggests that Lyman overestimated the number of Indians at the battle. Colonel Miles, in his reports of the battle, initially repeated Lyman's estimate but later stated that only 250 Indians attacked Lyman.[17] If Miles's estimate is closer to the actual number of Indians, then the percentage of Indians with firearms increases to 29.2 percent.

Overall, this analysis of cartridge cases and bullets suggests that the Indians were not as numerous and not as well armed as Captain Lyman's report indicates. Of course, several factors affected the number of cartridges we were able to recover from the site and, consequently, could affect our interpretations of the battle as well. These include the fact that 100 percent coverage of the site with the metal detectors was impossible to attain, and it is not known how many artifacts collectors previously removed from the site. Nevertheless, the patterns seem clear. If there were as many Indians at the site as Captain Lyman estimated, then, compared to the army, the Indians were not well armed or were being very conservative with their ammunition. The fact that the majority of the Indian cartridges are Spencers that were not manufactured after 1866 suggests that they were conserving the cartridges they had and even going to great lengths to curate their ammunition. Even if Lyman overestimated the number of Indians at the battle and Colonel Miles's estimate is closer to the actual number, it still appears that less than one-third of the Indians had firearms.

8

Outnumbered Twenty-Five to One

On the morning of September 12, 1874, about 125 of the warriors who had been participating in the siege of Capt. Wyllys Lyman's supply train decided to move south of the Washita River to join their families, who were on the move toward Gageby and Sweetwater creeks to the southwest with their ultimate destination being the sanctuary of Palo Duro Canyon farther south. As the warriors reached a small rise north of Gageby Creek, they ran into a detachment of six men from Colonel Miles's command who were riding with dispatches from Miles and were charged with finding Lyman's wagon train and directing it to Miles's new encampment on McClellan Creek. The detachment consisted of civilian scouts Billy Dixon (fig. 8.1) and Amos Chapman and four soldiers of the 6th Cavalry—Sgt. Zachariah T. Woodall and Pvts. Peter Rath, John Harrington, and George Smith. The ensuing engagement between the warriors and six men has come to be known as the Battle of Buffalo Wallow.[1]

The Battle of Buffalo Wallow

Sensing that the small group of men would be much easier prey than the soldiers at the wagon train, the Indians quickly encircled the couriers, stranding them with essentially no cover. The little group of men dismounted and prepared to fight the Indians the best they could. Private Smith was given all the horses' reins to hold, but within moments of the battle's outbreak he was shot in the chest and fell to the ground as the horses stampeded, taking with them all of the water, food, coats, and extra ammunition. With the horses gone, the men were completely vulnerable to the Indians. The Indians, however, did not charge down or close in on the whites, which they could have easily done. Instead, they decided to toy with them for a while, perhaps to try to count coup on the men.[2]

After about four hours of the Indians taunting and firing at them, all of the whites had been wounded. At some distance away, Dixon spotted a small buffalo wallow, a shallow depression on the plain where buffalo had lain and wallowed in the mud (fig. 8.2). Determined to make use of what little cover there was, Dixon decided to make a run for the wallow. He reached it, and three other men quickly joined him (fig. 8.3). Once there the men began digging with their knives to deepen the wallow, throwing the sandy soil up as a breastwork around the perimeter of the hole. The two men who remained outside the wallow were Private Smith, who had been shot first and was believed dead, and Chapman, who had suffered a crippling shot to his

Fig. 8.1. Scout William "Billy" Dixon was at the Battle of Buffalo Wallow. He was also at the Battle of Adobe Walls in June 1874, before signing on with the army. Courtesy Panhandle-Plains Historical Museum, Canyon, Texas

leg. After several attempts, Dixon was able to reach Chapman and carry him back to the wallow.[3]

As the afternoon wore on, the Indians settled into a game of cat and mouse, toying with the white men in the wallow, who began to run low on ammunition. The men decided that the revolver and ammunition belt should be retrieved from the body of the dead Private Smith. One of the soldiers, Private Rath, ran to the motionless body and recovered the items, but when he got back to the wallow he reported that Smith was still alive. Dixon and Rath made their way back to Smith and carried him back to the wallow (fig. 8.4), but it was obvious that he would not survive. "We could see that there was no chance for him. He was shot through the left lung and when he breathed the wind sobbed out of his back under the shoulder blade," Dixon wrote in his memoirs.[4]

The afternoon wore on and, despite twenty-five-to-one odds, the men had managed to hold the Indians at bay. As the afternoon temperature became hotter and hotter, the men in the wallow began to suffer from thirst; already weak from the loss of blood, they became weaker and weaker. They knew the fate that awaited them if they

Fig. 8.2. After a thunderstorm, buffalo will roll in the mud, as depicted by George Catlin in *Buffalo Bulls in a Wallow.* The dried mud helps deter biting flies and insects. These buffalo "wallows" were shallow depressions on the plains. Courtesy Smithsonian American Art Museum, Gift of Mrs. Joseph Harrison Jr.

Fig. 8.3. This Kiowa ledger drawing is probably a depiction of the Buffalo Wallow battle. Note that the drawing does not show scouts Billy Dixon and Amos Chapman. Courtesy Texas Memorial Museum, The University of Texas at Austin

were taken alive and, though wounded, they sat upright in the wallow to hide that fact and seem able to fight. By mid-afternoon a storm came up, and a heavy rain began to fall. The earlier scorching heat was now replaced with cold wind and rain as the norther blew in. As miserable as the men were in the wallow, the storm had an unseen benefit. With the advent of the inclement weather, the Indians broke off the fight and disappeared into the night. In the early morning hours of September 13, Private Smith died in his sleep.

Later that morning Dixon left the wallow on foot to seek help for the wounded

Fig. 8.4. In this Frederic Remington painting of the Buffalo Wallow battle, *The Last Stand,* the light-haired Amos Chapman is erroneously depicted as the one carrying Private Smith to the wallow. Courtesy The Museum of Fine Arts, Houston; The Hogg Brothers Collection, gift of Miss Ima Hogg

men. After a short while he encountered the 8th Cavalry under Major Price, who was in the area looking for his and Colonel Miles's supply trains. Price sent several soldiers and a surgeon to tend to the men in the wallow but then, incredibly, just left the men in their hole. He left no detail to protect them and gave them no ammunition, though he probably did not have any ammunition of the right caliber. His companies were using .50-caliber Sharps, and the 6th Cavalry men in the wallow had .45-caliber Springfield carbines (appendix B). That being the case, Price also refused to provide the men any additional arms. He did promise to let Colonel Miles know of their plight, and some of Price's men left them some dried beef and hardtack.[5]

Upon learning of their situation, Colonel Miles had the men rescued and severely scolded Major Price for his handling of the affair. In fact, just four days later Miles assumed command of Price's troops. The body of Pvt. George Smith was placed in the wallow and "[we] covered it with the dirt which we had ridged up with our hands and butcher knives for breastworks." Private Smith's remains were never removed from the buffalo wallow despite appeals from his family to have his body shipped to them in New York.[6]

The survivors of the battle were taken to Fort Supply, where they were treated for their wounds. Amos Chapman's leg was amputated above the knee, but he recovered and continued to serve as a scout. The others also recovered and the three surviving soldiers continued serving in the army. Billy Dixon continued to scout for the army until 1883. Colonel Miles recommended that all six men receive the Congressional Medal of Honor (appendix C). The medals were awarded, although Dixon's and Chapman's were later revoked because they were not officially enlisted in the army. In 1989, the Army Board for Correction of Military Records restored the medals to Dixon and Chapman.

Current Ownership and Land Use

In 1925, an acre of land in the northwest corner of section 30, Hemphill County, was deeded by D. E. Holt and A. B. Crump to the Panhandle-Plains Historical Society for the purpose of erecting a monument to mark the Buffalo Wallow battle (fig. 8.5). On September 20, 1927, a granite monument was unveiled on the site (fig. 8.6).[7] The placement of the monument was based primarily on the direction of Mrs. Olive Dixon, wife of the late Billy Dixon, who had taken Olive to the site at some point before he died in 1913. The monument is 1 mile south of Route 277 and 3.75 miles east of the intersection of Route 277 and U.S. Highway 83. An unpaved county-maintained road parallels the 1-acre plot on the west, and a private ranch road is situated along the south side of the site. A tree-lined windrow borders the north side of the property. The surrounding terrain to the north, east, and south is cultivated fields; that to the west is open pasture. There are several oil and gas wells and petroleum storage tanks in the immediate vicinity of the monument.

Archeological Investigations and Results

The Buffalo Wallow battle site is recorded in the state archeological site files as Site 41HH26. The archeological investigations of the site were conducted in May and June 1998. At the time of the metal detector survey, the area north, east, and south of the Buffalo Wallow monument was a cultivated field and ground surface visibility was good. The land west of the monument was pasture with tall grasses and weeds, which made it difficult to use the metal detectors. Though the cultivated fields allowed for a thorough examination of the terrain with the metal detectors, only one .50-caliber cartridge was found, approximately 750 m (820 yards) northeast of the monument (fig. 8.7).

On a small rise about 700 m (765 yards) to the northwest of the monument, seven additional cartridges were recovered. These were three Spencers and four .50/70 cartridges. Though efforts were made to conduct a thorough survey of the pastureland west of the monument, the tall grasses and weeds prevented it.

Artifact Descriptions and Analysis

Only eight fired cartridge cases were recovered from the Buffalo Wallow site. All of them are believed to be associated with the Indians at the battle. Five .50/70 cartridge cases were recovered (fig. 8.8). These are internally primed center-fire copper (Bloomfield Gilding Metal) cases, either Benét cup or Martin bar primers (table 8.1). Four of these cases (specimens 2, 3, 4, and 5) were fired in the Springfield Model 1868 or 1870 rifle, and all were all fired in the same rifle. Each shows some evidence of extractor slippage or extraction problems. It is likely that either the rifle or the cartridges were dirty at the time of firing, causing the extractor to pull the cases fully from the rifle's chamber. The remaining .50/70 cartridge case, specimen 8, has a square firing pin imprint and a firing pin drag mark consistent with being fired in a Sharps .50/70-caliber rifle.

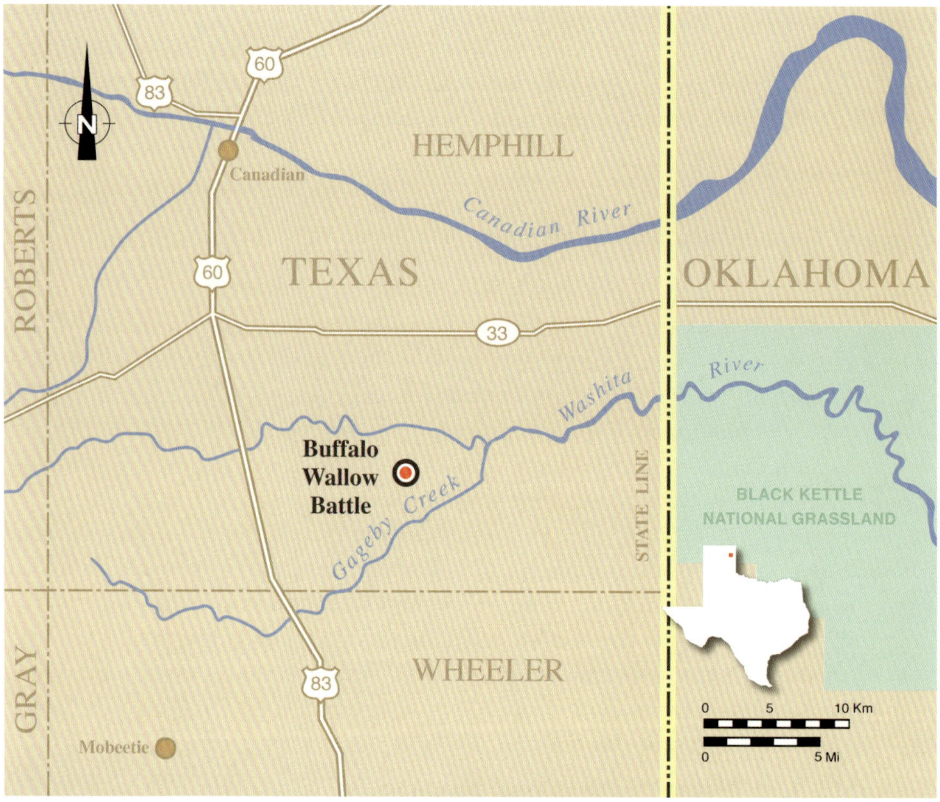

Fig. 8.5. The Battle of Buffalo Wallow took place in what is now southeastern Hemphill County, Texas. Illustration by Roland Pantermuehl

Fig. 8.6. A granite monument was erected in 1927 to honor the four soldiers and two scouts and marks the presumed battle site.

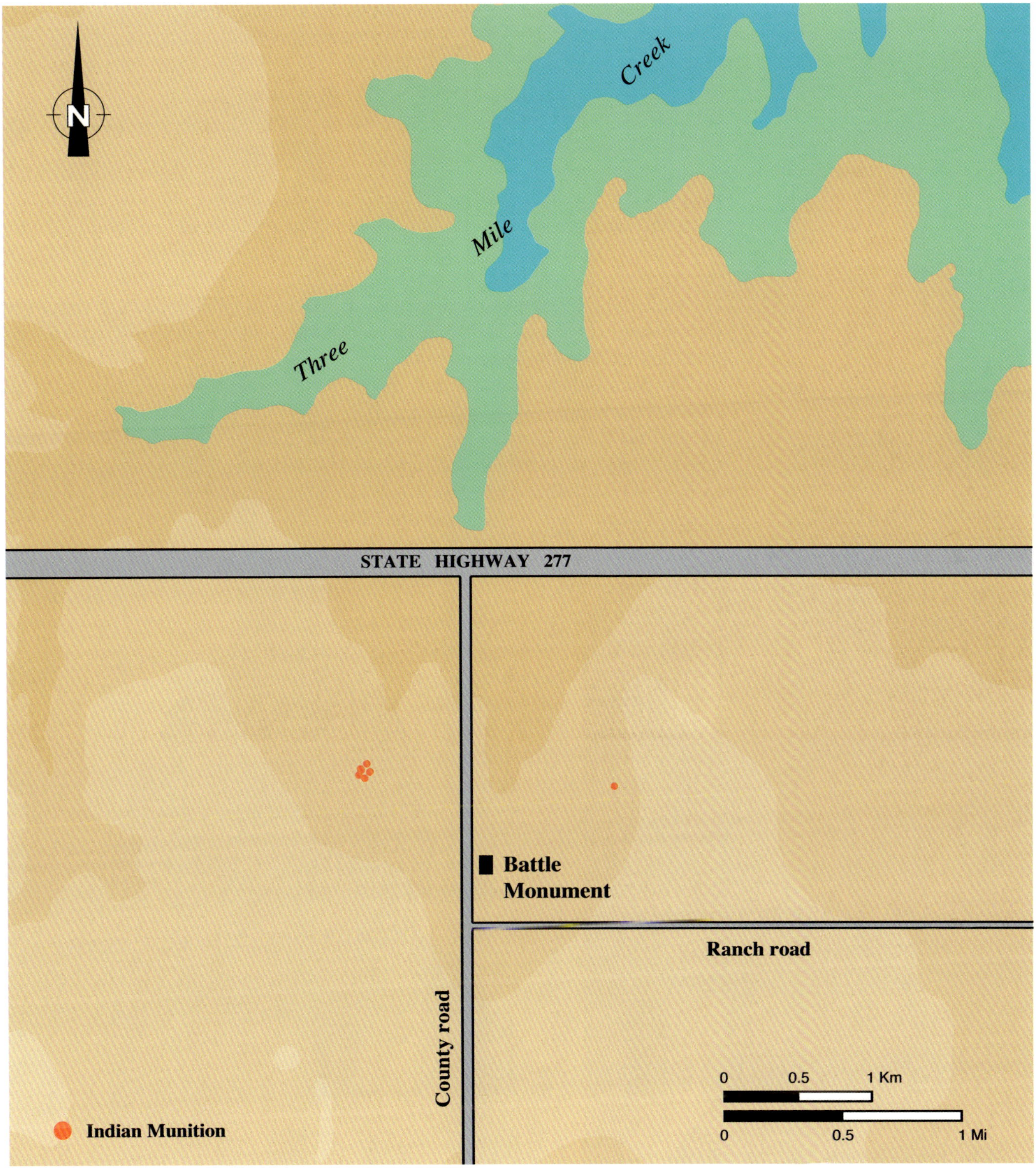

Fig. 8.7. Map showing the locations of the recovered cartridges in relation to the Buffalo Wallow monument. Illustration by Roland Pantermuehl

Three .50-caliber Spencer cases were also recovered (fig. 8.8), each fired from a different weapon. One case, specimen 6, has no head stamp; the other two (specimens 1 and 7) have the raised letter H stamped on the head. The H denotes manufacture by the New Haven Arms Company or the Winchester Company. Specimen 1 has no circle around the H; specimen 7 has the raised H set in a circle. The H on specimen 7 is the

Table 8.1. .50/70 Cartridge Cases from the Buffalo Wallow Site

Firearm	*Specimen*[a]	*Comments*
1	2br, 3br, 4b, 5b	2 and 3 extractor slipped; 4 and 5 rim torn by extractor, gun likely dirty, M1868 or 1870 Springfield rifle
2	8b	Square firing pin, firing pin drag, Sharps

[a]Letter following specimen number indicates primer type: b = Benét, br = bar.

same style, type, and dimension as the one on specimen 1. In all probability the lack of the depressed circle is nothing more than a manufacturing run error or a worn bunter used during the stamping process.

The non-head-stamped cartridge and the cartridge with the H in the depressed circle exhibit similar tool point marks. The tool point marks on these cases are in a roughly triangular configuration, with one mark at the one o'clock position, one at the four o'clock position, and one at the seven o'clock position. The tool point marks on a cartridge with the Winchester head stamp suggest that the non-head-stamped cartridge with the similar tool marks was also made by Winchester.

Discussion

The cartridge cases from the Buffalo Wallow site indicate that at least five separate firearms were used in the fight. The available cartridge cases indicate three Spencers and two .50/70-caliber rifles. One of the .50/70-caliber rifles was a Springfield Model 1868 or 1870 rifle and the other was a Sharps .50-caliber rifle. The artifacts recovered during the investigations, though few in number, appear to be associated with the Indian combatants at the Buffalo Wallow battle.

Though the investigations were not successful in locating the battle site precisely, the recovered artifacts suggest that the battle occurred in the near vicinity. Interviews with several area landowners revealed that collectors and metal detector hobbyists have collected cartridges from the areas surrounding the monument for many years, and it may be that most of the artifacts once associated with the battle have been removed from the site.

Fig. 8.8. Cartridge cases recovered at the Buffalo Wallow battle site: top row, Spencer 56/50-caliber; bottom row, .50/70-caliber.

9

The Indians Elude the 8th Cavalry

On August 24, 1874, Maj. William R. Price (fig. 9.1) and companies C, H, and K of the 8th U.S. Cavalry left Fort Union, New Mexico, and headed east toward the Texas Panhandle as the westernmost column in the campaign against the Southern Plains Indians. Upon reaching Fort Bascom, L Company of the 8th Cavalry joined the column. Price's command then consisted of 216 soldiers, five Navajo and three Mexican (Comanchero) guides, and one civilian blacksmith. The column also had twenty government six-mule wagons, one four-mule escort wagon, one ambulance with a surgeon, one four-mule battery forge, two mountain howitzers, thirty pack mules, and a contract train of twenty-four four- and six-mule teams. In his official campaign report, Major Price states that his wagons contained "10,000 rations, over fifty days for my command; about 80,000 pounds grain; 30,000 rounds each of Carbine and Pistol ammunition; 200 rounds canister and shell for howitzers; officers stores, company property, etc." He does not state how many men he dedicated to the howitzers or from which units they were detached. He also does not state whether limbers and caissons accompanied the howitzers, though his description of his wagon trains suggests that his howitzer rounds were being transported in the wagons rather than in limbers.[1]

Fig. 9.1. Maj. William R. Price, 8th U.S. Cavalry. Courtesy U.S. Army Military History Institute

Crossing the Texas Panhandle south of the Canadian River, the column followed the old Fort Smith–Santa Fe Road. On September 4, Price divided his command, directing Lt. Henry J. Farnsworth to take H Company, all of the wagons, and one howitzer toward Adobe Walls to establish a supply camp near there. In his report, Major Price writes, "With the Mexican teamsters he [Farnsworth] had a force of 110 men." If there were twenty-four contract wagons driven by the Mexican teamsters and one driver each for the escort wagon, ambulance, and battery forge, then Lieutenant Farnsworth would have had about eighty troopers, most of them from H Company, though he probably also had men from companies C, K, and L who drove the twenty government wagons.

Major Price took "the effective force of 'C' 'K' and 'L' companies, 130 men, one howitzer, and six days rations of hard bread, sugar, and coffee on pack animals" as the main column that moved southeast, expecting either to find Indians or to join Colonel Miles. Price dispatched twenty troopers to look for and intercept Miles's supply train, leaving 110 men remaining in his command. On September 7, Price found Colonel Miles still encamped on Battle Creek near the Red River. Miles immediately ordered Price to move northeast to find his and Price's own supply trains.

Fig. 9.2. Lone Wolf was the head chief of the Kiowa. Courtesy Panhandle-Plains Historical Museum, Canyon, Texas

The Battle of Sweetwater Creek

On September 12, plagued by driving rains and swollen streams, Price and his command were moving northeast between Sweetwater Creek and the Dry Fork of the Washita River (in what is now Wheeler County) when they encountered a large band of Kiowas and Comanches. These Indians, under the leadership of Lone Wolf (fig. 9.2), were some of the same Indians who had been participating in the siege on Lyman's wagon train.

According to Price, the Indians "selected their own ground on the crest of a steep ridge and awaited my attack." Price was unaware of it at the time, but the reason the Indians had taken their positions on the ridge in apparent readiness to engage a mounted force of cavalry, which was highly irregular for Plains Indians, was the same reason they had abandoned their siege of Lyman's wagon train. Their families were nearby, desperately trying to elude the soldiers, and the warriors had to delay the mounted troopers long enough to allow the villagers escape. One of the Indians present that day was Botalye, the young warrior who made the four daring dashes through the soldier's lines at the Battle of Lyman's Wagon Train. In relating his account of the battle to Wilbur S. Nye in 1937, Botalye stated, "We were anxious to start it [the battle] right then, but our chiefs were trying to keep us from shooting because our village, which at that time was packed and on the move, was so close still that it was risky for us to start anything."

Price had with him one mountain howitzer, which officer-of-the-day Lieutenant Fuller was detailed to guard with a platoon of twenty men. Because of the muddy conditions, the platoon was unable to keep up with the mounted troops, which Price had ordered to prepare for battle. Before the battle could start, however, one of the Kiowa war chiefs, Set-manun-te (Bear's Paw), rode out and across the front of the soldiers. The soldiers fired at him, but he was not hit. Then a Comanche rode out from a small creek toward two of the cavalry officers who were in front of the other soldiers. The officers, apparently believing that the Indian was approaching them to negotiate a peaceful solution to the impending encounter, holstered their pistols, at which point the Comanche fired at them. The troopers then opened fire at the Comanche as he raced back to the others. He was unhurt, but his horse was shot in the shoulder.

Price then ordered Captain Hartwell, Captain Morris, and Lieutenant Rogers with companies C, K, and L to charge the high ridge the Indians occupied and to sweep the Indians to the left. When the firing started, the Indians began making circling charges and breaking up into smaller groups of "forty or fifty" warriors to attack Price's flanks. One of the groups apparently was intent on taking the howitzer, for Lieutenant Fuller sent word to Price that "the Indians were concentrating on the gun, dismounting, and getting into ravines, and were getting his range and closing in on him." Price took a platoon to protect the gun, but the Indians continued to fight stubbornly and "were very bold, exposing themselves by rapidly riding on every side of us and firing at short range." The battle for the howitzer lasted for an hour and a half until the soldiers mounted a desperate charge and drove the Indians back.

The Indian warriors apparently were trying to lead the troops away from their women and children, keeping them occupied long enough to give their families time to escape, which they did successfully. Two days later, on September 14, as Lieutenant Farnsworth was passing west of the scene of the battle, he crossed the trail left by the fleeing Indians, which he reported was headed southwest and was more than a mile wide. He estimated there were a thousand head of stock with the Indians, and he killed or captured more than thirty horses the Indians had left.[2]

According to Price, there were 150–175 Indians at the battle, "all armed with long range guns, most of them breech-loaders," but the soldiers were able to clear the Indians "from every position they occupied" and "drove them for six or seven miles, occupying two hours and three quarters time when they fled in every direction." Price goes on to write that he was "confident the Indians received a very severe lesson," but, in fact, the warriors had succeeded in their apparent objective of decoying the soldiers away from the retreating Indian women and children. Price may not have won a great victory at the Battle of Sweetwater Creek, but his presence in the area did force the Indians to abandon their sieges of both the Lyman wagon train and the soldiers and scouts at Buffalo Wallow, though he was completely unaware of it at the time.

None of the 8th Cavalry soldiers were hurt in the battle, but fourteen of their horses received bullet wounds and ten of them later died. The Indians left no dead on the field, though some were seen to fall from their horses, only to be quickly surrounded and carried off by other warriors. Price's officers reported that eight Indians were killed or badly wounded, as were several Indian ponies. His scouts captured twenty Indian horses and colts. The next day Major Price and his command did not pursue the Indians. Instead, they moved some 8 miles east and north, where they found Billy Dixon and learned of the Buffalo Wallow battle. The large group of Indians that had fled the agency near Anadarko and held Colonel Miles's supply train under seize for four days, struck Miles's couriers at the buffalo wallow, and attacked Major Price and his 8th Cavalry had now successfully escaped to the southwest and were making their way to Palo Duro Canyon.

Current Ownership and Land Use

The Battle of Sweetwater Creek site is in northwest Wheeler County, north of the small community of Mobeetie (fig. 9.3). The site is situated between Sweetwater Creek to the south and Gageby Creek to the north and occupies approximately 18.35 square miles. For the most part, the site is privately owned. Only those portions that are traversed by two unpaved, county-maintained roads and where State Highway 48 bisects the site are publicly owned. Wheeler County is rural, with farming and ranching the primary sources of income. Most of the area encompassed by the battle site is pasture, though there are several small cultivated tracts. The terrain in the immediate area can be characterized as gently rolling with scattered smaller hills and higher ridges. The soils in the area are sandy loams, and the groundcover is mainly native grasses.

Archeological Investigations and Results

The precise location of the Battle of Sweetwater Creek was not known prior to our archeological investigations. Major Price had stated that his column was between Sweetwater Creek and the Washita River when they encountered the Indians, who had

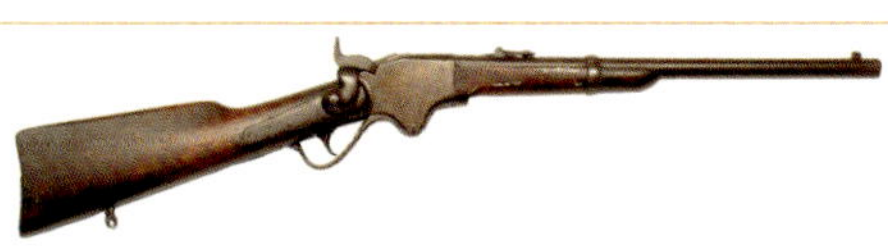

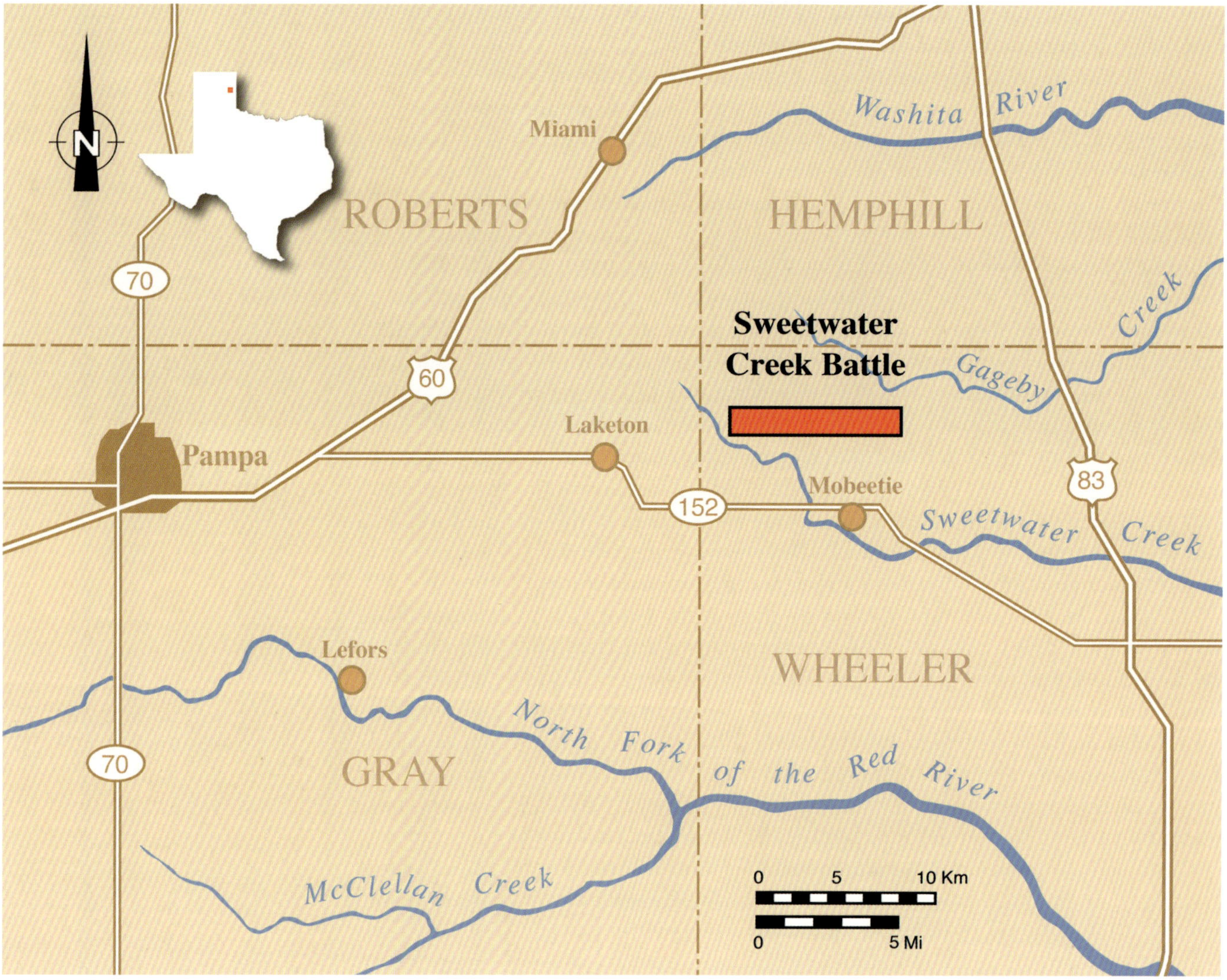

Fig. 9.3. The site of the Battle of Sweetwater Creek is in northwest Wheeler County, Texas. Illustration by Roland Pantermuehl

taken positions on a steep ridge to the north, and we identified an area in northwest Wheeler County that seemed to match that description. In addition, we examined an 1875 U.S. Army campaign map of the area that we assumed showed the location of a battle, marked by a pair of crossed sabers, situated between Sweetwater Creek and the Dry Fork of the Washita River (fig. 9.4). Using the map, we determined as precisely as possible the latitude and longitude indicated by the crossed sabers and entered this information into our GPS receiver, then used the GPS to lead us to that precise position, which turned out to be on top of a high ridge approximately 3 miles northeast of Sweetwater Creek. At this location, the archeological team quickly found several battle-related cartridges on the first day of the investigations (fig. 9.5). The Battle of Sweetwater Creek site is now recorded in the state site files as Site 41WE20, and it was listed in the National Register of Historic Places in August 2001.

The accounts of the battle given by Botalye and Major Price agree that the cavalry was operating in two groups, with the foremost group riding two abreast in a column and the rearward group of about twenty men escorting the howitzer. According to Price, he ordered three companies of the forward group to advance toward the ridge as forty to fifty Indians circled around his flanks, apparently in an attempt to separate the howitzer from the rest of the cavalry. When Price received word from Lieutenant

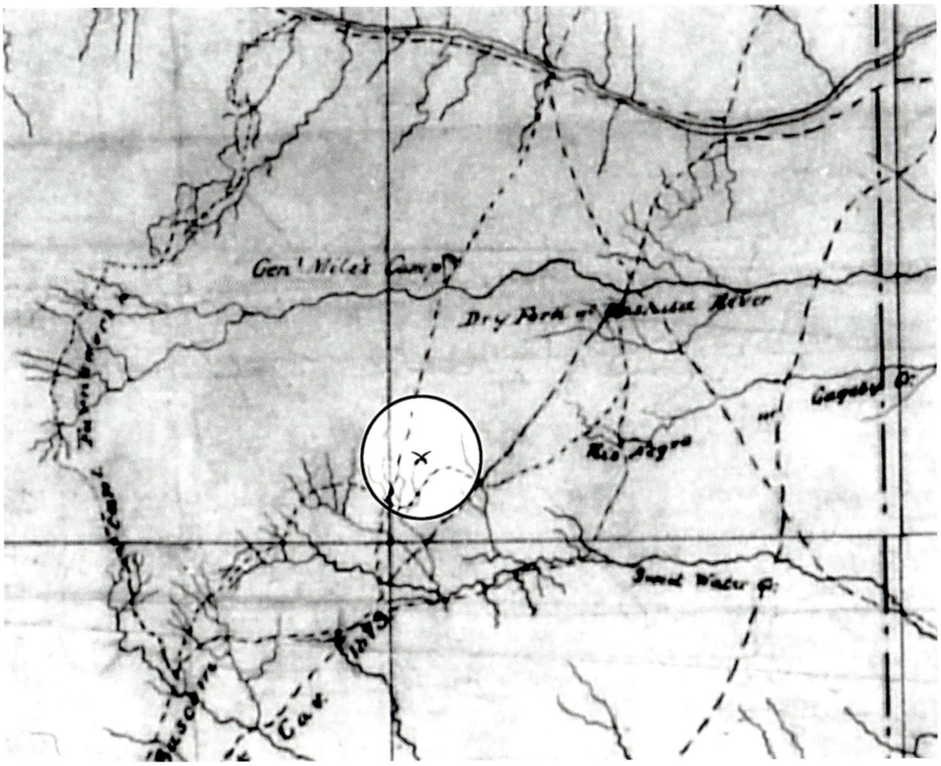

Fig. 9.4. A portion of an 1875 U.S. Army map shows the general location of the Battle of Sweetwater Creek. Map Files, Department Engineer, Southern Department, Fort Sam Houston, Texas, File No. 396.

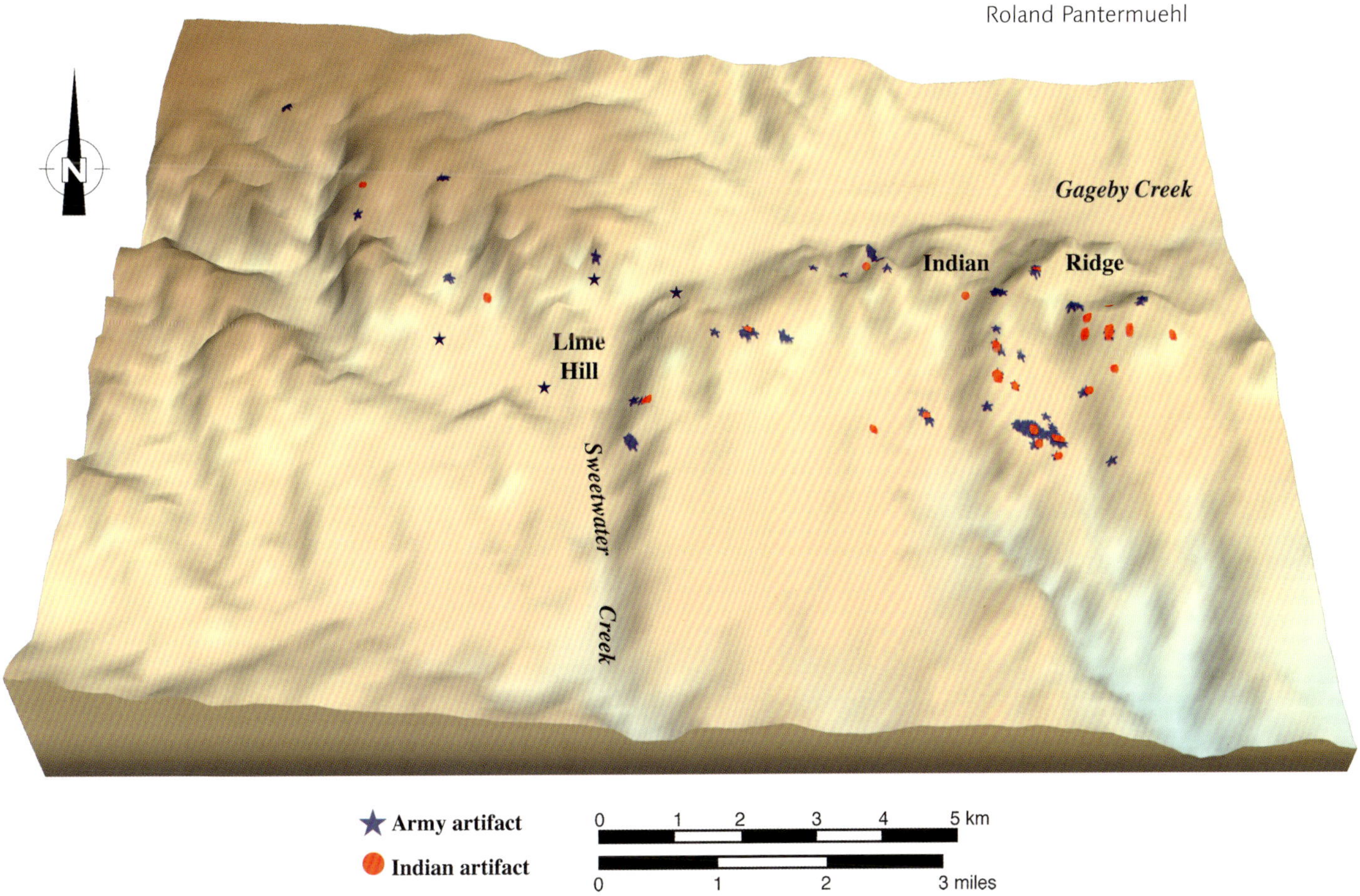

Fig. 9.5. Distribution of artifacts at the Battle of Sweetwater Creek site. When the battle opened, the Indians occupied the high ridge south of Gageby Creek as the 8th Cavalry moved northeast from Sweetwater Creek. Illustration by Roland Pantermuehl

Fuller that the Indians were concentrating on the cannon, he took a platoon of men back to the cannon to aid in its defense. From the description of the battle given by Major Price, it appears that the most intense fighting occurred around the howitzer. His statements that the Indians were dismounting from their horses, getting into the nearby ravines, and "firing at short range" suggest that initially the battle was somewhat stationary, with the Indians apparently intent on taking the cannon.

Major Price does not specifically state that the howitzer was used during the engagement. In fact, his statement that the howitzer "shot had become wet by the heavy rains, and was useless" has led some researchers to reasonably conclude that it was not used during the battle. Author and historian James Haley, for example, states that the howitzer was "useless" to Price. He further states, "If the howitzer had been serviceable it would have made things go very badly for the Indians, and it was just their good fortune that it had become a liability."[3]

The archeological investigations at the battle site tell a different story, however. On a small hill about a mile south of Indian Ridge, we found 141 spent .50-caliber Sharps cartridges (fig. 9.6). The .50-caliber Sharps was the principal firearm of the

Fig. 9.6. Archeological investigations confirmed that Major Price used his 12-pounder mountain howitzer during the battle. The distribution of lead shot suggests that at least two canister rounds were fired. Illustration by Roland Pantermuehl

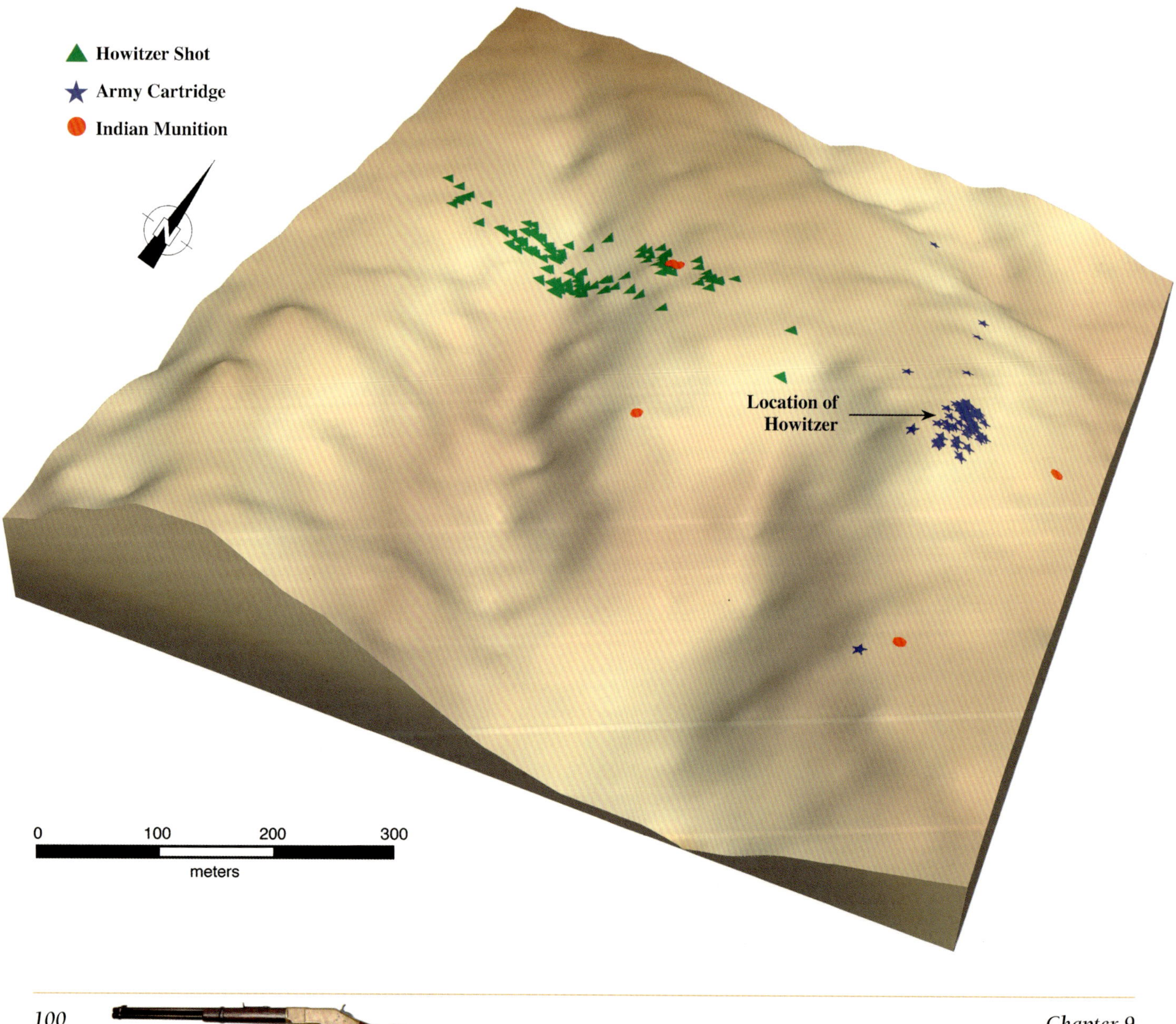

8th Cavalry in 1874 (appendix B). The cartridges were spread across the hilltop in a north–south orientation. Near the center of the cartridge cluster were a priming wire and a friction primer for a mountain howitzer. The friction primer is a small copper tube that was filled with powder and was the principal means of igniting the powder charge in the cannon. The priming wire was for piercing the bag that contained the powder charge prior to inserting the friction primer in the vent of the cannon. The friction primer and wire could have been lost without the howitzer actually having been fired, but the archeological investigations have established that the howitzer was indeed used during the battle, as indicated by recovered fragments of two exploded howitzer canisters and lead shot from the canisters. The canister fragments and shot were found in a small ravine about 300 m (328 yards) northwest of the friction primer, priming wire, and army cartridges.

The presence of howitzer canister fragments and lead shot contradicts the conclusions of other researchers that the 8th Cavalry did not use the howitzer during the battle. In light of the archeological evidence, a closer examination of Price's statement concerning the howitzer clarifies the confusion. Major Price writes, "I had with me . . . a howitzer with eight rounds of canister. My *shot* [emphasis added] had become wet with heavy rains, and was useless."[4] But the mountain howitzer was capable of firing both spherical shot and cylindrical canister.[5] Price states that he had both types with him, and it was the shot that had gotten wet and was not usable. The canister, however, as shown by the archeological evidence, was indeed used. In addition, in a letter to Lt. J. N. Mahnken in February 1875, Price confirms that the howitzer was used at the September 12 battle: "I fired the little mountain howitzer twice and have learned through the Indians that one shot did execution."[6]

Not being able to take the howitzer, the Indians apparently began to retreat toward the ridge to the north and west. The distribution of battle-related artifacts across the site suggests that the engagement now became a running battle, with the Indians breaking out into smaller groups and taking temporary positions on the higher elevations along the ridge. From these positions they apparently would fire a few shots at the soldiers before fleeing to the next position, trying to stay just out of range of the cavalry carbines. The Indian and army cartridges were recovered in small groups of only a few rounds, with these groups widely dispersed along the ridge for a distance of about 7 miles, precisely as Major Price reported. It appears that once the Indian warriors reached the high plains above the breaks of the Sweetwater Creek drainage, they broke off the engagement, since no artifacts were recovered above the breaks.

Artifacts Recovered

The archeological investigations of the Battle of Sweetwater Creek site recovered 578 battle-related artifacts (table 9.1). Of these, 405 artifacts are associated with the army combatants and 173 with the Indians. The analysis of the artifacts is included as appendix F. Most of the artifacts are munitions related and include 348 fired and eighty unfired rifle and pistol cartridge cases of various calibers. The fired cases include .44-caliber cartridges that were fired in Henry rifles, Model 1866 Winchesters, and Model 1873 Winchesters; .45-caliber Colt cartridges; .50-caliber cartridges fired in Sharps carbines; and Spencer .50- and .56-caliber cartridge cases. Sixty-five of the Spencer cartridge cases were unfired; all of these were found at a single location and apparently were lost during the battle, probably when one of the Indian combatants dropped the leather bag in which the cartridges were held.

Other items of interest include a friction primer and a priming wire used with the firing of the mountain howitzer, shrapnel and lead shot from exploded howitzer

Table 9.1. Artifacts from the Battle of Sweetwater Creek Site

Item	*Army*	*Indian*	*Total*
.44-caliber cartridge case, fired		15	15
.44/40-caliber cartridge case, fired		3	3
.45-caliber Colt cartridge case, fired	5		5
.45-caliber Colt cartridge, unfired	3		3
.45-caliber Springfield, fired in a Sharps		1	1
.50/70-caliber cartridge case, fired	256	21	277
.50/70-caliber cartridge, unfired	12		12
Spencer cartridge case, fired		47	47
Spencer cartridge, unfired		65	65
.44-caliber bullet		5	5
.44-caliber Colt bullet		1	1
.45-caliber Colt bullet	6		6
.50-caliber bullet	12	1	13
.44- or .45-caliber ball		2	2
.54-caliber ball		2	2
unidentified bullet		2	2
primer	1		1
priming wire	1		1
Howitzer friction primer	1		1
Howitzer canister fragments	24		24
Howitzer canister shot	83		83
iron arrowpoint		8	8
button, military	1		1
Total Artifacts	**405**	**173**	**578**

rounds fired by the army, an army uniform button, and metal arrowpoints. The majority of the artifacts were found in the precise locations where they were dropped some 130 years earlier.

Discussion

The distribution of Indian-associated cartridges suggests that, when the battle started, the Indians began to spread out into small groups along the ridge, some of them attacking the flanks and rear of the army column where the howitzer was positioned (fig. 9.7). Apparently, while some of the Indians were trying to take the howitzer, others stayed on the ridge in an attempt to draw some of the soldiers away from the cannon. Meanwhile, a large number of Indian women and children left behind the ridge escape to the southwest. When their families were out of immediate danger, the Indian warriors began to withdraw along the ridge, where the troops chased them for about 7 miles before the Indians scattered across the plains.

The analysis of cartridge cases and bullets recovered from the battle site indicates that at least twelve types of firearms were used in the fight (table 9.2), with at least fifty-one individual weapons used. A variety of firearm types are associated with the Indian combatants at the site. Of the firearm types represented, eleven were used by Indians, representing twenty-seven different firearms. The cartridge case analysis indicates that 67 percent of the Indian firearms were repeaters like the Henry and Winchester Models 1866 and 1873 and Spencer carbines, but they were also using single-shot rifles and even muzzle loaders.

Only two firearm types are associated with the army, representing twenty-four different firearms. These are the .50-caliber Sharps carbine and the .45-caliber Colt revolver. Unfortunately, ninety-one of the .50-caliber cartridges recovered were too oxidized for analysis. All of these cartridges were recovered from army positions at the site. The 186 .50-caliber cartridges that were analyzed were fired from twenty-six individual weapons. Thus, roughly one firearm was identified for every seven cartridges analyzed. Assuming a similar ratio, if the ninety-one oxidized cartridges could have been analyzed, an additional thirteen army-associated weapons would be expected from the analysis, for a total of thirty-seven individual army firearms.

The projected thirty-seven army guns represent 34 percent of the firearms used by the 110 soldiers in the battle. If the twenty-seven identified Indian-associated firearms also represent 34 percent of the firearms used by the Indians, then there would have been a projected seventy-nine Indian guns used at the battle. If Major Price's estimate of 150–175 Indians is accurate, then 45–53 percent of the Indians had firearms.

Of the 348 fired cartridge cases recovered from the site, 261 can be attributed to the 110 troopers, whereas only eighty-seven cartridges (mostly Spencers) can be attributed to the 150 or so Indians. This indicates that each soldier fired, on average, about 2.4 cartridges compared to only 0.6 cartridges per Indian warrior. Contrary to Major Price's statement that the Indians "were all armed with long range guns," the cartridge analysis suggests otherwise. Only four long-range Indian-associated guns

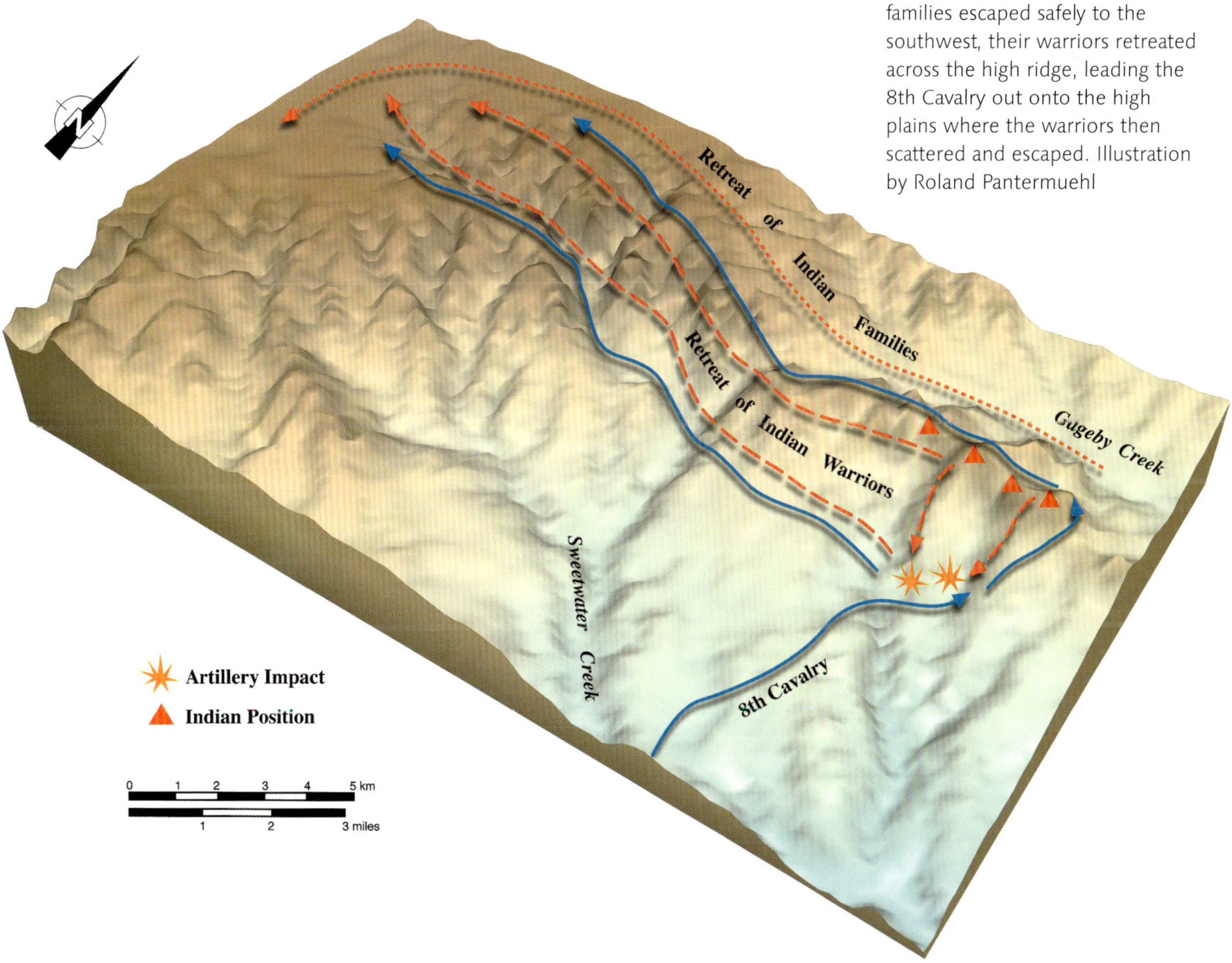

Fig. 9.7. Once the Indian families escaped safely to the southwest, their warriors retreated across the high ridge, leading the 8th Cavalry out onto the high plains where the warriors then scattered and escaped. Illustration by Roland Pantermuehl

Table 9.2. Firearm Types Used at the Battle of Sweetwater Creek

Firearm Type	*Army-Associated*	*Indian-Associated*	*Total*
.44-caliber Colt M1860 revolver		1	1
.44-caliber Henry or Winchester M1866 rifle or carbine		5	5
.44-caliber Winchester M1873 rifle or carbine		4	4
.44-caliber Ballard rifle		1	1
.44- or .45-caliber unidentified muzzle loader		1	1
.45-caliber Colt M1873 revolver	2		2
.50-caliber Springfield M1866 rifle		1	1
.50-caliber Springfield M1868 or 1870 rifle		2	2
.50-caliber Sharps rifle or carbine	22	1	23
.50- and .56-caliber Spencer carbine		9	9
.50-caliber Ballard rifle		1	1
.54-caliber unidentified muzzle loader		1	1
Total	24	27	51

are represented in the recovered cartridges, compared to eighteen shorter-range repeater rifles. A shorter-range repeater rifle can certainly have the advantage over a longer-range single-shot carbine when the firing distance is about 300 yards or less. However, the small number of Indian-associated cartridges recovered suggests that either the Indians were being very conservative with their ammunition or not as many of them were armed with rifles as Major Price believed.

The fact that the majority of the Indian cartridges are Spencers of types that were not manufactured after 1866 suggests that the Indians were conserving the cartridges they did have. In addition, four rifle balls for muzzle loaders were recovered at locations on the battlefield associated with the Indians, which indicates that at least some of the Indians were using firearms that would be considered obsolete by 1874. That some of the Indians were armed only with bows and arrows is evident from eight recovered iron arrowpoints. In short, it appears that less than half of the Indians at the battle had firearms, and those who did were not as well armed as Major Price stated.

10

The Turning Point of the War

Fig. 10.1. Col. Ranald S. Mackenzie commanded the 4th Cavalry. Courtesy Panhandle-Plains Historical Museum, Canyon, Texas

On August 23, 1874, Col. Ranald S. Mackenzie (fig. 10.1) and his "Southern Column" departed Fort Concho, Texas, and headed north toward the Texas Panhandle. Mackenzie's expedition included eight companies of the 4th Cavalry, four companies of the 10th Infantry, and one company of the 11th Infantry. The Southern Column consisted of forty-seven officers, 560 enlisted men, three acting assistant surgeons, and thirty-two scouts—six of them white men and the rest Seminole-Negroes and Lipan and Tonkawa Indians.[1]

On September 19, Mackenzie's forces reached Catfish Creek in present Crosby County, Texas, where they established a supply depot and their base of operations for the campaign against the Indians. Upon his arrival at the camp Mackenzie was informed that his scouts had spotted several Indian trails leading northwest. Leaving three companies of infantry to guard the supply base, Mackenzie led eight cavalry companies along with two infantry companies to protect the expedition's train of wagons and began following the Indian trails. He organized his cavalry into two battalions of four companies each. The 1st Battalion was composed of Companies D, F, I, and K and was commanded by Capt. Napoleon B. McLaughlin. The 2nd Battalion was made up of Companies A, E, H, and L and was commanded by Capt. Eugene B. Beaumont. Lt. William H. Thompson commanded the scouts.[2]

The Battle of Palo Duro Canyon

On September 26, after slogging through pelting rains and deep mud, Mackenzie's command camped near the head of Tule Canyon in present Briscoe County. That evening some of the scouts reported that a large Indian camp had been discovered in Palo Duro Canyon about 30 miles northwest. Later that night the army camp was attacked by some 250 Indians who apparently were attempting to stampede the cavalry's horses, but the soldiers were prepared for the attack and the attempt failed. The Indians took cover in nearby ravines and continued to fire periodically at the troops until morning.[3]

At daybreak, Mackenzie ordered Capt. Peter Boehm with Company E to counterattack while the rest of the command saddled and packed. Boehm charged the Indians, who retreated southwest in an apparent attempt to mislead the command concerning the location of their village. To give the appearance of being fooled by the Indians, Mackenzie followed them for several miles and then made camp as if for the night. When darkness fell, the command mounted and marched rapidly northwest toward

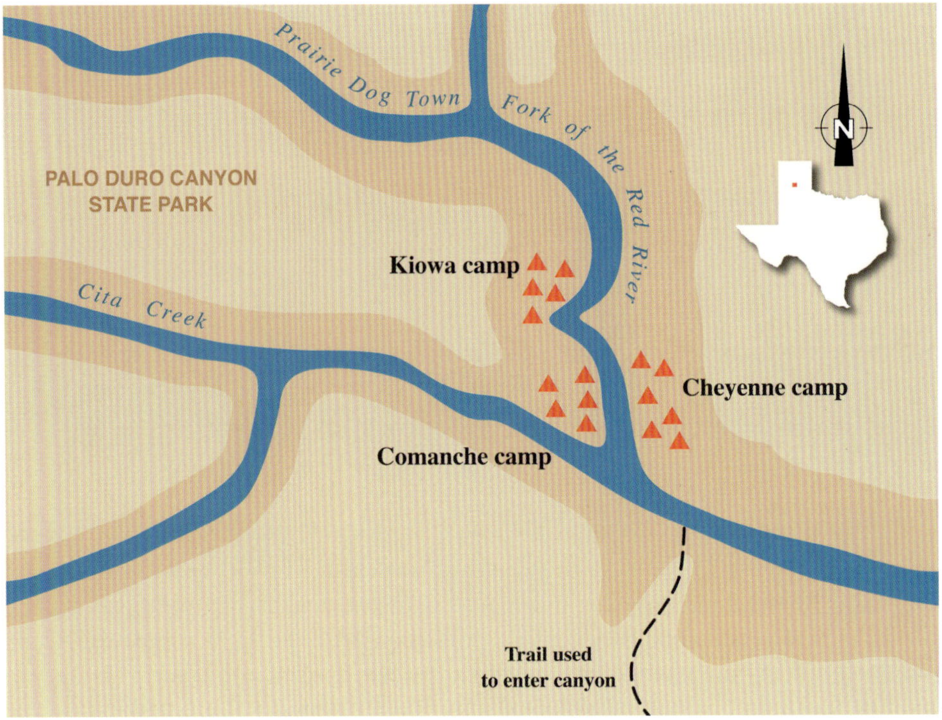

Fig. 10.2. On September 28, 1874, Mackenzie found several large Cheyenne, Comanche, and Kiowa camps in Palo Duro Canyon spread along the Prairie Dog Town Fork of the Red River. Illustration by Roland Pantermuehl

Palo Duro Canyon. About four o'clock on the morning of September 28, they reached the south edge of the canyon. At daybreak, they could see on the canyon floor—some 700 feet below them—a large number of Indian tepees strung out for several miles along the banks of the Prairie Dog Town Fork of the Red River where Cita Canyon joins Palo Duro Canyon (fig. 10.2). The Indian encampments consisted of a band of Southern Cheyenne led by Iron Shirt, a large band of Comanches under O-ha-ma-tai, and a Kiowa band led by Mamanti. It was Mamanti, the Owl Prophet, who had guaranteed the other camps that in Palo Duro Canyon they would be safe from the soldier's bullets and no harm would befall them. Notably, Quanah Parker's band of Kwahada Comanches was not present at the battle but was far to the south.[4]

Mackenzie realized he had caught the Indians asleep. He ordered the troops to descend the precipitous canyon walls and prepare to attack the villages. His plan of attack called for Lieutenant Thompson's Tonkawa and Seminole-Negro scouts to lead the charge. Companies A and E of Beaumont's 2nd Battalion would follow the scouts down the canyon walls, followed by Companies H and L under the personal direction of Mackenzie. McLaughlin's 1st Battalion, held in reserve, remained on the canyon rim. As the troops slowly made their way down the steep canyon wall in single file, an Indian sentry, Red Warbonnet (or K'ya-been), spotted them and fired his rifle, which aroused the sleeping Indians.[5] By the time the troopers reached the floor of the canyon, the panicked Indians were fleeing for safety. Women and children took what personal belongings they could carry and fled northwest, up Palo Duro Canyon.

Meanwhile, Thompson's scouts reached the canyon floor, where they were met by heavy fire. Thompson mounted a charge that scattered the Indian defenders and allowed Beaumont's 2nd Battalion the opportunity to take position on the canyon floor. Two of the 2nd Battalion companies joined the scouts in a sweep through the abandoned villages and up the canyon in pursuit of the fleeing Indians. The other two companies guarded the flanks. Thompson's charge carried him some 4 miles up the canyon in search of Indians, many of whom had taken refuge high up in the bluffs, where they could not be dislodged. Beaumont, meanwhile, rounded up 1,424 horses and mules—virtually the entire herd—and drove them back down the canyon. Finally, Indian resistance began to mobilize and one trooper, trumpeter Henry E. Hard of Company L, received a slug through the bowels. Though seriously wounded, he survived and was the only soldier casualty of the Palo Duro Canyon battle.[6]

Although some skirmishing continued for some distance up the canyon, the troops soon began to withdraw, but before they left the canyon Mackenzie ordered all the Indian lodges and winter supplies gathered up and burned. Companies D, I, and K of McLaughlin's 1st Battalion arrived on the canyon floor and formed a skirmish line to protect the soldiers engaged in destroying the Indian lodges and supplies. Meanwhile, Mackenzie dispatched Company H under Captain Gunther back to the rim. Gunther's force arrived just in time to beat back the efforts of warriors bent on reaching the trail out of the canyon, which would have blocked Mackenzie's escape route. With the lodges in flames, the troops drove the captured horse herd out of the canyon. Through the night the horses were driven some 30 miles back to the camp at Tule Canyon. The next morning, after allowing the scouts to select 376 of the best horses to keep, the remaining 1,048 were shot.[7] Mackenzie had learned from previous experiences that Indians would do everything in their power to recapture their horses if given the opportunity. By shooting the animals, Mackenzie denied them the chance to recapture the herd.

Mackenzie reported that, in addition to trumpeter Hard, he also had fourteen wounded horses. Four Indians were known to have been killed and several wounded. Despite the light casualties, the battle in Palo Duro Canyon was a catastrophe for the Indian bands there. Not only did they lose their horses and mules, they also lost their winter food supply. The Indians were demoralized. The loss was too heavy for many of them, and they turned to the Indian agencies and surrendered. Though some Indian bands from the various tribes were not at Palo Duro Canyon on September 28, 1874, the battle is viewed as a turning point in the Red River War when the will of a large number of free-roaming Southern Plains Indians was finally broken.

Current Ownership and Land Use

The area where the battle occurred is in Palo Duro Canyon, in the central Texas Panhandle in eastern Randall and western Armstrong counties. Most of the Battle of Palo Duro Canyon took place on land that in 2002 was privately owned property adjacent to the eastern boundary of Palo Duro Canyon State Park.[8] Efforts in 1998 by the Texas Historical Commission to gain access to this property to conduct the archeological investigations on this part of the battle site were not successful. Only a small portion of the battle took place on what is now state-owned park property, and it was on this area of the battle site that the archeological investigations were conducted (fig. 10.3). Palo Duro Canyon State Park consists of 18,438 acres some 12 miles east of Canyon, Texas, and 26 miles south and east of Amarillo.

Palo Duro Canyon formed as a result of millions of years of headward erosion by the Prairie Dog Town Fork of the Red River, which is the park's primary drainage system. This process has produced eroded canyons that reach depths of 213 m (700 feet) and elevations within the park that range from 1,061 m (3,481 feet) on the edge of the Llano Estacado to 815 m (2,674 feet) near Cita Creek at the park's southeast corner. Several of the canyons within the park still contain active springs.

A diversity of vegetation can be found within Palo Duro Canyon. Mesquite and short grasses dominate the upland portions, and evergreen shrubs, junipers, shin oaks, and taller grass varieties occupy the steep slopes of the canyons. Along the sandy

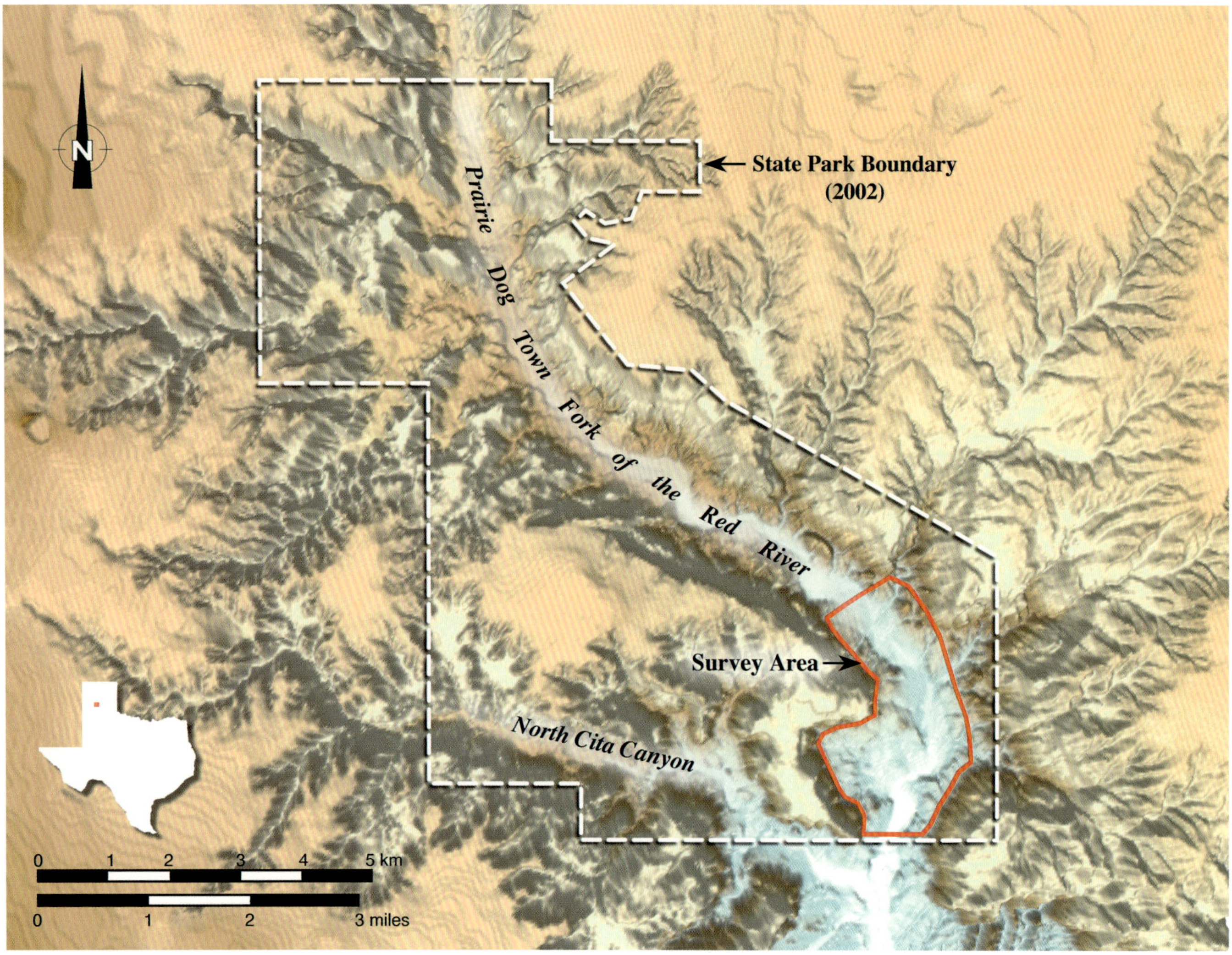

Fig. 10.3. Some of the Battle of Palo Duro Canyon took place within the boundaries of present-day Palo Duro Canyon State Park. Illustration by Roland Pantermuehl

terraces of the Prairie Dog Town Fork of the Red River, cottonwoods and tall grasses are found.

Archeological Investigations and Results

To provide an expanded understanding of park history and cultural resources, we undertook a metal detector survey of that portion of the battle site that lies within Palo Duro Canyon State Park on November 4 and 8, 2002, with one day of follow-up work on November 19. The survey area was determined initially by historical accounts and previous finds, but it evolved as new finds were made. In total, 41.5 person-days were utilized to survey approximately 111 acres. Even at this level of intensity (2.7 acres per person per day), however, full coverage of the project area was not possible; topographic and vegetation considerations limited actual coverage to approximately 50 percent. Nevertheless, the metal detector survey revealed that at least a portion of the battle took place within the survey area on what is state park property. The majority of the battle occurred outside park boundaries. The trail used by the cavalry to reach the canyon floor as well as the Indian encampments were east of the present park boundary. Most of the fighting appears to have occurred in these areas. Only a portion of the

Indian retreat up the canyon and the cavalry pursuit appear to have taken place within the present boundaries of the park.

Nevertheless, certain interpretations concerning the battle can be drawn from the distribution of the artifacts recovered during the survey. The recovered Indian artifacts (fig. 10.4) appears to mark the lines of retreat for at least some of the Indian families as they were fleeing up the canyon ahead of the army troopers. It seems that most of the Indians were on the north side of the river until they reached a point where the river makes a large horseshoe-shaped bend and the passage on the north side becomes very constricted. While some of the Indians apparently continued on the north side and made their way toward the protection offered by Tub Springs Draw, others crossed the river and continued up the canyon on the south side of the river. Some of the Indians that were now on the south side may have exited up the steep wall of the canyon, since Indian artifacts and army cartridges were recovered on a small, narrow ridge that leads up the south side of the canyon. This ridge is too narrow and steep to allow many people to have escaped, so it is likely that some Indians on the south side of the river now crossed back to the north side near the mouth of Tub Springs Draw and continued to flee up the draw (fig. 10.5).

The distribution of the U.S. Army artifacts, as expected, follows the same patterns as the Indian artifacts, since the troops were pursuing the Indians. At several locations, army cartridges were found among boulders above the margins of the canyon floor. This would seem to corroborate the army accounts that some of the troops tried to clear the Indians out of the rocks where they had taken refuge. As Sergeant Carter recalled, "As our skirmish line advanced, the Indians retired, springing from one rock to the protection of another, until finally they took to the inaccessible sides of the Cañon once more."[9]

Whether the artifacts recovered during the survey represent the extent of the battle within the park is not known. The military accounts state that some of the troops went as far as 4 miles up the canyon from the point they entered the canyon. Most of the artifacts recovered during the survey were found near or just south of the mouth of Tub Springs Draw, which is approximately 4 miles from the point the troops entered Palo Duro Canyon. The artifacts in the vicinity of the mouth of Tub Springs Draw may represent the extent of the battle within the park, but additional survey to the west of Tub Springs Draw should be conducted to better define the battle site boundaries. Additionally, the portion of North Cita Canyon owned by the state should be surveyed with metal detectors to seek any evidence of the battle there. It seems likely that some of the Indians fled up North Cita Canyon in their attempt to escape the 4th Cavalry troops.

Artifacts Recovered

A total of 218 battle-related artifacts were collected from 150 mapped locations (see fig. 10.4) within the park during our investigations. An additional twenty-two artifacts were collected by personnel with the Panhandle-Plains Historical Museum during earlier visits to the site. These earlier recoveries are included in the analysis presented in appendix G, for a total of 240 artifacts recovered from the site. Of the artifacts, 190 are considered associated with the Indians and fifty with the U.S. Army (table 10.1). The majority of the Indian artifacts (141, or 74.2 percent) are non-munitions items and were not used during the battle. Rather, these items are primarily domestic and household items that were most likely lost or discarded as the Indian families fled. These include a wide variety of metal items related to cooking (frying pan, spoons), clothing (buttons, clasp), horse tack (harness rings, bits, buckles, tacks), personal

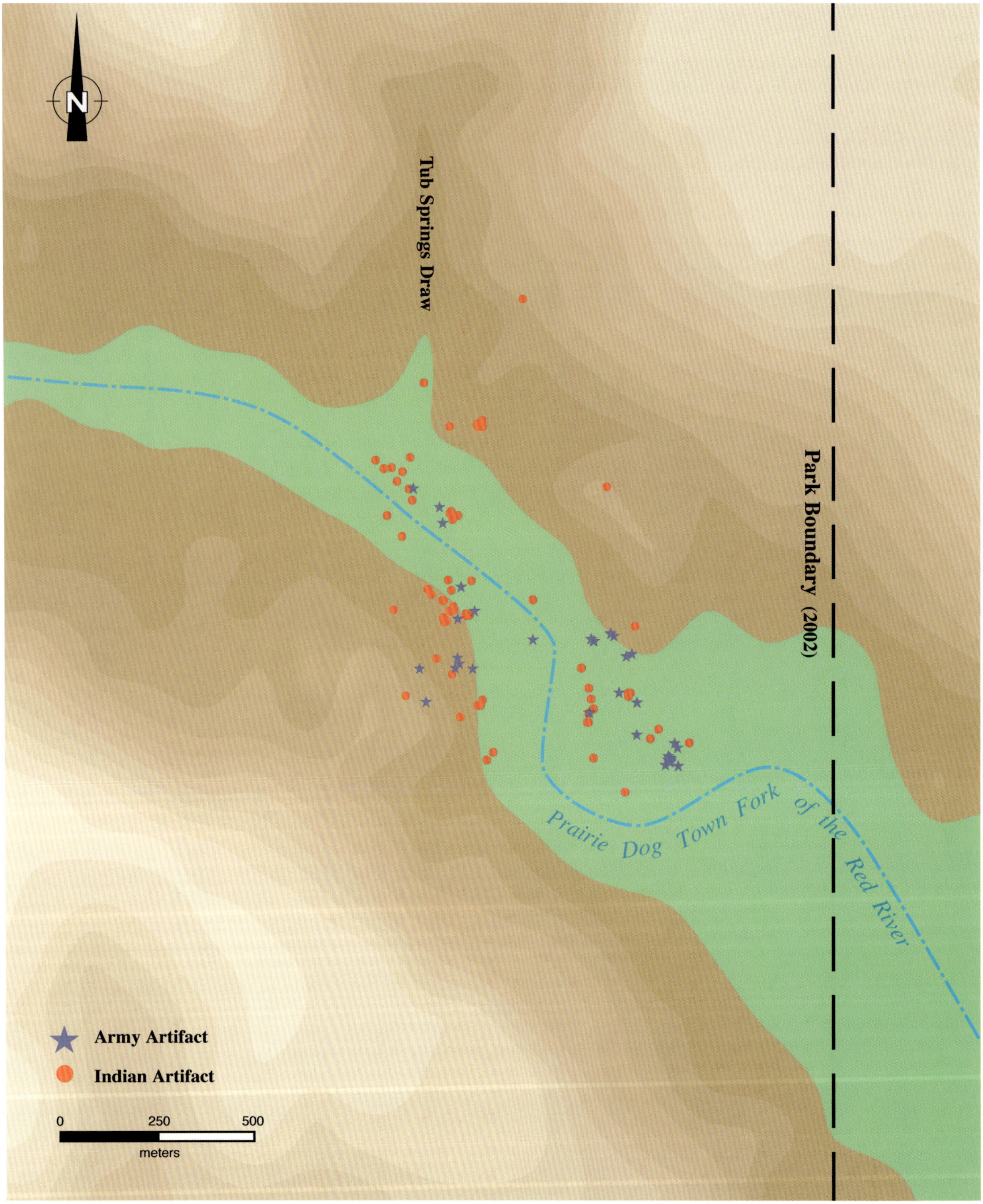

Fig. 10.4. Distribution of artifacts recovered at the Battle of Palo Duro Canyon site. Most of the Indian-associated artifacts are domestic and household items discarded by the Indian families as they escaped up the canyon. The majority of the army artifacts are cartridge cases. Illustration by Roland Pantermuehl

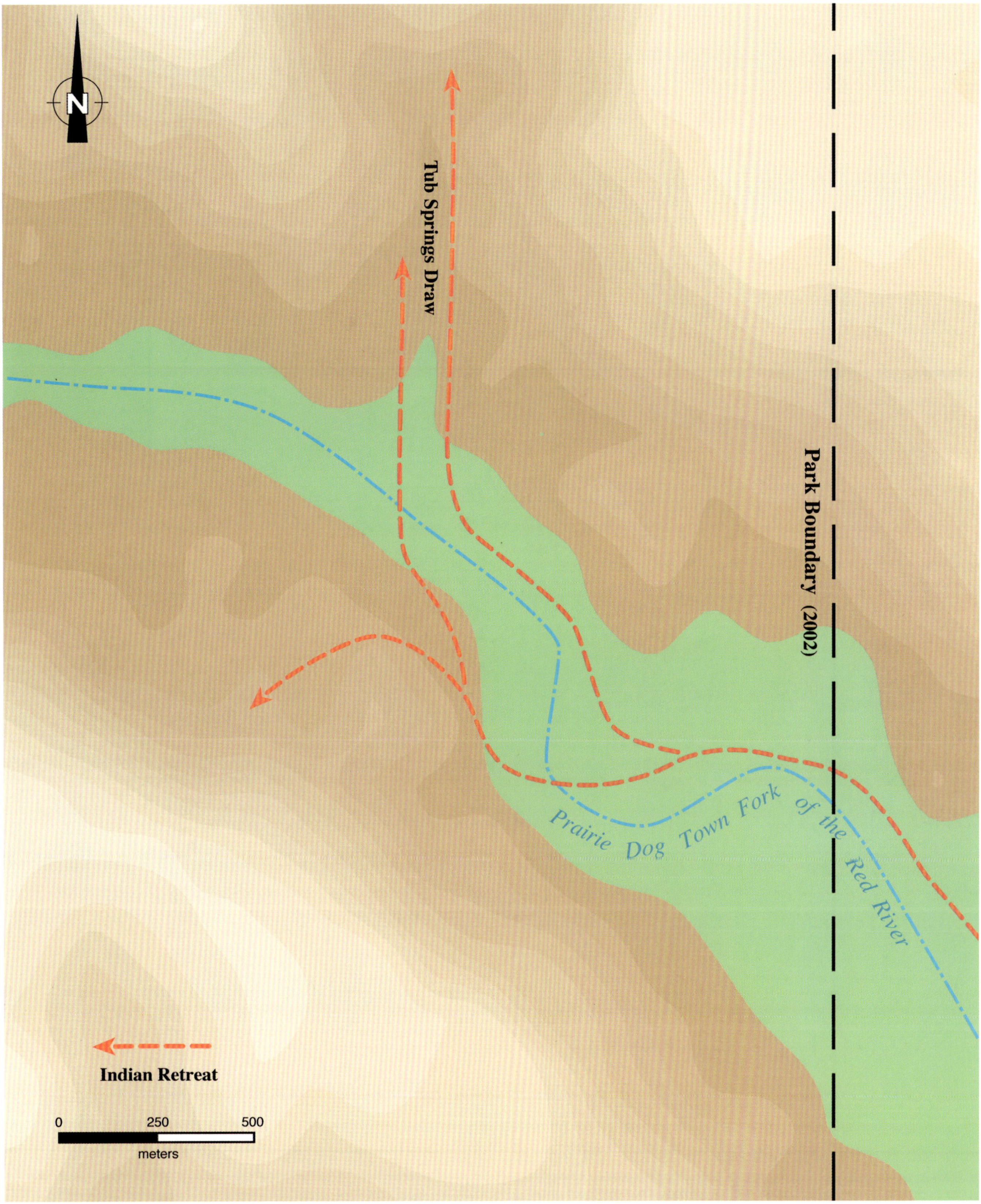

Fig. 10.5. The Indian-associated artifacts mark the lines of retreat for some of the Indian families as they fled up the canyon ahead of the army troops. Illustration by Roland Pantermuehl

Table 10.1. Artifacts from the Battle of Palo Duro Canyon Site

Item	*Army*	*Indian*	*Total*
Artifacts Related to Munitions			
.44-caliber Henry cartridge case, fired		1	1
.44-caliber Henry cartridge case, misfired		1	1
.44-caliber Smith & Wesson cartridge case, fired	2		2
.45-caliber Colt cartridge case, fired	1		1
.45/55-caliber cartridge case, fired in Springfield	42		42
.45/55-caliber cartridge case, fired in Sharps		7	7
.50/70-caliber cartridge case, fired in Springfield		2	2
.50/70-caliber cartridge case, fired in Sharps		3	3
56/50-caliber Spencer cartridge case, fired		4	4
56/56-caliber Spencer cartridge case, fired		3	3
56/56-caliber Spencer cartridge case, unfired		1	1
bullet (undetermined caliber)		2	2
.44-caliber bullet		2	2
.46-caliber rifle ball		1	1
.45-caliber bullet	2		2
.50-caliber bullet		4	4
iron arrowpoint		9	9
gun barrel (percussion)		1	1
gun screw		1	1
primer, Benét (.45 caliber)		7	7
Subtotal, munitions	47	49	96
Other Artifacts			
ax head		2	2
bead		1	1
bell and clapper		1	1
bit, snaffle		2	2
buckle		4	4
button		3	3
concha		1	1
cut metal		9	9
edged tools		3	3
file		1	1
food grater		2	2
frying pan		1	1
harness ring		2	2
horseshoe	3		3
horseshoe nail (unused)		10	10
nail, square		7	7
naja		1	1
pendant (token)		1	1
picket pin		4	4
pot leg		1	1
snap hook		1	1
spoon		2	2
tacks		24	24
tinkler		33	33
umbrella glider link		11	11
waist cinch buckle		1	1
wire		9	9
wood screw		3	3
unidentified		1	1
Subtotal, other	3	141	144
Total artifacts	**50**	**190**	**240**

adornment (pendants, medallions, tinklers), and utilitarian tools (axes, cut metal, knife, file, umbrella gliders).

Only forty-nine (25.8 percent) of the Indian-associated artifacts are munitions-related. These include twenty-two rifle cartridge cases, nine bullets, a broken gun barrel from a percussion type rifle, seven primers from .45-caliber cartridges, and a screw from an unidentified rifle. The cartridge cases are Spencer 56/50s, Sharps and Springfield .50/70s, .44-caliber Henrys or Winchesters, and .45-caliber Springfields. Nine metal arrowpoints were also recovered, but these were all found tightly clustered at one location. Two cut metal pieces that appear to be point preforms were found in association with the arrowpoints, suggesting that the points were not used during the battle but were probably in a bag or some other kind of container that was lost during the fight. The relatively small number of Indian-associated munitions supports the belief that the Indians were primarily fleeing rather than making concerted efforts to fight.

The fifty army-associated artifacts are primarily munitions-related: forty-two Springfield .45/55-caliber carbine cartridge cases, two .44-caliber Smith & Wesson cartridge cases, one .45-caliber Colt cartridge case, and two .45-caliber bullets. The remaining army artifacts are three horseshoes.

Discussion

The limited archeological investigations at the Battle of Palo Duro Canyon site confirm that at least a portion of the battle occurred on what is now state park property. The recovered artifacts are primarily domestic and personal artifacts associated with Indian villagers. The locations of the artifacts appear to mark the paths the villagers took as they were fleeing from the approaching army troops. As the villagers fled the canyon, items they had quickly gathered or packed were lost or abandoned along the way.

The relatively small number of munitions-related artifacts recovered indicates that during this late stage of the battle some firing was still taking place and some resistance by the Indian warriors remained, but the battle was drawing to a close. It is probable that by the time the villagers had reached this point in their flight up the canyon, some 4 miles from where the troopers had entered the canyon and the battle began, their horse herd had already been captured and the troopers were completing their destruction of the Indian lodges and beginning their retreat out of the canyon.

The munitions-related artifacts revealed that during the battle the Indians were using primarily repeater rifles such as the Spencer, Henry, and Winchester, though they also had single-shot Sharps and Springfields. Of interest are the seven .45-caliber cartridge cases that were fired in the larger-caliber Sharps and Springfield carbines. Apparently the Indians who fired these cartridges were unfamiliar with the caliber size of their weapons, or they were simply using whatever arms and ammunition they could acquire. There is some evidence that the Indians were still using muzzle loaders and percussion rifles during the battle. The recovered metal arrowpoints suggest that the bow and arrow also remained an important armament.

The army-associated munitions included the .45 Springfield carbine as the primary weapon, along with the .45 Colt and at least one .44-caliber Smith & Wesson pistol.

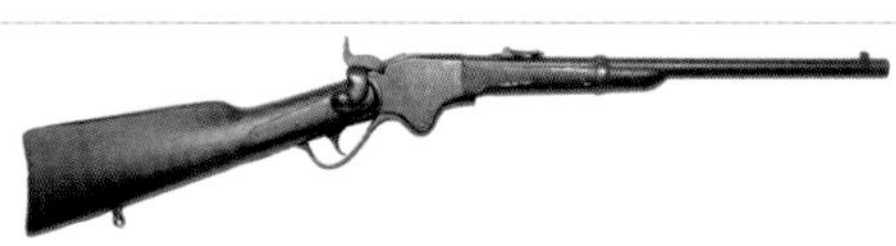

11

A Most Desperate Fight

Fig. 11.1. Lt. Henry J. Farnsworth of H Company, 8th Cavalry, commanded the twenty-eight-man scouting expedition that was attacked by Grey Beard's Cheyenne warriors on November 6, 1874. This photo was taken after Farnsworth had been promoted to major and inspector general in 1885. Courtesy U.S. Army Military History Institute

In late September 1874, Col. Nelson A. Miles established his headquarters and supply camp at a site on the Washita River in what is now Hemphill County, Texas, anticipating that the campaign against the Indians would extend into the coming winter months. From this camp, several scouting forays departed with the purpose of finding any Indian bands that had not returned to the reservations. One such scouting expedition, which departed the camp in early November, was commanded by 1st Lt. Henry J. Farnsworth (fig. 11.1) and was made up of twenty-eight troopers of the 8th Cavalry: twenty-four from Company H, two from Company C, and one each from Companies K and L. The troopers from Companies C, K, and L were to serve as packers for the expedition. The patrol was to take rations and supplies for five days packed on six mules. Accompanying the patrol was a Comanchero guide by the name of Anastacio Duran.[1]

Lieutenant Farnsworth received his orders from Maj. William R. Price on November 2 to undertake the scouting expedition after an Indian warrior was captured near the camp. Lieutenant Farnsworth was to take the patrol and scout the area to the west and southwest "to endeavor to learn if there were any Indians in the vicinity, of which the Indian captured was the outlaying picket."[2] The patrol departed on November 3 and proceeded southwest along the "Rio Negro" (present Gageby Creek) and the divide between the Washita and Canadian rivers. Farnsworth reported that the patrol reached "a point opposite Adobe Walls," which was probably south of the Canadian River somewhere on White Deer Creek. Here the patrol turned southward until, according to Farnsworth, they struck "the Rio Aranoso or McClellan Creek where, at about 1½ P.M. on the 6th inst. I engaged at least 100 Cheyennes well mounted and in full fighting trim, they were evidently appraised of my coming and had all the advantage of ground and fresh horses, while their arms were equally as good as mine and their supply of ammunition more abundant."[3]

The Battle of Round Timber Creek

Though Lieutenant Farnsworth wrote two brief reports on this engagement with the Cheyenne, he provided very few details of the circumstances of the battle. He does not explain how the battle was fought, whether the patrol was ambushed or whether they stumbled upon and attacked an Indian village, or even precisely where the battle took place. In his first report, written on November 7, one day after the battle, he states that the patrol fought the Indians until dark when, "my ammunition being exhausted as well as humanity for my wounded, compelled me to retreat under cover of the night." The troopers made their way back to the supply camp on the Washita River after traveling all night, a distance according to Farnsworth of at least 45 miles. He goes on to write that Pvt. William Densham was killed and Cpl. Thomas J. Thompson, blacksmith Henry Fields, trumpeter Herman Fehr, and Pvt. George Robinson were all wounded. In addition, he lost all six of his pack mules and six horses. He further writes that four Indians were killed and ten were badly wounded, as were many of the Indian horses, and "that they [the Indians] suffered severe punishment is evinced by their failure to persue me after reaching the plain."[4]

In his second report, written on November 12, Farnsworth provides a partial list of the men who made up the scout patrol and cites them for their gallantry (table 11.1). In this report he also states that a second man, Pvt. Rufus Hibbard, was killed by the Indians after he became detached from the command during the retreat back to the supply camp.[5]

On November 7, after Farnsworth and the surviving patrol members made it back to the supply camp, Major Price led two companies of the 8th Cavalry and Col. John

Table 11.1. Members of Lt. Henry J. Farnsworth's Scout Patrol, November 2–6, 1874

Name[a, c, d]	*Rank*	*Recognition*[a, b, d]	*Equipment Lost*[c]
Henry Joseph Farnsworth	First Lieutenant	Patrol commander	
Henry Bowers (Rowers?)	Private	recognized	1 great coat, 1 wool blanket
Owen Conway	Acting First Sergeant	recognized (horse killed under him)	
Andrew Cunningham	Private	deserving notice	
William Densham	Private	killed in action	
John Deary (Geary?)	Private		2 wool blankets
Herman Fehr	Trumpeter	recognized (wounded in breast)	
Henry Fields	Blacksmith	participated in two charges after being wounded twice in hip	
Daniel Haggerty	Private	recognized	
Martin Henman	Private	deserving notice	2 wool blankets
Rufus Hibbard	Private	killed in action	
Martin Huniaus	Private	deserving notice	
Charles W. Jones	Private	deserving notice	
Jonathan Kalber	Farrier	recognized	
Edward J. Kinney	Corporal	recognized	2 wool blankets
John Kitro	Private	deserving notice	1 great coat, 1 wool blanket
Thomas Manning	Private	deserving notice	2 wool blankets
Patrick McGuire	Corporal	deserving notice	
John Quigley (Sixley?)	Sergeant	deserving notice	1 great coat, 1 wool blanket, 1 poncho
Henry C. Redman	Private	recognized	
George Robinson	Private	recognized (wounded in hand)	1 great coat
John Ryan	Private	deserving notice	
Thomas J. Thompson	Corporal	recognized (wounded in side)	
Jonathan R. Williams	Saddler	recognized	1 great coat, 1 wool blanket
Anastacio Duran	Comanchero guide		1 great coat, 1 wool blanket
Brown Blackbird[e]	Cheyenne prisoner/guide		

[a]Farnsworth to Battalion Adjutant, Nov. 12, 1874 (RG 393, Part I, E–2601, NA).
[b]Marshall, *Miles Expedition,* 37–40.
[c]Farnsworth to Adjutant General, Nov. 27, 1874, in Taylor, *Indian Campaign,* 109–10.
[d]Price to Farnsworth, Nov. 2, 1874, Special Orders No. 36 (RG 393, Part I, E–2601, NA).
[e]Hyde, *Life of George Bent,* 362–63.

Davidson two companies of the 10th Cavalry back to the scene of the battle in an attempt to find the Indians. On November 8, while Price and Davidson were inspecting the battle site, they heard gun shots and explosions from artillery shells several miles away to the southwest and inferred that Colonel Miles or some part of his command were engaging the Indians. Davidson and his command proceeded toward the battle, but Major Price halted his command and actually moved east several miles away from the battle, though he had specific orders from Miles to find and pursue the Indians.

The next day Davidson encountered troops from the 5th Infantry and 6th Cavalry under the command of Lt. Frank Baldwin, who had engaged Chief Grey Beard's band of Cheyennes on November 8. This was the same group Farnsworth had fought two days earlier. After the battle with Farnsworth on November 6, Grey Beard and his band apparently reestablished their village near the head of the North Branch of McClellan Creek. It was here the Indians were accidentally found by Lieutenant Baldwin while he was escorting Colonel Miles's empty wagon train back to the headquarters camp on the Washita River for more supplies. At the ensuing battle, known as the Battle of McClellan Creek, the army troops routed Grey Beard's Cheyennes and rescued Adelaide and Julia German, then five and seven years old, who had been captured by the Cheyenne two months earlier.[6] For his actions at this battle, Lieutenant Baldwin was awarded his second Medal of Honor (appendix C).

Finding Farnsworth's Battle Site

Lieutenant Farnsworth's reports of his battle provide virtually no clues as to its precise location. His statement that the patrol engaged the Indians on "the Rio Aranoso or McClellan Creek" has led some to infer that the engagement occurred somewhere on McClellan Creek, which is a tributary of the North Fork of the Red River in present west-central Gray County, Texas. These researchers seem to view Farnsworth's "Rio Aranoso" as simply Spanish for McClellan Creek. This view would seem to have some validity, since the 8th Cavalry employed Navajo and Mexican guides when they left New Mexico to participate in the Indian campaign. These guides were not always familiar with the names of the streams and topographic landmarks of the Texas Panhandle, however, and they often applied Spanish names (e.g., Río Colorado, Río Negro, and Cañon Bonita), just as Farnsworth appears to have done in his report.

An alternate view is that Farnsworth was not sure which stream he was on, but he thought that it was either the Rio Aranoso or McClellan Creek. If this interpretation is correct, then the Rio Aranoso would be the North Fork of the Red River. Major Price, in his report to the assistant adjutant general the day after the battle, was apparently attempting to point out that the Rio Aranoso and McClellan Creek were not the same streams when he wrote, "Farnsworth encountered a large body of Indians on the Erenosa which is a branch of McClellan Creek."[7] If the Rio Aranoso (Price's Erenosa) is the North Fork of the Red River, then Major Price's statement would indicate that the battle was on the North Fork of the Red River rather than on McClellan Creek.

But the site of the battle continued to be a matter of confusion. George Bent (1843–1918), a mix-blood son of William Bent and Owl Woman, his Southern Cheyenne wife, wrote that Farnsworth and his men were attacked as they came in sight of a Cheyenne village on McClellan Creek. Yet J. T. Marshall, a newspaper reporter as well as a scout for Colonel Miles during the 1874 campaign, wrote that the battle occurred near the headwaters of Sweetwater Creek.[8] The few military reports and other accounts that mentioned the battle provide evidence that McClellan Creek, Sweetwater Creek, or the North Fork of the Red River are possible locations for Farnsworth's battle.

Additional clues for the battle's location came to light in 2001, during our archival research at the National Archives, in documents from a file containing the records of the court-martial of Major Price, Lieutenant Farnsworth's immediate commander.[9] At the court-martial proceedings that took place in June and July 1875, several 8th and 10th Cavalry soldiers gave testimonies both on the part of the prosecution (the U.S. Army) and for the defense (Major Price). The soldiers were from the companies under the commands of Major Price and Colonel Davidson that departed from the Washita camp on November 7 and returned to the scene of Farnsworth's battle in an attempt to find and pursue the Indians.

Presented below are the pertinent portions of those witness testimonies that proved significant in our search for, and ultimate discovery of, the site of Farnsworth's engagement with the Cheyenne on November 6, 1874. The testimonies provide details concerning mileages between certain points, directions traveled, and landmarks observed while en route to and at the location of Farnsworth's battle. They also make clear that the stream on which the battle occurred was in fact the North Fork of the Red River. The testimonies are presented in their original form, though some punctuation has been added for clarity. Our clarifications and interpretations follow, labeled as "Comment."

PAGES 300–302 OF THE COURT-MARTIAL PROCEEDINGS:
The proceedings of the 20th instant having been read and approved, 1st Lieutenant William R. Harmon 10th Cavalry a witness on the part of the prosecution being duly sworn testified as follows:

Ques. by J. A. [Judge Advocate]
Do you know the accused.

Ans. I do, Major Price of the 8th Cavalry.

Ques. by J. A. State where you were encamped on the morning of the 8th of November 1874.

Ans. At some Water-holes, near the head of the Sweet-water.

Ques. by J. A. About how far had been your previous days march and from what point.

Ans. We marched from the Washita, a distance of about 25 to 27 miles.

Comment: From the supply camp on the Washita, the command marched in a southwesterly direction 25–27 miles until they reached some waterholes near the head of Sweetwater Creek. The waterholes referred to are playa lakes, which are common on the Llano Estacado. This would place the November 7 camp of the command north of present Laketon near the Roberts-Gray county line.

Ques. by J. A. State what time of day you broke camp on the morning of the 8th of November—the general direction of your march that morning, and the principle occurrences.

Ans. We broke camp just about sunup. We marched about 8 miles to the Breaks of the Mesa, where Farnsworth had his fight. We were there about probably, half to three quarters of an hour, when we moved on an edge of the Mesa to another point, about a mile, where we stopped and rested probably for 15 minutes. Just as we were leaving—just after mounting,—we had probably gone three or four hundred yards, I heard the sound of guns, and called the commanding officer of my company, attention to it; who immediately notified Major Schofield, who was then in advance some short distance. We then moved on down to the valley, probably a mile and a half. There we received orders—Major Schofield joined us,—and we received orders to leave our animals and we then started in the direction of the firing. We travelled from that point about three miles and a half, to a point on the south side of the North Fork, and there halted.

Comment: Traveling south from the location of the November 7 camp, the only "breaks" one encounters are those of the North Fork of the Red River. Thus, Lieutenant Harmon's statement suggests that Farnsworth's battle was in the breaks on the north side of the North Fork. The sounds of guns heard on the morning of November 8 were those at the Battle of McClellan Creek between Lieutenant Baldwin's troops and Grey Beard's warriors.

PAGES 276–79:
Captain William B. Kennedy 10th U.S. Cavalry, a witness on the part of the prosecution being duly sworn, testified as follows:

Ques. by J. A. State where you were encamped on the night of the 7th and morning of the 8th of November 1874.

Ans. We were encamped under Major Price, at some water-holes on the Staked Plains, within about 8 miles of the North Fork of the Red River in the direction of our line of march. I presume however, the distance to the North Fork would be less by going directly South.

Ques. by J. A. About what time of day or night of the 7th of November did you arrive in that camp.

Ans. I can only form a judgment about that time. I presume it to be about between 11 and 12 oclock P.M. when our command arrived—the companies under the command of Major Schofield.

Ques. by J. A. State about what time you broke camp the next morning, and what direction you marched.

Ans. I think we broke camp just a little before sunrise or between day-light and sun-rise. We marched in a direction, I think, South of West.

Ques. by J. A. About how far until you halted.

Ans. I should say about South West, about 8 or 9 miles to where we halted.

Ques. by J. A. Go on and give the occurrences of that morning.

Ans. On arriving at the point where the horses that were killed belonging to Farnsworth's command, the command was halted, and an examination was made of the ground about there. The body of a dead soldier was found lying just below the crest of the plain. After some arrangement had been made as I observed, for the burial of the man, Major Price moved on down the ridge that appeared to have been the line of Lieutenant Farnsworth's fight leaving the valley of the North Fork.

I observed Major Price with his command going down that ridge while we remained on the crest, some distance off to his right. Some considerable delay was had there, and after a time Major Schofield and command, the 10th Cavalry of which I formed a part, moved on around the crest of the plain some considerable distance, say a mile or more, and we then moved down on an old road formed by some of the troops marching to and fro in that country and when about from 3 to 5 hundred yards from the crest of the plain on that ridge, we heard sounds off to our right as if volley-firing was taking place. . . .

Comment: In this testimony Captain Kennedy makes it clear that on the night of November 7 the command was camped at some playa lakes on the Llano Estacado and that on the morning of November 8 they marched 8–9 miles in a southwesterly direction, where they found dead horses and the body of a dead soldier that were killed during Farnsworth's engagement with the Cheyenne. The soldier was buried on the battle site. Captain Kennedy further states that Major Price went down a ridge that Farnsworth and his men used during the battle as they were retreating from the valley of the North Fork. Captain Kennedy's testimony leaves little doubt that Farnsworth's battle with the Cheyenne occurred on the north side of the North Fork of the Red River rather than on McClellan Creek or Sweetwater Creek. This is clear in the following testimonies as well.

PAGES 155–59:
Major G. W. Schofield 10th U.S. Cavalry, a witness on the part of the prosecution being duly sworn testified as follows:

Ques. by J. A. State if you know the accused and who he is.

Ans. I am acquainted with him. He is Major Price of the 8th Cavalry.

Ques. by J. A. State to what command you belonged during the fall of 1874 and where stationed.

Ans. I was under the command of Lieut. Colonel J. W. Davidson, then commanding post of Fort-Sill Ind. Territory; to make that exact, I should say from the 4th of October.

Ques. by J. A. State if during the month of November 1874, you formed part of Lieut. Colonel Davidson's command in the field.

Ans. I did, a part of November.

Ques. by J. A. State if you were directed at any time during the month of November to assist, reinforce, or support the accused in a movement to be made by him against certain Indians.

Ans. I was ordered on the 7th of November with two companies of the 10th Cavalry to co-operate with the accused on an expedition against hostile Indians.

Ques. by J. A. State where you were encamped on the night of November 7th 1874.

Ans. I was encamped at some ponds of water on the plain south of the Washita River, and probably about 8 miles North of the North Fork of the Red River.

Ques. by J. A. Was the accused encamped near you.

Ans. He was.

Ques. by J. A. State what hour you broke camp, on the morning of the 8th of November, and the prominent incicidents [*sic*] of your march that morning.

Ans. We broke camp not far from 7 oclock, to the best of my recollection, the sun being about half an hour high. We marched then nearly due south to the Breaks of the North Fork, and then changed the direction to a direction nearly west, which we continued for about 4 miles, to a point where we found some dead horses, and one dead soldier.

Ques. by J. A. What did you do at that point.

Ans. With the accused I passed over the ground, passing the body of the dead soldier, and down the slope towards the North Fork, for about 300 yards, when he gave an order to his column, the two companies of the 8th Cavalry, to move around the next ravine, and motioning down towards the river. He gave that order to the senior officer, I don't remember to which one, it was given,—one of the officers at the time with the column. My command having been halted by my order on the plain near where the dead soldier was found. Hearing the order of the accused to his command, I left him and rejoined my own; ordered them to mount and move forward, following the same course that had been pursued by Maj. Price's command; being for a mile, a little north of West, and nearly west I might say—it was substantially west,—to the point where his command had turned South, down an old trail, and directly towards the North Fork. I there halted my command. His command having passed out of my sight, down a slope toward the North Fork. Having halted for some time, I had ordered the "mount" and "forward" which had been sounded and the movement just commenced when the sound of distant firing was heard. I judged the sound to come from the south west. I immediately asked my Adjutant his opinion. He said he thought it was a cannon shot, and that it was from the West or Southwest as near as I can remember his words.

PAGES 251–53:
Captain L. H. Carpenter, a witness on the part of the prosecution being duly sworn, testified as follows:

Ques. by J. A. State where you were encamped on the morning of the 8th of November 1874.

Ans. On the morning of the 8th of November, my Company formed a portion of the Column commanded by Major Price, and was encamped at some rain water lakes, about 10 miles to the East of the North Fork of the Red River.

Ques. by J. A. State what the command you were with was composed of.

Ans. Composed of 2 companies of the 8th Cavalry and two companies of the 10th Cavalry, under the command of Major Schofield. The two companies of the 10th Cavy under command of Major Schofield were ordered to co-operate with the two companies of the 8th Cavalry under Major Price. The morning of the 8th of November, this column was in transit across from the Washita to the North Fork, in pursuit of certain Indians, and on the morning of the 8th of November they were in that camp. That is, we camped at night. We started out early in the morning of the 8th of November from that point.

Ques. by J. A. State what direction you marched after breaking camp on the morning of the 8th of November and the principle occurrences of that morning, to the best of your recollection.

Ans. On the morning of the 8th of November about sunrise we marched from that camp, in a direction west, and a little South of West, until we struck the Breaks of the North Fork—to a large mesa over-looking the North Fork. At that point, we found the body of one of the soldiers that had been killed in the fight of Lieutenant Farnsworth, a day or two before. We also found on the road, some of the horses, or ponies that were killed in that affair.

PAGES 518–19:
The examination of Charles A. Hartwell Captain 8th US. Cavalry, a witness on the part of the defence was resumed.

Ques. by accused State when you left camp the morning of the 7th of November 1874.

Answer As near as I could judge it was about 10 oClock. I had however no timepiece.

Ques. by accused When did you reach camp that night and how far had you traveled that day.

Answer We made Camp at a lagoona on the plains at about 11 oClock at night having marched I think 27 or 28 miles.

Ques. by accused State when you left camp and give the directions and distances, and principal incidents of the march.

Answer We left camp shortly after daylight I should think about seven o'Clock and marched for some time in a southerly direction seven or eight miles I should think, here coming to the breaks of the Arenosa we turned westward or a little south of west continuing around the heads of the breaks about four miles where we came on the scene of Farnsworth's fight, and found the dead body of a soldier at this point. Major Price ordered me to send a detail to bury the soldier and directed me to take the command around the breaks down towards the river while he himself would go over the ground fought over by Farnsworth. After leaving Major Price I marched for three or four miles down to the river bottom and I halted and dismounted for a rest. Shortly after dismounting I heard three cannon shot and in two or three minutes afterwards two more. The sound apparently came from my right or to the west and a little south.

Comment: In this testimony, Captain Hartwell says that the command came to the breaks of the Arenosa. From the testimonies of the previous witnesses, it is clear that the Arenosa is the North Fork of the Red River. When the command reached the breaks, they found the scene of Farnsworth's battle and the body of one of the dead soldiers. As Major Price was examining the battle site, Captain Hartwell led the command 3–4 miles down to the river, where they halted and rested. While the command was halted they heard five cannon shots from Lieutenant Baldwin's mountain howitzer, which was being fired several miles to the west at the Battle of McClellan Creek on the morning of November 8.

> EXHIBIT L. EXCERPTS FROM MAJOR PRICE'S DESCRIPTION OF FIELD ACTIVITIES DURING THE EARLY PART OF NOVEMBER (NO PAGE NUMBERS)
>
> We got started from here about 10 A.M. and marched steadily in a S. W. direction until 11 P.M., moved at daylight on the 8th and by 12 m. came to the scene of the fight—delayed only sufficient length of time to bury Private Densham and pushed on to discover the direction the Indians had taken, trails were running in every direction in the valley of the stream, both Col. Schofield's and my scouts were sent to find the trails of the teepeys. . . . At nearly Sun down the scouts reported that the teepey trails were concentrating in a S. direction and we concluded they had gone to McClellan creek or further south. Our animals were much jaded, and we went into camp on the trail at sundown.
>
> Gen. Davidson had followed the command closely and went into camp within two miles of us, that evening he sent me a note inviting my co-operation with him. I replied stating that the guns heard, and the wagons seen on our right were evidently Gen. Miles' command of several Companies, that his—Gen. D's—command would probably take the main trail south, and I thought there were more troops in one locality than were needed—that I would follow the trail on the left to see if any were going east down the north fork and go into the Camp on the Washitaw for forage, as my animals were very weak. . . .
>
> Gen. Davidson informed me that he burned one camp with fifty lodges standing—with buffalo skin coverings, many buffalo skins were stretched on the ground preparatory to tanning, they were making new cotton wood lodge poles—this camp was in the immediate vicinity of Capt. Farnsworth's fight and had been hurriedly abandoned, a rough sketch of the fight was found on a piece of paper and left in a crotch of a tree and indicating the direction the Indians had taken. There were evidences of encampments of at least 150 Indians on both sides of this stream.
>
> On my return I followed the entire course of Capt. Farnsworth's fight for eight miles and consider it a stubbornly contested and desperate fight. I make no estimate or give no opinion as to whether any Indians were killed. The Indians and troops were at all times in close bullet range of each other, and I know that there are cool daring men in the Company and good shots. The body of Private Hibbard, 8th Cavalry, was found and buried some distance this side of the fight. I am informed to day by General Miles that my actions have not met with his approval.

Major Price makes several interesting statements in this report. We learn that the body of the dead soldier mentioned in previous testimonies was that of Pvt. William Densham.[10] Price then states that the scouts sent to find the trails of the tepees found one that led in a southerly direction and concludes that the Indians broke camp and fled after the battle, then went on to McClellan Creek or farther south. One of the Indian trails, however, apparently led to the east down the North Fork of the Red River. Price decided to follow this trail rather than pursue the Indians to the west in the direction of the main Indian trail and the direction of the sounds of the cannon shots.

Price's comment that Miles did not approve of his decision is an understatement. Colonel Miles was enraged with Price for not pursuing the Indians and failing to render aid to Lieutenant Baldwin in his fight with the Cheyennes at McClellan Creek. On November 12, Miles had Price arrested and preferred charges against him, which resulted in Price's court-martial.[11]

Price goes on to say in his report that Colonel Davidson found and burned fifty tepees in an Indian camp that was "in the immediate vicinity of Capt. Farnsworth's fight and had been hurriedly abandoned," and that "there were evidences of encampments of at least 150 Indians on both sides of this stream." This statement indicates that Farnsworth's battle was very close to the Indian village, which was on both sides of a stream that Price did not identify. It is not likely that this stream is the North Fork of the Red River, which is in excess of 800 m (875 yards) wide in most places. Rather, it is probably one of several, small spring-fed streams that flow into the North Fork from the north. Apparently Davidson also found a piece of paper in a tree that had a sketch of the battle on it and indications as to the direction the Indians had fled. Lieutenant Farnsworth probably considered his situation with the Indians to be quite desperate, and he presumably left the paper in the tree for the troops to find in the event that he and his patrol did not survive the battle.

Finally, Major Price writes that on his return trip to the camp on the Washita River he followed the course of the battle for 8 miles, and that the soldiers and Indians were in close bullet range of each other the entire time. If Price followed the battle for 8 miles, then the battle was a long, running engagement that covered a relatively large area and would have extended, at a minimum, from the North Fork of the Red River northward through the breaks to the escarpment of the Llano Estacado, which is a distance of about 6 miles. Once on these high plains, the battle may have continued for some two more miles before the Indians abandoned the chase. Major Price, who wrote his report from the camp on the Washita River, also notes that the body of Private Hibbard, the second soldier killed during the battle, was found and buried "some distance this side of the fight." This account supports the statement by Lieutenant Farnsworth that Private Hibbard became separated from the command during the retreat back to the supply camp and was killed by the Indians. This may also be evidence that the battle continued for some distance once the command reached the plains.

Exhibit F in the Price court-martial file is a map titled "A Scout By Major Prices Comd Co's K. and L. 8th U.S. Cavy. Nov. 7th to Nov. 11th 1874." This map is reproduced as fig. 11.2. Though faint and of small scale, the map shows the route taken to the North Fork of the Red River by Major Price when he left the camp on the Washita River on November 7. On the map, the North Fork is labeled "Erenosa or North Fork of Red River," confirming that Farnsworth's reference to the Rio Aranoso is the North Fork of the Red River. The map also indicates the location of Farnsworth's battle. When the lower portion of the map is enlarged, as shown in fig. 11.3, it can be seen that Farnsworth's battle is indicated on the north side of the North Fork, as signaled by a pair of crossed sabers.

The testimonies and exhibits presented at Major Price's court-martial proceedings leave no doubt that Lieutenant Farnsworth's engagement with Grey Beard's Cheyennes on November 6, 1874, occurred somewhere on the north side of the North Fork of the Red River and not on McClellan Creek or Sweetwater Creek as previously thought by some writers. The testimonies indicate that the battle was a long, running engagement that took place primarily along a ridge that runs for several miles from the North Fork

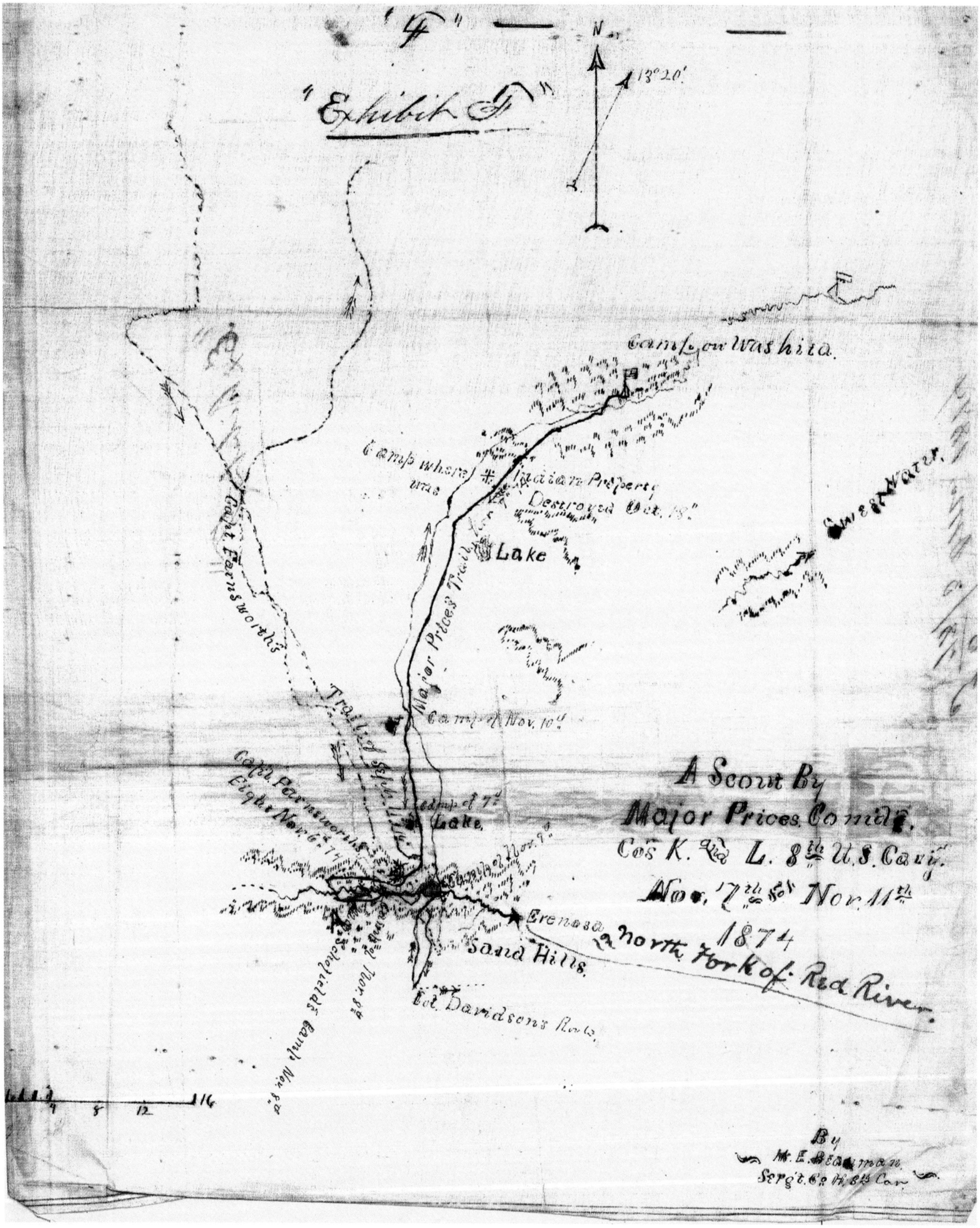

Fig. 11.2. This map was Exhibit F in Major Price's court-martial. It shows the route taken by Price to Farnsworth's battle near the North Fork of the Red River. Record Group 393, PP-4678, National Archives.

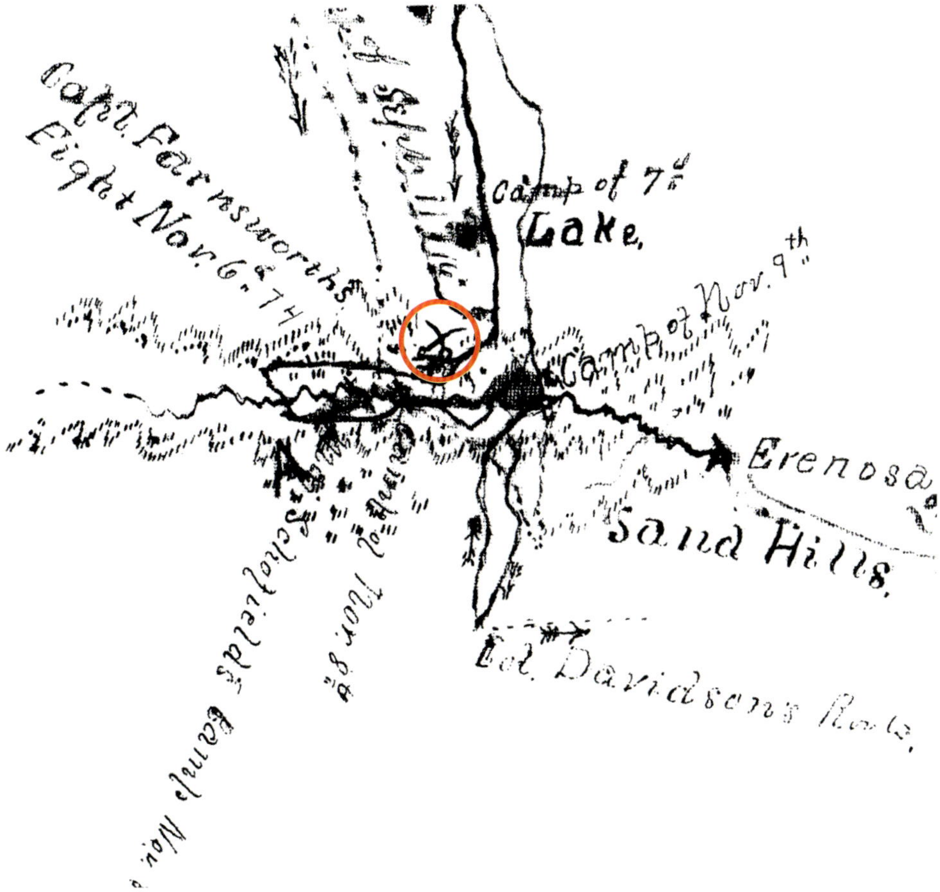

Fig. 11.3. Detail of the map in fig. 11.2, showing the location of Farnsworth's battle marked by a pair of crossed sabers.

up to the edge of the Llano Estacado escarpment. Apparently there was an Indian village close to the scene of the battle; this village may have been situated along one of the small streams that flow into the North Fork. If this were the case, the village would likely be on one of the spring-fed streams along the North Fork so that an ample supply of good water would be available. It would also be reasonable to expect the village to be situated closer to the mouth of the stream rather than in the steep, rough breaks of the escarpment, where there would be little grazing for horses.

Several of the soldiers who testified at Major Price's court-martial proceedings stated that on the morning of November 8, 1874, while they were examining the scene of Farnsworth's battle, they heard rifle and artillery fire at some distance to the southwest. They later learned that Lieutenant Baldwin and troops under his command were battling the Cheyenne on the North Branch of McClellan Creek. Although the distance from Baldwin's battle to where the men were when they heard the rifle and artillery shots is not stated, it must have been several miles, since Colonel Davidson and his troops moved in the direction of the firing but did not encounter any of Baldwin's troops or any Indians that day, and they went into camp that night on the North Fork of the Red River. In his report on the incidents of that day, Colonel Davidson writes, "During the afternoon the scouts with my command discovered the camp of the Indians who fought Farnsworth and followed the trail leading from it, toward McClellan Creek, about six (6) miles and which had entirely escaped the notice of the advance."[12] Davidson's scouts apparently followed the Indian trail 6 miles in the direction of McClellan Creek but likewise did not encounter any Indians or any of Baldwin's troops before they turned around and reported back to Davidson. This situation suggests that Baldwin's battle was more than 6 miles from the scene of Farnsworth's engagement.

In 1988, Gerald Wright of Pampa, Texas, identified the location of Baldwin's battle on McClellan Creek when he found and collected several hundred battle-related artifacts. Those artifacts are now at the White Deer Land Museum in Pampa. At its closest point, the Battle of McClellan Creek site lies roughly 9 miles southwest of the North Fork of the Red River. Because the soldiers who heard the rifle and artillery fire from Baldwin's battle were on the north side of the North Fork as they were inspecting Farnsworth's battle site, they were 9 miles or more from Baldwin's battle. That may seem like a long distance to be able to hear the sounds of guns and artillery, but the prevailing wind in this region is from the southwest, and this may have allowed the troopers to hear the sounds.

As to the location of Farnsworth's battle, one of the most important clues (overlooked by other researchers) is Lieutenant Baldwin's diary entry for November 9, 1874: "As I had been directed to conduct the train to Big Springs on N.F., I assumed charge of it and escort, arriving at the point designated about 2 P.M. and learning for the first time that Maj. Price was in close proximity to the scene of my fight yesterday and if he had moved up could have annihilated that band of Indians. . . . We camped here for the night."[13]

The camp that Baldwin refers to is at the Big Springs, on the North Fork of the Red River just west of the present community of Lefors in Gray County. A well-known and favored campsite for the military, the springs are mentioned in several military documents. Baldwin writes: "We hear today that Lieut. Farnsworth of the 8th Cav. had a fight with the Indians three or four miles below this [camp], and it is generally

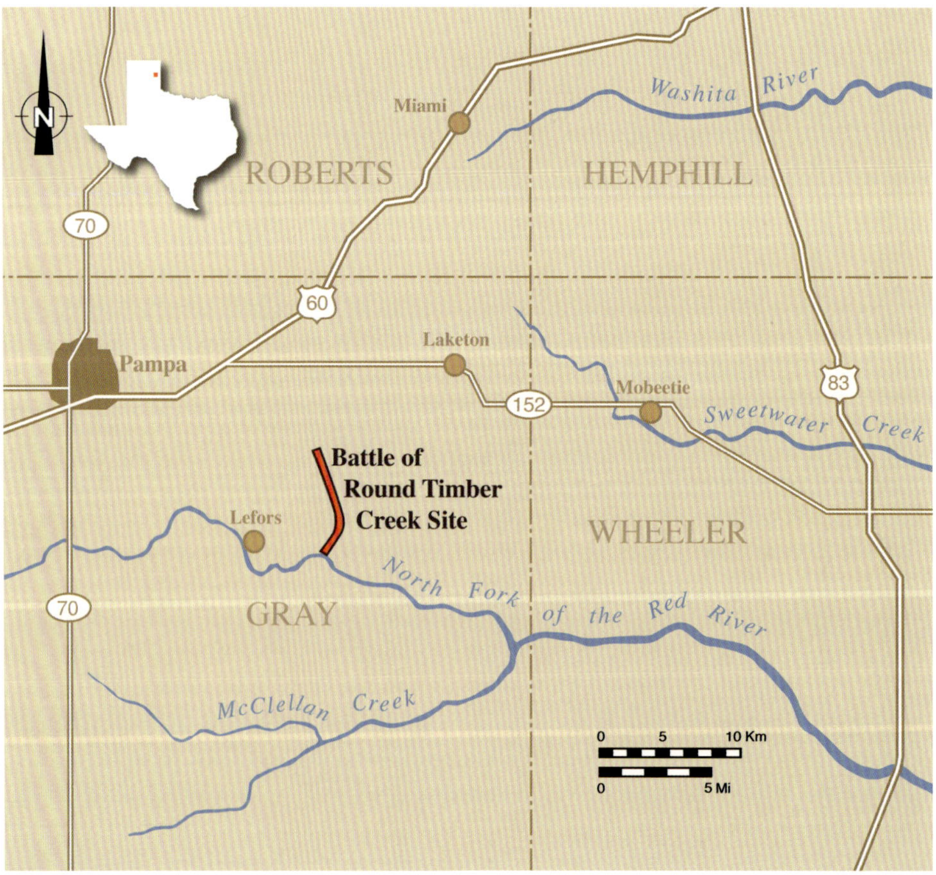

Fig. 11.4. The Battle of Round Timber Creek took place near the North Fork of the Red River in present Gray County, Texas. Illustration by Roland Pantermuehl

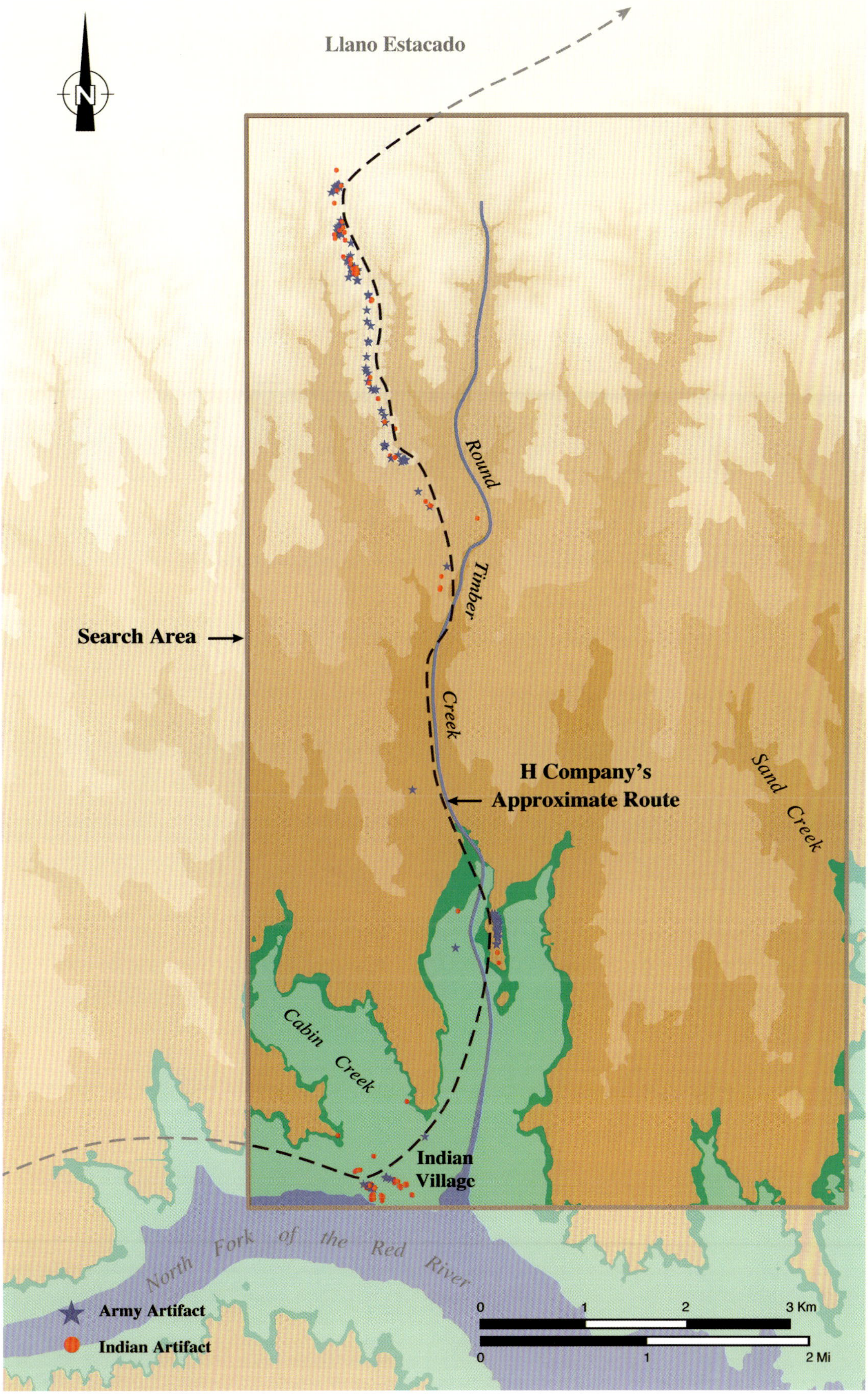

Fig. 11.5. The battle started at the site of Grey Beard's village near the mouth of Cabin Creek and continued northward up the valley of Round Timber Creek until the soldiers were able to reach the Llano Estacado, a distance of about 6 miles. Illustration by Roland Pantermuehl

believed that he was badly whipped. He claimed a grand victory though he lost everything he had in the shape of baggage, including ammunition, two men killed and six wounded—will probably learn more in time."[14]

Archeological Investigations and Results

Lieutenant Baldwin's statement that Farnsworth's battle took place 3–4 miles below or east of Big Springs—along with the other information gathered from the court-martial testimonies, exhibits, and reports—allowed us to identify an area in which to begin the archeological survey. This search area is in Gray County in the eastern Texas Panhandle about 15 miles southeast of the modern community of Pampa (fig. 11.4). The search area extended roughly from Cabin Creek on the west to Sand Creek on the east, and from the valley of the North Fork of the Red River on the south to the edge of the Llano Estacado escarpment on the north. The area measures approximately 6.4 km (4 miles) east–west and 9.7 km (6 miles) north–south (fig. 11.5).

The topography of the area is highly dissected, with numerous draws and streams that head along the edge of the escarpment of the plains and flow into the North Fork of the Red River. The ridges separating the draws and streams typically have steep sides and narrow crests. Several streams in the area are spring fed and usually flow, at least intermittently, all year. These include Thut Creek, Cabin Creek, and Cantonment Creek. Surface elevations across the area range from approximately 950 m (3,117 feet) above sea level along the edge of the escarpment to 823 m (2,700 feet) above sea level in the bed of the North Fork. Presently, the area from the edge of the plains to the valley of the North Fork is used primarily for cattle ranching, and the surface of the Llano Estacado is generally used for crop production, mainly wheat and grain sorghum. In the past, the area experienced extensive oil and gas exploration, but today these activities account for only a small portion of the local economy.

The archeological survey of the area was accomplished in April and May 2003. Near the mouth of Cabin Creek—in the southwest corner of the search area where several pipelines, a railroad grade, and Route 1321 have severely impacted the area—the archeological survey team found artifacts that suggested an occupation by a historic Indian group (fig. 11.6). In this area along both sides of Cabin Creek, the team recovered artifacts that included items usually considered unique to Indian village sites of the nineteenth century, including iron arrowheads, cut metal fragments, horseshoe nails, horse tack, knives, spoons, and buckles. In addition, there were cut pieces of brass kettles altered by filed serrations as hide-preparation tools and several iron objects altered by filing to serve a cutting or scraping purpose. Scattered among these Indian items were fired and unfired .50/70-caliber cartridge cases and fired Spencer and .44-caliber cartridge cases. These findings confirmed a late 1860s to mid-1870s occupation for the site. The Spencer and .44-caliber cartridge cases we found were typical of those associated with Indian firearms of the period. Because the 8th Cavalry was using only .50-caliber carbines, we believed that the majority of the .50/70 cartridge cases must have been fired by army carbines of the types that Company H of the 8th Cavalry was using in 1874—namely Sharps, Remingtons, Springfields, and Ward-Burtons (appendix B). This was later confirmed by the detailed analysis of the firing pin imprints on the cartridge case heads (see appendix H).

The recovered fired cartridge cases suggest that at least part of the November 6, 1874, engagement between the 8th Cavalry scout patrol and the Cheyenne warriors took place here, which the other recovered artifacts indicate was the site of the Cheyenne village. Lieutenant Farnsworth does not mention the Cheyenne village in either of his reports, but a statement by Major Price suggests that it played a prominent role in the battle. He reported that Colonel Davidson burned an Indian village that was "on both sides of this stream," was "in the immediate vicinity of Capt. Farnsworth's fight," and had been "hurriedly abandoned."[15] Furthermore, the sketch of the battle on the piece of paper Colonel Davidson found in a crotch of a tree while at the village site clearly establishes that Farnsworth and the patrol initially engaged the Indians at their village.

Whether the scout patrol attacked the Indian village or was ambushed by the Indian warriors as it approached the village is not entirely certain, but the consensus among the available accounts is that the Indians ambushed the patrol. Farnsworth seems to agree: "They [the Indians] were evidently appraised of my coming and had all the advantage of ground." Scout J. T. Marshall was not with Farnsworth at the battle but nevertheless states that the patrol was ambushed as it neared the village. Marshall, who claimed the Indian with Farnsworth was an Arapaho, wrote, "The Arrapahoe disappeared in the fight, and it is thought by some that he led the soldiers in this decoy [ambush]." Marshall also claimed that the Indians who attacked the patrol were Kiowas, though Farnsworth clearly states that they were Cheyennes. Finally, in his diary entry for November 11, 1874, Pvt. John Hechner of Company C, 5th Infantry, wrote, "They [men of the 6th Cavalry] confirmed the report that the Indians had succeeded in drawing 25 men of the 8th Cav. into an ambush and killing one & wounding several."[16]

The archeological evidence recovered at the village site suggests that the troopers did not remain in the village long before they began making a retreat. Only eighteen army cartridges and twenty-three Indian cartridges were recovered at the village location. It appears that from the village the patrol retreated northeast to the ridge that separates Cabin Creek and Round Timber Creek. On the crest of this ridge, the archeological survey team recovered five fired army-associated cartridge cases. Analysis of the firing pin imprints on the heads of the recovered cartridges shows that they were fired from five different guns. Apparently at least five soldiers stopped on the crest of the ridge long enough to fire one round each at the Indians, who were presumably in pursuit of the patrol. Still retreating to the northeast, the patrol made its way to the crest of another ridge on the east side of Round Timber Creek, where the soldiers stopped and took a defensive position (fig. 11.7). One can infer, based on the recovery here of 102 fired cartridge cases, that the patrol was apparently at this location for a substantial amount of time.

The common procedure for a cavalry defensive position was for the troopers to dismount and for every fourth soldier to hold and secure the horses. For a twenty-eight-man unit, at least seven men would be holding the horses and pack mules as the other twenty-one men fired at the Indians. The distribution and position of the recovered cartridges just below the crest on the east side of the ridge suggest that the troopers were firing in a west or southwest direction toward the terrace along Round Timber Creek. However, the survey team found no Indian-associated cartridges and only a single .50-caliber Sharps bullet on the terrace.

A closer examination of the area along Round Timber Creek where the bullet was found revealed that, at some point in the not-too-distant past, most of the terrace along the east side of Round Timber Creek had been mechanically removed in an apparent effort to straighten and rechannel the creek for flood control. The rechanneling may have been done in conjunction with the installation of a petroleum pipeline that now crosses the creek in this area. It appears that removal of the terrace took away the evidence that this was the primary Indian firing position. A single Indian cartridge was found west of the ridge on the west side of Round Timber Creek, and two additional Indian cartridges were found on the south end of the ridge where the army cartridges

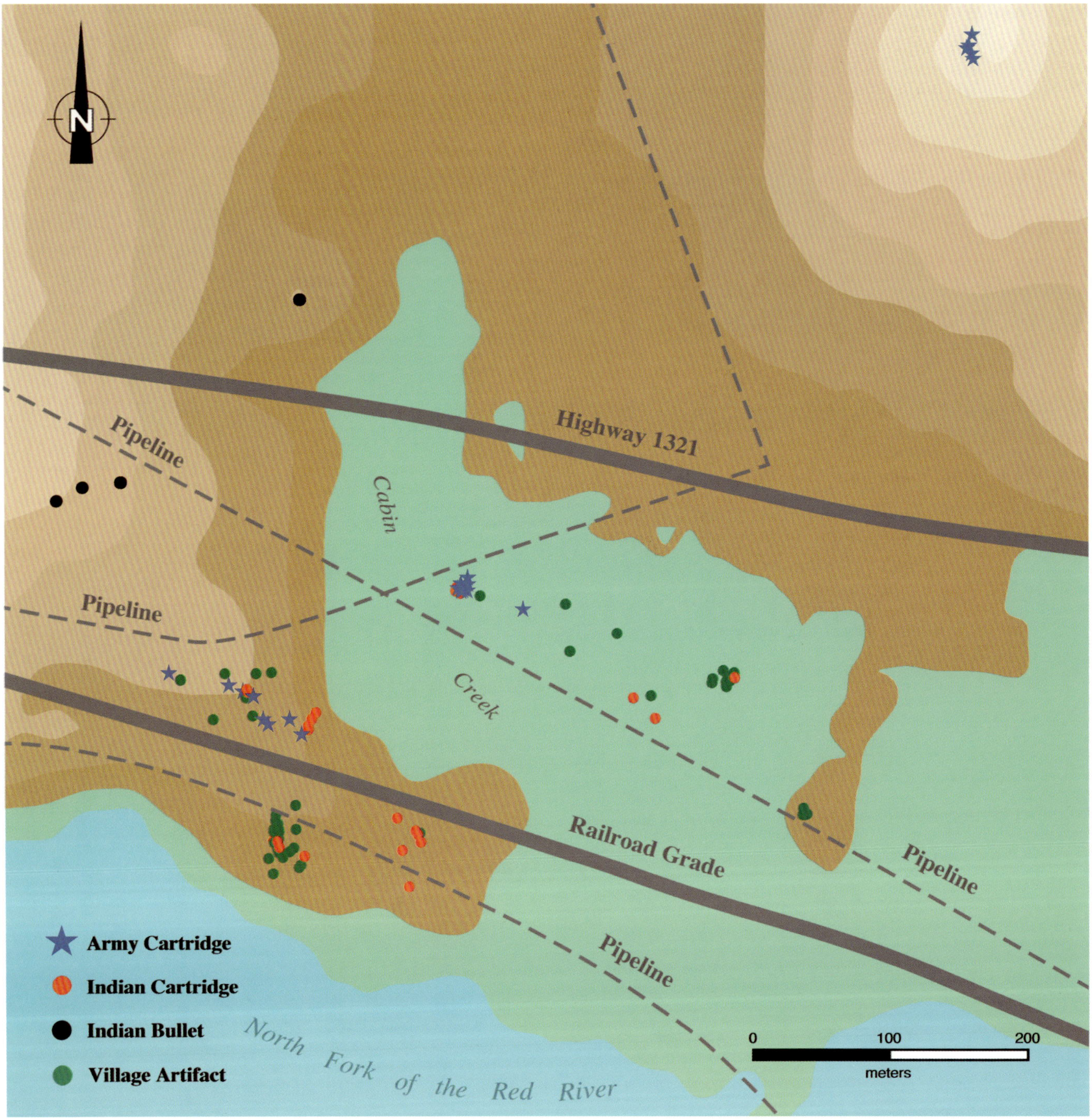

Fig. 11.6. Even though modern highway, railroad, and pipeline construction have severely impacted the site of Grey Beard's village, the mapped distribution of artifacts at the site helped confirm that the battle began here. Illustration by Roland Pantermuehl

were recovered. Though the Indian-associated cartridges indicate that at least some of the Indians were in these positions, we believe that most of the Indian combatants were situated along the bank of Round Timber Creek, southwest of the army's defensive position on the ridge.

The few Indian cartridges we recovered on the ridge near the army defensive position suggest that some of the Indians were on the west and south sides of the ridge and may have been trying to surround the troopers. At some point the troopers remounted and abandoned the ridge. It appears that upon leaving the ridge the troopers dropped down into the valley of Round Timber Creek and headed north (see fig. 11.5). Perhaps

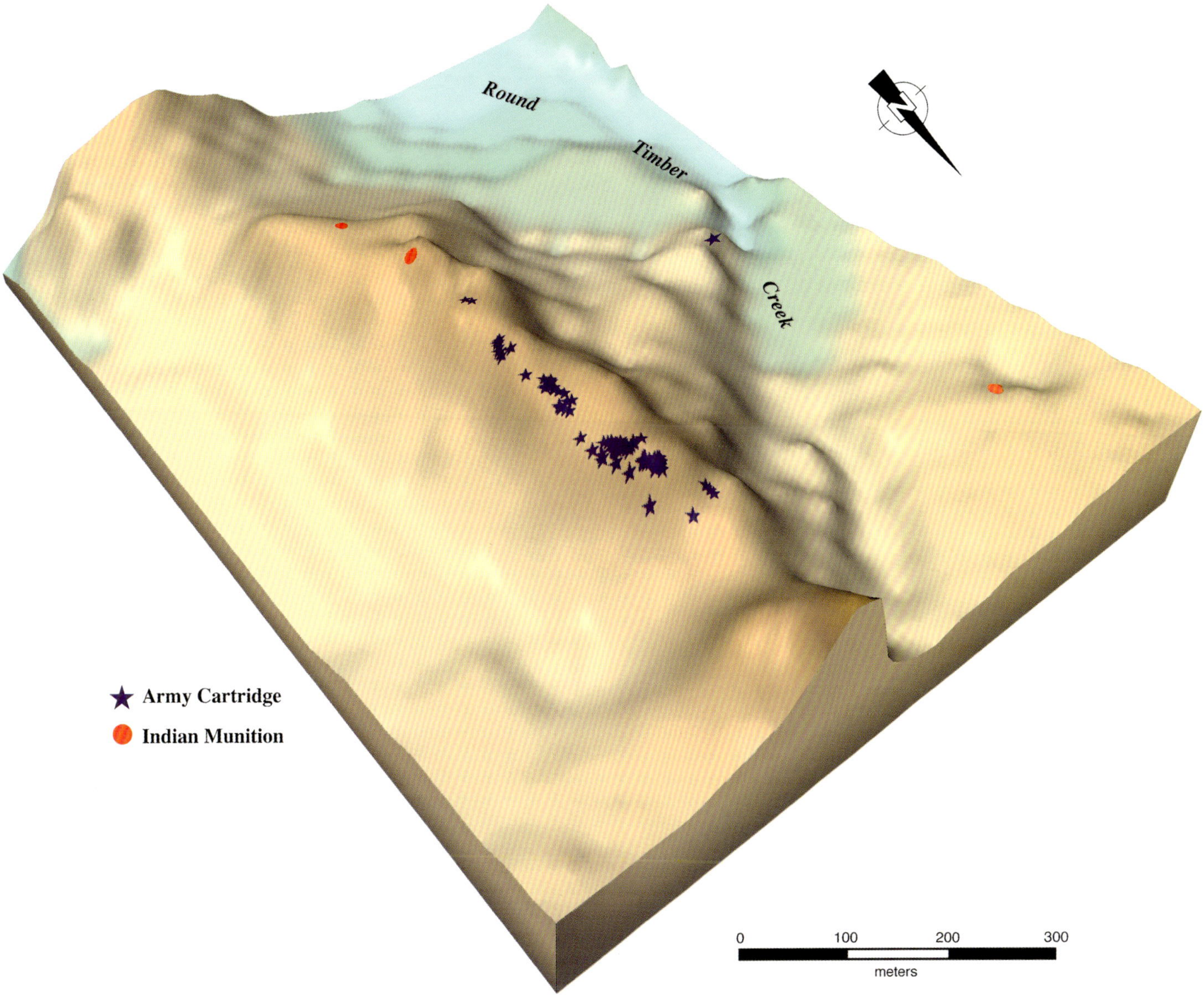

Fig. 11.7. On a ridge east of Round Timber Creek, the soldiers made their first defensive stance. Illustration by Roland Pantermuehl

the patrol decided to try to outrun the Indians and thought the valley of Round Timber Creek, rather than the more dissected ridge crests, would provide easier travel. The patrol made its way up the creek bed for approximately 3 km (1.86 miles), where, on the west side of Round Timber Creek, they reached the base of a high, narrow ridge they hoped would lead them out of the creek valley and onto the plains. Initially the patrol may have been able to outrun the Indians, for little fire was apparently exchanged while the patrol made its way up the creek valley. But the patrol had already traveled some 23 miles that morning before encountering the Indians; their horses were most likely thoroughly exhausted. The archeological remains provide evidence that, by the time the patrol reached the high ridge and began their ascent to the crest, the Indian pursuers had nearly caught up to them.

As the metal detector survey team worked its way up the slope of the high ridge, they found several fired .50/70-caliber cartridges as well as a few unfired .50/70 cartridges and .45-caliber Colt pistol cartridges. These artifacts confirmed that the troopers had used the slope to gain access to the ridge crest. When the survey team reached

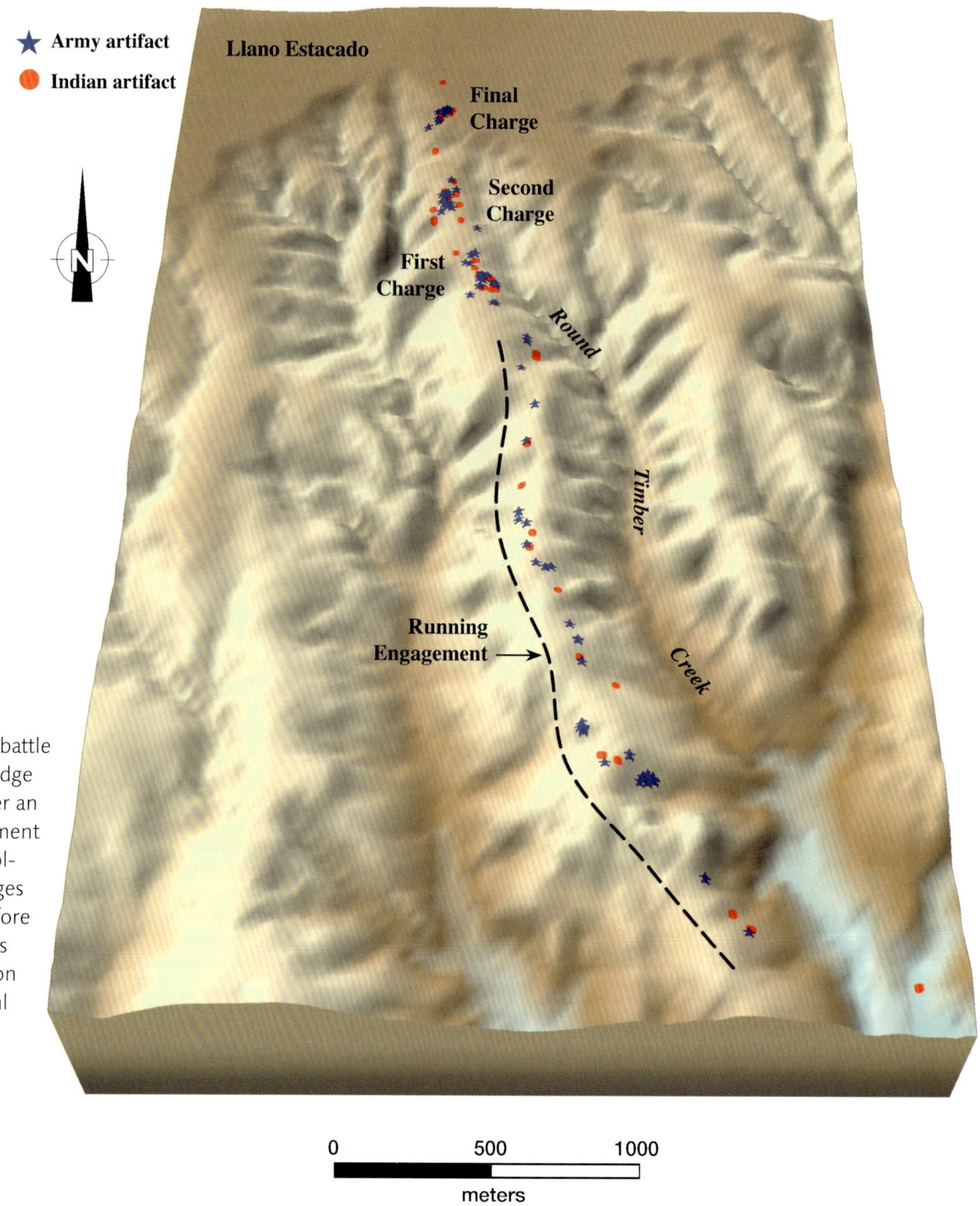

Fig. 11.8. Most of the battle took place on a high ridge west of the creek. After an initial running engagement on the ridgetop, the soldiers made three charges against the Indians before they reached the plains and escaped. Illustration by Roland Pantermuehl

the ridge crest, they discovered additional battle-related artifacts in a long linear pattern that stretched for more than 1.7 km (1.1 mile) along the ridge crest (fig. 11.8). Most of these artifacts were associated with the 8th Cavalry troopers and included nineteen fired .50-caliber Sharps and Springfield cartridge cases, a pocket knife, a butter knife, a dutch oven, a frying pan, five horseshoes, two mule shoes, a harness strap buckle, and a bridle buckle. Also discovered were thirteen Indian-associated artifacts: eleven fired cartridges (.44-caliber Henrys, .40/70 Sharps, and .56-caliber Spencers) and two .50-caliber rifle balls.

The long linear distribution of the relatively small number of artifacts suggests that the artifacts were deposited as a result of a running engagement, apparently when the

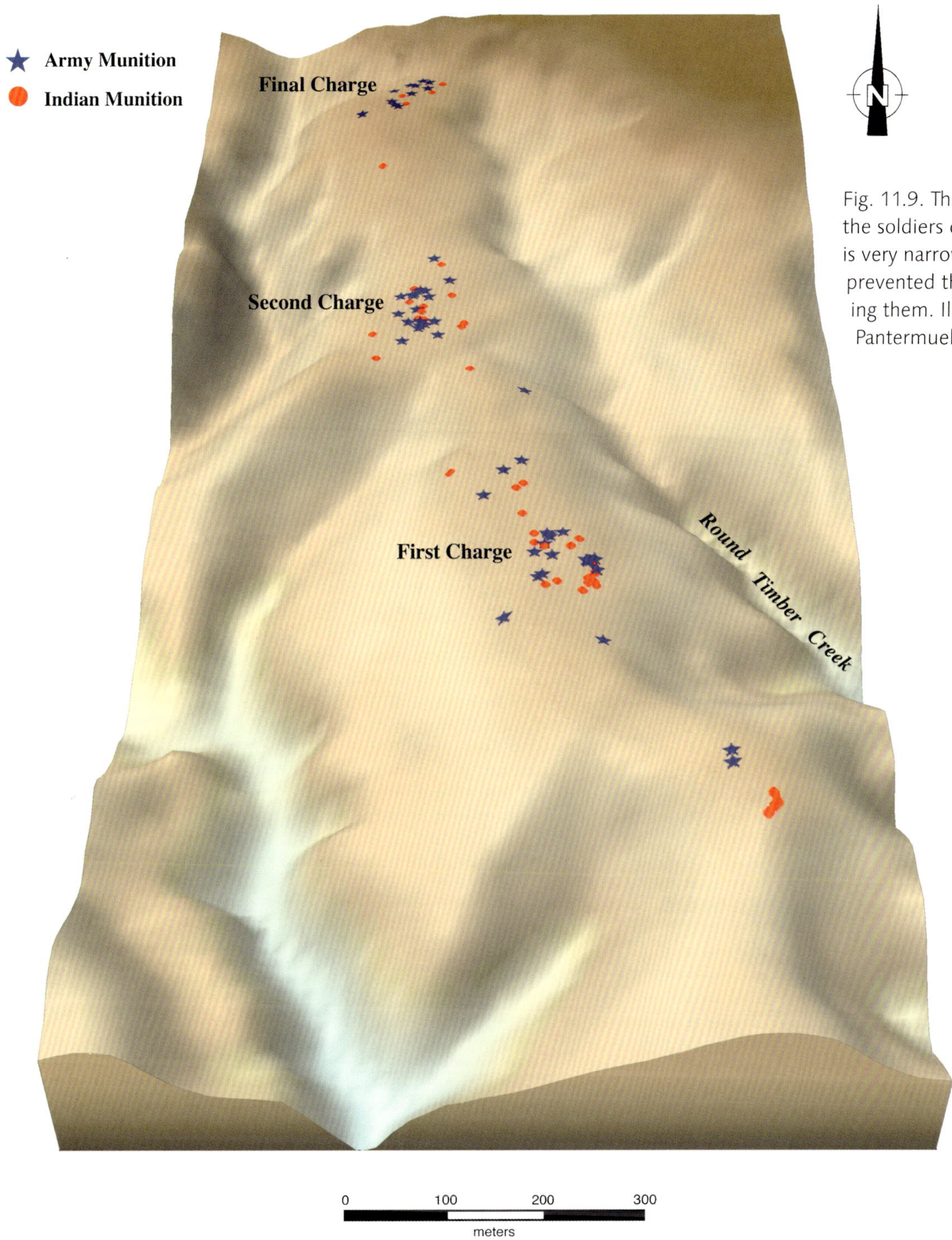

Fig. 11.9. The high ridge where the soldiers charged the Indians is very narrow, which may have prevented the Indians from flanking them. Illustration by Roland Pantermuehl

troopers were retreating northward along the narrow crest of the ridge (fig. 11.9). The frying pan, dutch oven, and butter knife are evidence that the troopers were losing some of their camp equipage during this portion of the engagement. In addition, at least one army horse and a mule may have been killed during this stage of the battle; four of the five recovered horseshoes were all found within a few feet of each other, as were the two mule shoes and the harness strap buckle. Apparently the Indians were quickly closing in on the retreating soldiers.

The running engagement between troopers and pursuing Indians appears to have

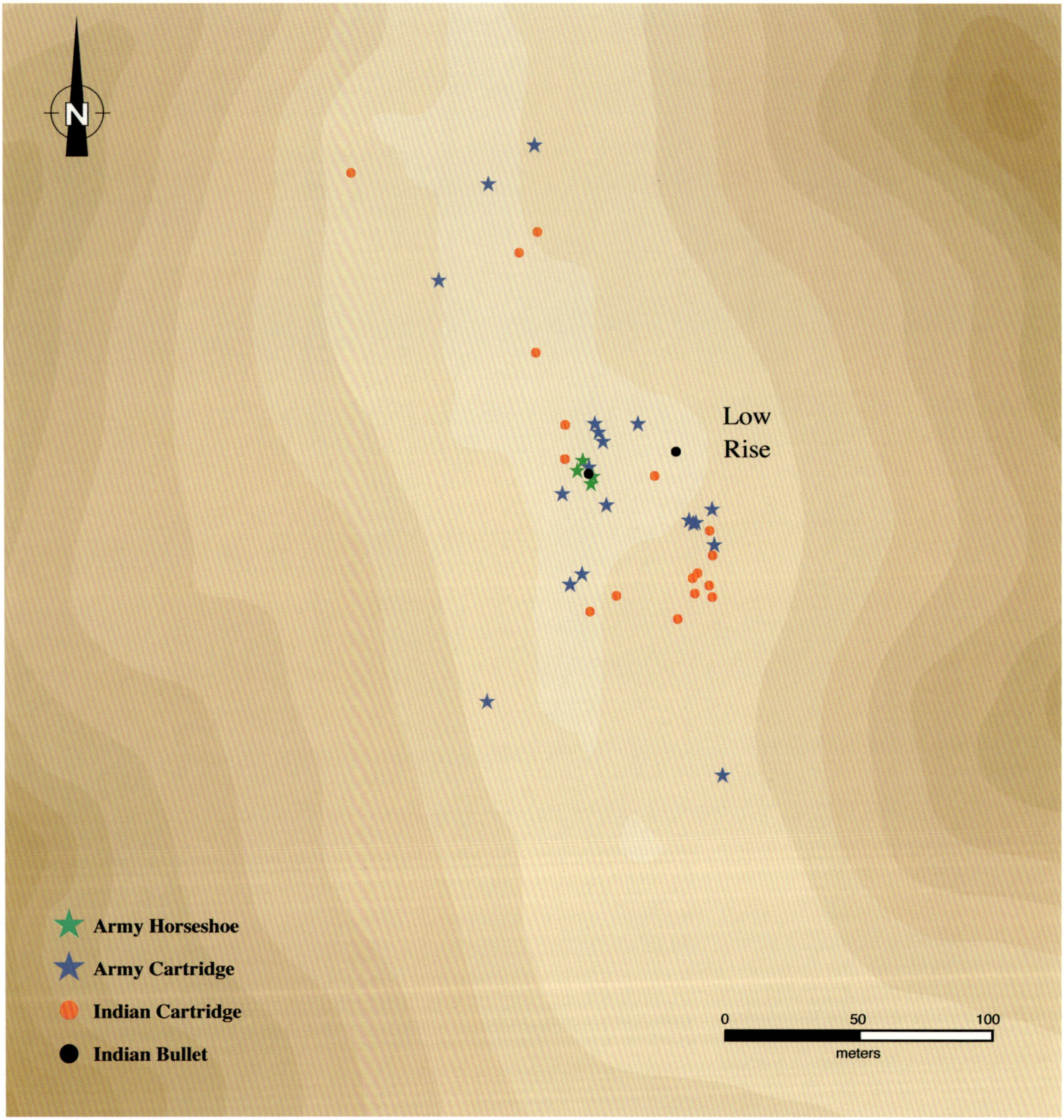

Fig. 11.10. At a low rise on the ridge, the soldiers made their first charge against the Indians. Illustration by Roland Pantermuehl

ended when the troopers reached a low rise on the ridge crest about 650 m (711 yards) south of the edge of the plains. Army- and Indian-associated cartridge cases were found on the rise, and the distribution of the recovered cartridges suggests that the troopers attempted to make a charge against the Indians (fig. 11.10). It is not clear why the troopers stopped here, but after the running engagement up the ridge they may have needed to rest their horses and allow any stragglers to catch up. Whatever the reason, it is apparent that the Indians closed in quickly and took cover behind the lower southeast side of the rise.

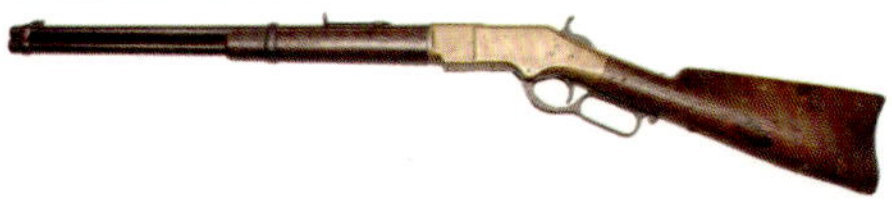

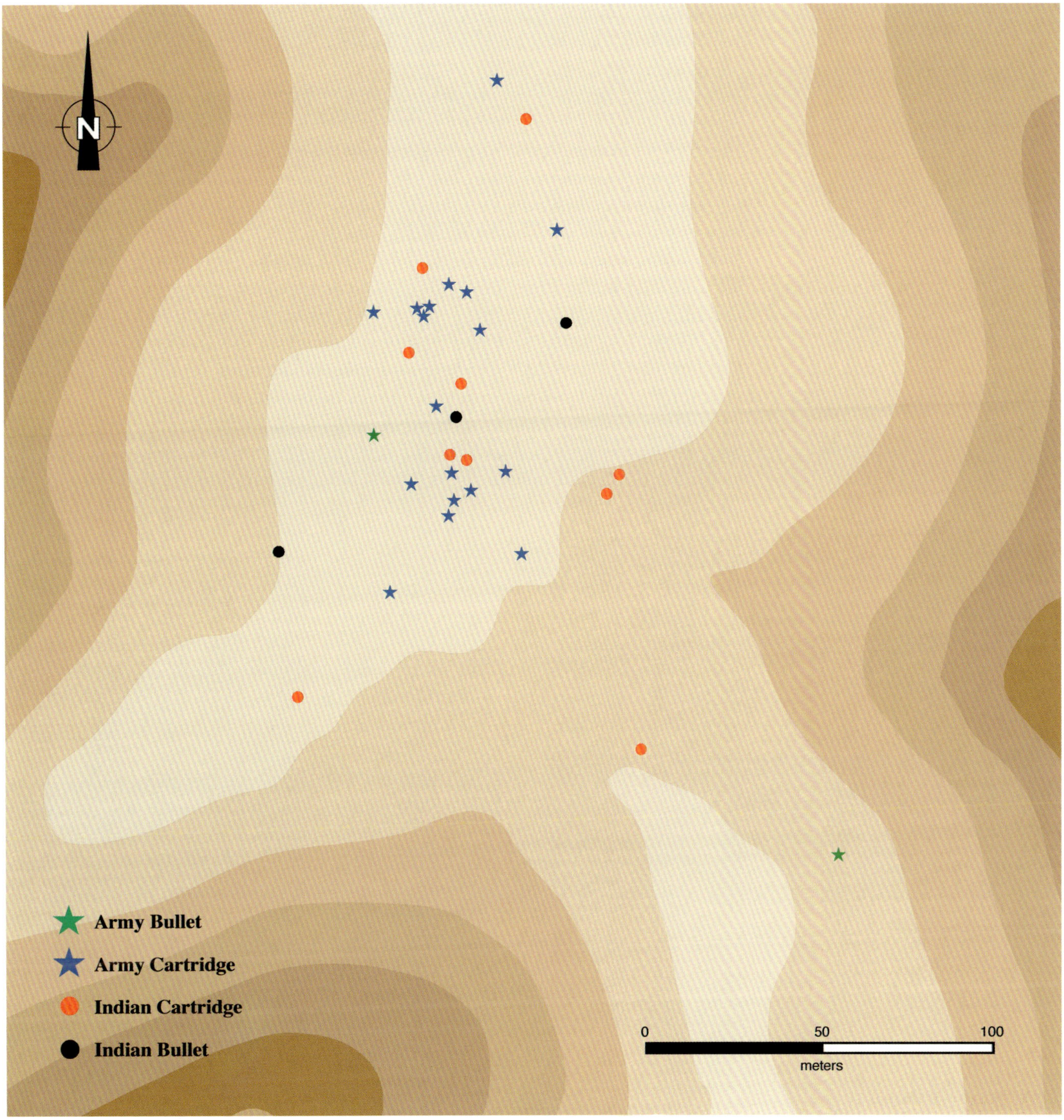

Fig. 11.11. The soldiers' second charge took place about 350 m north of the first charge. Illustration by Roland Pantermuehl

The distribution of recovered cartridges on this portion of the ridge indicates that the Indian positions were only 30–50 m (33–55 yards) from where most of the army cartridges were recovered on the low rise. It seems unlikely that the troopers would have allowed the Indians to get this close. Two scenarios could explain the apparent close proximity. In one, the troopers paused here just long enough to fire several rounds at the Indians, but they did not make any kind of concerted stand before continuing their retreat up the ridge. The Indians then moved up and used the low rise as cover while they fired several shots at the retreating troopers. In this scenario, the troopers and Indians would not have been in close proximity to each other and the low rise would have been used by both groups, but at different times.

In the second scenario, the troopers and Indians were in relatively close proximity at the low rise, and the troopers may have tried to charge the Indians and drive them back. Both Lieutenant Farnsworth and Major Price state in their reports that the troopers made several charges against the Indians. Farnsworth, for example, says that Henry Fields, the company blacksmith, participated in two charges even though he had already suffered two wounds.[17] Is this where the troopers made one of their charges? Several lines of evidence suggest that it is.

For one, if the troopers did not stop at the low rise, then the long, linear artifact distribution pattern, attributed to the running engagement on the southern portion of the ridge, most likely would have continued up to and beyond the low rise. But that is not the case; the artifacts on the low rise are more numerous and clustered together. The fact that the cartridge cases are clustered relatively close together indicates that at least some of the firing here occurred from more-or-less stationary positions.

Furthermore, the Indians were apparently close enough to the troopers to kill another army horse, as indicated by the recovery of four horseshoes grouped together and a bullet from an Indian's Spencer rifle near the center of the horseshoe cluster (fig. 11.10).

Finally, it appears that at least one of the soldiers charged the Indians who were behind the low rise, for several army-associated .50-caliber cartridges, all fired from the same Sharps carbine, were recovered there.

The nineteen army-associated cartridges recovered at the low rise were fired from eight individual guns, whereas the seventeen Indian-associated cartridges were fired from seven guns. It appears that the troopers' tactic here was for several of them to charge the Indian position while the others moved to the next position along the ridge, where they could then provide cover fire for the first group of soldiers as they completed their charge and fell back to the new position.

About 350 m (383 yards) north of the first charge, the second group of troopers took a position to provide cover fire for the group that made the first charge (fig. 11.11). The second group may have then made a charge toward the pursuing Indians, for here we found eighteen army cartridges fired from ten individual carbines. Three army carbines found at the locations of both charges were Sharps guns 1 and 8 and Springfield gun 2. Ten Indian cartridges from six individual guns were recovered here as well, including some of the Indian guns identified at the site of the first charge.

As the Indians pressed their attack, the troopers continued to move northward along the ridge crest. Just before they reached the plateau, the patrol made its third and final charge, approximately 300 m (328 yards) north of the second charge. Here ten army cartridges representing eight individual carbines and a .45-caliber Colt pistol were recovered (fig. 11.12). One unfired Colt cartridge was also recovered. Of the army carbines represented at this charge, only Sharps gun 5 was also represented at the location of the second charge. Only three Indian-associated cartridges, each fired from different guns, were found here, along with three bullets from Indian guns. Evidence from the archeological remains suggests that eight or so troopers either made a final charge toward the Indians or at least held this position long enough for the other members of the patrol, several of whom were now riding two men to a horse, to make their escape from the ridge and onto the plains.

By this time, the running battle had lasted four to five hours and darkness had settled over the battle site. According to Lieutenant Farnsworth, the patrol's ammunition was exhausted and they finally escaped the Indians under the cover of darkness. The patrol rode about 45 miles during the night and made it back to the headquarters

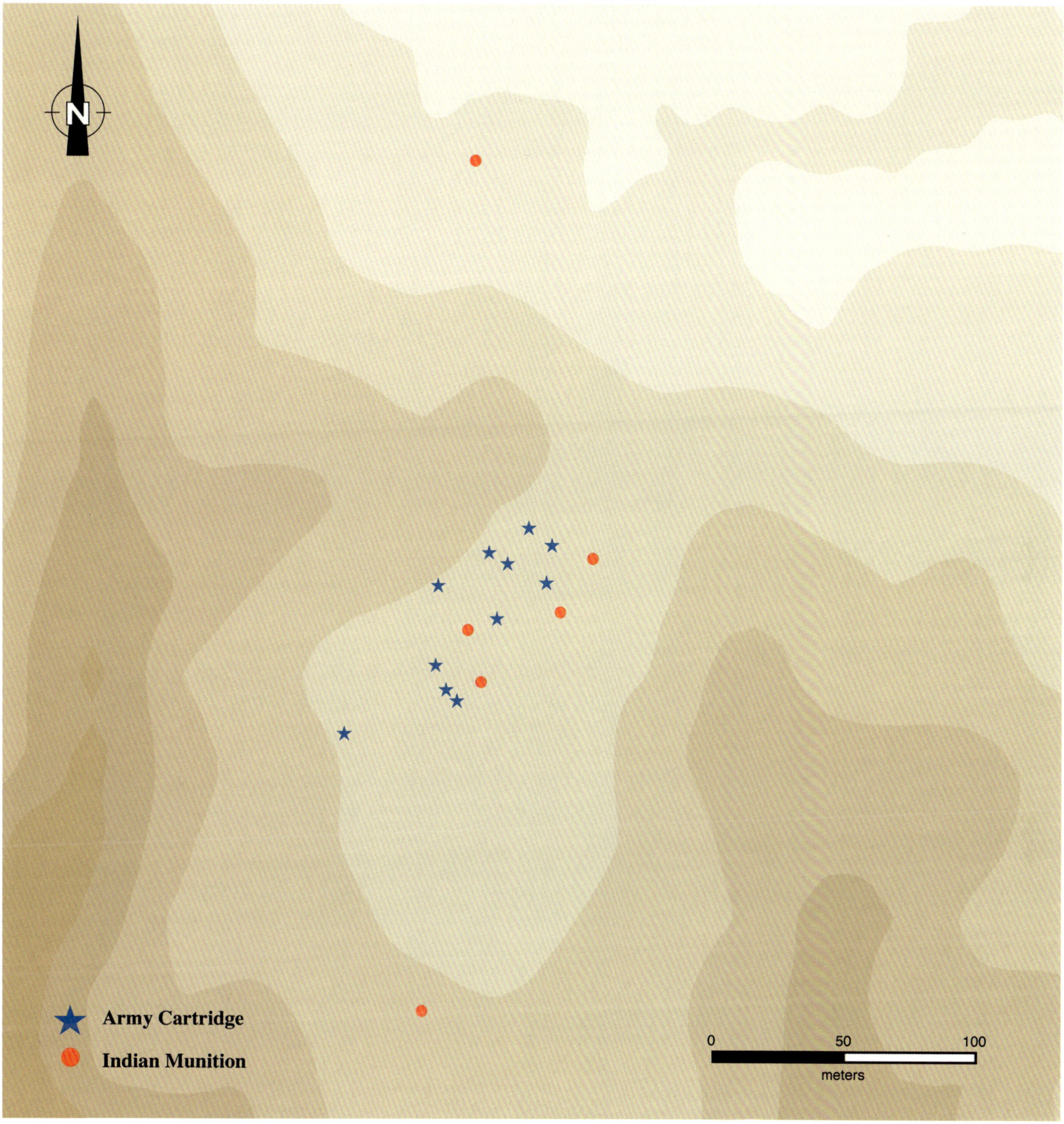

Fig. 11.12. In their third and final charge, just below the crest of the escarpment, the troopers finally made their escape. Illustration by Roland Pantermuehl

camp on the Washita River early the next morning. Pvt. William Densham was killed during the battle and left on the battlefield, as were all six pack mules and six horses. Losing six horses meant that some of the soldiers had to "double up" on the remaining horses both during the battle and on the retreat back to the Washita camp. Four soldiers were wounded (see table 11.1). At some point during the retreat, a second soldier, Pvt. Rufus Hibbard, became separated from the command and was killed by the Indians, who apparently continued to pursue the soldiers for some distance during the night before they broke off the engagement.

A decade later, in 1885, Henry J. Farnsworth, now a captain, was up for promotion to assistant inspector general with the rank of major. It was reported in two Washington, D.C., newspapers, however, that Gen. Nelson Miles had filed a protest against the promotion to President Cleveland. The *National Republican* reported, "General Miles charges that Captain Farnsworth, during the Cheyenne Indian war in Texas in 1874, showed cowardice in the face of the enemy." The following statement was published in the *Washington Critic*: "It is asserted that Gen. Nelson A. Miles will silently forward to President Cleveland, for his information, an official statement of an occurrence in the military history of the officer [Farnsworth] who was this week selected for appointment as major, which came under his own observation, and which will show the unfitness of the officer for such promotion."[18]

The assertions by General Miles, if he ever actually made them, would almost certainly have been related to Farnsworth's actions at the Battle of Round Timber Creek, since Farnsworth was not directly involved in any other battles or skirmishes during the 1874 campaign. Our examination of the military reports and official correspondence files failed to reveal anything specific that would indicate that Farnsworth "showed cowardice in the face of the enemy." It is curious, however, that on November 7, when Farnsworth wrote his first brief report about the November 6 encounter with the Cheyenne, he apparently was unaware Private Hibbard was missing from the command and had been killed. In his report he wrote that only Private Densham was killed during the engagement. Not until Farnsworth's second report, written on November 12, does he acknowledge that Hibbard was also killed when he became separated from the command during the retreat to the supply camp.

Is it possible that during the desperate retreat to escape the Indians, Farnsworth failed to ensure that all of his men were accounted for, abandoning Private Hibbard and leaving him to his own devices to make it back to the safety of the supply camp? This appears to be precisely what happened, as Pvt. John Hechner of Company C, 5th Infantry, who served under Colonel Miles, commented in his diary entry for November 14, 1874: "The Cav [8th Cavalry] was forced to retreat & leave the dismounted man [Private Hibbard] behind. Lt. Baldwin found him afterwards dead with his cartridge boxes empty."[19]

If General Miles ever formally made the protest against Farnsworth as reported in the newspapers, President Cleveland apparently chose to ignore it, because Farnsworth received the promotion. Maj. Henry J. Farnsworth served as assistant inspector general until his death on November 19, 1888. He is buried at Arlington National Cemetery.

Artifacts Recovered

During the archeological investigations of the Battle of Round Timber Creek site, a total of 308 battle-related artifacts were recovered (table 11.2). Of these, 209 are associated with the army and ninety-nine with the Indians. An additional fifty-eight Indian-associated items not related to the battle were found at the site of Grey Beard's village (table 11.3). The analyses of the artifacts recovered from the battle site and from Grey Beard's village site are included as appendix H. Most of the artifacts from the battle site are cartridges, including 242 fired and seventeen unfired cartridge cases. The fired cases are .40-caliber cases fired in Sharps carbines; .44-caliber cases fired in Henry or Winchester Model 1866 rifles; .44-caliber cases fired in a Smith & Wesson Russian Model revolver; .45-caliber Colt cases; .45/55 or .45/70 Springfield cases; .50-caliber cases fired in Remington, Sharps, Springfield, and Ward-Burton carbines; and Spencer cartridge cases in .50- and .56-calibers.

Table 11.2. Artifacts from the Battle of Round Timber Creek Site

Item	*Army*	*Indian*	*Total*
Artifacts Related to Munitions			
.40/70-caliber cartridge case fired in Sharps		3	3
.44-caliber cartridge case, fired		8	8
.44-caliber Smith & Wesson Russian, fired	3		3
.45-caliber Colt cartridge case, fired	1		1
.45-caliber Colt cartridge case, unfired	4		4
.45-caliber cartridge case fired in Springfield		2	2
.45-caliber cartridge case, unfired		1	1
.50/70-caliber cartridge case fired in Remington	7		7
.50/70-caliber cartridge case fired in Sharps	103	22	125
.50/70-caliber cartridge case fired in Springfield	28	3	31
.50/70-caliber cartridge case fired in Ward-Burton	23		23
.50/70-caliber unidentified cartridge case, fired		5	5
.50/70-caliber cartridge case, unfired	10		10
.56/50-caliber Spencer cartridge case, fired		4	4
.56/56-caliber Spencer cartridge case, fired		30	30
.56/56-caliber Spencer cartridge case, unfired		2	2
.44-caliber bullet		4	4
.45-caliber Springfield bullet		1	1
.50-caliber Spencer bullet		7	7
.50-caliber bullet	10		10
.50-caliber Minié ball		1	1
.50-caliber ball		4	4
percussion cap tin		2	2
Subtotal, munitions	189	99	288
Other Artifacts			
buckle, bridle	1		1
butter knife	1		1
carbine ring	1		1
carbine sling swivel	1		1
dutch oven	1		1
frying pan	1		1
horseshoe	10		10
mule shoe	2		2
nail, square	2		2
Subtotal, other	20		20
Total artifacts	**209**	**99**	**308**

Table 11.3. Artifacts from Grey Beard's Village Site

Item	*Total*
arrowpoint	2
buckle	6
button, military	6
button, clothing	1
can, leaded	2
chisel	1
combination tool	1
concha	1
curb chain	1
cut iron and brass	5
edged tool	7
file	1
food grater	3
horseshoe nail, unused	7
knife	3
nail, square	6
saddle ring	1
scissors	1
spoon	1
thimble	1
unidentified	1
Total artifacts	**58**

Bullets from the various cartridge types were also recovered, as well as a .50-caliber Minié ball and four .50-caliber rifle balls. These items suggest that at least some of the Indians were using old rifled muskets and muzzle loaders during the battle.

Other items recovered from the battle site and associated with the army include horse shoes, mule shoes, a carbine sling and swivel, a dutch oven, a frying pan, and a knife from an army mess kit. The horse and mule shoes and the camp equipment items mark where some of the army horses and mules were killed during the battle as well as where some of the army supplies and equipment were lost.

A variety of metal tools and other metal items were recovered from the Indian village site, including horse tack and equipment, metal edged tools, buttons, a thimble, spoon, scissors, file, chisel, and knives. Although modern construction activities have had a severe impact on the village site, a sufficient number of artifacts were recovered

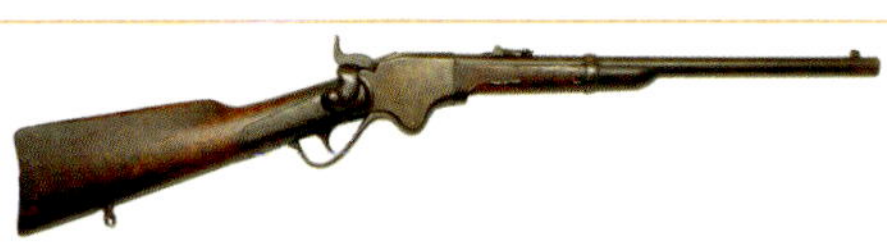

Table 11.4. Firearm Types Used at the Battle of Round Timber Creek

Firearm Type	*Army-Associated*	*Indian-Associated*	*Total*
.40-caliber Sharps rifle		1	1
.44-caliber Smith & Wesson Russian Model revolver	1		1
.44-caliber Henry or Winchester M1866 rifle or carbine		1	1
.45-caliber Colt M1873 revolver	1		1
.45-caliber Springfield rifle or carbine		2	2
.50-caliber Plains rifle or trade gun		1	1
.50-caliber muzzle loader musket or carbine		1	1
.50-caliber Springfield M1868 or 1870 rifle or carbine	9	3	12
.50-caliber Sharps carbine	28	10	38
.50-caliber Remington carbine	5		5
.50-caliber Ward-Burton carbine	14		14
.50-caliber unidentified carbine		2	2
.50- and .56-caliber Spencer carbines		8	8
Total	**58**	**29**	**87**

to identify the site and to provide at least a partial inventory of the types of artifacts associated with a Southern Cheyenne village site of the 1870s.

Discussion

Analysis of the cartridge cases and bullets from the battle site indicate that at least thirteen types of guns were used in the fight (table 11.4). Among these are Plains rifles or trade guns, muzzle loaders, pistols, and rifles or carbines in .40-, .44-, .45-, and .50-calibers. On the basis of cartridge case and bullet evidence, at least eighty-seven individual weapons were used in the fight.

Of the eighty-seven individual weapons, fifty-eight are associated with the 8th Cavalry troopers and twenty-nine with Indian combatants. The fifty-eight army-associated firearms present a puzzling question: how can fifty-eight firearms (two pistols and fifty-six .50-caliber carbines) be associated with twenty-eight soldiers? As unlikely as it seems, the most plausible explanation is that each of the soldiers carried two carbines. According to the 1874 ordnance returns (appendix B), Company H of the 8th Cavalry was primarily using .50-caliber Sharps carbines, but they also had .50-caliber Ward-Burton, Remington, and Springfield carbines. These carbines were considered experimental, and it may be that the troopers each carried two carbines in case the experimental models malfunctioned. It had been observed during field trials that all of these carbines experienced some problems, though the Springfield was often cited as the preferred weapon. As Captain Elijah Wells stated in a special report:

> I have used the experimental arms a long time, and find that the Sharps' carbine fouls in the breech by use, and, after being fired a number of times, the lever-bar does not work smoothly; also, the extractor does not extract the shells properly. The Remington, also, does not extract the shells properly. The extractor only draws the shell a short distance, when they have to be taken out with the fingers. Sometimes they expand, and cannot be withdrawn without considerable difficulty. The Ward-Burton fails often to explode the cartridge, which is caused by the firing-pin spring becoming weak. The extractor is good, but as the piece is always cocked, and there are so many motions which consume time in working

> the gun, it is not, in my opinion, adapted for the cavalry service. The Springfield has a good extractor. The firing-pin does not become weak, and it is no more liable to get out of order than either of the other guns. It is well made, and is, in my opinion, the best carbine for use in cavalry service.[20]

In principle, some of the identified army .50-caliber carbines could have been used by Indian combatants rather than troopers, but this does not appear to be the case, since the cartridges from the identified guns were recovered only from locations on the battle site that were clearly associated with soldiers. For example, at the first army defensive location identified on the ridge east of Round Timber Creek (see fig. 11.7), cartridge cases fired from forty-two of the fifty-six identified army carbines were recovered. None of the .50-caliber cartridge cases were fired from weapons identified as Indian firearms at other locations on the battle site.

In addition, two days after their battle with Farnsworth and the scout patrol, this same group of Indians participated in the battle against Lieutenant Baldwin and his troops on McClellan Creek. Baldwin and his troops from the 5th Infantry and 6th Cavalry were equipped with .45-caliber Springfields, so any .50-caliber cartridges at the battle would be associated with the Indian combatants, but there are no .50-caliber cartridge cases among the collection of artifacts at the White Deer Land Museum in Pampa recovered from that battle site. Apparently few if any of the Indians at the McClellan Creek battle had .50-caliber firearms, which suggests that most of the .50/70-caliber cartridge cases recovered at the Battle of Round Timber Creek site are indeed associated with the 8th Cavalry troopers.

A third possibility that must be considered is that some of the recovered cartridges, and thus some of the identified guns, are not associated with this battle at all but instead with a different battle. Though no other known battles of the Red River War took place in this vicinity, in 1872 Col. Ranald Mackenzie and 215 troops of the 4th Cavalry attacked a Comanche village somewhere on the North Fork of the Red River. The precise location of this battle has never been identified, but most researchers place it on the south side of the North Fork rather than on the north side. One researcher, however, places the Indian village attacked by the 4th Cavalry at the mouth of Cabin Creek and maintains that the battle extended all the way up to the creek's headwaters on the north side of the North Fork, though he provides no documentation to support this assertion.[21] In his report of the battle, Mackenzie wrote that the conflict occurred an estimated 7 miles above the confluence of McClellan Creek with the North Fork of the Red River.[22] This would place the battle closer to the mouth of Sand Creek, which is a little more than 3 miles east of Cabin Creek.

Furthermore, if some of the recovered cartridge cases are from Mackenzie's battle, then Mackenzie and his troops would have been following and fighting along the same route as Farnsworth and his men as they made their way up the ridge. But this was not the case, for Mackenzie clearly indicates that his men remained within the Comanche village where they captured a large number of horses and mules and took some 130 Comanche women and children prisoners. The soldiers then herded the livestock and prisoners several miles south of the North Fork, where they set up camp later that night. Clearly the two battles were not fought in the same area, and none of the cartridge cases recovered during the archeological investigations can be attributed to Mackenzie's 1872 battle. At present, then, it appears that the recovered cartridge cases are associated with the Battle of Round Timber Creek and that fifty-eight of the identified firearms—two pistols and fifty-six .50-caliber carbines—are associated with the 8th Cavalry troopers.

Of the 242 fired cartridge cases recovered, 170 (70 percent) were fired by the twenty-eight army troopers and seventy-two (30 percent) were fired by the Indian combatants. This is an average of 6.1 cartridges fired by each of the army personnel to less than one cartridge for each of the Indian warriors. It appears that the Indian combatants were being conservative with their ammunition and using it sparingly. It may be that efforts by the U.S. Army to control the illicit trade of firearms and ammunition to the Indians were having the desired effect and that by the fall of 1874 the Indians were finding it difficult to secure ample ammunition.

There are twenty-nine identified individual firearms associated with the Indian combatants. If Lieutenant Farnsworth's estimate of one hundred Indian warriors at the battle is accurate, then at least 29 percent of the Indian combatants had firearms. It is possible, however, perhaps even likely, that Lieutenant Farnsworth overestimated the number of Indian warriors—given that he arrived at his estimate during the heat of battle. Regardless of the exact number of warriors at the battle, of the identified Indian firearms nine are repeaters: eight Spencers and only one .44-caliber Henry or Winchester Model 1866. The other Indian firearms are a variety of single-shot carbines and old muzzle loaders and Plains trade guns; two are .45-caliber Model 1873 Springfield carbines that the Cheyenne warriors apparently captured from other army units in previous engagements.

If fewer than a third of the Indian warriors had firearms, what types of weapons were the other warriors using? Undoubtedly many of them were armed with traditional weapons such as bows and arrows, spears, knives, and tomahawks, even though little evidence was found on the battle site for the use of such weapons. Two metal arrowpoints were recovered at the site of Grey Beard's village, but none were found on the battle site. Many of the traditional Indian weapons were designed for hand-to-hand combat, and the opportunity may not have been available to the Indians to use them in what was, for the most part, a running battle. In addition, as long as their ammunition held out, the 8th Cavalry troopers, with their long-range .50-caliber guns, had superior firepower and may have been able to keep the Indians from getting close enough to use their bows and arrows or spears.

The cartridge and bullet analyses suggest that only about 29 percent of the Indian warriors had firearms. This is consistent with our findings at the other battle sites investigated during the project. At this battle, it appears that only about 31 percent of the Indian firearms were repeaters. Perhaps if more of the Cheyenne warriors had repeater carbines during the battle, where much of the fighting seems to have been at close range, then the 8th Cavalry soldiers might have suffered more casualties or not escaped at all.

12

Conclusions and Legacy

The archeological evidence retrieved from the Red River War battle sites tells a compelling story of struggle between two opposing cultures. On one side were the Plains Indians, whose free-roaming culture and dependence on the buffalo simply did not allow for an understanding of the concept of strict territorial boundaries or reservations. Their lifestyle, indeed their very survival, depended on their ability to pursue and hunt the great bison herds wherever they went. The Indians viewed the indiscriminate slaughter of buffalo by Anglo hunters and the encroachment of railroads and Anglo settlers as a direct and intolerable threat.

On the other side were the Anglo-Americans who believed that it was their god-given right to take, occupy, and exploit any land they saw fit, especially if that land was occupied by people they regarded as inferior and savage. To help them drive the "savages" from the land, they turned to the U. S. Army with its modern artillery, firearms, and almost unlimited supplies, ammunition, and manpower. The result of these two opposing forces on the Southern Plains in 1874 was armed conflict that ended with the defeat of the Indians, the imprisonment of many of their leaders, and the demise of a once proud culture.

The Red River War Battle Sites Project has provided an unprecedented amount of new information on the more significant battles of the Red River War. When the project was initiated in 1998, the primary goals were to locate precisely and document the battle sites through archeological investigations and to use the results of the investigations to fill some of the "gaps" and correct some of the bias of the historical documents that relate to the war. By the time the fieldwork portion of the project was completed in 2003, six of the better-known battle sites had been located and at least partially investigated and more than 3,700 artifacts recovered.

Several research objectives were formulated for the investigations at each of the battle sites. The primary objective for each site was to establish the chronology of battle events. This was accomplished by recording and mapping the precise location of each battle-related artifact. By analyzing the artifact types and plotting their placement across the battle site, it was possible to determine whether each artifact was associated with Indian or army combatants. Thus, by examining the artifact patterns across the battle sites and comparing these patterns with the historical documents, it became possible to trace combatant movements and establish the chronology and placement of battle events.

Another objective was to examine the tactics used both by the army and the Indians at the various battle sites. By 1874, the post–Civil War U.S. Army had developed and adopted new battle tactics, primarily in response to improvements in firearms such as the development of rapid-fire repeating rifles, which made it impracticable for opposing armies to line up face-to-face and fire at each other as they had done during the Civil War. Another reason new tactics were developed was that the army was now facing a new type of conflict and an enemy that was more flexible, had better knowledge of the terrain, and was more mobile. One of the tactics developed was the deployment of skirmishers who typically dismounted, established a line, and engaged the enemy by firepower. The use of skirmishers was evident in several of the investigated battles, including Red River, Sweetwater Creek, Lyman's Wagon Train, and Round Timber Creek.

Not all of the army's tactics were new, however. Some tactics had been employed for years and would not have been out of place on a Civil War battlefield. At the Battle of Red River, for example, Colonel Miles used his battalions in long linear formations with his artillery in the center to move across the battle ground and push the Indians from the field. Also, at the Battle of Round Timber Creek the mounted cavalrymen appear to have made successive charges to scatter the Indians and force them back as the soldiers attempted to make their escape along the narrow ridgetop.

The archeological evidence for the tactics used by the Indian combatants is consistent with hit-and-run guerilla-style warfare. At most of the sites the Indian-associated cartridge cases were typically found in small groupings of two to three, which were widely spread across the battle site. This pattern appears to be the result of the Indian warriors breaking into small groups and dispersing across the landscape in order to make it more difficult for the soldiers to ascertain where they would next appear. At virtually every battle the primary concern for the Indian warriors was the protection of their families; in almost every instance the warriors were trying to lead the soldiers away from their villages or delay the advance of the soldiers long enough to allow their families time to escape. Only at battles such as Lyman's Wagon Train and Buffalo Wallow, where the Indian warriors greatly outnumbered the soldiers, did the Indians commit to close-range fighting or attempt to overpower the soldiers. But even at these battles, when the Indians were unable to overrun the soldiers initially they were content to pull back out of range of the soldier's rifles, eventually abandon their attacks altogether, and then typically disperse across the landscape, often burning the prairie behind them to make pursuit by the soldiers more difficult.

One of the most important objectives for the project was to determine the types and quantities of armaments the Indians used at the battles. Several army documents make reference to the Indians' use of firearms, but few provide specific details regarding type or quantity of Indian weapons. There is no doubt that the Indians used firearms during the Red River War, but the questions of what types of firearms and in what quantities remained unanswered. The only viable means to assess these questions was through examination of the recovered artifacts. By utilizing modern firearms identification procedures, we were able to determine the minimum number of firearms per weapon type used at each battle site. The identified weapon types that were not associated with the army based on official army records and ordnance returns we assumed to be from Indian firearms.

The firearm analysis identified thirty firearm types used at the battles by both the army and the Indians. The individual firearm counts are conservative estimates in that only those cartridges and bullets that could be sorted and identified with certainty were counted. In addition, there were numerous cartridge cases that were too oxidized to be analyzed. There is little doubt that, if the round balls and problematic cartridge cases could have been identified further, the number of individual firearms would have been considerably higher. The figures obtained from the firearms analysis represent only the minimum number of firearms that could be identified from the archeological evidence. No doubt many more firearms were used by the combatants. Nonetheless, of the firearm types identified, the Indian combatants used at least twenty-six types, and nine types were used by the army combatants.

The twenty-six Indian-associated types represent an impressively diverse array of firearms, including obsolete muzzle loaders and trade guns, single-shot carbines, revolvers, and repeater rifles or carbines such as the Henry or Winchester and the Spencer. Despite this diversity, the analysis of identified firearms suggests that the Indians were not well armed. Generally it was found that only 30–50 percent of Indian combatants at any battle had firearms of any kind. The Spencer carbine was the most common firearm represented among the Indian guns, followed by Henry or Winchester Model 1866 and 1873 rifles. Together, these repeater models account for about 53 percent of the Indian firearms overall. Approximately 36 percent of the Indian firearms were single-shot rifles or carbines of various models and calibers, 8 percent were old trade guns and muzzle loaders, and 3 percent were revolvers. The trade guns and muzzle loaders are probably underrepresented since groups of rifle balls, such as the .44-, .50-, and .54-caliber, were counted as representing only one gun in each type.

The types and numbers of Indian firearms appear consistent with what archeologists have found at other late nineteenth-century Indian wars battle sites. At the Battle of the Little Bighorn site, for example, the firearms analysis of archeologically derived cartridge cases concluded that 50 percent or fewer of the estimated 1,500 Indian warriors at the battle had firearms. Of the identified Indian firearms, it was statistically projected that 45–54 percent were repeaters and a similar 45–54 percent were muzzle loaders and single-shot rifles or carbines.[1]

The nine army-associated firearm types identified at the Red River War battle sites represent a surprising array of weapons in light of the fact that in 1873 the army adopted the .45-caliber Springfield as the standard firearm for cavalry and infantry troops and the .45-caliber Colt as the standard revolver. However, as discussed in chapter 5, sufficient numbers of new weapons simply could not be produced and issued to all the army units prior to the start of the campaign against the Southern Plains Indians in August 1874. As a result, the troops that did not receive new firearms either continued to use what they had on hand, such as the .50-caliber Sharps carbine and the .50-caliber Springfield Model 1868 or 1870 carbine, or they were issued experimental .50-caliber Ward-Burton and Remington carbines.

The firearms analysis identified the Model 1873 Springfield rifle or carbine as the firearm most often used by the army combatants. This firearm represents 42 percent of all army guns identified. The next most common army weapon was the .50-caliber Sharps (27 percent), followed by the Springfield Model 1868 or 1870 (13.7 percent) rifle or carbine, and the Ward-Burton carbine (7.4 percent). The Colt Model 1873 revolver accounts for 6.8 percent of the army weapons identified. At least one soldier, perhaps an officer, carried a .44-caliber Smith & Wesson Russian Model revolver.

Another objective for the project was to ascertain the degree of accuracy and bias of the army records. For the most part, the archeological data correlate well with the historical documents. The cartridge case data recovered from the various battle sites allowed us to identify cartridge case groups that can be associated with historically known army unit positions. For example, at the Battle of Red River site we identified the location of Major Compton's charge as well as the hill where Captain Chaffee and his men made their charge using their pistols. At the Lyman Wagon Train site we identified where the wagon train made its defensive circle, just as Lyman described it. We also found the Indian positions on the ridges at the precise distances detailed by Lyman in his report. At the Battle of Sweetwater Creek site we identified the precise position of the army howitzer during the battle and established that it was fired at least two times. At the Battle of Round Timber Creek we identified the site of Grey Beard's village, where the battle started, and the 8th Cavalry's various defensive positions and where they charged the Indians, just as Lieutenant Farnsworth said they had done. Even without the historical documentation of the various army company locations at each of the battles, we could have identified discrete unit assemblages and traced their movements. This is precisely what we did with the Indian-associated firearms data from each battle site.

Even though the archeological data generally corroborate the historical data, they do not support statements made by some army personnel, primarily officers, concerning the number of Indian combatants at each battle and how well armed the Indians were. Based on the archeological data, it appears that there were not as many Indians as the officers indicate and that the Indians who were at the battles were not as well armed as army documents suggest. That being the case, the army documents are still invaluable for interpreting the events of each battle and as aids for interpreting the archeological data gathered from the battles.

Other Red River War Sites

Other Red River War-related sites await field identification and documentation, including battle sites, army supply and base camps, and Indian villages (fig. 12.1). Of the battle sites, most were small skirmishes that are mentioned briefly in the military documents with few details. The general locations of these battles are, however, shown on one or more of the military campaign maps. The maps and documents may provide sufficient information to allow for these sites to be found and documented. The one battle that was not a small skirmish, and the location of which is known, is the Battle of McClellan Creek in present Gray County. It was at this battle on November 8, 1874, that Lt. Frank Baldwin and troops of the 5th Infantry and 6th Cavalry attacked a Cheyenne village on North McClellan Creek and rescued Adelaide and Julia German.[2]

The smaller and lesser-known battles include Col. Ranald Mackenzie's engagement on the night of September 26 and the morning of September 27 with Kiowa and Comanche warriors near Tule Canyon in present Briscoe County.[3] This battle was a prelude to the engagement on September 28 in Palo Duro Canyon. A little more than a month later, Mackenzie was far to the south near Tahoka in present Lynn County, where, on November 3, his command found a small camp of Comanche Indians. The troopers charged the camp, killed two warriors, captured nineteen women and children, and rounded up 144 horses. On November 5, after having moved 10 miles east, the command discovered another small camp where two more Indians were killed and twenty-six additional horses and mules were captured.[4]

Lieutenant George P. Buell and his command out of Fort Griffin struck a small Indian camp on October 9 near the headwaters of the Salt Fork of the Red River, probably in present Donley County. The troopers killed one warrior and destroyed the Indian lodges. Farther up the river, the soldiers burned Kiowa and Cheyenne villages of fifteen, seventy-five, and four hundred lodges.[5] Capt. Adna Chaffee, with a combined force of infantry and cavalry, attacked "a considerable body of Indians" between Gageby and Sweetwater creeks, probably in present southeastern Hemphill County, Texas, or in western Roger Mills County, Oklahoma. The lodges of the Indians were destroyed, as was much property, and the Indians were pursued to near the Cheyenne Agency.[6]

Capt. C. A. Hartwell and troops of the 8th Cavalry attacked a force of 40–50 Cheyenne warriors on November 29 near the head of Muster (Bonita) Creek in present

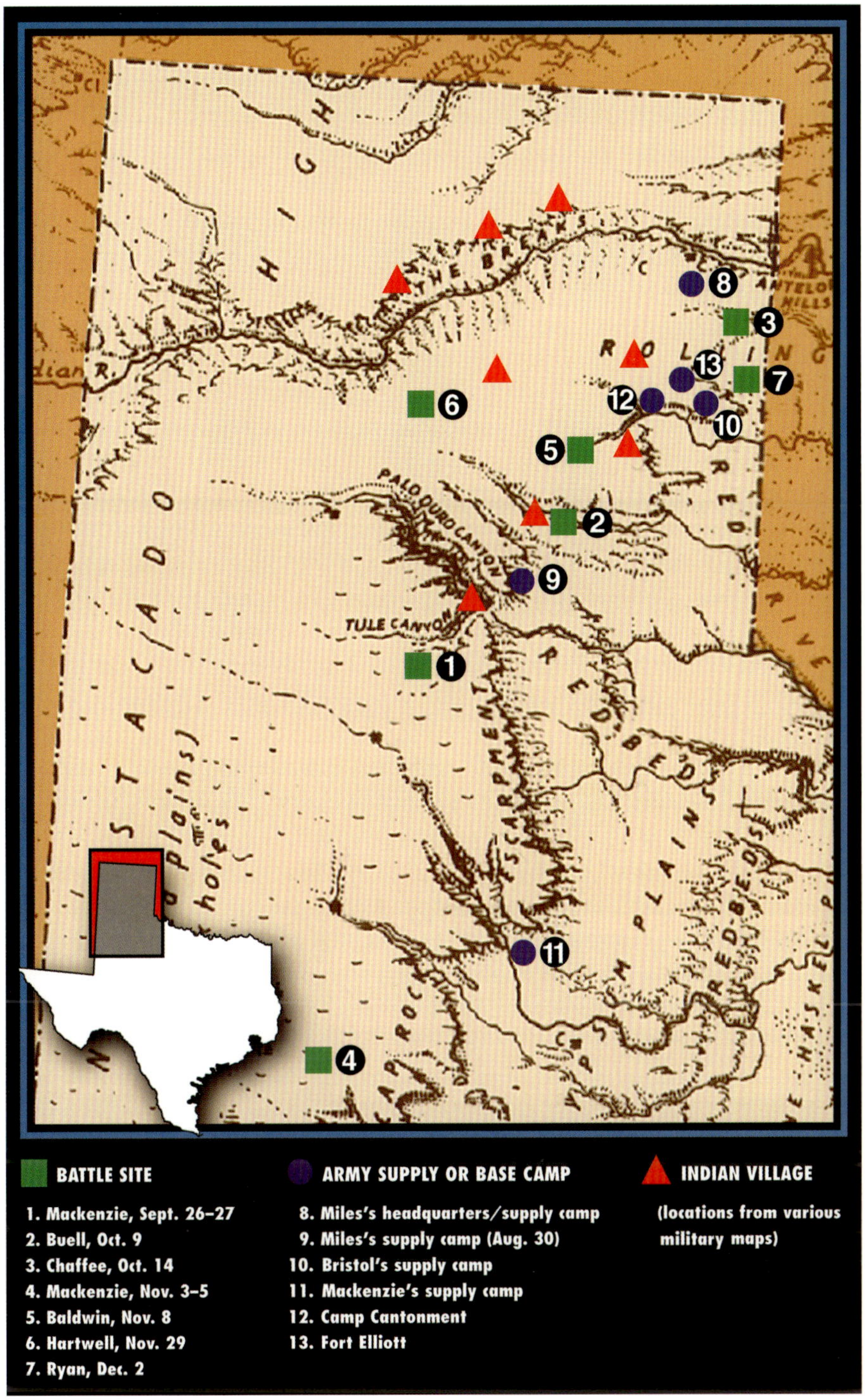

Fig. 12.1. Additional battle sites, army supply and base camps, and Indian village sites related to the Red River War. Illustration by Roland Pantermuehl

Potter County. The running battle covered a distance of about 12 miles, and two Cheyenne warriors were killed.[7] On December 2, 1874, Sgt. Dennis Ryan and sixteen troops of the 6th Cavalry surprised a band of Cheyennes south of Gageby Creek in present Wheeler County. Ryan pursued the Indians for some 10 miles, captured or killed horses, and destroyed a large amount of Indian property. Sergeant Ryan received a Congressional Medal of Honor for this action.[8]

During the 1874 Indian campaign, numerous army camp sites were used only briefly and were not mentioned in the military documents or shown on military maps.

Of more concern are the army supply and base camps that were occupied from several days to several months. These camps are often described in the military documents and their locations shown on military campaign maps. Field identification and documentation of these sites would provide details on size and layout of the camps and should afford insights into the daily activities that took place there.

One of the first supply camps Col. Nelson Miles established was after his battle at the Red River on August 30, 1874. At this temporary supply camp on Battle Creek (Armstrong County), what few supplies the command had were unloaded and the empty wagons, under command of Captain Lyman, sent back toward Camp Supply for additional provisions. The camp on Battle Creek was in use from August 30 until September 8, when Miles began moving his command back north to the Washita River.

After reaching the Washita River in mid-September, Colonel Miles established his headquarters and supply camp a few miles west of the scene of the Lyman Wagon Train battle in present Hemphill County. This camp was occupied for only a short time before being reestablished at a more favorable location several miles up the river. This site was used for several months and was the primary destination for supplies coming from Camp Supply. Also in mid-September, Miles ordered Capt. H. B. Bristol to "select some good position on South side of Sweetwater [Creek], not East of our crossing point, establish your command and make all preparations for defence."[9] This post, in present Wheeler County, was occupied for about a month and was visited by Colonel Davidson and his command on September 21, at which time Lt. Richard Pratt observed "one Parrott Gun in position, surrounded by earth work, and rifle pits on hills near," suggesting that Captain Bristol had indeed made preparations for defense of the camp.[10]

Another large military supply camp was established by Colonel Mackenzie in Blanco Canyon in what is now Crosby County, Texas. This camp was first used by Mackenzie during his campaign against the Comanches in 1871, and he reestablished it as his base of operations in 1874. The precise location of this camp has been previously identified by artifact collectors, and, fortunately, the Crosby County Pioneer Memorial Museum in Crosbyton, Texas, has been the recipient of a substantial number of artifacts recovered from the site.

Two other military camps or installations should be mentioned: Camp Cantonment and Fort Elliot. Camp Cantonment was established in early 1875 on what came to be called Cantonment Creek, a tributary of the North Fork of the Red River in eastern Gray County. Camp Cantonment was a small post, the purpose of which was to guard the region and prevent Indians at the reservations from returning to the area and to control or prevent additional outbreaks by the Indians in the region. The camp would be used for only a few months until Fort Elliott was established in June 1875, a few miles to the northeast on Sweetwater Creek near the present community of Mobeetie in western Wheeler County. First known as New Cantonment, the name of the post was officially changed to Fort Elliott on February 21, 1876, in honor of Maj. Joel Elliott, who had been killed at the Battle of the Washita six years earlier. Fort Elliott guarded the western edge of Indian Territory for fifteen years until it was abandoned by the army in 1890. The post buildings were sold at public auction on March 20, 1900.[11]

Legacy of the Red River War

The Red River War and the events surrounding the U.S. Army's Indian Campaign of 1874 have been largely overlooked by historians of the American West. The events of the Red River War were not insignificant, however; they had profound impacts on the Indian tribes of the Southern Plains and on the subsequent settlement of the region by Anglo-Americans. Perhaps one of the reasons the Red River War has gone largely unnoticed is the efficiency and effectiveness with which the U.S. Army completed its mission during the campaign. Within only a few months of the army troops taking the field, many of the Indians had returned to the reservations, and in less than a year from the time the secretary of war gave approval for the army to begin the campaign the last of the Indian holdouts had surrendered. Another reason the Red River War has received less attention than other Indian war conflicts is that relatively few deaths were incurred by the army or the Indians. Certainly there were no "massacres" on either side to draw much notice by the public.

Today, none of the Red River War battle sites or other related sites can be visited by the public, save for portions of the Battle of Palo Duro Canyon in Palo Duro Canyon State Park and the Adobe Walls and Buffalo Wallow sites, which are owned by the Panhandle-Plains Historical Society. All of the other sites are privately owned on working ranches. There are, however, several museums and other facilities in the region that offer exhibits and information about the Red River War (fig. 12.2). By far the largest of these is the Panhandle-Plains Historical Museum in Canyon, Texas. Often regarded as the foremost historical museum in the state, the visitor here can view exhibits on the Southern Plains Indians, the Adobe Walls site, and virtually every other aspect of history and prehistory related to the Texas Panhandle.

The White Deer Land Museum in Pampa has artifact displays from the battles of McClellan Creek and Round Timber Creek as well as from Camp Cantonment. At the Roberts County Museum in Miami is an exhibit on the Battle of Buffalo Wallow, and the Old Mobeetie Jail Museum in Mobeetie has exhibits and artifact displays on Fort Elliott and information on several participants in the Red River War. The River Valley Pioneer Museum in Canadian has a display of artifacts from the Lyman Wagon Train battle site. The Wolf Creek Heritage Museum in Lipscomb has a small exhibit on Amos Chapman, a scout for the army and participant at the Buffalo Wallow battle. The Hutchinson County Historical Museum in Borger has exhibits related to Adobe Walls and the Red River War in general. Other museums with small exhibits related to the Red River War include the Saints' Roost Museum in Clarendon, the Armstrong County Museum in Claude, the Swisher County Archives and Museum in Tulia, and the Crosby County Pioneer Memorial Museum in Crosbyton. The visitor's center at Palo Duro Canyon State Park has a small exhibit on the Red River War and the Battle of Palo Duro Canyon.

These eleven museums and Palo Duro Canyon State Park have recently formed a coalition with plans to enhance, enlarge, and integrate their Red River War exhibits so that each museum within the "Red River War heritage corridor" of the Texas Panhandle can tell a part of the compelling story of the Red River War. Artifacts recovered by the Texas Historical Commission during the archeological investigations of the battle sites will be integrated into these exhibits. Some of the planned museum exhibits will focus on the events leading up to the war; others will examine the various treaties and promises that were made and broken, the deplorable conditions the Indians faced at the reservations, and the importance of the buffalo to the tribes. Still other exhibits will explore the overall strategy of the army and the various military columns that took the field, the battles of the war, the weapons used by the military and the Indians, the important Indian and white participants of the war, the confinement of the tribes to the reservations and imprisonment of the Indian leaders, and the settlement of the region by Anglo-Americans. Visitors to the museums and the park will be encouraged to visit the other museums to better understand the entire story of the events surrounding the Red River War.

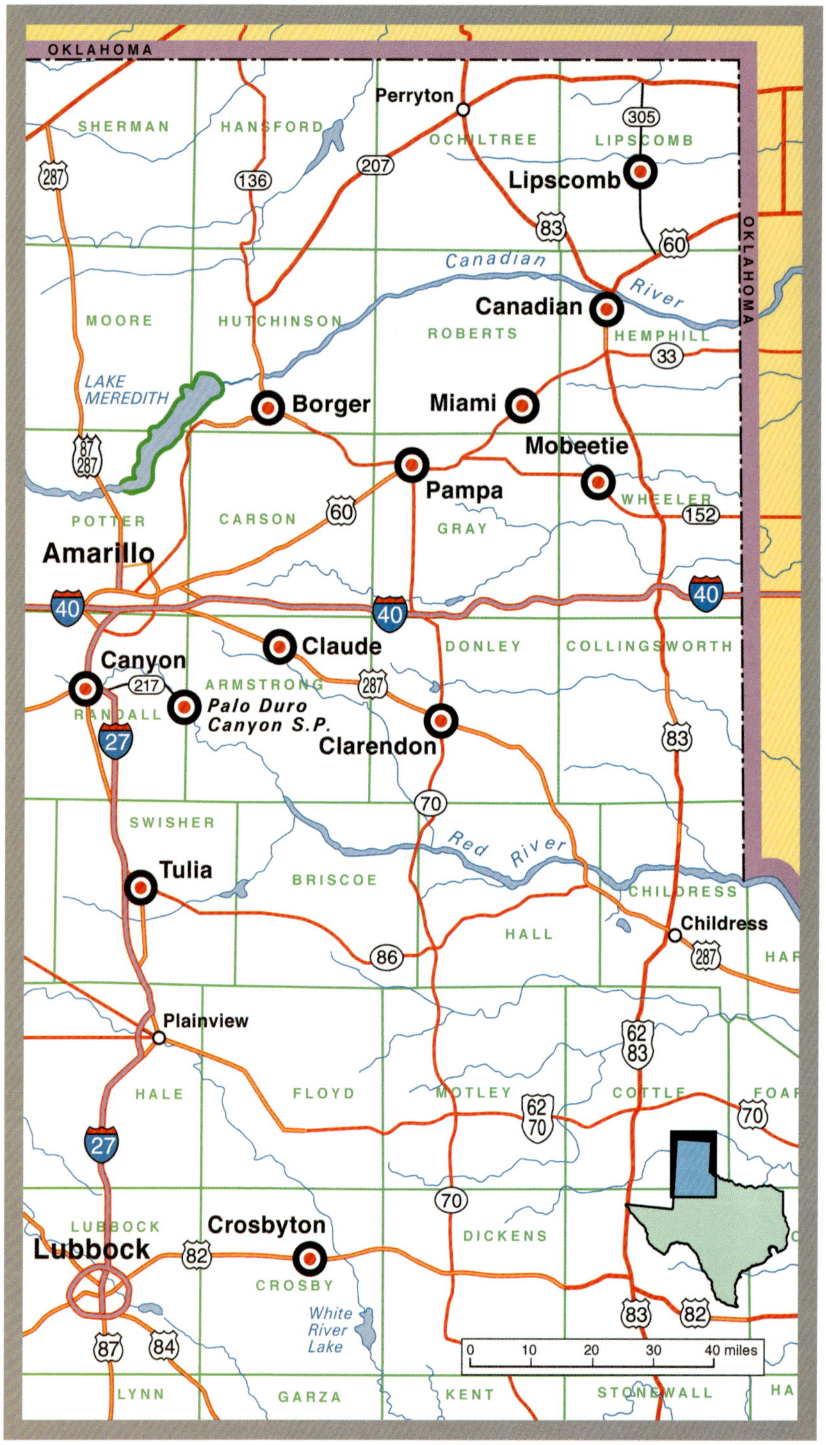

Fig. 12.2. Museums with Red River War exhibits. Illustration by Roland Pantermuehl

The interpretations of the archeological investigations of the battle sites have provided new insights on the battle events and important data on the type and quantity of Indian firearms. New light has been shed on the struggle in 1874 between the Southern Plains Indian tribes and the U.S. Army—a struggle that quickly brought an end to the nomadic and free-roaming lifestyle of the Indians and placed them, rightly or wrongly, on the slow, tedious, and often painful path of assimilation into the society of the white man.

Appendix A

Report of Indian Prisoners confined in Ft. Marion, St. Augustine, Florida, during the month of May, 1875 (Facsimile)

Report of 1st Lt. Richard H. Pratt for the month of May 1875, Central Superintendency, Letters received by the Office of Indian Affairs, Microcopy No. 234, Roll 66, 1875, Frames 831–832, Oklahoma Historical Society.

			Arrested		
No.	**Names**	**Rank**	**Date**	**Place**	**Offence~Remarks**
	Cheyennes				
1	Heap of Birds	Chief	Apr. 3, 1875	Chey. Agency	Ringleader
2	Bear Shield	Chief	3 Apr. '75	Chey. Agency	Ringleader-Murder
3	Minimic	Chief	3 Apr. '75	Chey. Agency	Ringleader
4	Medicine Water	Leading Warrior	5 Mch. '75	Chey. Agency	Ringleader-Murder
5	Long Back	Sub Chief	18 Mch. '75	Chey. Agency	Held and abused Germain girls
6	White Man	Warrior	5 Mch. '75	Chey. Agency	Accomplice in murders
7	Rising Bull	Warrior	5 Mch. '75	Chey. Agency	Accomplice in murders
8	Cahoe	Warrior	19 Jany. '75	Chey. Agency	Accomplice in murders
9	Bear's Heart	Warrior	14 Dec. '74	Chey. Agency	Accomplice in murders
10	Big Mocassin	Warrior	3 Apr. '75	Chey. Agency	Accomplice in murders
11	Star	Warrior	3 Apr. '75	Chey. Agency	No offence charged
12	Howling Wolf	Warrior	3 Apr. '75	Chey. Agency	Ringleader
13	Making Medicine	Warrior	3 Apr. '75	Chey. Agency	Ringleader
14	Antelope	Warrior	3 Apr. '75	Chey. Agency	Ringleader
15	Come-uh-see-vah (Wolf-marrow)	Warrior	3 Apr. '75	Chey. Agency	Ringleader
16	Little Medicine	Warrior	3 Apr. '75	Chey. Agency	Ringleader
17	Shave Head	Warrior	3 Apr. '75	Chey. Agency	Ringleader
18	Roman Nose	Warrior	3 Apr. '75	Chey. Agency	Ringleader
19	Big Nose	Warrior	3 Apr. '75	Chey. Agency	Ringleader
20	Squint Eye	Warrior	3 Apr. '75	Chey. Agency	Ringleader
21	Little Chief	Warrior	3 Apr. '75	Chey. Agency	Ringleader
22	Matches	Warrior	3 Apr. '75	Chey. Agency	Ringleader
23	Starving Wolf	Warrior	3 Apr. '75	Chey. Agency	Ringleader
24	Spotted Elk	Warrior	3 Apr. '75	Chey. Agency	Ringleader
25	Buffalo Meat	Warrior	3 Apr. '75	Chey. Agency	Ringleader
26	Buzzard	Warrior	3 Apr. '75	Chey. Agency	Ringleader
27	Soaring Eagle	Warrior	25 Dec. '74	Ft. Wallace, Ks.	Murder
28	Macouista	Warrior	25 Dec. '74	Ft. Wallace, Ks.	Murder
29	Left Hand	Warrior	25 Dec. '74	Ft. Wallace, Ks.	Murder
30	Mochi (Squaw)	Wife of Medicine Water	5 Mch. '75	Chey. Agency	Accomplice in murder
31	Chief Killer	Warrior	24 Sep. '74	On the Plains at Head of McClellan Creek	Accomplice in murder
	Arapahoes				
1	Packer	Warrior	5 Mch. '75	Chey. Agency	Murder
2	White Bear	Warrior	5 Mch. '75	Chey. Agency	Attempt to kill
	Kiowas				
1	Woman's Heart	Chief	3 Oct. '74	Chey. Agency	Ringleader-murder
2	Bird Chief, alias, Bird Medicine, alias Bad Eye	Leader	3 Oct. '74	Chey. Agency	Murder

No.	Names	Rank	Arrested		Offence~Remarks
			Date	Place	
3	White Horse	Chief	17 Dec. '74	Fort Sill, I. T.	Ringleader-murder
4	Wo-Haw (Beef)	Warrior	3 Oct. '74	Chey. Agency	Murder
5	Ah-ke-ah, alias Pah-o-ka (coming to the grove)	Warrior	3 Oct. '74	Chey. Agency	Murder
6	Double Vision	Sub Chief	3 Oct. '74	Chey. Agency	Ringleader-Murder
7	La-a-mi-a-da (Bear in the Clouds)	Leader	3 Oct. '74	Chey. Agency	Ringleader-Murder
8	Lone Wolf	Chief	18 Feb. '75	Salt Fork of the North Fork of Red River	Ringleader-Murder
9	Zo-tom (Biter)	Warrior	18 Feb. '75	Salt Fork of the North Fork of Red River	Murder
10	Mah Mante, alias Swan (Man who walks above ground)	Chief	18 Feb. '75	Salt Fork of the North Fork of Red River	Ringleader, Murder, Robbery, Theft
11	Ou-ko-eht (Ankle)	Warrior	18 Feb. '75	Salt Fork of the North Fork of Red River	Murder-Theft
12	O-het-toint (High Forehead)	Warrior	18 Feb. '75	Salt Fork of the North Fork of Red River	Murder
13	E-tah-dle-uh (Boy)	Warrior	18 Feb. '75	Salt Fork of the North Fork of Red River	Murder
14	Zo-po-he (Toothless)	Warrior	18 Feb. '75	Salt Fork of the North Fork of Red River	Murder
15	Tsah-dle-tah (White Horse)	Warrior	18 Feb. '75	Salt Fork of the North Fork of Red River	Murder
16	Zove-ke-uh (Teeth)	Warrior	18 Feb. '75	Salt Fork of the North Fork of Red River	Murder
17	Beah-ko (Old Man)	Warrior	18 Feb. '75	Salt Fork of the North Fork of Red River	Robbery and Theft
18	To-me-ke-uh (Good Talk)	Warrior	18 Feb. '75	Salt Fork of the North Fork of Red River	Theft and Murder
19	Ko-lah (Wild Horse)	Warrior	18 Feb. '75	Salt Fork of the North Fork of Red River	Theft
20	Th-pa-yah (Straightening an Arrow)	Warrior	18 Feb. '75	Salt Fork of the North Fork of Red River	Theft
21	Maw-ko-peh (Flat Nose)	Warrior	18 Feb. '75	Salt Fork of the North Fork of Red River	Theft
22	Aw-lih (Wise)	Warrior	18 Feb. '75	Salt Fork of the North Fork of Red River	Murder, Robbery, Theft
23	Ko-ho (Kicking)	Warrior	18 Feb. '75	Salt Fork of the North Fork of Red River	Murder, Robbery, Theft
24	To-o-sape (Bull with holes in his ears)	Warrior	18 Feb. '75	Salt Fork of the North Fork of Red River	Murder, Theft
25	Tsait-kope-ta (Bear Mountain)	Warrior	18 Feb. '75	Salt Fork of the North Fork of Red River	Robbery, Theft, Murder
26	Pedro	Warrior	18 Feb. '75	Salt Fork of the North Fork of Red River	Murder, Robbery, Theft
Comanches					
1	Quoi-yo-uh	Warrior	8 Apr. '75	Ft. Sill, I.T.	Theft
2	Pavoor-iti (Little Prairie Hill)	Warrior	25 Dec. '74	Wichita Agcy.	Theft-Attempt to kill
3	Eck-ewah-ats (Buck Antelope)	Warrior	26 Oct. '74	Elk Creek, I.T.	Raiding-Theft
4	Wy-a-ko (Dry Wood)	Warrior	26 Oct. '74	Elk Creek, I.T.	Raiding-Theft

No.	Names	Rank	Arrested		Offence ~ Remarks
			Date	Place	
5	Black Horse	Chief	7 Mch. '74	Ft. Sill, I.T.	Talking defiantly—killed white man in 1867
6	Had-a-with-t	Warrior	7 Mch. '74	Ft. Sill, I.T.	Raider-Theft
7	Ta-a-way-ite (Telling something)	Warrior	18 Apr. '75	Ft. Sill, I.T.	Raiding-Theft
8	Pe-eh-chip (Tail Feathers)	Warrior	18 Apr. '75	Ft. Sill, I.T.	Shot his father, War path man
9	Tis-cha-kah-da (Always setting down on a bad place)	Warrior	18 Apr. '75	Ft. Sill, I.T.	Raider-Theft
	Caddoes				
1	Hu-wah-nee	Prominent man	7 Apr. '75	Ft. Sill, I.T.	Murder of E. B Osborne, Black Beaver's son-in-law
	Absent				
1	Lean Bear	Warrior	3 Apr. '75	Chey. Agency	No offence charged. Stabbed himself and then two of the guards en route, May 19, '75. Left at Nashville in dying condition.
Died					
	Cheyennes				
1	Grey Beard	Chief	3 Apr. '75	Chey. Agency	Ringleader—Jumped from cars en route near Houston, Fla., May 21, '75, and was shot by the guard—died in two hours.
	Kiowas				
1	Co-a-vote-ka (Sun)	Warrior	23 Oct. '74	Sulphur Creek, I.T.	Murder—Died of Pneumonia in hospital at St. Augustine, May 24, '75.

The foregoing is a correct report.

R. H. Pratt
1st Lt. 10th Cavalry
In charge of Indian Prisoners.

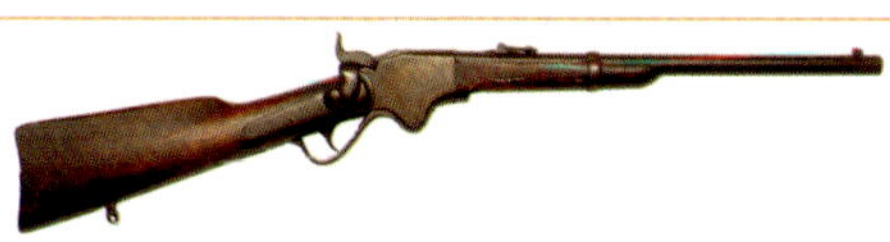

Appendix B

Summary of Ordnance and Ordnance Stores in the Hands of Troops in the Service of the United States during the 3rd Quarter Ending Sept. 30, 1874 (Facsimile)

Record Group 156–159, Microfilm Roll 1281, National Archives.

4th U.S. Cavalry			Small Arms					Ammunition	
			Carbines	Pistols		Sabers and Swords	Equipments & Accouterments	Carbines	Pistols
Date of Receipt at Ordnance Office	Letter of the Company	Station	Springfield, Cal. .45	Smith & Wesson's, Cal. .44	Colt Revolver, Cal. .45	Light Cavalry	Cavalry Equipment, Sets of	Carbine Ball, Cal. .45	Revolver Ball, Cal. .45
Dec. 19, 1874	A	In the field, Camp _____ Canyon, Tex.	79		80	78	50	4,487	7,310
Dec. 19, 1874	D	In the field, Texas	79	1	80	77	50	5,635	8,398
Feb. 8, 1875	E	In the field, Texas	78		75	70		2,920	5,350
Dec. 19, 1874	F	In the field, Texas	78		77	65		9,620	8,050
Dec. 19, 1874	H	In the field near Ft. McKavett, Tex.	79		80	70		6,173	8,040
Dec. 19, 1874	I	In the field, Camp on Staked Plains near Ft. Clark Tex.	75	1	77	82	50	8,000	6,000
Nov. 30, 1874	K	In the field, Camp at Tule Canyon, Tex.	75	2	77	83		5,040	7,920
June 19, 1874	L	In the field near Ft. Griffin, Tex.	78		76	80		5,052	7,606

6th U.S. Cavalry

			Small Arms					Ammunition			
			Carbines			Pistols	Sabers and Swords	Carbines		Pistols	
Date of Receipt at Ordnance Office	Letter of the Company	Station	Springfield, Cal. .45	Sharps, Cal. .50	Spencer, Cal. .50	Colt Revolver, Cal. .45	Light Cavalry	Carbine Ball, Cal. .45	Rifle & Carbine Blank, Cal. .45	Revolver Ball, Cal. .45	Revolver Blank, Cal. .45
Oct. 27, 1874	A	In the field near Camp Supply, I. T.	76			75	82	13,270		2,900	
Dec. 4, 1874	D	Camp near Canadian River, I. T.	83	1		82	82	20,000		8,000	
Nov. 20, 1874	F	In the field near Ft. Dodge, Kas.	69		4	66	71	12,457	4,500	12,490	5,000
Dec. 4, 1874	G	Fort Dodge, Kas.	67			71	82	8,940		5,652	
Jan. 6, 1875	H	Fort Lyon, C. T.	83			84	88	3,192		14,300	
Nov. 16, 1874	I	In the field with Indian Territory Expedition	78			69	84	22,920	10,000	9,956	
Oct. 22, 1874	L	Camp on Canadian River, Tex.	79			75	80	6,290		5,770	
Dec. 26, 1874	M	Fort Lyon, C. T.	80			71	80	8,806	3,400	14,801	2,760

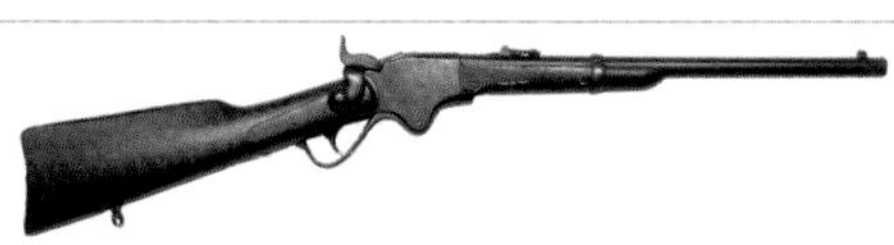

8th U.S. Cavalry			Small Arms							Ammunition		
			Carbines				Pistols		Sabers and Swords	Carbines		Pistols
Date of Receipt at Ordnance Office	Letter of the Company	Station	Springfield, Cal. .50	Remington, Cal. .50	Sharps, Cal. .50	Ward-Burton, Cal. .50	Remington's using percussion cap, Cal. .44	Colt Revolver, Cal. .45	Light Cavalry	U.S. Center Fire, Cal. .50	U. S. Blank, Cal. .50	Revolver Ball, Cal. .45
March 30, 1874	C	Camp near Antelope Hills, Tex.			81		75	55	77	18,255		4,800
April 16, 1874	H	In the field, Indian Territory and Texas	15	13	50	11	20	59	84	20,660	2,980	3,776
Oct. 27, 1874	K	Camp Wingate, N.M.			69		34	47	29	18,697		3,000
Oct. 27, 1874	L	Oasis Creek, I.T. near Fort Union, N.M.			68		74	66	79	10,940		2,000

9th U.S. Cavalry			Small Arms						Ammunition			
			Carbines			Pistols		Sabers and Swords	Carbines			Pistols
Date of Receipt at Ordnance Office	Letter of the Company	Station	Sharps, Cal. .50	Springfield, Cal. .45	Ward-Burton, Cal. .50	Remington's using percussion caps, Cal. .44	Colt's for Metallic Ammunition, Cal. .44	Light Cavalry	U.S. Center Fire, Cal. .50	Carbine Ball, Cal. .45	U.S. Blank, Cal. .50	Colt's Altered, Cal. .44
Nov. 18, 1874	A	Fort Concho, Texas	23	41			34	71	11,428	6,755		3,736
Jan. 27, 1875	D	Fort Concho, Texas		60		49	34	72		9,600		5,000
May 21, 1875	E	Fort Concho, Texas	15	49	4	42		79	346	8,900	1,790	
Aug. 6, 1874	F	Blank	52			52		82	11,144	8,600		
March 4, 1875	K	In the field near Ft. Sill, I.T.	78	59		38		85	11,661	11,000		

10th U.S. Cavalry

			Small Arms					Ammunition	
			Carbines		Pistols		Sabers and Swords	Carbines	Pistols
Date of Receipt at Ordnance Office	Letter of the Company	Station	Sharps, Cal. .50	Springfield, Cal. .45	Remington's using percussion caps, Cal. .44	Colt Revolver, Cal. .45	Light Cavalry	Carbine Ball, Cal. .45	Revolver Ball, Cal. .45
Jan. 18, 1875	A	Fort Griffin, Texas		84		84	84	8,740	10,800
Oct. 28, 1875	B	Fort Sill, I.T.		84		74	74	10,000	10,000
Dec. 23, 1875	C	Fort Sill, I.T.		52		67	75	16,975	11,591
Nov. 18, 1875	D	Fort Sill, I.T.	1	83	1	84	128	9,095	10,700
Dec. 30, 1874	E	In the field, Texas		73		84	66	20,982	23,400
Jan. 2, 1875	F	Fort Sill, I.T.		76		75	47	10,420	11,180
Oct. 27, 1875	H	Fort Sill, I.T.		81		83	80	19,415	11,615
Oct. 30, 1875	K	Fort Sill, I.T.	1	84		60	76	17,500	4,300
Oct. 27, 1875	L	Camp in the field near Fort Sill, I.T.		84		84	51	27,800	20,500

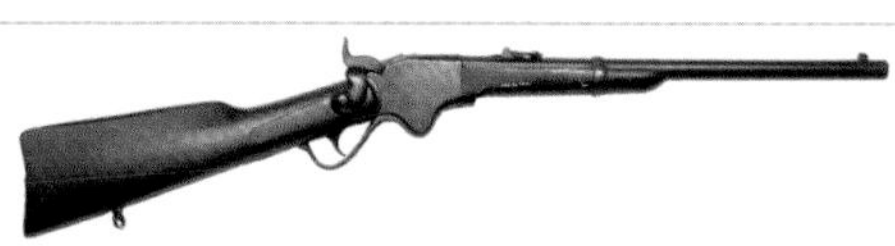

5th U.S. Infantry			Muskets		Sabers and Swords	Equipments & Accouterments	Ammunition	
Date of Receipt at Ordnance Office	Letter of the Company	Station	Springfield, Cal. .50 M1868	Springfield, Cal. .45	Travel Bayonets	Infantry Equipment, Sets of	U.S. Center Fire, Cal. .50	Springfield, Cal. .45
Oct. 16, 1874	C	Camp Supply, I.T.	59	60	15	57	13,691	11,468
Oct. 13, 1874	D	Camp on Oasis Creek, Tex.		52		50		14,150
Dec. 4, 1874	E	Camp on Washita River, Tex.		54		60		7,580
Dec. 10, 1874	I	Camp on Washita River, Tex.		54		58		10,500

10th U.S. Infantry			Muskets		Equipments & Accouterments	Ammunition			
Date of Receipt at Ordnance Office	Letter of the Company	Station	Springfield, Cal. .50 M1868	Springfield, Cal. .50 M1870	Infantry Equipment, Sets of	U.S. Center Fire, Cal. .50	U.S. Center Fire, Cal. .50 Martin	U.S. Center Fire, Cal. .50 Berdan	U.S. Blank, Cal. .50
Nov. 19, 1874	A	Camp Tulle Springs, Tex	40	26	30	7,847	2,232		3,825
Feb. 17, 1874	C	Field near Ft. McKavett, Tex.	52	11	38	7,109		3,630	
Nov. 19, 1874	I	In the field, Tex.	75		32	10,075			
Dec. 19, 1874	K	Fort Clark, Texas	66		34	13,510			

11th U.S. Infantry

Date of Receipt at Ordnance Office	Letter of the Company	Station	Muskets: Springfield, Cal. .50 M1868	Muskets: Springfield, Cal. .50 M1870	Equipments & Accouterments: Infantry Equipment, Sets of	Ammunition: U.S. Center fire, Cal. .50	Ammunition: U.S. Center fire, Cal. .50 Martin	Ammunition: U.S. Center fire, Cal. .50 Berdan	Ammunition: U.S. Blank, Cal. .50	Ammunition: Metcalf Block
Oct. 14, 1874	A	Field near Ft. Griffin, Tex.	41	14	33	4,744	5,000	1,050		
Oct. 21, 1874	C	Fort Sill, I.T.	53		34	8,236			1,610	
Dec. 22, 1874	E	Fort Sill, I.T.	59	10	31	9,820				279
Dec. 26, 1874	F	Fort Griffin, Tex.	60		50	3,532		8,750		
Feb. 8, 1874	H	Field near Ft. Concho, Tex.	61		30		6,850		290	

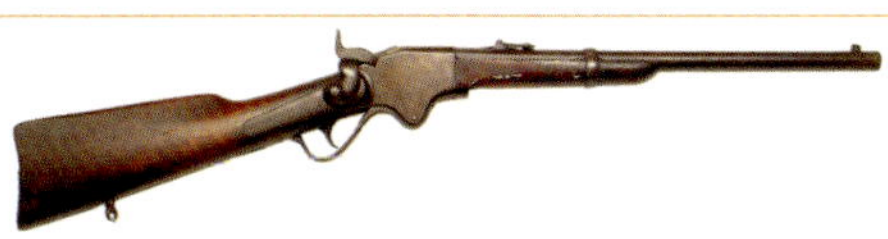

Appendix C

Red River War Medal of Honor Recipients

Public Information Division, U.S. Army, *Medal of Honor,* 206–38; Taylor, *Indian Campaign;* Neal, *Valor across the Lone Star.*

James F. Ayers. *Rank and organization*: Private, Company H, 6th U.S. Cavalry. *Place and date*: Sappa Creek, Kansas, April 23, 1875. *Entered service*: He first enlisted in the 16th U.S. Infantry on November 13, 1868, was later with the 5th and 6th U.S. Cavalries, and finally with the 20th U.S. Infantry. *Birth*: circa 1845 at Collinstown, Virginia. *Date of issue*: November 16, 1876. *Citation*: Rapid pursuit, gallantry, energy, and enterprise in an engagement with Indians. *Death*: January 18, 1895, at Fort Riley, Kansas.

Frank D. Baldwin. *Rank and organization*: First Lieutenant, 5th U.S. Infantry. *Place and date*: McClellan Creek, Texas, November 8, 1874. *Birth*: June 26, 1842, near Manchester, Michigan. *Entered service*: Constantine, Michigan, to serve in the 19th Michigan Infantry during the Civil War. He received a regular army commission in 1866 and retired from the army in 1903 as a brigadier-general. *Date of issue*: December 3, 1891. *Citation*: Rescued, with 2 companies, 2 white girls by a voluntary attack upon Indians whose superior numbers and strong position would have warranted delay for reinforcements, but which delay would have permitted the Indians to escape and kill their captives. *Death*: April 22, 1923 at Denver, Colorado. *Note*: This was Baldwin's second Medal of Honor. His first was awarded for action during the Civil War at Peach Tree Creek, Georgia on July 12, 1864.

Frederick Bergerndahl. *Rank and organization*: Private, Band, 4th U.S. Cavalry. *Place and date*: Staked Plains, Texas, December 8, 1874. *Entered service*: Boston, Massachusetts, in November 1871. *Birth*: February 26, 1851, at Goteborg, Sweden. *Date of issue*: October 13, 1875. *Citation*: Gallantry in a long chase after Indians. *Death*: January 31, 1924, at Goteborg, Sweden.

Amos Chapman. *Rank and organization*: Scout (Civilian), 6th U.S. Cavalry. *Place and date*: Washita River, Texas, September 12, 1874. *Birth*: March 15, 1837, at Kalamazoo, Michigan. *Date of issue*: November 4, 1874. *Citation*: Gallantry in action. *Death*: July 28, 1925, near Seiling, Oklahoma. *Note*: In 1916, the general review of all Medals of Honor deemed nine hundred unwarranted; Amos Chapman's was one of them. In June 1989, the U.S. Army Board of Correction of Records reinstated Chapman to the Medal of Honor Roll.

John W. Comfort. *Rank and organization*: Corporal, Company A, 4th U.S. Cavalry. *Place and date*: Staked Plains, Texas, November 5, 1874. *Entered service*: Philadelphia in 1870. *Birth*: circa 1845 at Philadelphia, Pennsylvania. *Date of issue*: October 13, 1875. *Citation*: Ran down and killed an Indian. *Death*: November 29, 1893 at Philadelphia.

Michael Dawson. *Rank and organization*: Trumpeter, Company H, 6th U.S. Cavalry. *Place and date*: Sappa Creek, Kansas, April 23, 1875. *Entered service*: He served three enlistments with the army. *Birth*: circa 1846 at Boston, Massachusetts. *Date of issue*: November 16, 1876. *Citation*: Gallantry in action. *Death*: unknown.

William DeArmond (awarded posthumously). *Rank and organization*: Sergeant, Company I, 5th U.S. Infantry. *Place and date*: Mortally wounded at Upper Washita, Texas, September 9, 1874. *Entered service*: New York City in 1866. *Birth*: February 1842 near Okeana, Ohio. *Date of issue*: April 23, 1875. *Citation*: Gallantry in action. He was buried where he fell in what is now Hemphill County, Texas.

William Dixon. *Rank and organization*: Scout (Civilian) 6th U.S. Cavalry. *Place and date*: Washita River, Texas, September 12, 1874. *Birth*: October 25, 1850, near Wheeling, West Virginia. *Date of issue*: November 4, 1874. *Citation*: Gallantry in action. *Death*: March 9, 1913 in Cimarron County, Oklahoma. *Note*: In 1916, the general review of all Medals of Honor deemed nine hundred unwarranted. Billy Dixon's was one of them. In June 1989, the U.S. Army Board of Correction of Records reinstated Dixon to the Medal of Honor Roll.

Peter W. Gardiner. *Rank and organization*: Private, Company H, 6th U.S. Cavalry. *Place and date*: Sappa Creek, Kansas, April 23, 1875. *Entered service*: New York City in 1872. *Birth*: circa 1846 at Carlisle, New York. *Date of issue*: November 16, 1876. *Citation*: With 5 other men he waded in mud and water up the creek to a position directly behind an entrenched Cheyenne position, who were using natural bank pits to good advantage against the main column. This surprise attack from the enemy rear broke their resistance. *Death*: 1883 near Fort Lowell, Arizona.

John Harrington. *Rank and organization*: Private, Company H, 6th U.S. Cavalry. *Place and date*: Washita River, Texas, September 12, 1874. *Entered service*: unknown, 1870. *Birth*: circa 1848 at Detroit, Michigan. *Date of issue*: November 4, 1874. *Citation*: While carrying dispatches was attacked by 125 hostile Indians, whom he and his comrades fought throughout the day. He was severely wounded in the hip and unable to move. He continued to fight, defending an exposed dying man. *Death*: 1905 at San Antonio, Texas.

Frederick S. Hay (a.k.a. Frederick H. Schwabe). *Rank and organization*: Sergeant, Company I, 5th U.S. Infantry.

Place and date: Upper Washita, Texas, September 9, 1874. *Entered service*: unknown, 1873. *Birth*: circa 1850 at Sterlingshire, Scotland. *Date of issue*: April 23, 1875. *Citation*: Gallantry in action. *Death*: January 14, 1914 at Highlands, New Jersey.

Simpson Hornaday. *Rank and organization*: Private, Company H, 6th U.S. Cavalry. *Place and date*: Sappa Creek, Kansas, April 23, 1875. *Entered service*: unknown, 1870. *Birth*: March 24, 1851 at Hendricks, Indiana. *Date of issue*: November 16, 1876. *Citation*: With 5 other men he waded in mud and water up the creek to a position directly behind an entrenched Cheyenne position, who were using natural bank pits to good advantage against the main column. This surprise attack from the enemy rear broke the resistance. *Death*: July 9, 1923, at San Diego, California.

John James. *Rank and organization*: Corporal, 5th U.S. Infantry. *Place and date*: Upper Washita, Texas, September 9–11, 1874. *Entered service*: Albany, New York, on June 6, 1872. *Birth*: circa 1838 near Manchester, England. *Date of issue*: April 23, 1875. *Citation*: Gallantry in action. *Death*: May 23, 1902 at Washington, D.C.

John J. H. Kelly. *Rank and organization*: Corporal, Company I, 5th U.S. Infantry. *Place and date*: Upper Washita, Texas, September 9, 1874. *Entered service*: unknown, 5th Infantry, August 19, 1872. *Birth*: December 27, 1850, at Rushville, Illinois. *Date of issue*: April 23, 1875. *Citation*: Gallantry in action. *Death*: February 4, 1907, at Springfield, Illinois.

Thomas Kelly. *Rank and organization*: Private, Company I, 5th U.S. Infantry. *Place and date*: Upper Washita, Texas, September 9, 1874. *Entered service*: New York City on April 8, 1858. *Birth*: circa May 1836 in Mayo County, Ireland. *Date of issue*: April 23, 1875. *Citation*: Gallantry in action. *Death*: March 21, 1919, at Leavenworth, Kansas.

George Krause Kitchen. *Rank and organization*: Sergeant, Company H, 6th U.S. Cavalry. *Place and date*: Upper Washita, Texas, September 9, 1874. *Entered service*: unknown, July 20, 1870. *Birth*: October 5, 1849, near Pottsville, Pennsylvania. *Date of issue*: April 23, 1875. *Citation*: Gallantry in action. *Death*: November 22, 1922, at San Antonio, Texas.

John W. Knox. *Rank and organization*: Sergeant, Company I, 5th U.S. Infantry. *Place and date*: Upper Washita, Texas, September 9, 1874. *Entered service*: unknown. *Birth*: circa 1849 near Des Moines, Iowa. *Date of issue*: April 23, 1875. *Citation*: Gallantry in action. *Death*: unknown.

William Koelpin. *Rank and organization*: Sergeant, Company I, 5th U.S. Infantry. *Place and date*: Upper Washita, Texas, September 9, 1874. *Entered service*: Brooklyn, New York on December 1, 1870. *Birth*: October 6, 1848, at Stebbin, Germany. *Date of issue*: April 23, 1875. *Citation*: Gallantry in action. *Death*: January 2, 1912, at Brooklyn, New York.

James Lowthers. *Rank and organization*: Private, Company H, 6th U.S. Cavalry. *Place and date*: Sappa Creek, Kansas, April 23, 1875. *Entered service*: unknown. *Birth*: circa 1850 at Boston, Massachusetts. *Date of issue*: November 16, 1876. *Citation*: With 5 other men he waded in mud and water up the creek to a position directly behind an entrenched Cheyenne position, who were using natural bank pits to good advantage against the main column. This surprise attack from the enemy rear broke their resistance. *Death*: unknown.

Gregory Mahoney. *Rank and organization*: Private, Company E, 4th U.S. Cavalry. *Place and date*: Near Red River, Texas, September 26–28, 1874. *Entered service*: Boston, Massachusetts, on November 8, 1871. *Birth*: May 2, 1850, at Pontypool, South Wales, Great Britain. *Date of issue*: October 13, 1875. *Citation*: Gallantry in attack on a large party of Cheyennes. *Death*: unknown.

William McCabe. *Rank and organization*: Private, Company E, 4th U.S. Cavalry. *Place and date*: Near Red River, Texas, September 26–28, 1874. *Entered service*: unknown, February 3, 1874. *Birth*: circa 1845 at Belfast, Northern Ireland. *Date of issue*: October 13, 1875. *Citation*: Gallantry in attack on a large party of Cheyennes. *Death*: unknown.

John Mitchell. *Rank and organization*: First Sergeant, Company I, 5th U.S. Infantry. *Place and date*: Upper Washita, Texas, September 9–11, 1874. *Entered service*: unknown, 1867. *Birth*: circa 1846 at Dublin, Ireland. *Date of issue*: April 23, 1875. *Citation*: Gallantry in engagement with Indians. *Death*: May 1, 1904, at San Francisco, California.

William W. Morris. *Rank and organization*: Corporal, Company H, 6th U.S. Cavalry. *Place and date*: Upper Washita, Texas, September 9–11, 1874. *Entered service*: unknown, 1872. *Birth*: 1846 near Dover, Tennessee. *Date of issue*: April 23, 1875. *Citation*: Gallantry in engagement with Indians. *Death*: unknown.

Frederick S. Neilon (a.k.a. Frank Singleton). *Rank and organization*: Sergeant, Company A, 6th U.S. Cavalry. *Place and date*: Upper Washita, Texas, September 9–11, 1874. *Entered service*: Chicago, Illinois, 1872. *Birth*: June 22, 1846, at Boston, Massachusetts. *Date of issue*: April 23, 1875. *Citation*: Gallantry in action. *Death*: September 13, 1916, at Boston, Massachusetts.

John O'Sullivan. *Rank and organization*: Private, Company I, 4th U.S. Cavalry. *Place and date*: Staked Plains, Texas, December 8, 1874. *Entered service*: New York, New York, on March 22, 1870. *Birth*: circa 1856 in Kerry County, Ireland. *Date of issue*: October 13, 1875. *Citation*: Gallantry in a long chase after Indians. *Death*: May 19, 1907, at New York City.

Adam Paine (a.k.a. Payne). *Rank and organization*: Private, Seminole-Negro Indian Scout, 4th U.S. Cavalry. *Place and date*: Canyon Blanco tributary of the Red River, Texas, September 26–27, 1874. *Entered service*: Fort Duncan, Texas, 1873. *Birth*: circa 1842 near Alachua, Florida. *Date of issue*: October 13, 1875. *Citation*: Rendered

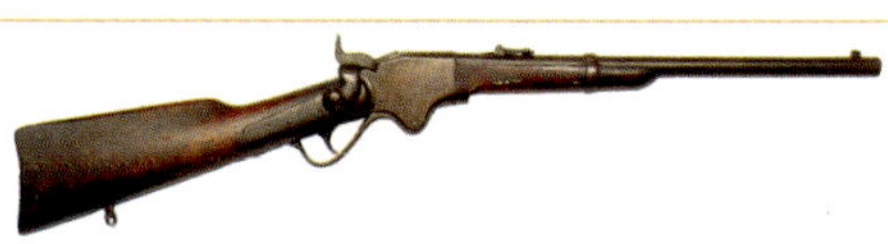

invaluable service to Col. R. S. Mackenzie, 4th U.S. Cavalry, during this engagement. *Death*: January 1, 1877, at Brackettville, Texas.

Josiah Pennsyl. *Rank and organization*: Sergeant, Company M, 6th U.S. Cavalry. *Place and date*: Upper Washita, Texas, September 11, 1874. *Entered service*: unknown, January 17, 1871. *Birth*: September 22, 1852, near Rainsburg, Pennsylvania. *Date of issue*: April 23, 1875. *Citation*: Gallantry in action. *Death*: January 22, 1920, at Pima, Arizona.

Edwin Phoenix. *Rank and organization*: Corporal, Company E, 4th U.S. Cavalry. *Place and date*: Near Red River, Texas, September 26–28, 1874. *Entered service*: Kentucky, January 5, 1867. *Birth*: May 15, 1844, at St. Louis, Missouri. *Date of issue*: October 13, 1875. *Citation*: Gallantry in action. *Death*: September 5, 1932, at Los Angeles, California.

Frederick Platten. *Rank and organization*: Sergeant, Company H, 6th U.S. Cavalry. *Place and date*: Sappa Creek, Kansas, April 23, 1875. *Entered service*: New York City on February 8, 1871. *Birth*: circa 1855 in Ireland. *Date of issue*: November 16, 1876. *Citation*: With 5 other men he waded in mud and water up the creek to a position directly behind an entrenched Cheyenne position, who were using natural bank pits to good advantage against the main column. This surprise attack from the enemy rear broke their resistance. *Death*: March 2, 1939, near Williams, Arizona.

Marcus M. Robbins. *Rank and organization*: Private, Company H, 6th U.S. Cavalry. *Place and date*: Sappa Creek, Kansas, April 23, 1875. *Entered service*: Boston, Massachusetts, on August 1, 1872. *Birth*: July 25, 1851, near Elba, Wisconsin. *Date of issue*: November 16, 1876. *Citation*: With five other men he waded in mud and water up the creek to a position directly behind an entrenched Cheyenne position, who were using natural bank pits to good advantage against the main column. This surprise attack from the enemy rear broke their resistance. *Death*: June 21, 1924, at Pittsfield, Massachusetts.

Peter Rath. *Rank and organization*: Private, Company A, 6th U.S. Cavalry. *Place and date*: Washita River, Texas, September 12, 1874. *Entered service*: New York City on April 8, 1870. *Birth*: June 5, 1850, at Beffendorf, Germany. *Date of issue*: November 4, 1874. *Citation*: While carrying dispatches was attacked by 125 hostile Indians, whom he and his comrades fought throughout the day. *Death*: January 18, 1907, at Rottenmunster, Germany.

Dennis Ryan. *Rank and organization*: First Sergeant, Company I, 6th U.S. Cavalry. *Place and date*: Gageby Creek, Indian Territory, December 2, 1874. *Entered service*: New York City, 1871. *Birth*: circa 1848 at Cork, Ireland. *Date of issue*: April 23, 1875. *Citation*: Courage while in command of a detachment. *Death*: circa 1912 at New York City.

Edward C. Sharpless. *Rank and organization*: Corporal, Company H, 6th U.S. Cavalry. *Place and date*: Upper Washita, Texas, September 9–11, 1874. *Entered service*: unknown, November 17, 1872. *Birth*: circa 1853 in Marion County, Ohio. *Date of issue*: April 23, 1875. *Citation*: While carrying dispatches was attacked by 125 hostile Indians, whom he (and a comrade) fought throughout the day. *Death*: January 12, 1934, at Mountainair, New Mexico.

George W. Smith (awarded posthumously). *Rank and organization*: Private, Company M, 6th U.S. Cavalry. *Place and date*: Washita River, Texas, September 12, 1874. *Entered service*: New York, January 31, 1870. *Birth*: circa 1848 at Brooklyn, New York. *Date of issue*: November 4, 1874. *Citation*: While carrying dispatches was attacked by 125 hostile Indians, whom he and his comrades fought throughout the day. Pvt. Smith was mortally wounded during the engagement and died early the next day. He was buried where he fell in present Hemphill County, Texas.

Richard L. Tea. *Rank and organization*: Sergeant, Company H, 6th U.S. Cavalry. *Place and date*: Sappa Creek, Kansas, April 23, 1875. *Entered service*: unknown, February 1, 1858. *Birth*: circa 1841 at Philadelphia, Pennsylvania. *Date of issue*: November 16, 1876. *Citation*: With 5 other men he waded in mud and water up the creek to a position directly behind an entrenched Cheyenne position, who were using natural bank pits to good advantage against the main column. This surprise attack from the enemy rear broke their resistance. *Death*: September 14, 1911, near Whipple Barracks, Arizona.

Ernest Veuve. *Rank and organization*: Farrier, Company A, 4th U.S. Cavalry. *Place and date*: Staked Plains, Texas, November 3, 1874. *Entered service*: New Orleans, Louisiana, on December 17, 1869. *Birth*: March 19, 1843, at Cernier, Canton of Neucastle, Switzerland. *Date of issue*: October 13, 1875. *Citation*: Gallant manner in which he faced a desperate Indian. *Death*: June 17, 1916, at Missoula, Montana.

Lewis Warrington. *Rank and organization*: First Lieutenant, 4th U.S. Cavalry. *Place and date*: Muchaque Valley, Texas, December 8, 1874. *Entered service*: Washington, D.C. *Birth*: November 12, 1847, at Washington, D.C. *Date of issue*: April 12, 1875. *Citation*: Gallantry in a combat with 5 Indians. *Death*: January 4, 1879, at San Antonio, Texas.

Zachariah T. Woodall. *Rank and organization*: Sergeant, Company I, 6th U.S. Cavalry. *Place and date*: Washita River, Texas, September 12, 1874. *Entered service*: unknown, January 24, 1871. *Birth*: September 1849 at Alexandria, Virginia. *Date of issue*: November 7, 1874. *Citation*: While in command of 5 men and carrying dispatches, was attacked by 125 Indians, whom he with his command fought throughout the day, he being severely wounded. *Death*: September 12, 1899, at Cabana Fortress, Havana, Cuba.

Appendix D

Descriptions and Analysis of Artifacts from the Battle of Red River Site and Indian Village Site (41BI544) in Tule Canyon

A total of 1,214 artifacts were recovered from the site of the Battle of Red River, and a total of 181 artifacts were recovered from Site 41BI544. A total of 1,012 of these artifacts are munitions related. Additionally 383 non-munitions artifacts were recovered, 64 Indian-associated and 319 associated with the U.S. Army.

Arms and Ammunition

.44-Caliber Cartridge Cases

The .44-caliber Henry rimfire cartridge (fig. D.1a) was developed in the late 1850s by B. Tyler Henry, the plant superintendent for Oliver Winchester at the New Haven Arms Company.[1] The company's name was changed to Winchester Repeating Arms Company in the mid-1860s. Henry also developed the first successful repeating rifle that would fire this cartridge by improving Smith & Wesson's Volcanic repeating arms, which were failures because of the small caliber and extraction problems. Henry's conception of a flexible claw-shaped extractor was probably the most important single improvement leading to the success of the Henry repeating rifle and its .44-caliber rimfire cartridge. This extractor principle is still being used today in the Ingram submachine gun.[2]

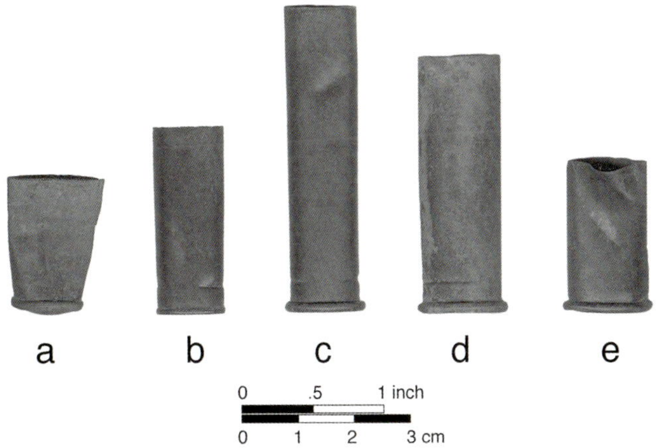

Fig. D.1. Cartridge case types recovered: a, .44 Henry; b, .45 Colt; c, .45/55 or .45/70; d, .50/70; e, 56/50 Spencer.

The first Henry cartridges were manufactured by the New Haven Arms Company. The cartridge had a copper case, a length of 0.82 inches, a round nose lead projectile with a 0.443-inch diameter, and a weight of 210 grains, with a black powder charge of 25 grains. The total length of the cartridge was 1.363 inches. The base of the case had no head stamp. In 1862, the company introduced another Henry cartridge and referred to it as the .44 Henry Flat because of its flat-nose bullet. It weighed 216 grains. This was the first cartridge case to bear the letter H as a head stamp in honor of Henry.[3] The raised letter H is in a circular depression in the center of the head of the case (fig. D.2). The flat-nose bullet variation was designed to lessen the danger of explosion in the magazine tube. Manufacture of this cartridge after 1865 was on a wide scale in the United States and Europe, owing to the popularity of the Henry rifle and the Winchester Model 1866, the latter being an improvement of the Henry. With such a large number of manufacturers, the cartridge had at least nine different variations in dimension and projectile shape.[4]

Fig. D.2. Some cartridges were stamped with the mark of the company that manufactured them. These Spencer cartridges are stamped with (from left to right) F.V.V&Co., for Fitch, Van Vechten and Company; S.A.W. for Sage Ammunition Works; and H (in a depressed circle) for New Haven Arms Company or Winchester Company.

The tendency for this rimfire ammunition to misfire was a serious problem in the early development of cartridge firearms. Henry designed a double firing pin for his repeating rifle that would strike the rim of the cartridge at points on opposite sides. The wedge-shaped firing pins were on one side of the breech pin collar. The collar was threaded into the breech pin, which was designed to move a fraction of an inch forward and rearward during firing. Both the Henry rifle and its improved version, the Model 1866 Winchester, had firing pins that were exactly alike in shape and dimensions. The firing pins were less pointed on some Model 1866s between serial numbers 24,000 and 26,000 but were changed back to their original shape because of misfire problems.[5]

Even with the double firing pin, these weapons were still prone to misfire. If the breech pin was dirty or rusty, a very hard blow was required before the firing pins would penetrate the rim of the cartridge deeply enough to detonate the primer.

There were twenty-four .44-caliber cartridge cases recovered from the battle site and an additional eleven from the Indian village site. All are of New Haven Arms Company (Winchester) manufacture. Case dimensions are the same as found in Winchester-manufactured ammunition. Microscopic firearms identification revealed that the twenty-four battle site cases were fired in Henry rifles or Model 1866 Winchesters. Both rifles are lever-action magazine-fed repeaters. Both could hold up to sixteen rounds in the magazine and chamber. Individual characteristics of the firing pins in the archeologically recovered .44-caliber Henry cartridge cases indicate that the cases were fired in at least three individual weapons, all of which are associated with the Indian combatants.

An additional four Indian-associated guns are represented by the cartridge cases from Site 41BI544. Cases 1 and 18 were fired in the same Winchester; cases 4 and 13 were fired in another Winchester; case 5 was fired in a third gun; and cases 101, 102, and 103 represent the fourth Winchester. Cases 2, 3, and 6 were too oxidized for comparison.

.45-Caliber Colt Cartridge Cases

The collection contained sixteen fired and forty-two unfired Colt Benét primed cartridges from the battle site and an additional three unfired cartridges from Site 41BI544 (fig. D.1b). Benét primed cartridges are internally primed centerfire cartridges. Two of the unfired Colt cartridges from the battle site are blanks. Of the fired Colt cases, specimens 396, 488, 639, 642, and 651 were too oxidized for comparison. The remaining fired cases represent at least nine different Colt Model 1873 revolvers. These nine revolvers are associated with the army troops. A single case represents a firearm for the following cartridge cases: 635, 763, 878, 1199, 1200, 1208, 1210, and 1211. Cartridge cases 638, 876, and 877 were fired in the remaining Colt Model 1873 revolver.

.45/55 or .45/70-Caliber Cartridge Cases

The vast majority of cartridge cases recovered are nominally the .45/55 or .45/70-caliber. There are 349 fired and 228 unfired .45/55 or .45/70 Benét primed cartridges (fig. D.1c) in the collection from the battle site and an additional thirteen unfired cartridges from Site 41BI544, all of which are associated with the army troops. Benét primed cartridges exhibit a wide crimp mark around the base to hold the Benét cup primer in position (see fig. 3.4). The firing pin and extractor marks on the fired cartridge cases indicate that they were fired in the Model 1873 Springfield rifle or carbine made by the U.S. Army Springfield Arsenal. This was the principle firearm of the army beginning with its distribution to field units in late 1873.[6]

The analyzed cartridge cases from the site revealed that at least thirty-nine Springfield Model 1873 firearms were used in the engagement. It is entirely possible that many more firearms were used in the fight, but the number of heavily oxidized and other problematic cases that could not be compared likely reduced the number of weapons identified. There were 133 cartridge cases unsuitable for analysis because of excessive oxidation. Table D.1 lists the firearm matches among the .45/55 and .45/70 cartridge cases by specimen number.

.50/70-Caliber Cartridge Cases

The .50/70 cartridge (fig. D.1d) was developed for the army's first service-wide adoption of a cartridge weapon. The round was used in various Springfield model rifles and carbines from 1866 to 1873. It was also a popular commercial cartridge, with Sharps, Remington, and other arms manufacturers chambering single-shot firearms for this caliber. The army also had 33,734 Sharps percussion weapons converted to fire .50/70 cartridges.[7]

This cartridge is .50-caliber with 70 grains of black powder as a propellant and a 450 grain conical lead bullet. The .50/70 cartridge was the subject of much experimentation in developing a center-fire primer. There are more than twenty varieties of primers known, the most common being internally primed Martin bar, Disk-anvil, and Benét cup and externally primed Berdan, Boxer, Martin folded-head, and Millbank for Winchester-made ammunition.

There were forty-three fired .50/70 cartridge cases and one misfired round (case head missing) recovered from the battle site. One unfired cartridge was recovered from Site 41BI544. On thirty-nine of the fired cartridge cases, the firing pin and extractor marks are consistent with firing from a Gatling gun. The cases and extractor marks represent the firing bolts of ten separate barrels (table D.2), which is also consistent with firing in the multibarreled Gatling gun.

Thirty variants of the Gatling gun were developed over a forty-year period. Six models were chambered for the U.S. government's .50/70-caliber round: Models 1866, 1871, and 1874 (with variations in 1875, 1876, and 1877). The bolt mechanism breech faces, firing pins, and extractors are nearly the same form in each model, so it is not possible to distinguish specific Gatling gun models from firing pin or extractor marks.[8]

The majority of the fired .50/70 cartridge cases from the Battle of Red River site are Benét primed, although the Berdan and bar primer types are also present. The single misfired .50/70 round (specimen 43) is a bar-primed cartridge. The case head has separated from the body, exposing the iron bar primer (fig. D.3). This is an excellent example of how a bar primer is placed in the case. Microscopic examination of the cartridge indicates that the round was chambered in a Gatling gun. The case rim shows crushing in two locations (fig. D.4) that are consistent with a Gatling gun extractor. This suggests that the round was chambered in the gun and misfired, perhaps causing the head to separate

Table D.1. Springfield .45/55 or .45/70 Cartridge Case Matches, Battle of Red River

Firearm	*Specimen Matches*	*Comments*
1	29, 123, 125, 132, 149, 186, 338, 340, 341, 412,597, 599, 619, 973, 986, 987	
2	32, 95, 1250, 1272	
3	49, 50, 222, 223, 348, 349, 1178, 1185	348 extractor problem
4	51, 52, 97, 116, 1232, 1240, 1265, 1281, 1283	
5	53, 66, 100, 101, 114, 216, 368, 417, 1213	53, 66, 100,101,114 extractor problems
6	67, 99, 105, 119, 201, 206	
7	94, 117, 228, 230, 231, 1234, 1242, 1290	228 extractor problem; 230 cut off and extractor problem
8	102, 127, 129, 133, 141, 144, 187, 1235	
9	109, 115, 150, 189, 190, 200, 203, 234, 265, 414	
10	120, 124, 131, 139, 220, 267, 961, 962, 1001, 1102, 1103, 1104, 1188, 1189, 1198	
11	122, 134, 138, 140, 142, 148, 283, 963, 1207, 1236, 1238, 1239, 1251, 1252, 1262, 1263, 1278, 1285, 1286, 1297, 1306	
12	128, 236, 237, 238, 239, 261, 263, 264, 1267, 1291	
13	153	
14	188, 258, 951, 952, 965, 969, 979, 985, 1212	
15	192, 998	
16	194, 270, 274, 285, 413, 415, 416, 594, 1145, 1150,1156, 1179, 1186	
17	195, 960, 968, 1008, 1041, 1261	
18	196, 405, 409, 423, 1004	
19	232	
20	271, 272, 277, 281, 1254	
21	276, 282, 287	
22	286	
23	334, 335, 336	Dirty firing pin
24	371, 598	
25	372, 407, 457, 1214, 1216	372 struck twice
26	408	
27	605	
28	950, 959 967, 984	
29	974, 991, 992, 1227, 1237, 1282	
30	989, 990	
31	996, 1003	
32	1002, 1244, 1275, 1276, 1277, 1284	
33	1038	
34	1092	
35	1098, 1215, 1246	
36	1101, 1124, 1182, 1183, 1184, 1187	
37	1201, 1202, 1204, 1205	
38	1231	
39	1253	

from the case body. It is likely that the extractor pulled past the weakened rim and may have required hand manipulation to reseat and extract the misfired round.

The presence of Berdan primed cartridge cases fired from barrels 4 and 9 suggests that commercially manufactured ammunition was issued to the gun battery. The box to the gun's magazine usually fed the cartridges. If this routine pattern was followed at the Battle of Red River, then it seems that at least one box of Berdan primed ammunition was fired in the course of the fight. The same can also be said for the Arsenal-made bar-primed cases fired in barrel 7. The drag marks (fig. D.5) present on cartridge cases fired in barrels 7 and 10 as well as the crushed case fired in barrel 7 are suggestive of dirty or malfunctioning bolts associated with those barrels. Specimen 634 exhibits battering, crushing, and gouges made by a sharp instrument, indicating that this round required hand removal probably by manipulating it with a knife. The extreme nature of the gouging

Table D.2. .50-Caliber Gatling Gun Cartridge Cases, Battle of Red River

Barrel	*Specimen Matches*[a]	*Comments*
1	6, 7, 8, 9, 11, 47	11 a possible match, heavily oxidized
2	10, 12, 213, 214	
3	15, 48, 600	
4	44, 45, 46, 198, 212, 233	198 and 233 Berdan primed
5	83, 373, 374, 375, 376	
6	215	
7	327, 329, 330, 634, 641, 643, 644, 645	All have drag marks except 641; 634 crushed and extracted with sharp instrument; 643, 644, and 645 bar primed
8	328, 377	
9	428, 648	428 Berdan primed
10	646, 647	646 and 647 have drag marks

[a]Cartridge cases that match by group. Each cartridge case has a deep, circular firing pin imprint and distinct edge crushing indicative of a Gatling gun extractor. Each group is indicative of cases fired from the same barrel. All cartridge cases are Benét primed unless otherwise noted.

Fig. D.3. The iron bar primer is visible in this misfired .50/70 cartridge case. The case head has separated from the case body to expose the primer.

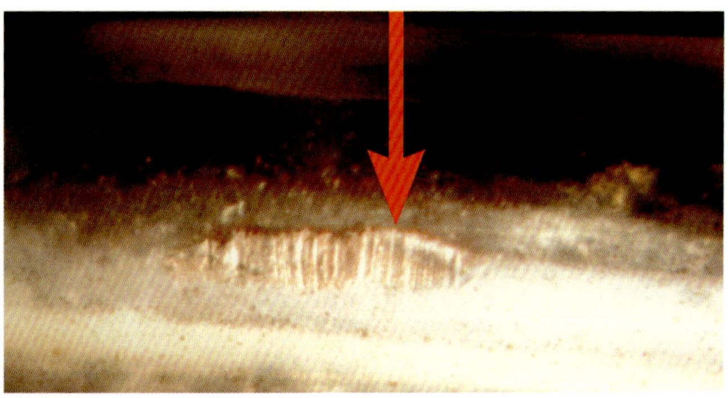

Fig. D.4. Microscopic view of the extractor mark on the edge of a .50/70 cartridge case. The extractor mark is consistent with that of a Gatling gun extractor.

suggests that the gun jammed when this round failed to extract properly, thus causing some delay to remove the round and get the gun in operation again.

Except for the Gatling gun cartridges, only four additional .50/70 fired cartridge cases and one case head were recovered from the battle site. Each of these specimens represents a separate firearm. Specimens 677, 761, and 1147 are Berdan primed Winchester-made cartridge cases. Specimen 677 was fired in a Remington-manufactured firearm, probably a rolling block rifle. Specimens 761 and 1147 were each fired in a different Springfield Model 1868 or 1870 trapdoor rifle. The last specimen (1168) is a Frankford Arsenal bar-primed case that was fired in a Sharps rifle. The head from a fired case (specimen 1296) is also present. The head appears to have been blown from a fired round,

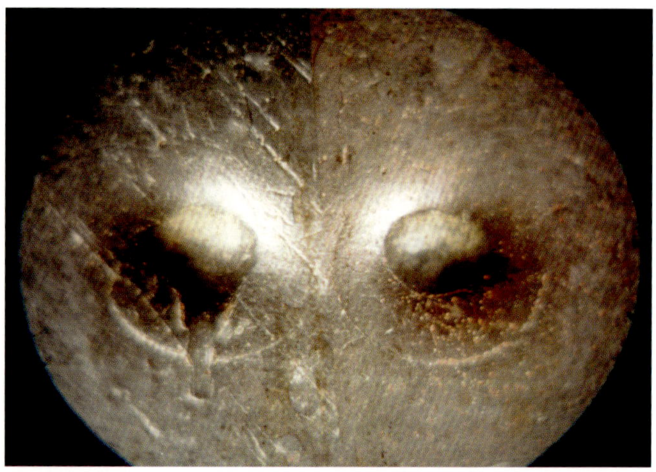

Fig. D.5. This microscopic view of two .50/70 Gatling gun cartridge cases shows that they were fired in different barrels of the gun. The left case shows clear drag marks, which are the result of a malfunctioning firing pin.

but the firing pin imprint is too distorted to determine weapon type.

Spencer 56/50 and 56/56-Caliber Cartridges

The Spencer repeating rifle and carbine were originally chambered for the reliable Spencer 56/56 caliber rimfire cartridge. In 1864, Spencer's army contracts were modified to have the chamber and bore reduced in size for the smaller diameter 56/50 caliber cartridge. As a result, the Model 1865 carbine and rifle emerged. In addition, Spencer developed a 56/52 caliber cartridge for the civilian market. The army canceled its contracts for further procurement of additional Spencer patent repeaters in late 1865, and the final deliveries under the existing contracts were made in 1866.[9]

Unlike most cartridge designations, in which caliber is listed first and black powder load second (e.g., .45/70), the Spencer designation is based on other nomenclature. The 56 in the 56/50 cartridge refers to an old designation for the No. 56 Spencer ammunition. The appellation remained and was applied to the .50-caliber ammunition as well. The 56/50 and the 56/52 cartridges were interchangeable, and both could be fired in the 56/56 Spencer. The interchangeability did not work in reverse, however; the 56/56 could not be fired in the other two firearms.

Twenty-one Spencer cartridge cases (fig. D.1e) were recovered from Indian combatant positions at the battle site. Cartridge cases in two calibers, .50 and .56, were noted in the collection of recovered specimens. One variety, of which there are nine specimens, has no head stamp. Ten cartridges are head stamped with the letter H (fig. D.2), denoting manufacture by the New Haven Arms Company or the Winchester Company; one cartridge case has the impressed letters S.A.W., denoting the Sage Ammunition Works; and one case is impressed F.V.V&Co., for Fitch, Van Vechten and Company. The latter company manufactured both .50- and .56-caliber cartridges for the federal government until 1866.[10]

Dennis C. Sage and his Sage Ammunition Works contracted with the army to supply Spencer cartridges beginning early in 1864. His last delivery of Spencer ammunition is not precisely known, but the company ceased operations in 1866. The New Haven Arms Company and Winchester produced rimfire ammunition from 1867 to the early twentieth century.[11]

Some non-head-stamped cartridge cases have tool marks (fig. D.6) on their heads left by tool points of the power head used to hold the case during the bullet crimping process. There are two varieties of tool marks present. The most common are two vertical lines at the twelve o'clock and six o'clock positions on the case head. Several manufacturers used similar tool points, but this variety appears most consistent with that attributed to the U.S. Army's Frankford Arsenal.[12] The head-stamped cases with the H in the depressed circle also have tool point marks present. There are three marks in a roughly triangular configuration on these cases, with one mark at the one o'clock position, one at the four o'clock position, and one at the seven o'clock position. This tool point mark is not otherwise documented for Winchester-made ammunition.

All of the fired cartridge cases were subjected to microscopic firearms identification procedures. The cases represent nine different Spencer firearms (table D.3). Three weapons experienced at least one cartridge case extraction problem, suggesting that some firearms became dirty or were not well maintained (see fig. 3.5 for examples of cartridge cases exhibiting evidence of extraction problems). One cartridge matched to Spencer gun 6 exhibits multiple firing pin strikes, indicating initial misfires with the ammunition. Table D.4 provides information on the head stamps and tool marks identified on the Spencer cartridges recovered from the battle site.

Bullets

Ninety bullets were recovered (fig. D.7) from the battle site, and an additional seven were recovered at Site 41BI544. The bullets were comparatively few relative to the number of cartridge cases recovered. Table D.5 shows the caliber of each bullet as well as the weapon type from which it was fired. Of interest are six .50-caliber bullets that exhibit a 6-right narrow land and wide groove pattern that is typical of Gatling gun barrels (fig. D.8). Though the 6-right land-and-groove pattern is also found in weapons produced by other arms manufacturers such as Sharps and Remington, the land-and-groove widths on the six .50-caliber bullets are unique to the Gatling gun and are identical to barrel characteristics measured on a Model

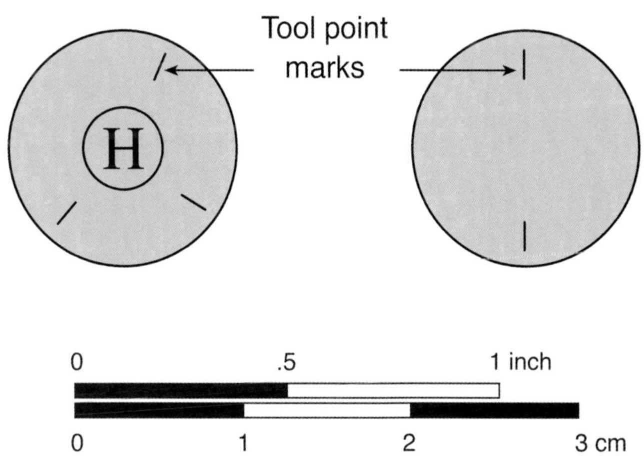

Fig. D.6. Some cartridge case heads have linear marks as a result of the manufacturing process when the power head holds the cartridge while the bullet is inserted into the case. Shown here are examples of tool point marks on the heads of Spencer cartridge cases. Illustration by Roland Pantermuehl

1877 Gatling gun on exhibit at the Frontier Army Museum in Fort Leavenworth, Kansas.[13]

Also of interest are twenty-four round balls recovered from the battle site. Round balls were usually fired in muzzle loader firearms, which were considered obsolete by 1874. It is somewhat surprising then that the round balls make up 26.7 percent of the total number of bullets found at the site. Two of the round balls were fired from .44-caliber 1858 New Model Army Remington pistols, and the other balls are .50- and .54-calibers that are undoubtedly associated with the Indians. It seems that the Indians were continuing to use muzzle-loading weapons, perhaps because lead and powder were generally easily obtainable whereas cartridges of an appropriate caliber could not always be obtained.

Table D.3. Spencer Cartridge Case Matches, Battle of Red River

Firearm	*Specimen Matches*	*Comments*
1	17	
2	86	
3	676, 1125	1125 extraction problem
4	1009	Extraction problem
5	1093, 1095, 1096, 1097, 1191	
6	1094, 1166	1166 two firing pin strikes
7	1165, 1167	
8	1192, 1193, 1195, 1197	1192 extraction problem
9	1194, 1196, 1270	

Of the other bullets from the battle site, four are .40-caliber fired from a Sharps, ten are .44-caliber from a Sharps, seven are .44-caliber fired from Henry or Winchester Model 1866 or 1873 rifles, seven are .45-caliber fired from Colt Model 1873 pistols, seventeen are from .45-caliber Springfield carbines or rifles, seven are .50-caliber fired from a Sharps, and eight are unidentifiable fragments or deformed bullets for which the caliber and weapon type could not be determined.

It is interesting to note that 67 percent of the balls and bullets recovered from the battle site are associated with the Indian combatants, compared to 33 percent associated with the U.S. Army. These percentages are in stark contrast to the fired cartridge cases recovered from the battle site, where army-associated cartridges account for 90.1 percent of the total recovered, compared to 9.9 percent Indian-associated. One reason that may account, at least in part, for this discrepancy has to do with the firepower of the weapons being used by the army and Indian combatants and the resulting distance a bullet would travel. For example, the U.S. Army Springfield .45-caliber rifle was capable of firing a bullet that would travel 1,100 m or more, whereas the smaller caliber .44 Henrys or Winchesters being used by the Indians could launch a bullet perhaps half as far. Even the larger .50- and .56-caliber Spencers used by some of the Indians were capable of firing a bullet only 366–457 m because of the heavier bullet and smaller amount of powder these cartridges held. In short, the greater firepower of the army weapons resulted in the bullets from those weapons traveling greater distances from the point the weapons were fired. If the troopers missed or overshot their targets, then a greater proportion of the army bullets might not have

Table D.4. Spencer Head Stamps and Tool Marks, Battle of Red River

Specimen	*Caliber*	*Head Stamp*	*Tool Mark*
676	56/50	None	2 at 12 and 6 o'clock
1009	56/56	None	None
1093	56/50	H in depressed circle	3 at 1, 4, and 7 o'clock
1094	56/50	H in depressed circle	3 at 1, 4, and 7 o'clock
1095	56/50	H in depressed circle	3 at 1, 4, and 7 o'clock
1096	56/50	H in depressed circle	3 at 1, 4, and 7 o'clock
1097	56/50	H in depressed circle	3 at 1, 4, and 7 o'clock
1125	56/50	H in depressed circle	None
1165	56/50	None	2 at 12 and 6 o'clock
1166	56/50	F.V.V&Co.	None
1167	56/50	None	None
1191	56/50	H in depressed circle	3 at 1, 4, and 7 o'clock
1192	56/56	None	None
1193	56/56	None	None
1194	56/50	H in depressed circle	3 at 1, 4, and 7 o'clock
1195	56/50	H in depressed circle	3 at 1, 4, and 7 o'clock
1196	56/50	H in depressed circle	3 at 1, 4, and 7 o'clock
1197	56/56	None	None
1270	56/50	S.A.W.	None

Table D.5. Balls and Bullets by Associated Firearm Type, Battle of Red River and Site 41BI544

Specimen	*Item and Caliber*	*Firearm Type*	*Comment*	*Association*
Battle of Red River				
590	ball, .44-caliber	Remington	1858 New Model Army	Indian
591	ball, .44-caliber	Remington	1858 New Model Army	Indian
204	ball, .50-caliber	unknown	faceted lead ball	Indian
205	ball, .50-caliber	unknown	faceted lead ball	Indian
240	ball, .50-caliber	unknown	faceted lead ball	Indian
241	ball, .50-caliber	unknown	faceted lead ball	Indian
242	ball, .50-caliber	unknown	faceted lead ball	Indian
243	ball, .50-caliber	unknown	faceted lead ball	Indian
244	ball, .50-caliber	unknown	faceted lead ball	Indian
246	ball, .50-caliber	unknown	faceted lead ball	Indian
247	ball, .50-caliber	unknown	faceted lead ball	Indian
248	ball, .50-caliber	unknown	faceted lead ball	Indian
249	ball, .50-caliber	unknown	faceted lead ball	Indian
250	ball, .50-caliber	unknown	faceted lead ball	Indian
251	ball, .50-caliber	unknown	faceted lead ball	Indian
252	ball, .50-caliber	unknown	faceted lead ball	Indian
253	ball, .50-caliber	unknown	faceted lead ball	Indian
254	ball, .50-caliber	unknown	faceted lead ball	Indian
255	ball, .50-caliber	unknown	faceted lead ball	Indian
256	ball, .50-caliber	unknown	faceted lead ball	Indian
257	ball, .50-caliber	unknown	faceted lead ball	Indian
245	ball, .54-caliber	unknown	faceted lead ball	Indian
499	ball, .54-caliber	unknown	faceted lead ball	Indian
1112	ball, unidentified	unknown	deformed ball	Indian
623	bullet, .40-caliber	Sharps		Indian
653	bullet, .40-caliber	Sharps		Indian
660	bullet, .40-caliber	Sharps		Indian
668	bullet, .40-caliber	Sharps		Indian
689	bullet, .44-caliber	Sharps	smooth body, long	Indian
890	bullet, .44-caliber	Sharps	smooth body, long	Indian
958	bullet, .44-caliber	Sharps	smooth body, long	Indian
1109	bullet, .44-caliber	Sharps		Indian
1126	bullet, .44-caliber	Sharps		Indian
1129	bullet, .44-caliber	Sharps		Indian
1141	bullet, .44-caliber	Sharps		Indian
1152	bullet, .44-caliber	Sharps	smooth paper patch body	Indian
1177	bullet, .44-caliber	Sharps	smooth paper patch body	Indian
26	bullet, .44-caliber	Winchester	Henry Model 1866 or 1873	Indian
1070	bullet, .44-caliber	Winchester	Henry Model 1866 or 1873	Indian
1071	bullet, .44-caliber	Winchester	Henry Model 1866 or 1873	Indian
1072	bullet, .44-caliber	Winchester	Henry Model 1866 or 1873	Indian
1073	bullet, .44-caliber	Winchester	Henry Model 1866 or 1873	Indian
1074	bullet, .44-caliber	Winchester	Henry Model 1866 or 1873	Indian
1110	bullet, .44-caliber	Winchester	Henry Model 1866 or 1873	Indian
1051	bullet, .44 or .45	Sharps		Indian
589	bullet, .45-caliber	Colt 1873		Army
1048	bullet, .45-caliber	Colt 1873		Army
260	bullet, .45-caliber	Colt 1873		Army
595	bullet, .45-caliber	Colt 1873		Army
1036	bullet, .45-caliber	Colt 1873		Army
1161	bullet, .45-caliber	Colt 1873		Army
1170	bullet, .45-caliber	Colt 1873		Army
70	bullet, .45-caliber	Springfield		Army
185	bullet, .45-caliber	Springfield		Army
199	bullet, .45-caliber	Springfield		Army
208	bullet, .45-caliber	Springfield		Army

Table D.5, *continued*

Specimen	*Item and Caliber*	*Firearm Type*	*Comment*	*Association*
209	bullet, .45-caliber	Springfield		Army
259	bullet, .45-caliber	Springfield		Army
331	bullet, .45-caliber	Springfield		Army
481	bullet, .45-caliber	Springfield		Army
618	bullet, .45-caliber	Springfield		Army
620	bullet, .45-caliber	Springfield		Army
1114	bullet, .45-caliber	Springfield		Army
1123	bullet, .45-caliber	Springfield		Army
1142	bullet, .45-caliber	Springfield		Army
1158	bullet, .45-caliber	Springfield		Army
1162	bullet, .45-caliber	Springfield		Army
1163	bullet, .45-caliber	Springfield		Army
1176	bullet, .45-caliber	Springfield		Army
456	bullet, .50-caliber	Gatling gun		Army
476	bullet, .50-caliber	Gatling gun		Army
477	bullet, .50-caliber	Gatling gun		Army
478	bullet, .50-caliber	Gatling gun		Army
479	bullet, .50-caliber	Gatling gun		Army
480	bullet, .50-caliber	Gatling gun		Army
72	bullet, .50-caliber	Sharps	smooth body	Indian
378	bullet, .50-caliber	Sharps	smooth body	Indian
395	bullet, .50-caliber	Sharps		Indian
424	bullet, .50-caliber	Sharps		Indian
673	bullet, .50-caliber	Sharps		Indian
1091	bullet, .50-caliber	Sharps		Indian
1225	bullet, .50-caliber	Sharps	smooth paper patch body	Indian
73	bullet, unidentified	unknown	fragment	Indian
202	bullet, unidentified	unknown	fragment	Indian
655	bullet, unidentified	unknown	fragment	Indian
659	bullet, unidentified	unknown	fragment	Indian
954	bullet, unidentified	unknown	fragment	Indian
1019	bullet, unidentified	unknown	fragment	Indian
1113	bullet, unidentified	unknown	deformed	Indian
1119	bullet, unidentified	unknown	fragment	Indian
Site 41BI544				
71	ball, .36-caliber	Colt	Colt Model 1860?	Indian
12	ball, .61-caliber	unknown	copper, probably homemade	Indian
56	bullet, .44-caliber	Winchester	Henry Model 1866 or 1873	Indian
77	bullet, .44-caliber	Winchester	Henry Model 1866 or 1873	Indian
162	bullet, .50-caliber	Sharps		Indian
181	bullet, .50-caliber	Sharps		Indian
171	bullet, unidentified	unknown	fragment	Indian

even landed within what we established as the boundaries of the battlefield. In contrast, the shorter firing range of the Indian weapons would have resulted in more of their bullets landing within the boundaries of the battlefield and, consequently, being found by the archeologists.

The seven bullets recovered from Site 41BI544 are one .61-caliber copper ball, one .36-caliber ball possibly from a Colt Model 1860 pistol, one .44-caliber bullet fired from a Henry or Winchester Model 1866 or 1873 rifle, one .50-caliber bullet from a Henry or Winchester Model 1866 or 1873 rifle, two .50-caliber Sharps bullets, and one unidentified bullet fragment. The .61-caliber copper ball (fig. D.9) has been beaten round and was apparently made by one of the Indians.

Gunflint

A single gunflint (fig. D.10a) found on the surface at Site 41BI544 appears to be a British-made single-ridge flint fashioned from a square, dark gray flint blade. All four edges of the gunflint show use wear. The gunflint measures

25.6 mm long by 23.4 mm wide and is 9.7 mm thick. These measurements suggest that the flint was for a trade gun rather than a fowler, a musket, or a pistol.[14]

British gunflints were produced from the late 1700s to the early 1900s. They are characterized by the use of a gray to black glassy flint and a micro-burin technique for separating flint blades into square segments to form the shape of the gunflint. British flints also usually exhibit single or double ridges along their back surfaces.[15]

Flintlock trade guns (fig. D.11) remained in use long after the appearance of percussion caps in 1820, apparently because they were economical to use, requiring only a few flints, a small quantity of gun powder, and lead for the production of balls. Though repeating rifles such as Spencers, Winchesters, and Henrys became the most popular among Plains Indians after the Civil War, it appears that the Indians used any type of firearm they could acquire, including obsolete flintlocks.

Hotchkiss Artillery Shell Shrapnel

A total of 145 pieces of shrapnel representing nine different artillery shells were recovered from the battle site. Though Colonel Miles clearly states that he used a 3-inch Parrott rifle during the battle, the shrapnel pieces recovered from the battlefield during the archeological investigations were from Hotchkiss shells, not Parrott shells. The recovered pieces include brass fuses designed for the 14-second Bormann-Wright combination fusing system commonly used in Hotchkiss shells (fig. D.12b) and 14-second Hotchkiss-Bormann time fuses (fig. D.12c). As the name

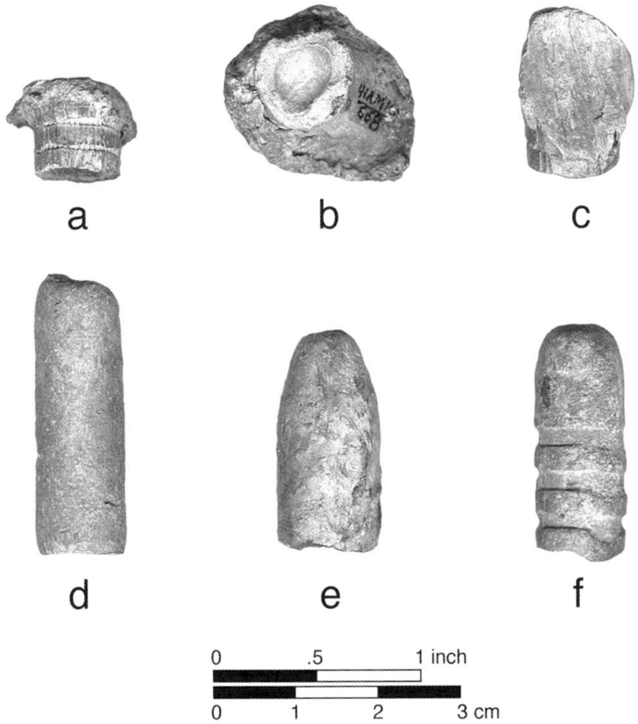

Fig. D.7. Bullet types recovered: a, .44 Winchester; b, .40 Sharps; c, .45 Colt; d, .44 Sharps; e, .50 Sharps; f, .45 Springfield.

Fig. D.8. The land-and-groove marks on these .50/70-caliber bullets are indicative of being fired from a Gatling gun.

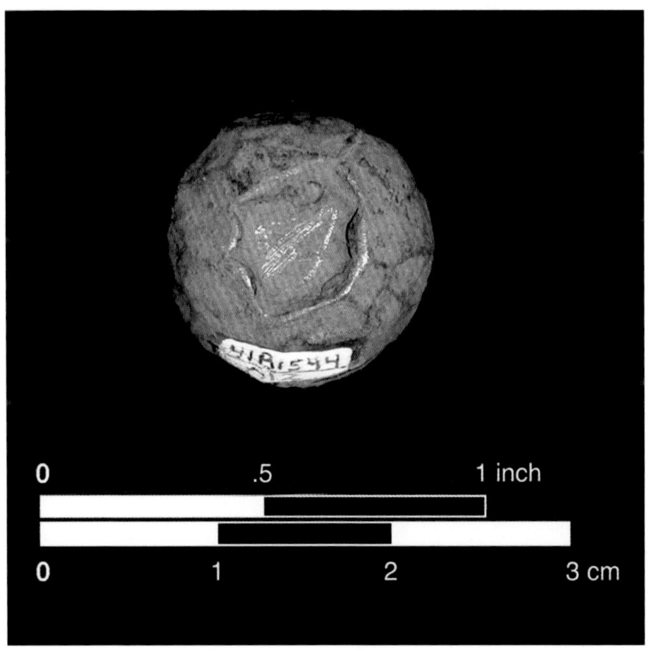

Fig. D.9. This .61-caliber copper rifle ball was made by hammering it to the approximate shape and intended caliber.

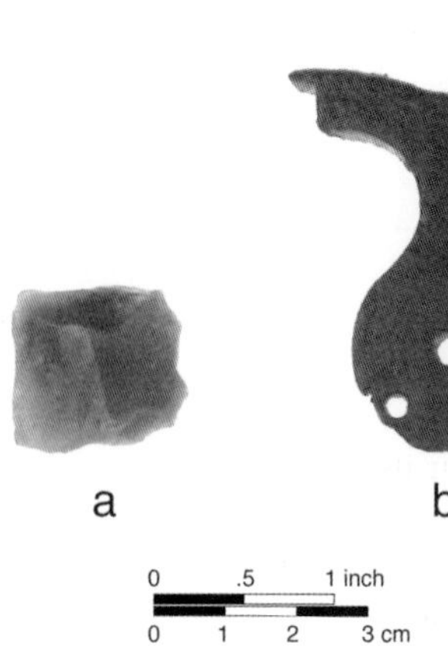

Fig. D.10. This gunflint (a) was probably made in England and shipped to the United States as a trade item. This gun hammer (b) is from a Colt Model 1860 Army revolver.

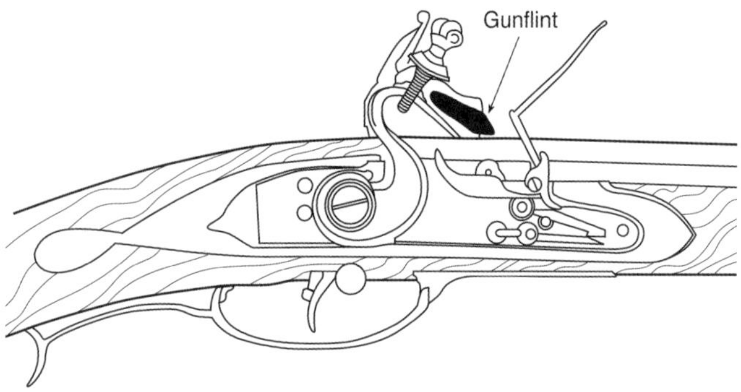

Fig. D.11. The flintlock rifle had a piece of flint clamped onto the gun's hammer. When the trigger was pulled, the flint struck the hinged cover of the pan, spraying sparks into the priming powder, which ignited the powder in the breech. Illustration by Roland Pantermuehl

Fig. D.12. Exploded Hotchkiss shell fragments: a, base cup showing the three flame grooves; b, brass fuse for the 14-second Bormann-Wright combination fusing system; c, 14-second Hotchkiss-Bormann time fuse.

implies, this fuse system was a combination of the time fuse and percussion fuse systems. The basic premise of the combination fuse was that the fuse was set to a specific detonation time prior to being fired. When the projectile was fired from the cannon tube, the inertia of the firing caused a plunger to slide down and strike a chemical composition against a metal platform, causing a flame to ignite the powder train inside the shell. If the projectile struck an object before the time element was completed, the system was designed to activate as a percussion fuse.[16]

Also recovered were several base cups from shells (fig. D.12a). The base cups have three flame grooves, which ran the full length of the shell. The function of the flame grooves was to aid the propellant charge flame to travel more readily past the shell body and light the paper time fuse. The shell fragments recovered from the battle site are from common shells. The base cups of the recovered shells have a diameter of 2.94 inches. Hotchkiss common shells of this diameter were 6 5/16 inches long and weighed 8 pounds 14 ounces (fig. D.13).[17]

Hotchkiss common shells were manufactured with a sabot made of lead. The sabot was attached directly onto the projectile and served as the driving band for the projectile. When the gun was fired, the gases from the propellant charge caused the sabot to expand into the rifling grooves inside the bore of the gun. This, in turn, caused the projectile to rotate, which extended its range and improved stability. Several pieces of lead sabots were recovered during the investigations.

Metal Arrowpoints

Eight iron arrowpoints were recovered from the battle site (fig. D.14) and six other metal arrowpoints and a point preform were recovered at Site 41BI544 (fig. D.15). Metal arrowpoints, most often made of iron, were a common trade item from the early 1600s to as late as the early twentieth century. Some metal points were commercially made by European and American cutlery firms, and some were apparently made by trading post blacksmiths, but the greatest number of them appear to be of Indian manufacture using metal chisels, axes, and files to cut and shape the points from strap iron or other similar material. Metal arrowpoints had virtually supplanted chipped stone arrowpoints by the mid-nineteenth century.[18]

Of the iron arrowpoints recovered, all but specimen 944 from the battle site, which is broken and appears to have never been completed, have stems. The stem on specimen 438 is unique in that it has shallow basal serrations. Specimen 505 from the battle site and specimen 168 from Site 41BI544 have straight shoulders, whereas all the other complete points, except specimen 140, have shoulders that angle upward. On specimen 140 one of the shoulders angles up and the other shoulder angles down. Specimens 510, 943, and 944 obtained from the battle site are particularly corroded and in poor condition.

The arrowpoints recovered from the battle site have

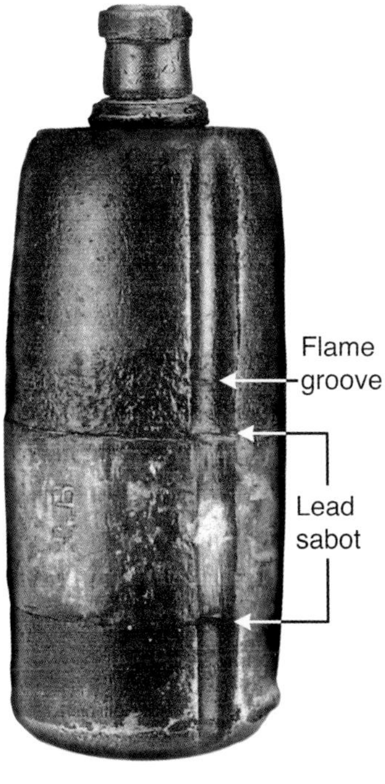

Fig. D.13. 2.94-inch-diameter Hotchkiss artillery shell. Note the lead sabot and flame grooves that run the length of the shell. Courtesy Jack Melton

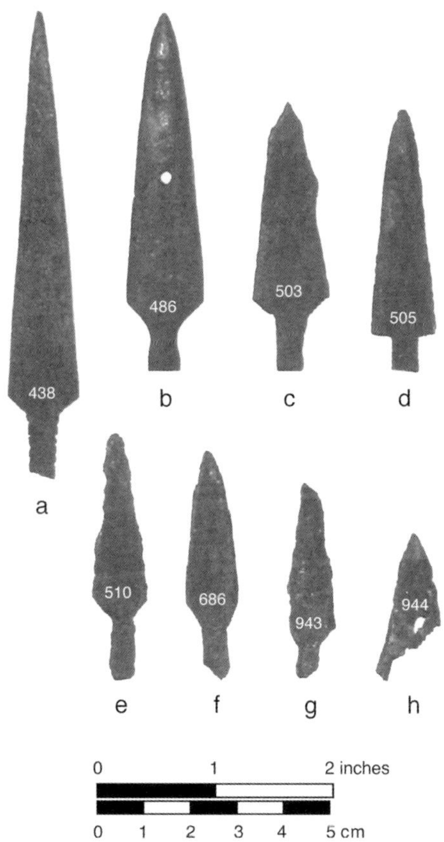

Fig. D.14. By the mid-1800s, iron and steel had replaced stone as the material from which Indians made points for their arrows. The metal arrowpoints recovered from the Battle of Red River site include (a) one that may have been commercially made and traded to the Indians and seven (b–h) that were made by the Indians.

an average length of 5.36 cm, an average width of 1.44 cm, and an average thickness of 1.9 mm (table D.6). The arrowpoints from Site 41BI544 are slightly smaller overall, averaging 3.51 cm in length, 1.52 cm in width, and 1.7 mm in thickness. All but one of the arrowpoints recovered from both sites appear to be Indian made. The Indian-made points are somewhat asymmetrical and were apparently cut from scrap pieces of metal or fashioned from metal barrel hoops, as illustrated by specimen 486 (fig. D.14b), which has a small hole near its center. The hole appears to be where the brad held the metal hoop onto the barrel.

The only arrowpoint recovered that may be commercially made is specimen 438 (fig. D.14a). This point is substantially longer than the other arrowpoints, at 9.11 cm, and is symmetrical in outline. It has a straight, serrated stem. The base of the stem is angled, but it appears that the stem has been broken and reworked. This point is almost identical in outline and symmetry, though shorter in length, to one recovered in southwest Kansas that was stamped with a trademark indicating English manufacture in the latter half of the nineteenth century (fig. D.16).[19]

The arrowpoint preform (specimen 165, fig. D.15g) from Site 41BI544 is chisel-cut from a piece of flat iron. It is triangular in outline and measures 4.81 cm in length, 1.87 cm in maximum width, and 1.4 mm in thickness. The metal arrowpoints and point preform recovered from both the battle site and the village site clearly indicate that even as late as 1874 the Indians were relying heavily on the bow and arrow not only for hunting but also in warfare. Obviously, firearms were being acquired and used by the Indians, but they had not completely supplanted the use of the bow and arrow.

Table D.6. Arrowpoints, Battle of Red River and Site 41BI544

Site	*Specimen*	*Length (cm)*	*Width (cm)*	*Thickness (cm)*
41AM10	438	6.87	1.76	0.26
	486	4.47	1.19	0.21
	503	9.11	1.67	0.17
	505	5.15	1.71	0.15
	510	5.08	1.43	0.19
	686	3.71	1.33	0.21
	943	4.71	1.25	0.17
	944	3.77	1.21	0.19
	average	5.36	1.44	0.19
41BI544	29	4.05	1.62	0.18
	134	3.05	1.25	0.18
	136	4.16	1.65	0.16
	137	4.48	2.02	0.17
	140	2.57	1.24	0.15
	168	2.72	1.31	0.15
	average	3.51	1.52	0.17

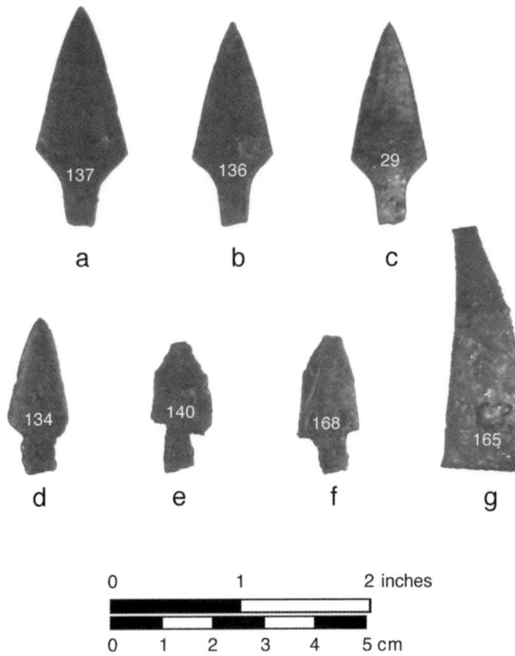

Fig. D.15. Iron arrowpoints were also recovered from Site 41BI544: a–f, Indian-made points; g, preform for a point.

Muzzle Loader Barrel

A portion of a rifle barrel from a .50-caliber muzzle loader was recovered at the extreme southern end of the battle site. The length of the barrel is 50.6 cm. The stock and hammer are missing, and the end of the octagonal barrel has been broken.

As the Indian villagers fled from the advancing U.S. Army troops, they apparently destroyed much of their property they could not take with them. Lieutenant Baldwin states that the Indians had burned their lodges and their contents and "had destroyed everything."[20] Despite Baldwin's statement, it is unlikely that the Indians were the ones who broke the muzzle loader, because firearms of any kind would have been among the more prized Indian possessions. It is more likely that the weapon was lost or dropped by the fleeing Indians and the army troops found and destroyed it.

Pistol Hammer

A hammer from a Colt Model 1860 Army revolver (fig. D.10b) was recovered at Site 41BI544. The Colt Model 1860 revolver was a six-shot, .44-caliber percussion revolver. It is believed that the hammer is associated with the Indian occupants of the site rather than the army personnel because the army troops were carrying the Colt Model 1873 .45-caliber revolver, and no .44-caliber revolvers are listed on the ordnance returns for any of the companies that participated in the battle (see appendix B).

Ramrod

A complete ramrod for a Model 1868 or 1870 .50/70 Springfield rifle was recovered from the battle site (fig. D.17). Though referred to as a ramrod, the rod was actually used for cleaning the barrel of the rifle. The rod measures 90.4 cm in total length. The head of the rod has an opening through which a rag could be inserted and then wrapped around the shank of the rod and inserted into the rifle barrel to clean it.

Other Indian-Associated Artifacts

Awls

A small awl fashioned from a square nail was recovered from the battle site, and four other awls were found at Site 41BI544 (fig. D.18). Awls were a domestic tool for sewing or working with leather. Like the awl from the battle site, two of the awls from the village site were fashioned from square nails. On these awls, both ends of the nail were sharpened to a point to form the awl. The two square nail awls from 41BI544 are burned and heavily corroded. Of the other awls from 41BI544, one was made from a short piece of round wire, and the other was fashioned from an unused horseshoe nail. The overall lengths of the awls range from 5.2 cm to 9.6 cm.

Bells

A small brass bell and a "hawk" bell (fig. D.19) were recovered from the battle site. The diameter of the brass bell at its base is

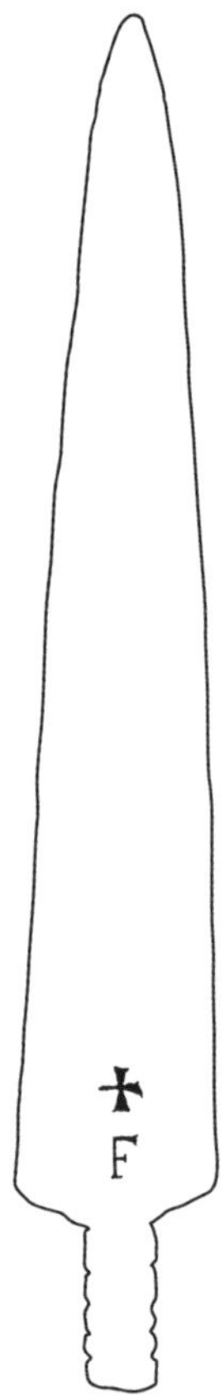

Fig. D.16. Commercially made iron arrowpoint stamped with a maker's mark indicating manufacture in England. Note the similarity between this point and that shown in Fig. D.14a. Adapted from Taylor, "Preliminary Study of Metal Arrowpoints," fig. 13.

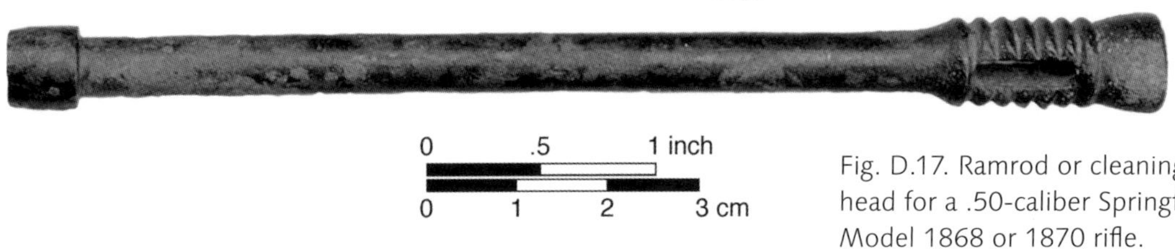

Fig. D.17. Ramrod or cleaning rod head for a .50-caliber Springfield Model 1868 or 1870 rifle.

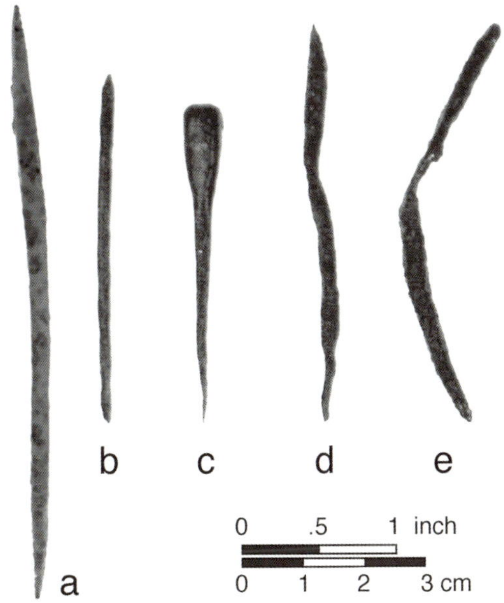

Fig. D.18. Iron awls, used for sewing and in leatherwork. Specimens a, d, and e were fashioned from square nails, specimen b was made from a piece of round wire, and specimen c was made from a horseshoe nail.

4.65 cm, and it is approximately 3.2 cm in height. The bell's clapper was recovered next to the bell. The clapper is a small flat piece of iron and appears to be a replacement rather than the original clapper.

The round hawk bell is made of thin brass and has a hole in the top for the attachment eye. On the bottom of the bell are two round holes cut through the sheet brass, and a slit connects the holes. The bell has a diameter of 1.5 cm. As a trade item, the Indians used hawk bells for decorations on numerous items such as clothing and cradleboards, and they also wore them in their hair.

Bore Cleaning Brushes

Two brass bore cleaning brushes were recovered, one from Site 41BI544 (specimen 26, fig. D.20a) and a similar specimen from the battle site (specimen 1030, fig. D.20b). No bristles remain on either brush. The brushes are two variations of Civil War–era carbine cleaning or wiping brushes. Specimen 26 is a male-threaded brush that screwed into a brass, female-threaded tip that was attached to a long leather thong (generally about 3 feet in length), which allowed the brush to be pulled through the bore of the carbine. On specimen 1030 the brass female-threaded tip is still attached to the brush, but the leather thong is missing. The bristle area length of the brush from the village is 10.6 cm long; that from the battle site measures 9.3 cm. These lengths suggests that the brush diameter was about 1.9 cm, suitable to clean the bores on .50-caliber and larger guns like the Spencer.[21]

Fig. D.19. Bells were a common trade item to the Indians. Two types of bells were recovered: left, brass hawk bell; right, brass round bell.

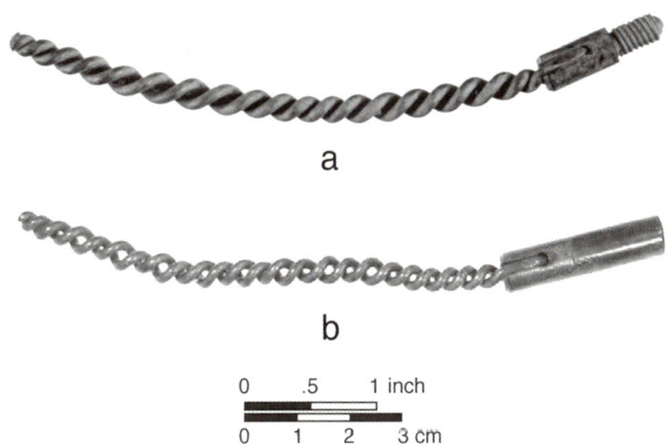

Fig. D.20. Bore cleaning brushes were used to clean the inside of a carbine or rifle barrel: a, male-threaded brush; b, female threaded tip still attached to the brush.

Buckle and Cinch Ring Tongue

One D-shaped buckle from Site 41BI544 was recovered (fig. D.21a). The buckle is for a three-quarter-inch strap and is most likely from a bridle. The tongue from a saddle cinch ring (fig. D.21b) was recovered near the buckle. Both of these horse-related items were found in an area of the site where other Indian-associated artifacts were recovered, and they are presumed to be associated with the Indian occupants of the site.

Buttons

Ten metal clothing buttons associated with the Indians were recovered, six from the battle site and four from the village site. The six buttons from the battle site are iron, jean-style buttons (fig. D.22e–j). None of them have back marks. The buttons range from 14 mm to 17 mm in diameter. These buttons were found in an area where several Indian-associated cartridges were recovered.

The buttons from Site 41BI544 are all of different types. Specimen 124 is an iron two-piece, four-hole button 16.4 mm in diameter (fig. D.22a). Specimen 0.2 is a brass and gilded button with clasp ties that measures 20.3 mm in diameter (fig. D.22b). The front of this button is decorated with a bow design. This may have been on a woman's dress. Specimen 49 is brass with a staff type shank on the back and measures 12.5 mm in diameter. It is decorated with an incised star and a dimpled border (fig. D.22c). It is backmarked HORSTMANN BROS&CO. PHILA, and the button was manufactured between 1859 and 1863. This button may have been used on women's blouses or vests. Specimen 186 is an iron one-piece button with a loop or shank back. It measures 25.4 mm in diameter and is decorated with a large flower design (fig. D.22d). Although specimens 0.2, 124, and 186 have not been dated, they are believed to be associated with the Indian occupants of the site.

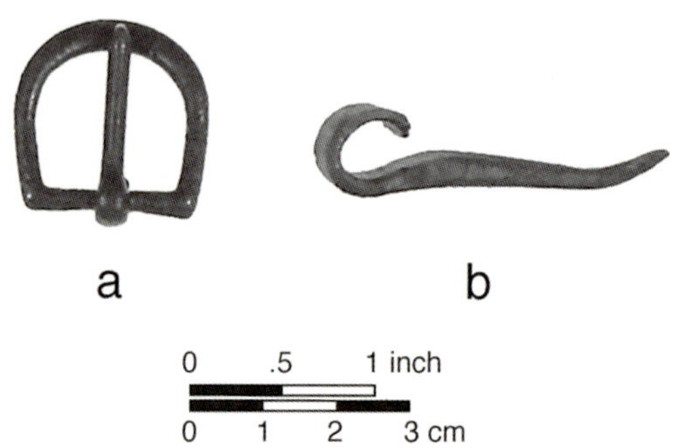

Fig. D.21. (a) bridle buckle and (b) tongue from a saddle cinch ring.

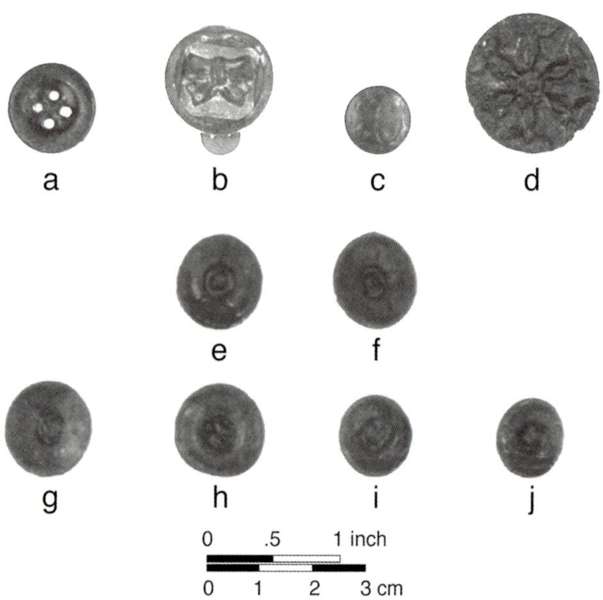

Fig. D.22. Indian-associated buttons.

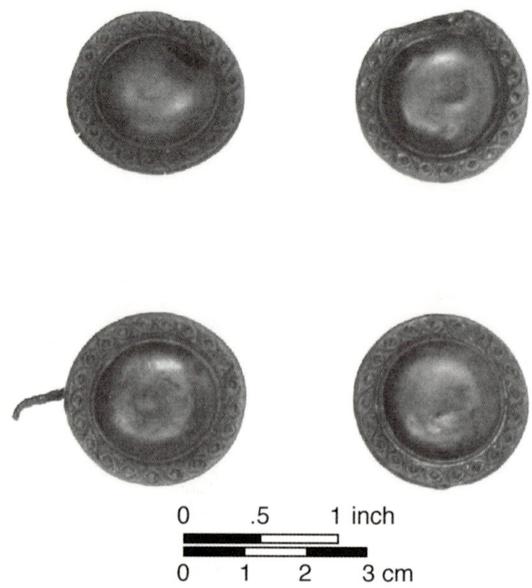

Fig. D.23. Conchas were used to decorate Indian clothing, horse bridles, and pouches.

Conchas

Four nickel-plated brass conchas (fig. D.23) were recovered from the battle site. The four conchas are identical. They are slightly domed in the center and have a looped weave pattern around their edges. Each concha is 2.9 cm in diameter. They have nickel-plated copper attachment wires soldered to the center of their backs.

The conchas were all recovered within a few feet of one another from a small hill near the southern end of the site. Several Indian-associated cartridges were also recovered here. Conchas were popular items used to decorate belts, pouches, leggings, and bridles.

Coscojos

Two *coscojos* were recovered during the investigations of the battle site and three more were found at Site 41BI544 (fig. D.24a). A *coscojo* is a metal jingle attached to a bridle or bit.[22] *Coscojos* were made from flat strips of iron with a loop at one end and were hung like pendants. They would have been hung from the headstall plate or chains of a Spanish or Mexican style ring bit.

Rein Chains and Ring

A section of a bridle rein chain (fig. D.24b) consisting of six S-shaped wire links was recovered from the battle site. The length of the chain is 14.2 cm. Another section of a rein chain consisting of four links and measuring 11.7 cm long was found at Site 41BI544. The rein chains would have attached to the shank of the ring bit on one end and usually to a brass ring on the other end. One such brass ring (fig. D.24c) was recovered at 41BI544. It has an inside diameter of 2 cm and was attached between the rein chain and the reins of the bridle.

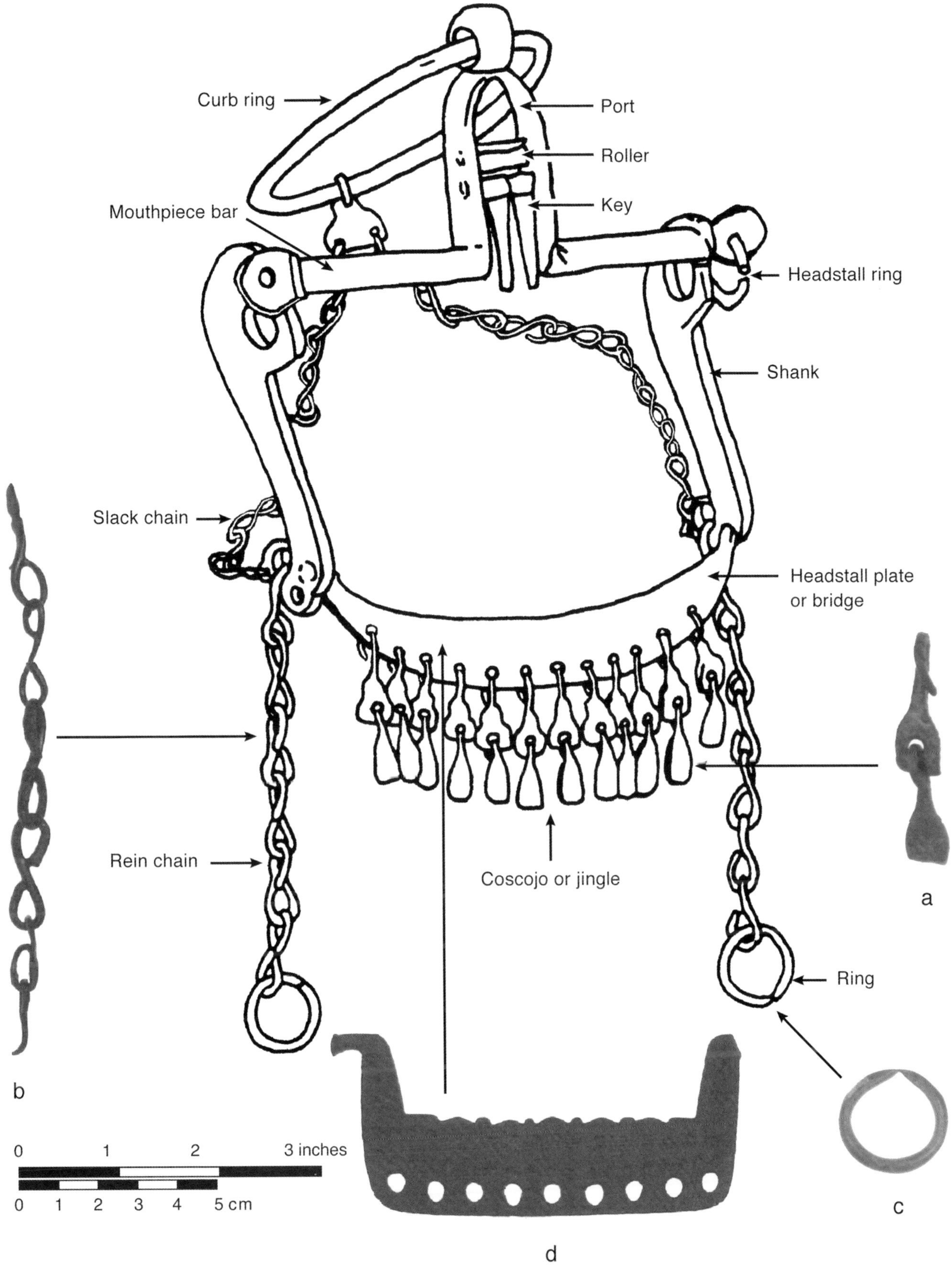

Fig. D.24. Components of a Mexican-style ring bit: a, *coscojos;* b, rein chain; c, rein chain ring; d, headstall plate. Adapted from Simmons and Turley, *Southwestern Colonial Ironwork*, fig. 1, p. 101.

Headstall Plate or Bridge

Many Native American bridles were ornamented with a metal headstall plate that connected between the shanks of the bridle. A rectangular headstall plate was recovered from the battle site (fig. D.24d). This plate has nine holes across its lower edge, from which *coscojos* would have been suspended. Above these holes are two rows of small five-pointed stars that have been stamped into the plate. There are nineteen stars in one row and seventeen in the other. There are also three stars in a single vertical line on each shank of the plate. The end of the right shank is broken.

The horse trappings recovered from both sites, which include the headstall plate, rein chains, rein chain ring, and *coscojos,* are testament to the reliance and importance the Southern Plains Indians placed on horses.

Cut Iron and Brass

Six pieces of iron and three pieces of brass that had been cut or worked were recovered from Site 41BI544. The cut iron specimens are all strap pieces of various sizes and lengths. All of the pieces appear to have been cut by chisel and hammer. The pieces range in width from 1.5 cm to 2.5 cm and in thickness from 0.8 mm to 1.5 mm. The ends of two of the cut iron pieces are concave and exhibit use wear and smoothing within the concavity (fig. D.25). The use wear on these pieces appears to be the result of the pieces being used in a scraping motion on a rounded object such as a small tree branch or wooden shaft.

One of the cut brass pieces (specimen 164) has also been utilized as a scraping implement. This specimen (fig. D.26a) was cut with sheers from a thin-walled object such as a kettle or pan. One edge of the specimen is serrated with five shallow V-shaped notches, probably produced with a small file. The serrated edge is worn and smoothed from use as a scraper. Specimen 120 is a brass corner bracket (fig. D.26b) from a small box or chest that has had one end cut off with a chisel. Several cut marks are evident on the other end of the bracket, but they have not cut through the bracket. No other evidence of use is on the bracket. The remaining cut brass item (specimen 144, fig. D.26c) is a 6.2 cm long bar that has been hammered flat. The bar is 8.2 mm wide and approximately 2.4 mm thick. Both ends of the bar appear to be chisel-cut. The bar appears smoothed and polished but shows no other evidence of use. Its function is not known.

Fleshers

Two iron fleshers were recovered from the battle site. Fleshers were used to strip and scrape the flesh from the hides of animals. One of the fleshers (fig. D.27a) measures 30.5 cm long and was made on a squared flat strap that varies in thickness from 5 mm to 8 mm. The piece has three holes in it, one on either end and one in the middle. In the middle hole is an iron brad or rivet that is bent down against the tool. One end of the piece has been flattened, and small notches have been filed into the end (fig. D.28a).

Fig. D.25. Indians often used pieces of iron straps, possibly from barrel hoops, to make tools. The two strap pieces on the left show evidence of use as scraping implements.

The other flesher (fig. D.27b) is 38.1 cm long and was made on a heavy iron shank that has seven holes offset along its length. The shank has been hammered to flatten it and, like the other flesher, this one has a series of small notches cut into the end of the shank to form the working end of the tool, though the notches on this specimen are deeper and more pronounced than on the other specimen (fig. D.28b).

Kettle Bail Ears

A bail ear from a brass kettle was recovered at Site 41BI544 (specimen 70, fig. D.29a), and a similar bail ear was found at the battle site (specimen 1149, fig. D.29b). Both bail ears are of cast brass and are similar in construction. The lower end of each is rectangular, with two brass rivets that attached the ear to the kettle. The upper end of the bail ears are rounded and perforated for the bail attachment. Between the bail perforation and the rectangular lower part, the body of the ear bulges outward, creating a channel on the inside. Presumably the rim of the kettle fitted into this channel. The perforation on specimen 1149 is extensively worn, resulting in it being more oblong rather than round.

Though the two bail ears are similar, specimen 70 is slightly larger. Maximum length of this bail ear is 4.45 cm, and the maximum width of the lower rectangular part is 4.0 cm. The thickness is variable, ranging from 4 mm to 8 mm.

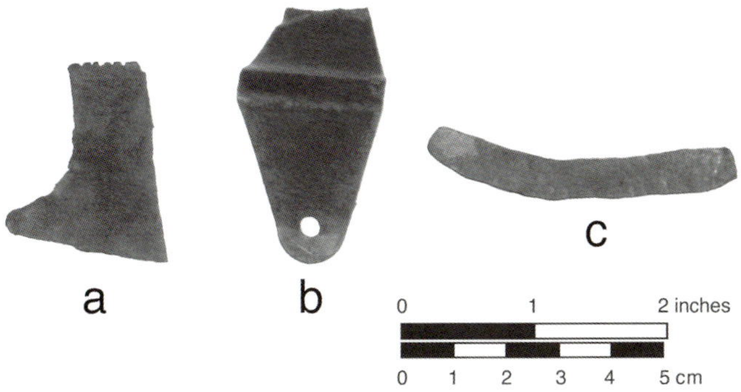

Fig. D.26. Indians utilized any metal object they could acquire. Here a piece of brass (a) has been serrated for use as a scraping tool, a brass corner bracket (b) from a chest has been cut with a chisel, and a small brass bar (c) has been hammered flat and cut with a chisel.

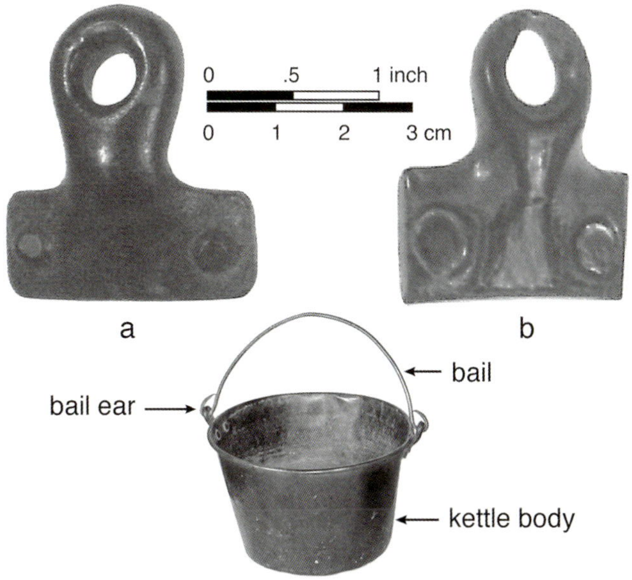

▲Fig. D.29. Brass kettles were desirable trade items for the Southern Plains Indians. Shown here are bail ears from two brass kettles.

▼Fig. D.27. Fleshers were tools used to strip and scrape the flesh from the hides of animals. The fleshers shown here were fashioned from pieces of iron.

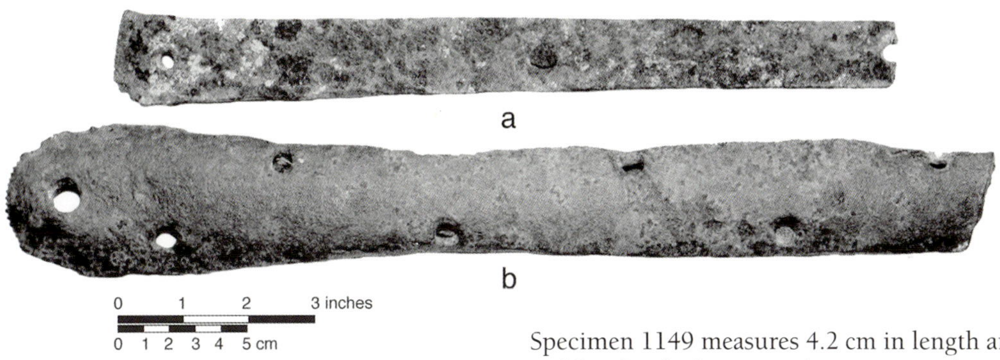

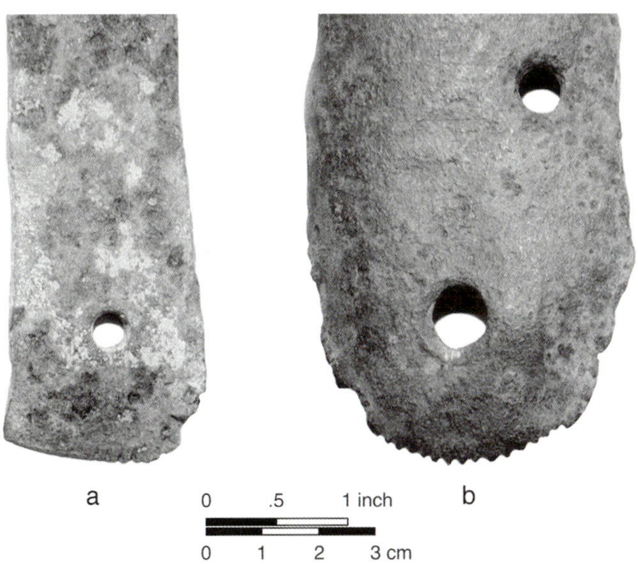

Fig. D.28. The serrations on the ends of these metal fleshers were most likely made with a small file.

Specimen 1149 measures 4.2 cm in length and 3.5 cm in width. The thickness on this ear varies from approximately 3 mm to 7 mm.

Brass kettles were desirable trade items for the Southern Plains Indians because they were more durable and easier to carry than fragile pots made of clay. Also, kettles had value even after they wore out and could no longer be used as containers. For example, kettles could be cut up to make tinklers, pendants, scraping tools, and arrowpoints.

Percussion Cap Tin

A small tin container for holding percussion caps was found at Site 41BI544. The container measures 3.24 cm in diameter and is 1.27 cm tall. When the container was opened in the laboratory, several small beads of mercury were found inside.

Percussion caps were used with percussion firearms, which were developed in the early 1800s and began replacing flintlock firearms during the first quarter of the nineteenth century. The percussion rifle required no flint and no priming powder like the flintlock rifle. Instead, a percussion cap was placed on a hollow cone or nipple that led to the powder in the gun's breech. The percussion cap was a small copper cup that contained a priming compound of fulminate of mercury, which is extremely explosive. The gun's hammer was shaped to strike the cap on the nipple, which caused a small explosion that traveled down the nipple to the powder.

Punch

A hexagonal iron punch 23.3 cm long was recovered from the battle site (fig. D.30a). The specimen is complete, though the head of the punch is well hammered and battered. The punch was found in an area of the battle site where several other Indian-associated domestic items were recovered. The punch, like the other items, apparently was discarded as the Indian families fled toward Tule Canyon.

Tinklers

One tinkler, or jingle, as they are sometimes referred to, was recovered from the battle site, and two others were found at Site 41BI544 (fig. D.31). Metal tinklers are conical ornaments made by cutting sheet metal into triangles and curling them into cones. They were often used by Native Americans to adorn clothing, moccasins, bags, and quivers. Multiple tinklers were sometimes attached to an item of clothing where they would strike each other when in motion, producing a tinkling sound. The recovered tinklers range in length from 2.4 cm to 3.3 cm.

When tinklers are curled, the edges either meet in the center or overlap to the right or left, probably according to individual preference (fig. D.32). Specimens 57 and 657 are center curled, whereas specimen 166 has a right curl.

Utensils

There are twelve specimens included in the category of utensils. Eleven of these were recovered from the battle site, and a single spoon cup was recovered at Site 41BI544. The utensils are five spoon or fork handles, three spoon cups, one fork tine, and three knife fragments (fig. D.30b–c). Two of the knife pieces are blade fragments of butter knives. The other knife is a butcher knife that is approximately 85 percent complete, with three brass rivets still in place in the shank of the handle. This knife probably had a wooden handle, which has deteriorated. The blade measures 13 cm long and has several nicks and chips along the cutting edge.

Other Army-Associated Artifacts

Buckles

Seven iron buckles were recovered from the battle site. Four are roller buckles (fig. D.33b, d, f, g) and could have been used on packsaddles or cartridge belts. The other three buckles are small center-bar buckles (fig. D.33a, c, e) that may have been used on a horse bridle, link strap, or carbine socket.[23]

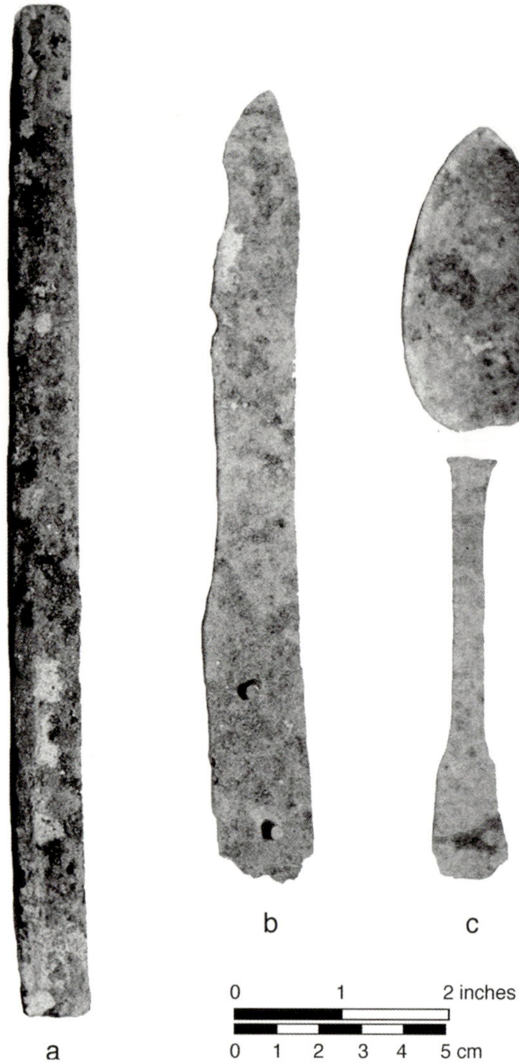

Fig. D.30. Discarded utensils and other metal tools marked the route of the retreating Indian families: a, large punch; b, butcher knife; c, spoon bowl and handle.

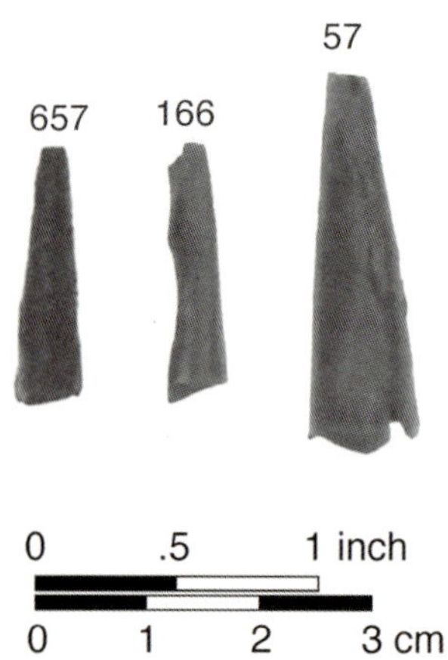

Fig. D.31. Iron tinklers were used to adorn clothing, bags, and quivers.

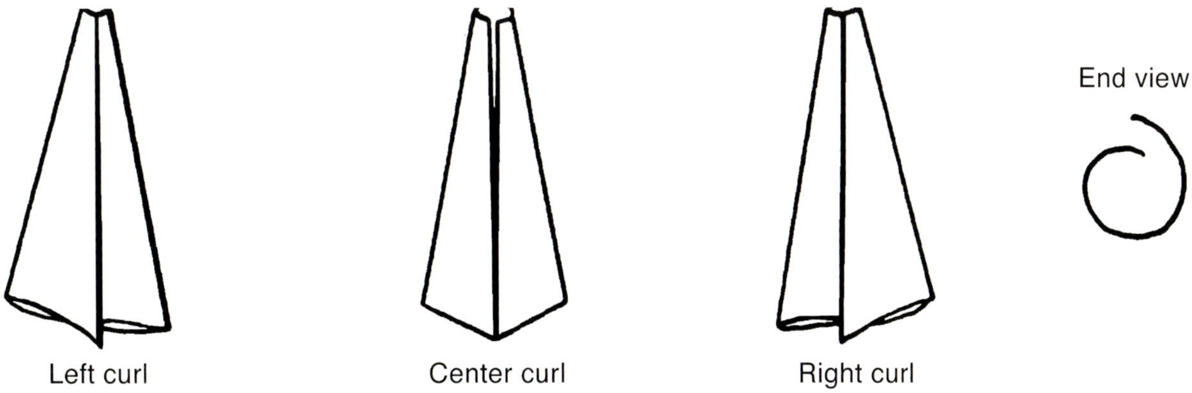

Fig. D.32. Tinklers were curled so that their edges overlap to the left, meet in the center, or overlap to the right.

Buttons

Five army-associated buttons were recovered (fig. D.34). Four of these are uniform buttons and one is a rain slicker or poncho button. One of the military uniform buttons (specimen 326) was recovered from the battle site, and the other three (specimens 153, 156, and 184) are from Site 41BI544. The military brass general service uniform button bears a stamped eagle on the front piece, with the eagle's head turned to its right and its wings and legs extended. The eagle has a raised spade-shaped shield on its chest and grasps three arrows in its left talon and a laurel branch in its right.

The military uniform buttons are represented in two sizes, both of which were used on uniforms of enlisted men. Specimen 153, the smallest button, is 14.5 mm in diameter. It is backmarked SCOVILLS & CO. EXTRA, a backmark used from 1840 to 1850 by the Scovill Company. This button size was used on blouse cuffs, caps, and hats. The larger buttons (specimens 156, 184, and 326) are 19.4 mm in diameter. These buttons would have been used on coats. Specimen 184 is backmarked SCOVILL MFG CO WATERBURY, which was used by the Scovill Company from 1850 to 1865.[24]

The other army-associated button from the battle site, specimen 186, is a large two-piece, two-holed rain slicker button that has a brass-covered face and bears the backmark TOWERS WIRE FASTENED. This button has a diameter of 23 mm. The Abner J. Tower Company manufactured rain slickers and other oiled clothing in Boston, Massachusetts, between 1873 and 1956.[25]

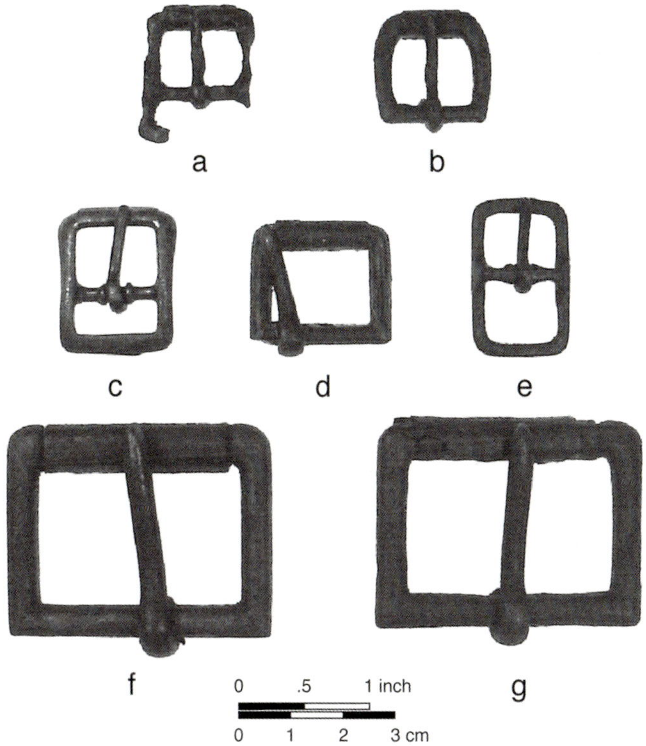

Fig. D.33. These army buckles were likely used on pack-saddles, cartridge belts, and horse tack.

Cans

Fragments of five tin cans with lead-soldered side seams and one leaded can lid were recovered from the battle site. Fragments from an additional nineteen cans were found at Site 41BI544. Most of the can fragments from the village site are burned and, with only a few exceptions, the fragments are not complete enough to determine the sizes of the cans. Of the few determinable cans, most are No. 2 cans (8.7 cm by 11.5 cm), which held 20 ounces. For the most part, the cans appear to be hole-in-cap types with lead-soldered lap side seams and stamped or flanged ends (fig. D.35).[26] Most of the recovered cans were opened by using a knife or other sharp tool to cut an X pattern through one end, which resulted in four triangular pieces that could then be lifted up. The tin cans were probably used for rations or other provisions.

Fig. D.34. Army-associated buttons.

Fig. D.35. Flattened lead-soldered lap side seam No. 2 can. Cans such as this held army provisions.

Canteen Chains and Stopper Rings

Three canteen chains, two with the stopper rings and tin washers for the now-missing cork still attached, were recovered from the battle site. Each chain measures approximately 9.7 cm long. The canteen chains and stopper rings (fig. D.36) could be from either the Model 1858 canteen or the Model 1874 canteen, which have identical chains and stopper rings. The 1874 army used a tin canteen covered with kersey cloth.[27]

Fig. D.36. Several canteen stopper rings and chains were recovered. Many of the soldiers were out of water by the time the battle ended; the temperature on August 30, 1874, was in excess of 100 degrees. Illustration by Roland Pantermuehl

Curry Comb

One curry comb (fig. D.37) was recovered from the battle site. It is similar to Civil War–era combs, with a square body and a Y-shaped handle riveted onto the body with three rivets. Dirt knockers extend from the sides of the body. The iron handle shank would have been inserted into a wooden handle and secured in place with a brass ferrule. The body of the comb measures 10.2 cm by 12.1 cm. The shank of the handle extends 10.2 cm out from the body.

The Model 1874 curry comb was curved on the sides, and the back was reinforced with wrought iron plates. The handle was also wrought iron and had a hoof hook attached to it.[28]

Harmonica Reed Plates

Three harmonica reed plates (fig. D.38) were found on the battle site. The reed plates in a harmonica sit on top and below the body or comb of the instrument and contain the reeds that produce the harmonica's sound when air is blown into the comb. The recovered reed plates apparently were from harmonicas soldiers carried with them onto the battlefield and lost during the battle. The plates are brass and each measures 10 cm in length. Each of the plates contains ten reed slots. Specimen 1014 is actually two plates that

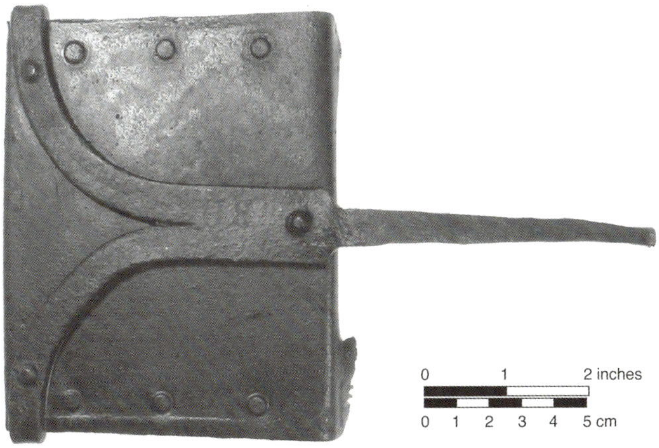

Fig. D.37. Civil War–era curry comb. Each cavalry soldier carried a curry comb in his saddle bag.

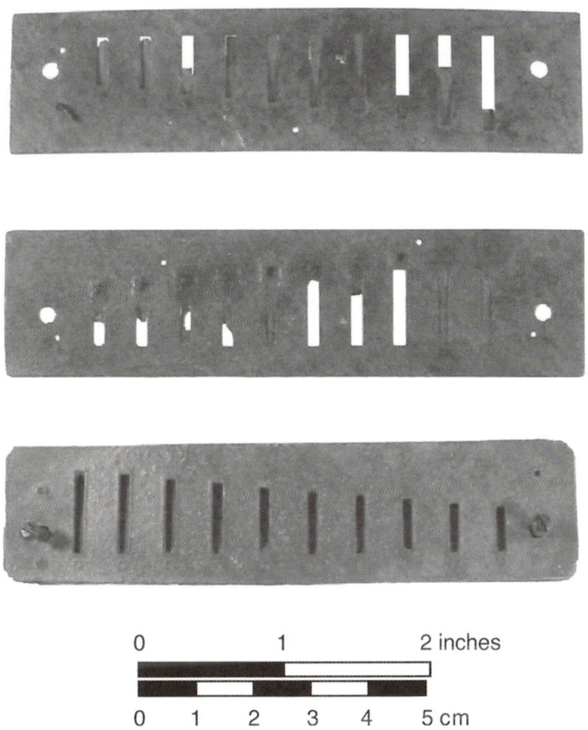

Fig. D.38. The harmonica was a common item carried by soldiers. Shown here are harmonica reed plates. Several reeds are missing on specimens 386 (top) and 459 (middle). Specimen 1014 (bottom) is actually two plates that are still connected, and all of the reeds remain intact.

are still connected, the comb having disintegrated over the years. All of the reeds are still intact on this plate, whereas on specimens 386 and 459 several reeds are missing.

Horseshoes and Mule Shoe

There were twenty-nine horseshoes (fig. D.39) recovered from the battle site and six from Site 41BI544. In addition, one mule shoe was recovered from 41BI544. All of the horseshoes appear to be of the Burden pattern. The Burden horseshoe pattern was introduced just before the Civil War and issued to the U.S. Army.[29] Of the horseshoes, eleven are worn in half—a testament to the excessive use these shoes received; as a general rule of thumb, army horseshoes were to be replaced on a monthly basis. Six horseshoes still have at least one nail present. Three of the shoes have toe caulks. The farrier often added caulks to the shoe to give the horse better traction.

Horseshoe Nails

A surprisingly large number of horseshoe nails were recovered. Of the 168 horseshoe nails recovered from the sites, 149 are unused (fig. D.39). Of the unused nails, seventy-two were recovered from a single location on the battle site and probably represent a container of nails lost out of a supply wagon. The other unused nails were probably lost from the soldiers' saddlebags during the battle. Mounted troops were required to carry two extra horseshoes and fifteen extra horseshoe nails in their saddlebags while on the march. All of the recovered horseshoe nails are of the Ausable variety, which had a rounded head with sides that angle inward to the nail shank. Ausable nails were made for the Burden horseshoe.[30]

Nails and Tacks

Sixty square nails and tacks (fig. D.40) ranging in size from 2d to 40d were recovered at Site 41BI544 (table D.7). Cut square nails in the 4d size dominate the nail assemblage. The concentration of these nails near army-related artifacts suggests that they are associated with the army occupation of the site. Army hardtack ration boxes and ammunition boxes were constructed of wood and nailed and screwed together. Period ammunition boxes used 4d nails in their construction, and ration boxes probably did as well.[31] The fact that no wood screws, which were also used in ammunition boxes, were recovered from the site may suggest that the nails are from ration boxes. Ration boxes at the site would be expected, since part of Miles's troops camped there for nine days after the battle.

Picket Pins

Portions of two Model 1859 army-issue picket pins (fig. D.41) were recovered at Site 41BI544. Picket pins were driven into the ground to tether the army horses and mules. Typically, near the top of the pin a ring was attached, to which the animal was tied. On the Model 1859 picket pin this ring was shaped like a figure eight.

Specimen 179 is nearly complete but lacks the figure eight tether ring. This specimen measures 31.3 cm in length. Specimen 107 is the lower portion of a bent and broken picket pin shaft.

Pommel Ornament

A brass pommel ornament (fig. D.42a) from a McClellan saddle was recovered from Site 41BI544. The shield-shaped

Fig. D.39. A horseshoe (left) and horseshoe nails (right). Mounted troops were required to carry extra horseshoes and horseshoe nails in their saddlebags.

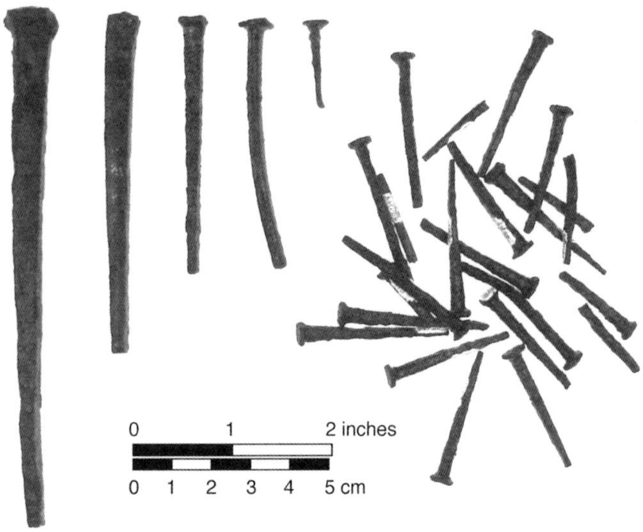

Fig. D.40. A variety of square nails and tacks, probably from army ration and supply boxes.

Table D.7. Nails and Tacks, Site 41BI544

Size	*Number*	*Specimen*
2d	7	34, 163 (six specimens)
4d	32	67 (24 specimens), 76, 83, 84, 96, 100, 110, 116, 176
7d	2	113, 121
8d	5	36, 79, 87, 88, 154
16d	1	75
40d	1	188
Fragments	12	20, 58, 98, 111, 112, 122, 123, 135, 155, 167, 175, 177

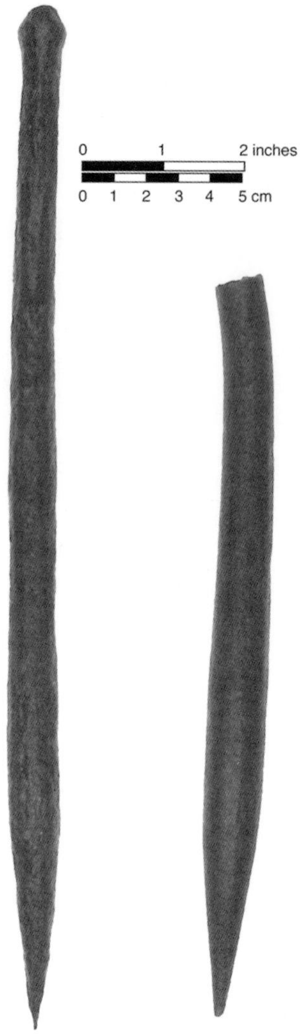

Fig. D.41. Model 1859 army-issue picket pins. Specimen 179 (left) is complete except for the tether ring. Specimen 107 (right) is most of the shaft of the pin.

pommel ornament is stamped 11 INCH SEAT, indicating the length of the seat of the saddle. The pommel ornament would have been centered near the top of the saddle's pommel and attached with three brass screw-pins.[32]

Rivet

A single small brass rivet was recovered from the battle site. The rivet has a flat head and may have been used on a variety of equipment, such as a horse halter, girth straps, soldiers' waist belts, or holsters.

Saddle Rings

Two saddle O-rings and two D-rings were recovered from the battle site. The O-rings are skirt rings (fig. D.42b), and the D-rings are saddle girth rings (fig. D.42c). Skirt rings served to attach the various pieces of pack equipment to the saddle. The girth ring attached to the cinch strap to secure the saddle on the horse.

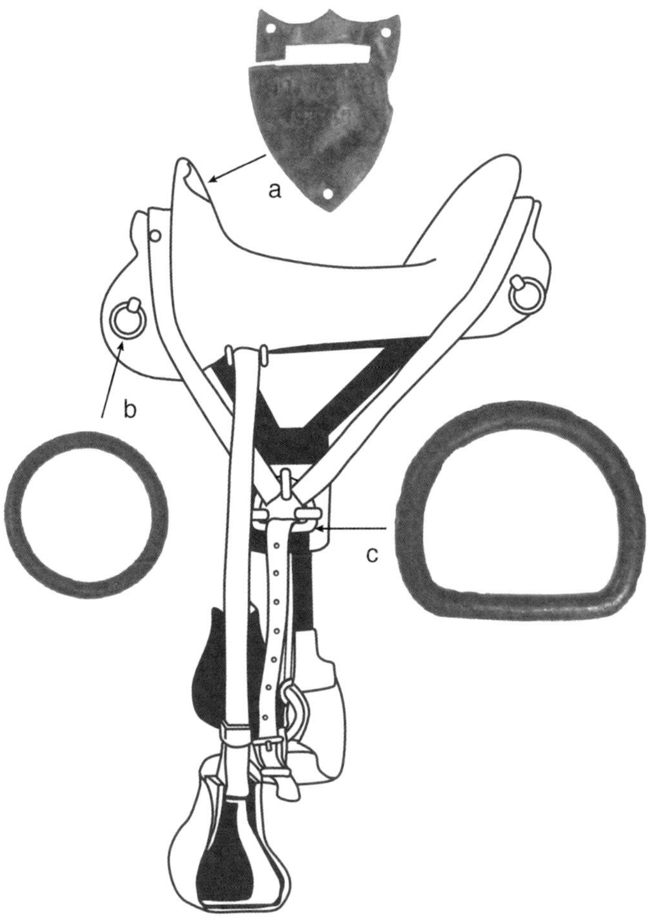

Fig. D.42. Various saddle parts and their placement on a saddle: a, brass pommel ornament from a McClellan saddle; b, skirt ring; c, girth D-ring. Illustration by Roland Pantermuehl

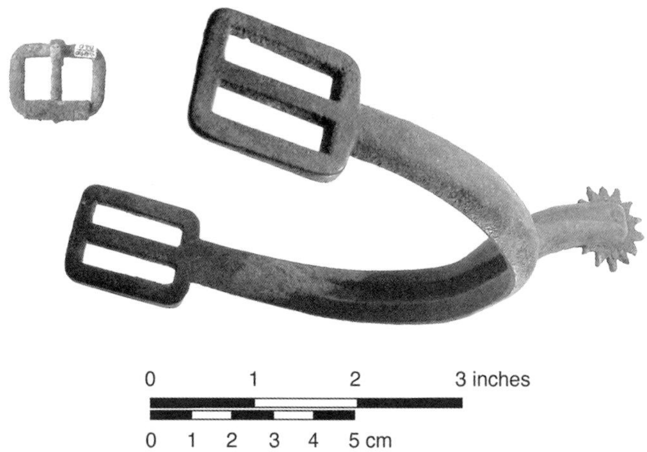

Fig. D.43. Model 1859 brass cavalry spur and spur strap buckle.

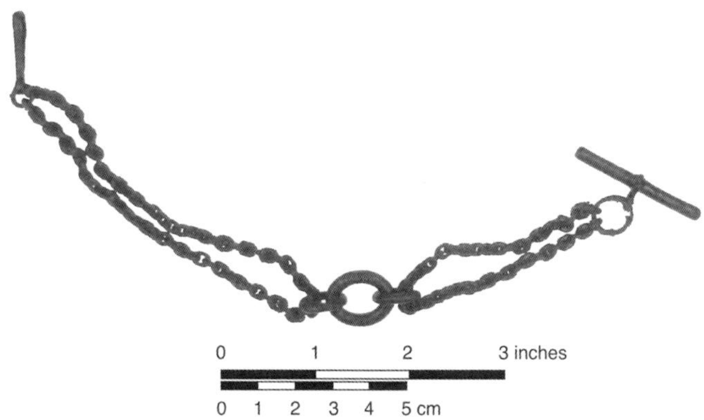

Fig. D.44. Pocket watch chain.

Cavalry Spur

One cavalry spur and associated strap buckle (fig. D.43) were recovered from the battle site. The brass spur is the regulation Model 1859 pattern with a small iron rowel and slots for attaching the spur to a boot. The iron strap buckle is a roller buckle that was recovered adjacent to the spur.

Harness Chain

One harness neck chain was recovered. It is 132 cm long and has two circular ring connectors near each end and another free-moving ring in the middle. A swivel connector is on one end. The harness neck chain would have been used with one of the mule-drawn army wagons.

Watch Chain

Specimen 25 is a pocket watch chain (fig. D.44) recovered from Site 41BI544. The double-strand chain has the T-bar on one end and the watch clasp on the other end. Approximately 8 cm from the T-bar is an iron ring that connects the double strands of the chain. The overall length of the chain is 22.2 cm.

If the watch chain is associated with the army occupation of Site 41BI544, then it most likely belonged to one of the officers. On the other hand, the chain may have been obtained by one of the Indians and subsequently lost when the Indians abandoned the site.

Appendix E

Descriptions and Analysis of Artifacts from the Battle of Lyman's Wagon Train Site

A total of 1,176 artifacts were recovered from the Battle of Lyman's Wagon Train site, 892 associated with the army and 284 with the Indians. Most of the artifacts are cartridges, among them 852 fired and forty-eight unfired cases of various calibers used by the army and Indians. Other than cartridges and bullets, 174 other artifacts were recovered from the site. Because the site area has never been used for any purpose other than ranch pasture, these artifacts are assumed battle-related. Of these, 170 were recovered within the area of the army defense site and were apparently associated with the wagon train personnel. The other four items were recovered from Indian locations at the site.

Arms and Ammunition

.44-Caliber Cartridge Cases

Eighteen .44-caliber cartridge cases were recovered, all of them from Indian positions. The cartridges are all of New Haven Arms Company (Winchester) manufacture (table E.1). Case dimensions are the same as found in Winchester-manufactured ammunition. Microscopic examination of the class characteristics on each cartridge case indicated that eight of the cases were fired in a Henry rifle or Model 1866 Winchester. Both are lever-action magazine-fed repeating rifles that could hold up to sixteen rounds in the magazine and chamber. Individual characteristics of the firing pin marks on the cartridge cases indicate that five Henrys or Winchester Model 1866 rifles fired the eight cases.

The Henry and Winchester Model 1866 rifles were prone to misfire. This problem is evident on cartridge cases B56 and B327, which have eight sets and two sets of firing pin marks, respectively. Some of the .44-caliber cases show bulging of the head, which is commonly found on fired .44 Henry cases. This is the result of the failure of the breech bolt, in either the Henry or Model 1866, to fit snugly against the face of the chamber and is not the result of being fired in one model or the other.

The presence of two cases indicating misfires brings up some interesting observations. Spacing of the firing pin marks on these cases indicates that they were rotated in the chamber slightly each time they were fired. This was not an easy task to perform with loaded cartridges in a Henry or Winchester Model 1866 rifle, as experimentation has shown. If the finger lever is gently thrown down when extracting the cartridge, the case drops back onto the cartridge lifter and can be inserted by hand back into the chamber. One must also look at the base of the case and rotate the misfire marks away from the firing pins. This all takes time.

The remaining .44-caliber cases were fired in two other firearm types. The .44 Henry was a popular round, and many other manufacturers chambered one or more models of their firearms for the Henry. A Colt Model 1872 Open Top revolver is represented by cases B59 and B61. It is interesting to note that these two revolver cartridges are the only pistol cartridge cases observed in the entire collection.

Table E.1. .44-Caliber Cartridge Case Matches, Battle of Lyman's Wagon Train

Firearm	*Specimen*	*Type*	*Comment*
.44 Henry			
1	B56, B370	Henry	Short, raised H, 8 firing pin marks on B56
2	B136, B137, B326	Henry	Long, no head stamp
3	B322	Henry	Short, raised H
4	B327	Henry	Long, raised H, 2 firing pin marks
5	C57	Henry	Long, raised H
.44 Colt Open top			
1	B59, B61	M1872 Colt Open Top	Long, no head stamp
.44 Ballard			
1	B261, B268, B270,B304	Ballard	Long except B268 (Short), no head stamps
2	B294, B295, B296,B297	Ballard	Short except B294 and B297 (Long); raised H head stamp on B294 and B297; rifle had breech face defect

Two different Ballard single shot rifles are represented by cartridge groups B261, B268, B270, and B304 and cartridges B294, B295, B296, and B297.

.45/55 or .45/70-Caliber Cartridge Cases

The vast majority of cartridge cases recovered from the Lyman Wagon Train battle site are nominally the .45/55 or .45/70-caliber. There are 518 fired .45-caliber cartridges and thirty-six unfired .45-caliber cartridges from the site. All of the unfired cartridges and all fired cartridge cases are Benét primed (an internally primed center-fire cartridge), and all cartridges and cartridge cases exhibit a wide crimp mark around the base to hold the Benét cup primer in position. The firing pin and extractor marks on the fired cartridge cases indicate that all but three were fired in the U.S. Army Springfield Arsenal–made Model 1873 Springfield rifle or carbine. The three exceptions are cases B21, B25, and B63, which are .45-caliber cartridges that were fired in Model 1868–1870 .50-caliber Springfield rifles. When these cases were fired in the larger-diameter chamber of the Model 1868–1870 Springfield rifles, they expanded and split lengthwise. These cartridge cases were recovered adjacent to several Indian-associated .50-caliber cartridge cases, and the firing pin marks on the .45-caliber cases indicate that they were fired from three separate Model 1868–1870 Springfield rifles.

Of the thirty-six unfired .45/55/70 rounds, five cartridges deserve further comment. Extractor failure was an oft-repeated complaint with the early issue .45/55 and .45/70 rounds.[1] Interestingly, only two of the recovered cases exhibit any evidence of extractor failure, but both are rather spectacular. On Specimen A547 the extractor tore the case head nearly off the body (fig. E.1a). The head remains barely attached, exposing the base of the Benét cup primer. In the second example, Specimen A142 has had the cartridge case head pulled completely off during the extraction process (fig. E.1b). The case body has been crushed at the head by some type of sharp force, probably a knife, which the operator apparently used to remove the jam from the rifle's chamber.

Specimen A345 has a dented case (fig. E.1c), and its bullet has apparently been ripped from the case mouth, as indicated by the deformation present there. The configuration of the denting and tearing of the metal suggests that a bullet struck this cartridge during the battle. Specimen A723 is an intact round but has had the bullet cut off immediately above the case mouth (fig. E.1d). In addition, one oxidized and broken unfired round has the remains of the cardboard wad exposed (fig. E.2b), indicating that it is a .45/55-caliber cartridge. This was the only cavalry caliber round identified in the analysis.

The cartridge cases analyzed revealed that a minimum of forty-one Springfield Model 1873 rifles were used in the engagement. It is entirely possible that many more were used in the fight, but the numbers of heavily oxidized and other problematic cases that could not be compared likely reduced the number of firearms identified. Of the .45/55 and .45/70 cartridge cases recovered from the site, 187 were unsuitable for analysis because of excessive oxidation and other factors. Table E.2 lists the matches among the .45/55 and .45/70 cartridge cases.

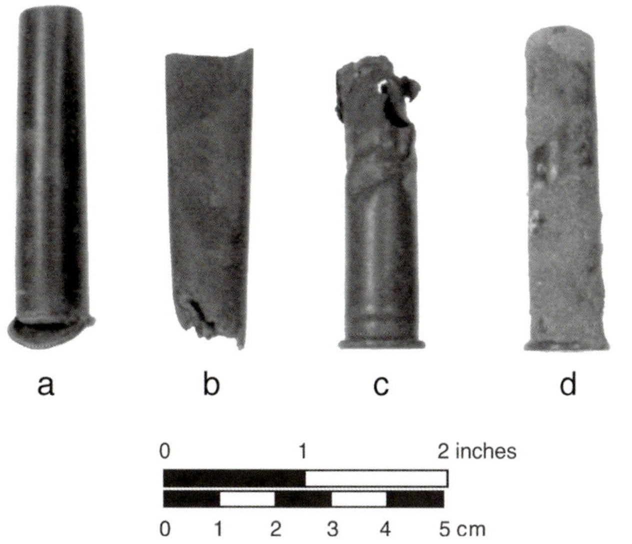

Fig. E.1. Some of the recovered .45/55 or .45/70 cartridge cases exhibited problems: a, cartridge case with a torn head as a result of extraction failure; b, cartridge case with the head torn completely off and evidence of prying to remove the case from the gun; c, cartridge that was struck by a bullet; d, unfired cartridge that has had the bullet cut off immediately above the case mouth.

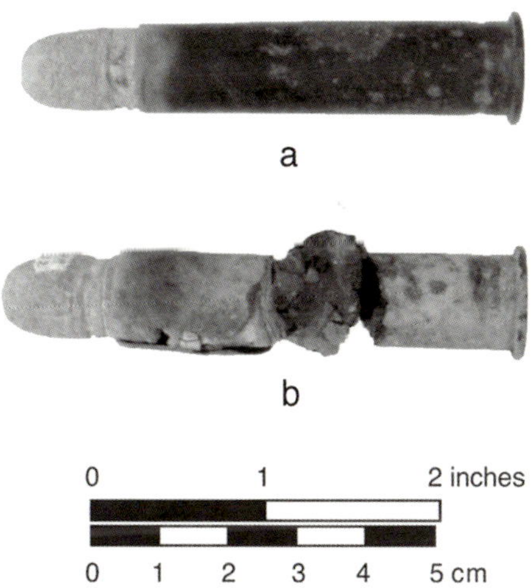

Fig. E.2. a, unfired .45/55 or .45/70 cartridge; b, oxidized and broken unfired round with the remains of the cardboard wad exposed, indicating that the cartridge is .45/55-caliber.

.50/70-Caliber Cartridge Cases

There are 143 fired and eleven unfired .50/70 cartridges from the Lyman Wagon Train site. Of these, ninety-six

Table E.2. Springfield .45/55 or .45/70 Cartridge Case Matches, Battle of Lyman's Wagon Train

Firearm	*Specimen Matches*
1	A000.03, A000.08, A12, A13, A14, A199, A336, A472
2	A000.07
3	A000.09, A22, A23, A43, A316, A333, A335, A343, A346, A357, A382, A408, A410, A418, A422, A474, A484
4	A3, A264, A265, A275, A278, A280, A287, A313, A327, A340, A380, A381, A383
5	A6, A9, A60, A246, A249, A271, A272, A273, A279, A282, A283, A305, A307, A309, A311, A325, A326, A378, A386, A557, B195, B197, B198, C19, C22, C25, C30, C49, C54
6	A8, A20, A161, A251, A254, A267, A284, A286, A288, A295, A415, A417, A433, A434, A439, A447, A459, A469,A477, A478, A479, A480, A485, A510, A537, A582, A594, A597, A609, A828, A831, C46
7	A21, A107, A207, A220, A285, A298, A583, C8, C23
8	A33, A202
9	A37, A215, A218, A245, A270
10	A38, A131, A186, B199, B291, B310
11	A39, A219, A242, A565
12	A41, A104, A304, A317, A328, A329, A334, A384, A385, A395, A400, A404, A406, A409, A486, A511, A677, C9, C10
13	A185, A402, A508, A512, A513, A525, A567, A592, A601, A608, A689
14	A188, A196, A680, A762, B243, B244
15	A191, A337, A347, A360, A373
16	A193, A420, A440, A453, A464, A473, A490, C24, C27
17	A209, A573
18	A290, A291, A292, A293, A294, A299, A500, A501, A541, A543, A668, A739, A761, A823, A826, C33, C43, C45
19	A300, A301, A362, B292
20	A306, A321, A330, A359, A379, A393
21	A310, A312, A376, A377, A452, A455, A482, A487, B242
22	A315, A363, A368, A372, A374, A387, A394, A397, C32
23	A318, A342
24	A338, A339, A571, A581, A587
25	A341, A348, A349, A365, A369, A411, A441, A442, A443, A467, A483, A488, A585
26	A350, A375, A398, A465
27	A355, A498, A505, A509, A520, A556, A604, A611, A619, A691, C50
28	A403, A449, A454, A489, A574, A593, B193
29	A506, A507, A562, A566, A600, A605, A628, A637, A638, A639, A640, A672, A678, A693, C31
30	A595
31	A606, A620
32	A613, A625
33	A616, A618
34	A621, A627, A630
35	A626
36	A629, A683
37	A740, A827
38	A760
39	A830
40	C7, C17, C44
41	C29, C34

cartridges representing fifteen different firearms are associated with the army combatants, and fifty-eight cartridges representing seventeen different firearms are associated with the Indian combatants. The .50/70 cartridges are mostly internally primed center-fire copper cases, although a few external Berdan primed brass cases are also present. These were commercially manufactured rounds made by Winchester and Remington. Several cases are the Martin folded-head variety, a Frankford Arsenal–made case used by the army for several years. The internally primed varieties include the Benét cup primer and the Martin bar primer. The Martin bar primer was developed at Frankford Arsenal and manufactured between October 1866 and March 1868 for use in the Model 1866 Springfield breechloading rifle, or the so-called 2nd Allin Conversion.[2] The .50/70 cases from the site were fired in at least three different rifle types: the U.S. Models 1866 (table E.3), 1868 or 1870 (table E.4), and Sharps-made rifles (table E.5).

Several of the Indian-associated Sharps-fired cases are of interest. Some cases representing several different rifles show misfires or multiple firing pin drag marks, indicating firing and extraction problems. One case in particular is interesting. Case B153 is a 56/56 Spencer that someone initially attempted to fire in a Sharps rifle, but the cartridge failed to fire. It was later fired in a Spencer rifle. There are several possible explanations for this situation, including lack of familiarity with the noninterchangeability of rimfire and center-fire ammunition or a simple mix-up in the heat of battle.

Two other Sharps are also of interest. The cases represented by Sharps rifles 4 and 7 (table E.5) have square firing pin imprints. Sharps firearms were not made with square firing pins. The most likely explanation for this interesting arrangement is that the firing pins on these rifles either broke or became inoperable and an incipient Indian gunsmith fashioned a new firing pin from some bar stock or refashioned the firing pins by filing them nearly square. The square marks on the cases representing the two rifles appear to have been formed in a similar manner, and quite likely by the same hand. Whoever the incipient gunsmith was, he made the two rifles operational, and they performed their intended functions well. There are eleven unfired .50/70-caliber cartridges in the collection and five other cartridges that are missing the head. Twenty-one of the .50/70-caliber cases were too oxidized to analyze.

Table E.3. Model 1866 Springfield Cartridge Matches, Battle of Lyman's Wagon Train

Firearm	*Specimen Matches*[a]	*Association*
1	A000.4m, A000.7b, A134m	Army
2	A133b	ArmyA133b
3	A704be	ArmyA704be
4	B100b, B154b	IndianB100b, B154b
5	B269br	IndianB269br

[a]Letter following lot number indicates primer type; b = Benét, be = Berdan, br = bar, m = Martin folded-head.

Spencer 56/56-, 56/52-, and 56/50-Caliber Cartridge Cases

There are 173 Spencer cartridge cases from the Lyman Wagon Train battle site. All of these cartridges are associated with the Indian combatants. Cases in all three calibers—.56, .52, and .50—were noted in the collection. One variety (fig. E.3), of which there are ninety-seven specimens, has no head stamp; three cartridge cases have the impressed letters S.A.W., denoting the Sage Ammunition Works; two cartridge cases are impressed with the letters J.G., for the firm Joseph Goldmark; three cartridge cases are impressed with the head stamp C.D.L., for the firm of

Table E.4. Model 1868–1870 Springfield Cartridge Matches, Battle of Lyman's Wagon Train

Firearm	*Specimen Matches*[a]	*Comments*
Army-Associated		
1	A18br, A97b, A108br, A179m, A190b, A713br, C6br, C11br, C12br, A713	Oxidized and a probable match
2	A45m, A57m, A73br, A74br, A75br, A77br, A078br, A080br, A136m, A167be, A323br, A358be, A431b, A470be, A702br	
3	A99m	
4	A137be, A204m, A239be, A703br	
5	A139m, A436be, A471be	
6	A164be	
7	A166m, A168be, A423b, A424br, A437b, A707br, A708b, A750m, B301b, B302b	
8	A205m, A388m, A426m, A427m, A429m, A430m, A432m	
9	A210m	
10	A216b	
11	A266m, A367br, A370br, A371br, A392m, A413br, A425m	
12	A742	Head of case only
Indian-Associated		
13	B21b, B64b, B201br, B21	.45 cartridge fired in .50-caliber gun; case split
14	B25b, B299b,B25	.45 cartridge fired in .50-caliber gun; case split
15	B63b, B65br, B202b,B63	.45 cartridge fired in .50-caliber gun; case split
16	B300b	

[a]Letter following lot number indicates primer type; b = Benét, be = Berdan, br = bar, m = Martin folded-head

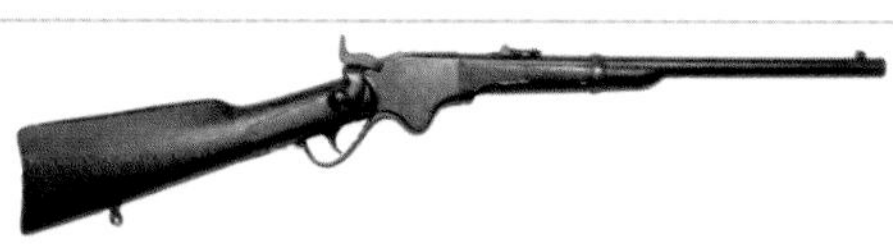

Table E.5. .50-Caliber Cases Fired in Sharps-Made Guns, Battle of Lyman's Wagon Train

Firearm	*Specimen Matches*[a]	*Comments*
Army-Associated		
1	A177m, A250be	
Indian-Associated		
2	B5b	Case misfired; 2 firing pin marks
3	B6m, B74br, B86b, B303m	B6 and B303 have multiple drag marks indicating misfires or extraction problems
4	B17b, B31b, B84b, B88b, B153, B170b	All have square firing pin marks; B153 is 56/56 Spencer fired in Sharps
5	B66b, B97b, B101b, B148m, B186b, B259br	B66, B148, and B186 have multiple drag marks indicating misfires or extraction problem
6	B67m, B94b, B95b, B102b, B138b, B143br, B168b, B169b	B67, B94, and B143 have multiple drag marks indicating misfires or extraction problem
7	B152m, C53br	Square firing pin marks
8	B176be	
9	B177b	Head separating; multiple drag marks indicating misfire
10	B203be, B307be	Square firing pin marks
11	B256br	
12	B336b, B363b	B336 struck twice by firing pin; multiple drag marks indicate misfire
13	B356br	

[a]Letter following the lot number indicates the primer type; b = Benét, be = Berdan, br = bar, m = Martin folded-head

Fig. E.3. Spencer cartridge case head stamps: top, left to right: no head stamp type from Frankford Arsenal, plain H, raised H in a circle; bottom, left to right: J.G., C.D.L., S.A.W.

C. D. Leet; and fifty-nine have the letter H, denoting manufacture by the New Haven Arms Company or the Winchester company.

The Joseph Goldmark firm (often erroneously identified as Jacob Goldmark) manufactured Spencer ammunition for the U.S. Army during the Civil War and completed its last delivery to the army on December 31, 1866.[3] Goldmark-manufactured ammunition had a reputation for misfiring and was the subject of several complaint letters from army officers stationed in the West between 1866 and 1869. The army finally recalled the Goldmark Spencer ammunition, condemning it and destroying thousands of cases or crates of ammunition.

C. D. Leet manufactured Spencer ammunition from 1860 to 1866, but the C.D.L. head stamp was used only from 1864 to 1866, when production ceased.[4] The cartridge cases in the collection made by this company have two head stamp varieties. One variety, found on fifty-six cases, has a raised H in a depressed circle, a common head stamp for Winchester. The second variety, present on three cases, is a raised H without the circle. The H is the same style, type, and dimension as the one in the depressed circle. In all probability the lack of the depressed circle is nothing more than a manufacturing run error or a worn bunter used during the stamping process.

Some non-head-stamped cartridge cases have tool marks on the head of the cartridge as a result of the tool points of the power head used to hold the case during the bullet crimping process. There are two varieties of tool marks present. The most common one, found on seventy-seven cartridge cases, is two vertical lines at the twelve o'clock and six o'clock positions on the case head. Several manufacturers used similar tool points, but this variety appears most consistent with that attributed to the U.S. Army's Frankford Arsenal.[5] There are four cases with multiple marks nearly encircling the head. This mark is consistent with the tool point used by C. D. Leet and Company. Thirty cases with the raised H in the depressed

Table E.6. Spencer Cartridge Case Matches, Battle of Lyman's Wagon Train

Firearm	*Specimen Matches*	*Comment*
1	B11, B38	
2	B10, B53, B131, B135, B191, B359	B53 extraction problem
3	B12, B13, B15, B19, B47, B345	
4	B20, B29, B30, B32, B55, B71, B91, B365	
5	B22, B28, B51, B116	
6	B23, B35, B52, B124, B306, B314	
7	B24, B36, B37, B40, B44, B58, B60, B62,B147, B153, B158, B159, B160, B339, B346	B153 attempted to fire in Sharps
8	B27, B33, B34, B41, B43, B45, B49, B50, B81,B189, B265, B266, B267, B317, B348	B27 and B317 hit twice; B266 extraction problem
9	B39, B42, B48, B92	
10	B46, B80, B85, B122, B258, B320	B320 hit twice and extraction problem
11	B69, B118, B119, B120, B125, B127, B145, B334, B335	B69 hit twice, extraction problem
12	B72, B76, B77	
13	B83, B115, B123, B129, B132, B144	
14	B90, B134, B139, B260	
15	B140, B142, B149, B178, B319	B178 extraction problem
16	B146, C52	
17	B190	
18	B255, B315, B340, B366	
19	B257, B367	
20	B262	
21	B264	
22	B305, B338	
23	B323, B328, B329, B330, B331, B347, B353,B364	
24	B318, B321, B324, B325, B332, B343, B350	B324 extraction problem; B332 hit twice in two different guns
25	B333	
26	B349	Misfire, extraction problem
27	B351 (probable match) C55	C55 extraction problem
28	C56, C58	
29	B332	B332 hit twice in two different guns (see 24 above)

circle also have tool point marks, which appear in a roughly triangular configuration with one mark at the one o'clock position, one at four o'clock, and one at seven o'clock. This tool point mark is not otherwise documented for Winchester-made ammunition.

The head-stamped and non-head-stamped tool point–marked cases indicate that ammunition from five separate manufacturers was used in the battle. At least three of these, Leet, Sage, and Goldmark, had not made Spencer ammunition since 1866. These three varieties were probably old stock remaining after the Civil War. The predominate cartridge types are the government's own Frankford Arsenal–loaded rounds and the Winchester loaded rounds.

The base of an unfired and corroded cartridge (B352) and two misfired cartridges (B298 and B349) were also recovered. Nineteen Spencer cartridges, including one misfired cartridge, could not be analyzed because of extensive oxidation.

All fired cartridge cases and the misfired rounds were subjected to microscopic firearms identification procedures. As noted above, some had become too oxidized to study for individual characteristics. The cartridge cases suitable for comparison represent twenty-nine different Spencer firearms (table E.6). In several instances, only a single cartridge case represents a rifle, but the majority have multiple matches.

Cartridge case matches representing rifles 7, 8, 10, 14, and 15 indicate that these rifles fired at least one full magazine and were reloaded at least once during the battle. Eight rifles experienced cartridge case extraction problems, which suggests that some rifles became dirty or were not well maintained. Cartridge cases from five rifles exhibit multiple firing pin strikes, indicating initial misfires with the ammunition. One cartridge case (B332) is especially interesting in that it bears the firing pin impressions of two different Spencer rifles. Apparently the round initially failed to fire, but when it was placed in a second rifle it did fire.

Within the collection are nine Spencer cases with a

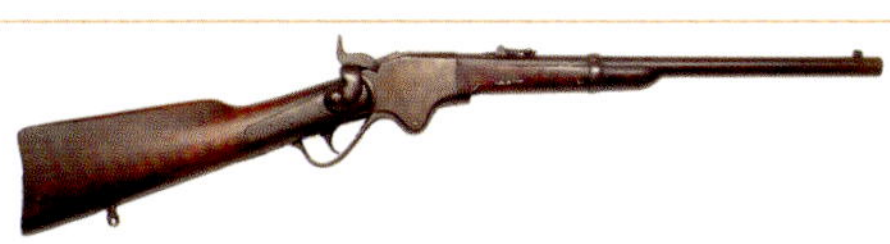

Table E.7. **Spencer Head Stamps and Tool Marks, Battle of Lyman's Wagon Train**

Specimen	*Caliber*	*Head Stamp*	*Tool Mark*	*Gun Type*	*Comment*
B4	56/50	None	None	Jocelyn	
B7	56/50	None	None	Jocelyn	
B8	56/50	None	None	Jocelyn	
B9	56/56	H in depressed circle	3 at 1, 4, and 7 o'clock	Spencer	
B10	56/50	None	None	Jocelyn	
B11	56/56	None	None	Spencer	
B12	56/56	H in depressed circle	3 at 1, 4, and 7 o'clock	Spencer	
B13	56/56	None	None	Spencer	
B15	56/56	None	None	Spencer	
B16	56/56	H in depressed circle	None	Spencer	
B18	56/56	H in depressed circle	3 at 1, 4, and 7 o'clock	Spencer	
B19	56/56	H in depressed circle	3 at 1, 4, and 7 o'clock	Spencer	
B20	56/56	None	2 at 12 and 6 o'clock	Spencer	
B22	56/56	H in depressed circle	3 at 1, 4, and 7 o'clock	Spencer	
B23	56/56	H in depressed circle	3 at 1, 4, and 7 o'clock	Spencer	
B24	56/56	H in depressed circle	3 at 1, 4, and 7 o'clock	Spencer	
B26	56/50	H in depressed circle	None	Spencer	
B27	56/50	J.G.	None	Spencer	Struck twice, extraction problem
B28	56/56	None	2 at 12 and 6 o'clock	Spencer	
B29	56/50	None	None	Spencer	
B30	56/50	S.A.W.	None	Spencer	
B32	56/56	H in depressed circle	None	Spencer	
B33	56/56	C.D.L.	None	Spencer	
B34	56/56	H in depressed circle	None	Spencer	
B35	56/56	H in depressed circle	None	Spencer	
B36	56/56	H in depressed circle	None	Spencer	
B37	56/56	H in depressed circle	3 at 1, 4, and 7 o'clock	Spencer	
B38	56/56	None	None	Spencer	
B39	56/56	H in depressed circle	3 at 1, 4, and 7 o'clock	Spencer	
B40	56/56	None	2 at 12 and 6 o'clock	Spencer	
B41	56/56	None	None	Spencer	
B42	56/56	H in depressed circle	3 at 1, 4, and 7 o'clock	Spencer	
B43	56/56	H in depressed circle	3 at 1, 4, and 7 o'clock	Spencer	
B44	56/56	H in depressed circle	None	Spencer	
B45	56/56	H in depressed circle	3 at 1, 4, and 7 o'clock	Spencer	
B46	56/56	H in depressed circle	3 at 1, 4, and 7 o'clock	Spencer	
B47	56/56	H in depressed circle	3 at 1, 4, and 7 o'clock	Spencer	
B48	56/56	None	None	Spencer	
B49	56/56	C.D.L.	5–11 pairs	Spencer	
B50	56/50	None	5 pairs	Spencer	
B51	56/50	None	None	Spencer	
B52	56/56	H in depressed circle	3 at 1, 4, and 7 o'clock	Spencer	
B53	56/56	None	None	Spencer	Extraction problem
B55	56/56	H in depressed circle	3 at 1, 4, and 7 o'clock	Spencer	
B58	56/56	None	None	Spencer	
B60	56/56	None	None	Spencer	
B62	56/50	None	None	Spencer	
B68	56/56	None	None	Jocelyn	
B69	56/50	None	None	Spencer	Struck twice
B71	56/50	None	None	Spencer	
B72	56/56	None	None	Spencer	
B73	56/56	None	None	Ballard	
B75	56/50	None	None	Jocelyn	
B76	56/56	None	None	Spencer	
B77	56/56	None	5 pairs	Spencer	
B78	56/56	H in depressed circle	None	Spencer	
B79	56/56	None	None	Jocelyn	

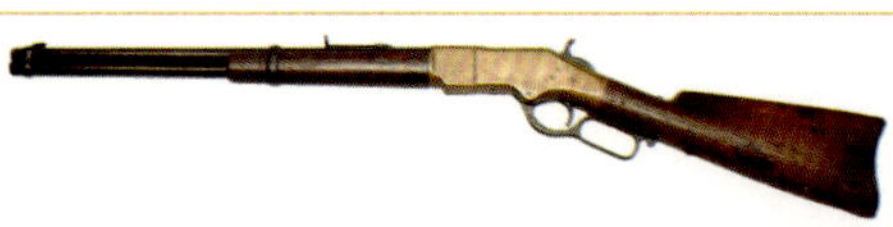

Table E.7, *continued*

Specimen	*Caliber*	*Head Stamp*	*Tool Mark*	*Gun Type*	*Comment*
B80	56/56	H in depressed circle	None	Spencer	
B81	56/56	H in depressed circle	3 at 1, 4, and 7 o'clock	Spencer	
B82	56/50	None	None	Jocelyn	
B83	56/56	None	None	Spencer	
B85	56/56	None	None	Spencer	
B90	56/56	H in depressed circle	3 at 1, 4, and 7 o'clock	Spencer	
B91	56/56	None	None	Spencer	
B92	56/56	None	None	Spencer	
B93	56/56	H in depressed circle	3 at 1, 4, and 7 o'clock	Spencer	
B99	56/56	None	None	Spencer	
B103	56/50	None	None	Spencer	
B115	56/56	H in depressed circle	None	Spencer	
B116	56/50	None	None	Spencer	
B117	56/56	None	None	Spencer	
B118	56/56	None	None	Spencer	Extraction problem
B119	56/50	None	None	Spencer	
B120	56/50	None	None	Spencer	
B122	56/56	H in depressed circle	3 at 1, 4, and 7 o'clock	Spencer	
B123	56/56	H in depressed circle	3 at 1, 4, and 7 o'clock	Spencer	
B124	56/56	H in depressed circle	3 at 1, 4, and 7 o'clock	Spencer	
B125	56/56	H in depressed circle	3 at 1, 4, and 7 o'clock	Spencer	
B127	56/56	H in depressed circle	3 at 1, 4, and 7 o'clock	Spencer	
B129	56/56	None	None	Spencer	
B131	56/56	H in depressed circle	None	Spencer	
B132	56/56	None	None	Spencer	
B133	56/50	None	None	Spencer	
B134	56/56	H in depressed circle	None	Spencer	
B135	56/50	None	None	Spencer	
B139	56/56	None	None	Spencer	
B140	56/50	H in depressed circle	None	Spencer	
B141	56/56	H in depressed circle	None	Spencer	
B142	56/56	None	None	Spencer	
B144	56/56	None	2 at 12 and 6 o'clock	Spencer	
B145	56/56	None	None	Spencer	
B146	56/56	H in depressed circle	None	Spencer	
B147	56/56	None	None	Spencer	
B149	56/50	H in depressed circle	None	Spencer	
B151	56/56	H in depressed circle	None	Spencer	
B153	56/56	None	None	Spencer	Attempted to fire in Sharps
B158	56/50	None	None	Spencer	
B159	56/50	None	None	Spencer	
B160	56/50	None	None	Spencer	
B162	56/56	None	None	Spencer	Extraction problem
B178	56/56	None	None	Spencer	Extraction problem
B181	56/56	None	5 pairs	Spencer	Extraction problem
B189	56/50	None	2 at 12 and 6 o'clock	Spencer	
B190	56/56	None	2 at 12 and 6 o'clock	Spencer	
B191	56/56	H in depressed circle	None	Spencer	
B255	56/56	H in depressed circle	None	Spencer	
B257	56/56	None	None	Spencer	
B258	56/56	H in depressed circle	None	Spencer	
B260	56/50	J.G.	None	Spencer	
B262	56/50	None	2 at 12 and 6 o'clock	Spencer	
B264	56/56	None	2 at 12 and 6 o'clock	Spencer	
B265	56/56	None	None	Spencer	
B266	56/56	None	None	Spencer	Jocelyn
B267	56/56	None	2 at 12 and 6 o'clock	Spencer	

Table E.7, *continued*

Specimen	*Caliber*	*Head Stamp*	*Tool Mark*	*Gun Type*	*Comment*
B298	56/56	H in depressed circle	3 at 1, 4 and 7 o'clock	Spencer	Misfire
B305	56/56	None	None	Spencer	
B306	56/56	None	None	Spencer	
B314	56/56	Raised H, no circle	None	Spencer	
B315	56/56	Raised H, no circle	None	Spencer	
B316	56/56	None	None	Spencer	
B317	56/56	None	None	Spencer	Struck twice
B319	56/56	None	None	Spencer	
B320	56/56	None	None	Spencer	Struck twice, extraction problem
B321	56/56	None	None	Spencer	
B323	56/50	None	None	Spencer	
B324	56/56	None	None	Spencer	Extraction problem
B325	56/56	None	None	Spencer	
B328	56/50	None	None	Spencer	
B329	56/56	None	None	Spencer	
B330	56/56	H in depressed circle	None	Spencer	
B331	56/56	H in depressed circle	None	Spencer	
B332	56/56	None	None	Spencer	Attempted to fire in two different guns
B333	56/56	H in depressed circle	None	Spencer	
B335	56/50	None	None	Spencer	
B338	56/56	None	5 pairs	Spencer	
B339	56/56	None	2 at 12 and 6 o'clock	Spencer	
B340	56/56	None	None	Spencer	
B341	56/56	None	2 at 12 and 6 o'clock	Spencer	
B343	56/56	None	None	Spencer	
B345	56/50	H in depressed circle	3 at 1, 4 and 7 o'clock	Spencer	
B346	56/56	None	None	Spencer	
B347	56/56	None	None	Spencer	
B348	56/50	None	None	Spencer	
B349	56/50	S.A.W.	None	Spencer	Misfire and extraction problem
B350	56/56	None	None	Spencer	
B351	56/52	None	None	Spencer	
B352	56/56	S.A.W.	None	Spencer	Unfired base only
B353	56/56	H in depressed circle	None	Spencer	
B357	56/56	H in depressed circle	3 at 1, 4, and 7 o'clock	Spencer	
B358	56/56	None	None	Spencer	
B359	56/56	Raised H no circle	None	Spencer	
B364	56/56	H in depressed circle	None	Spencer	
B365	56/56	None	2 at 12 and 6 o'clock	Spencer	
B366	56/50	None	None	Spencer	
B367	56/56	None	2 at 12 and 6 o'clock	Spencer	
B368	56/56	C.D.L.	5–11 pairs	Spencer	Extraction problem
B369	56/56	H in depressed circle	3 at 1, 4, and 7 o'clock	Spencer	
C52	56/56	H in depressed circle	3 at 1, 4, and 7 o'clock	Spencer	
C55	56/56	None	None	Spencer	Extraction problem
C56	56/50	None	2 at 12 and 6 o'clock	Spencer	
C58	56/50	None	2 at 12 and 6 o'clock	Spencer	

single block firing pin imprint (table E.7). These represent six different firearms chambered for the Spencer round, but from other manufacturers. Cartridge cases B4, B7, B8, and B68 were fired in a Jocelyn carbine. Cases B10, B75, B79, and B82 also represent Jocelyn carbines, but each case represents a different firearm. Finally, cartridge case B73 bears a nearly square firing pin imprint that was probably made by a Ballard rifle.

Bullets

The 102 bullets and pistol and rifle balls (fig. E.4) recovered from the battle site were comparatively few relative

Table E.8. Identified Bullets and Associated Firearm Type, Battle of Lyman's Wagon Train

Specimen	*Caliber*	*Firearm Type*	*Comment*	*Association*
A000.5	.45	Springfield	Mushroomed	Army
A132	.50	Unidentified	Sand embedded	Indian
A135	.44	Colt	Round ball, ram	Indian
A232	.50	Unidentified	Sand and mushroomed, cloth patch	Indian
A233	.50	Unidentified	Flattened	Indian
A236	.50	Springfield		Indian
A354	.50	Springfield		Indian
A390	.50	Springfield		Indian
A457	.50	Unidentified		Indian
A615	.50	Unidentified	Round ball	Indian
A676	.50	Unidentified	Round ball	Indian
A697	.36	Colt	Round ball, ram	Indian
A698	.40	Unidentified	Homemade, elongate	Indian
A699	.44	Unidentified	Round ball, chewed	Indian
A700	.50	Springfield		Indian
A701	.50	Unidentified	Mushroomed	Indian
A730	.44	Unidentified	Chewed	Indian
A832	.44	Colt	Round ball, ram	Indian
B1	.54	Unidentified	Round ball	Indian
B3	.45	Springfield		Army
B54	.45	Springfield		Army
B87	.45	Springfield	Rushroomed	Army
B89	.45	Springfield		Army
B96	.45	Springfield		Army
B98	.50	Sharps	Mushroomed, sand embedded	Army
B121	.50	Springfield	Mushroomed	Army
B161	.45	Springfield		Army
B164	.44	Winchester		Indian
B165	.50	Springfield		Army
B167	.50	Unidentified	Round ball	Indian
B175	.45	Springfield		Army
B182	.50	Springfield		Army
B183	.50	Springfield		Army
B184	.50	Springfield		Army
B185	.45	Springfield		Army
B187	.50	Unidentified		Army
B188	.45	Springfield		Army
B208	.45	Springfield		Army
B209	.50	Sharps		Army
B210	.45	Springfield		Army
B211	.45	Springfield		Army
B212	.50	Unidentified		Army
B213	.45	Springfield		Army
B214	.50	Springfield		Army
B215	.45	Springfield		Army
B216	.45	Springfield		Army
B217	.45	Springfield		Army
B218	.50	Springfield		Army
B219	.50	Springfield		Army
B220	.50	Springfield		Army
B221	.45	Springfield		Army
B222	.45	Springfield		Army
B223	.45	Springfield		Army
B224	.50	Springfield		Army
B225	.45	Springfield		Army
B226	.50	Springfield		Army
B227	.45	Springfield		Army

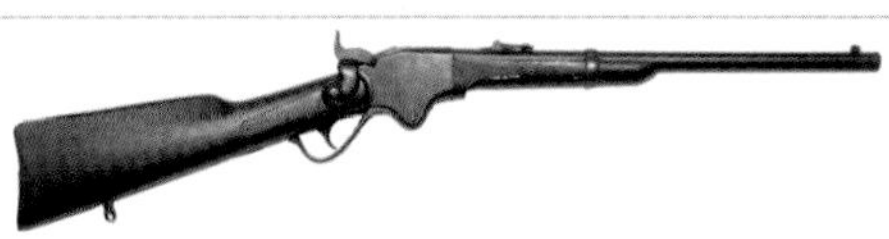

Table E.8, *continued*

Specimen	*Caliber*	*Firearm Type*	*Comment*	*Association*
B228	.45	Springfield		Army
B229	.45	Springfield		Army
B231	.45	Springfield		Army
B232	.45	Springfield		Army
B233	.45	Springfield		Army
B234	.45	Springfield		Army
B235	.45	Springfield		Army
B237	.50	Springfield		Army
B238	.45	Springfield		Army
B239	.45	Colt		Army
B241	.45	Springfield		Army
B245	.45	Springfield		Army
B246	.45	Springfield		Army
B247	.50	Springfield		Army
B248	.45	Springfield		Army
B249	.50	Springfield		Army
B250	.50	Springfield		Army
B251	.45	Springfield		Army
B252	.45	Springfield		Army
B253	Unknown	Unidentified	Deformed lead fragment	Army
B254	.50	Springfield		Army
B272	.50	Sharps		Army
B275	.45	Springfield		Army
B276	.45	Springfield		Army
B277	.45	Springfield		Army
B279	.45	Springfield		Army
B278	.50	Sharps		Army
B280	.45	Springfield		Army
B281	.50	Springfield		Army
B282	.50	Springfield		Army
B283	.45	Springfield		Army
B284	.50	Sharps		Army
B288	.50	Springfield		Army
B289	.50	Springfield		Army
B290	.50	Sharps		Army
B293	.45	Springfield		Army
B308	.45	Springfield		Army
B311	.45	Springfield		Army
B313	.45	Springfield		Army
B337	.45	Springfield		Army
B342	.45	Springfield		Army
B344	.45	Springfield		Army
B354	.45	Springfield		Army
C48	.41	Colt		Indian

Fig. E.4. Bullets and balls: top left, .45-caliber; bottom left, .50-caliber; right, rifle and pistol balls of various calibers.

Fig. E.5. a, iron arrowpoint; b–d, Indian-associated metal butcher knives.

to the number of cartridge cases analyzed. Table E.8 lists the artifact number and identification of the caliber and weapon type in which the bullet was fired. The bullets include the following: one .41-caliber Colt, two .44-caliber of which one was fired from a Winchester rifle and the other is too mashed to identify the weapon type, one .45 Colt Model 1873 revolver, six .50-caliber fired from a Sharps, fifty-one .45-caliber Springfield, twenty-four .50-caliber Springfield, seven .50-caliber unidentified, and one fragment of a bullet that could not be identified as to caliber or firearm type.

Also recovered were nine rifle and pistol balls: one .36-caliber from a Colt percussion cap revolver, one .40-caliber ball that appears to be homemade and fired from a Plains rifle or trade gun, two .44-caliber from Colt percussion cap revolvers and one .44-caliber from an unidentified firearm, three .50-caliber balls from unidentified firearms, and one .54-caliber ball fired from a Plains rifle or trade gun. As at the Battle of Red River site, the presence of rifle balls indicates that some of the Indians were still using the older muzzle loaders.

Of the bullets recovered from the battle site, twenty-one are associated with the Indian combatants and eighty-one with the U.S. Army. The Indian-associated bullets reflect a variety of firearm calibers and types, including all of the rifle and pistol balls, .44-caliber Winchester rifles, a .41-caliber Colt pistol, and .50-caliber Springfield rifles. The army-associated bullets were fired from a .45-caliber Colt Model 1873 revolver, .45-caliber Springfield rifles or carbines, .50-caliber Springfield rifles or carbines, and .50-caliber Sharps rifles.

The small number of pistol bullets recovered during the investigations suggests that hand guns played only a minor role in the Battle of Lyman's Wagon Train.

Other Indian-Associated Artifacts

Metal Arrowpoint

One iron arrowpoint (fig. E.5a) was recovered from the battlefield. It is slightly asymmetrical with rounded shoulders and a long, squared stem. The total length of the arrowpoint is 6.88 cm, its maximum width is 2.25 cm, and it has a maximum thickness of 2.1 mm. An Indian probably made the arrowpoint from a portion of a barrel hoop.

Knives

Three butcher knives (fig. E.5b–d) were recovered from the site. One knife is complete except the handle, which was probably wood and has deteriorated. The total length of this specimen is 26 cm, with the blade measuring 14.3 cm. A brass handle guard is still intact, as are three brass bolsters that would have held the wooden handle in place. The thickness of the knife blade ranges from 1.5 mm at the tip to 3 mm at the handle. The width of the handle is 2.5 cm.

The second specimen is more corroded and is not complete. The portion remaining, which is the blade and a small portion of the handle, is 19 cm long. The blade measures approximately 14 cm. There are three brass bolsters still intact on the handle. The thickness of the blade is 3 mm at the handle and 1.5 mm at the tip. The blade has a width of 2.5 cm.

The third knife recovered is a handle that measures 12.5 cm in length and is 2.8 cm wide. The thickness of the handle is 3 mm. There is an iron guard still intact, which is 2 cm wide and extends 1.2 cm both above and below the blade. Four bolsters that held the wooden handle in place remain on the handle. The butcher knife was a very popular trade item, serving as a utilitarian tool, scalping knife, and

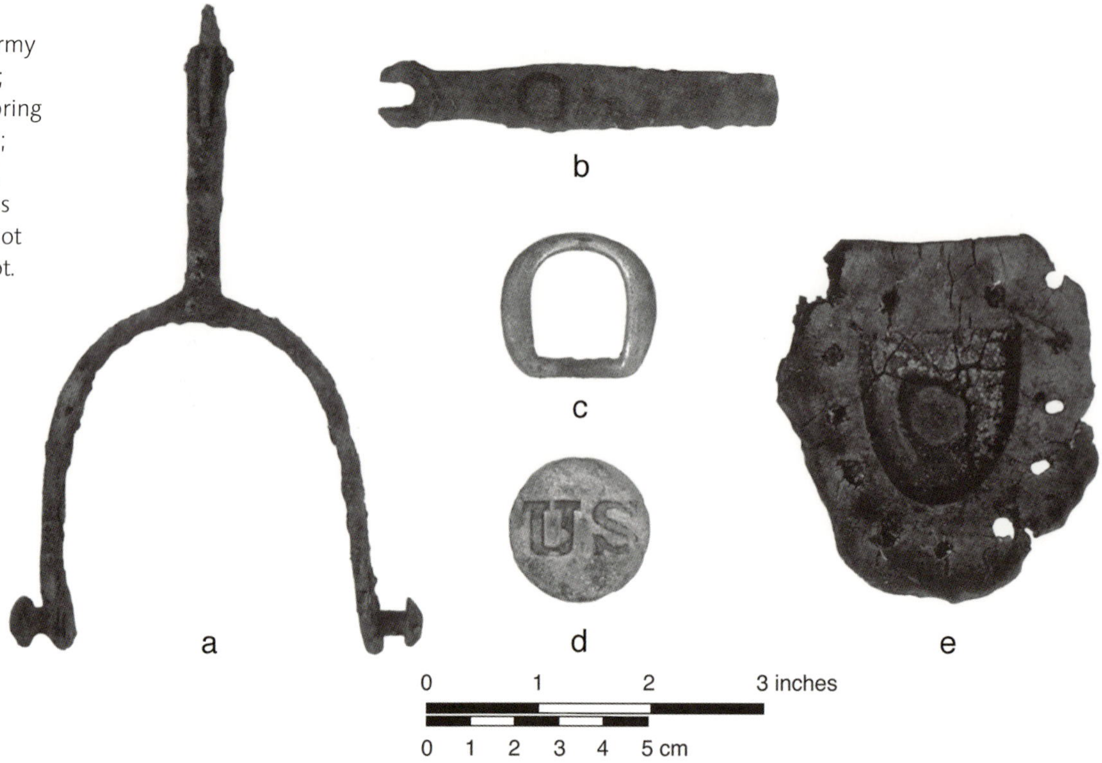

Fig. E.6. Army-related artifacts: a, spur (not army regulation equipment); b, Model 1870 mainspring clamp and screwdriver; c, D-shaped buckle; d, bridle boss of cast brass and stamped US; e, boot heel from an army boot.

weapon. The three butcher knives recovered from the battle site were found in or near Indian rifle pits. Apparently the knives were used to facilitate the digging of the pits and were lost.

Fig. E.7. Army general service uniform button. The letter C on the eagle's shield indicates that the button was from a cavalryman's uniform.

Other Army-Associated Artifacts

Benét Cup Primer

A single Benét cup cartridge primer was found in the area of the circled wagon train. This internal primer was used in .45- and .50-caliber cartridges. The primer was evidently dislodged from its cartridge case by the force of the explosion that fired the cartridge. The Benét primers have two holes in the body, designed to transmit the flash of the primer charge to the black powder propellant.

Boot Heels

Two leather boot heels were recovered from the battlefield. One specimen 5.5 cm long and 4.1 cm wide comprises only one leather counter and retains three 2.4 cm heel nails. The other boot heel (fig. E.6e) is larger, more intact, and comprises several leather heel counters. The length of this specimen is 8 cm and the width is 7 cm. This boot heel retains seven 2.4 cm heel nails.

Bridle Boss

A bridle boss (fig. E.6d) of cast brass and stamped US was found within the area of the circled wagon train. It has a diameter of 3.3 cm and is 5.1 mm thick. Four small pins on the back attached the boss to the bridle.

Buckles

One brass buckle (fig. E.6c) was found. It is a D-shaped buckle 3.2 cm long, 3.5 cm wide, and 3 mm thick. The tongue is missing. This buckle appears to be from a waist or pant belt. One iron center-bar buckle was also recovered. It is 2.6 cm long and 2.4 cm wide. This buckle is probably from a bridle.

Buttons

One general service army button (fig. E.7) was recovered within the area of the wagon train. It is 19 mm in diameter and has the letter C (for cavalry) on the eagle's shield. One iron two-piece, four-hole button that measures 1.5 cm in diameter was also recovered. This button is the type used to close the fly on a soldier's trousers.[6]

Combination Gun Tool

One Model 1870 combination gun tool (fig. E.6b) 9 cm long and 1.4 cm wide was recovered on the infantry ridge west of where the wagon train was circled. This tool was modified from the Model 1863 combination tool. The modification included the grinding down of the screwdriver bit on the swinging blade to fit the smaller screws found in the breech of the Model 1868 and 1870 series longarms. This gun tool incorporated a mainspring clamp and two screwdrivers.[7]

Firearm Trigger

One corroded and broken iron trigger, 2 cm long, was found. The firearm type is not known.

Chains and Chain Links

One mule harness neck chain, another longer harness chain, and three breast chains were recovered within the area of the circled wagon train.[8] The harness neck chain is 132 cm long and has two circular ring connectors near each end and another free-moving ring in the middle. A swivel connector is on one end. The other harness chain is 168 cm long. The links on one end of this chain are larger than the links on the rest of the chain. Three breast chains (fig. E.8), which are part of the mule harness, were also recovered. Two of the chains measure 61 cm in length, and the third chain is 66 cm long. Two chain links, both broken, were also recovered; they are probably from a harness chain.

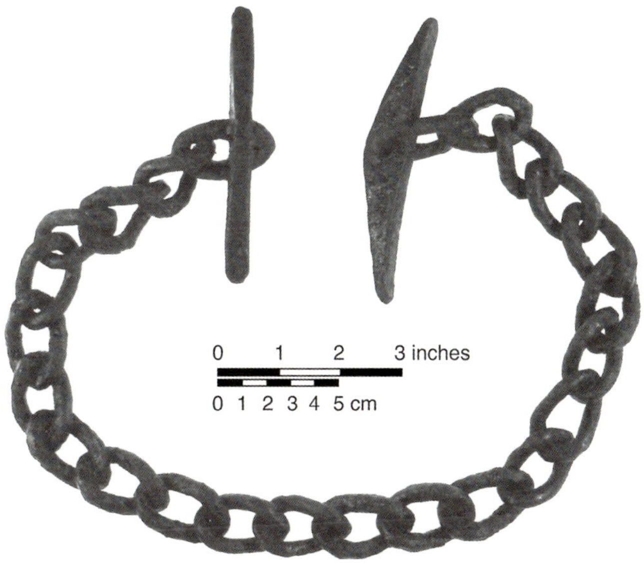

Fig. E.8. Harness breast chain from a mule harness. Twenty-two army mules were killed during the battle.

Leaded Tin Cans and Can Lids

Thirteen leaded tin cans (fig. E.9) of various sizes were recovered from the battlefield, as were numerous pieces of cans. These were probably used for rations or other provisions. Four of the cans were excessively corroded, flattened, and too fragmented to analyze further. The remaining nine cans, though somewhat bent and flattened, were sufficiently intact to allow further analysis. There are eight No. 2 cans. These cans are hole-in-cap types with lead-soldered lap side seams and stamped or flanged ends. Of the No. 2 cans, five were opened by cutting an X across the top and lifting the cut pieces up. The tops of the other three cans appear to have been cut out. The remaining can is large, measuring 27 cm tall and 20 cm in diameter. The top of this can has been removed. Numerous other pieces of cans as well as fragments of can lids were also recovered from the site.

Fig. E.9. Leaded tin cans recovered from the battle site held army rations and provisions.

Horse and Mule Shoes

Eight mule shoes and two Burden horseshoes were recovered from the site. Two of the mule shoes and one of the horseshoes are worn in half. The relatively high number of mule shoes recovered from the site is not too surprising given that twenty-two of Lyman's mules were killed during the battle.

Picket Pin and Picket Line Stake

One broken picket pin (fig. E.10), with the tether ring attached to the shaft, was found. The picket pin is square and the portion remaining is 15.3 cm long. This picket pin is similar to the Model 1874 Lyon type, but the tether

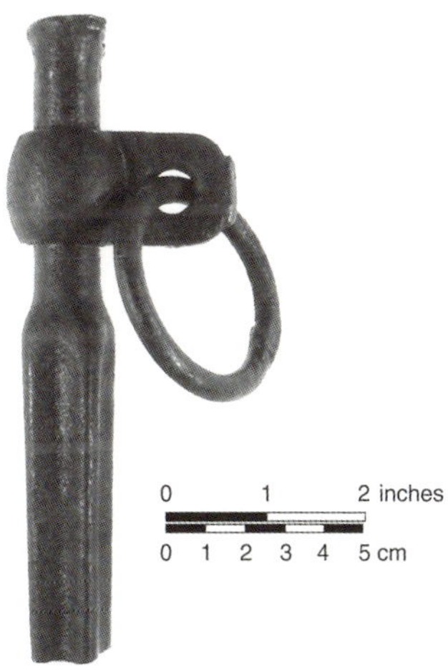

◀ Fig. E.10. This broken picket pin is similar to the Model 1874 Lyon type.

▼ Fig. E.11. Large picket line stake, used to help secure the line on which a group of horses or mules were picketed.

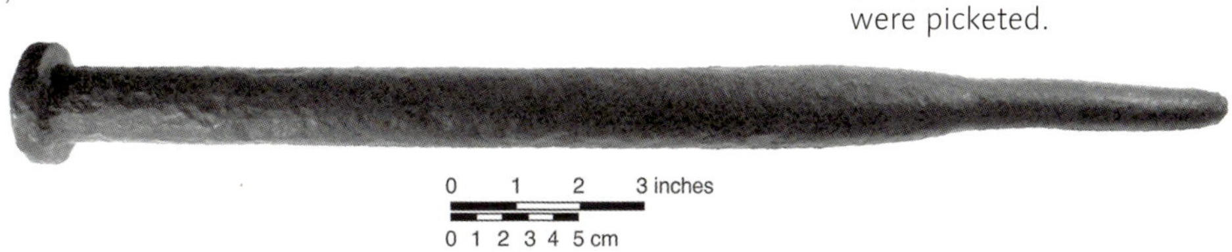

ring on this pin does not swivel as on the Lyon pin. A larger picket line stake (fig. E.11) was also recovered. It measures 48.4 cm long. This large stake was driven into the ground to help secure the line on which a group of horses or mules were picketed.

Wagon Hardware

Two wagon plates were found during the investigations. One plate has two small holes and one larger hole in the middle with a diameter of 2.5 cm. The plate is rectangular, measuring 4 cm by 6.5 cm. A larger wagon plate, 9 cm by 10.5 cm, has four holes, each 5 mm in diameter, one in each corner. A larger hole is off center and has a diameter of 3.2 cm.

One wagon screw pin 13 cm long and 1.5 cm in diameter was found. A nickel-plated peerless eyelet, used to clinch a wagon curtain fastener, was also recovered. It is 2.2 cm by 2.9 cm and is 3 mm thick.

Five wagon bolts were found. Three are similar and 9.5 cm in length. Two of these have been burned. The other two bolts have square heads and are 16 cm and 17 cm in length. Several other recovered items are probably associated with wagons, including one iron washer, two square nuts, three round nails, one cotter pin, one unidentified iron pin, two unidentified wire fragments, and five unidentified iron fragments.

Square Nails

The U.S. Army utilized square nails for supply boxes, ammunition boxes, and ration boxes. There were seventy-eight square nails recovered, ranging in size from 2d to 9d (2.5 cm to 7 cm). Most of the nails are 2d size. Thirty-eight of the nails have been burned, probably as a result of the soldiers using the empty ammunition and ration boxes for firewood.

Wood Screws

Nine wood screws were recovered, all 5 cm long. Several are burned. The wood screws were probably used in ammunition boxes.

Straps

Three metal straps were collected from the battlefield. The specific functions of the straps are not known, but they are likely from ammunition boxes or crates.

Spur

One spur (fig. E.6a) was recovered. It measures 14 cm long by 7 cm wide. The spur is not army regulation. It has a small spiked rowel and studs instead of slots for attaching the straps.

Cookware Handle

A wire cookware handle, 33 cm long, was recovered from within the area of the circled wagon train. The handle is most likely from a dutch oven or related cookware.

Leather

Fifteen leather fragments were recovered. Some of the pieces have stitching on them and may be parts of a harness.

Glass

Two fragments of a light blue, widemouth bottle with a bead neck finish were recovered. The bottle dates from 1865 to 1890. A small fragment of a green container was also found and dates to around 1865. One amber piece recovered is from a beer or whiskey bottle. This type of vessel was in general use after 1860.[9]

Appendix F

Descriptions and Analysis of Artifacts from the Battle of Sweetwater Creek Site

Arms and Ammunition

.44-Caliber Cartridge Cases

Eighteen .44-caliber rimfire cartridge cases (fig. F.1a–b) were recovered from Indian positions at the battle site. All were manufactured by the New Haven Arms Company. Case dimensions are the same as found in Winchester-manufactured ammunition. Microscopic firearm characteristics on each cartridge case indicated that three different types of rifles fired the cartridges. Individual characteristics of the firing pins on the recovered cartridge cases indicate that five Henrys or Winchester Model 1866 rifles fired fourteen of the cases. One rifle fired specimens 62, 65, 66, 69, 70, 73, 75, and 76. The remaining cartridge cases were fired in four other rifles. Specimens 111 and 116 were fired in one rifle, specimens 112 and 114 in another, and specimens 109 and 611 were each fired in a different rifle. Specimen 611 is the head of a cartridge only. It may have blown off the cartridge case at the time of firing. Specimens 62 and 109 have two and four firing pin strikes, respectively, which indicate that the cartridges did not fire on the initial strike, possibly because of malfunctioning ammunition or—more likely—dirty firearms.

Specimen 82 has a single block firing pin imprint. This small imprint was made by a Ballard-manufactured firearm. There are three other .44-caliber cartridge cases in the collection (specimens 223, 250, and 252), each fired in a different .44/40-caliber Winchester Model 1873 rifle or carbine.

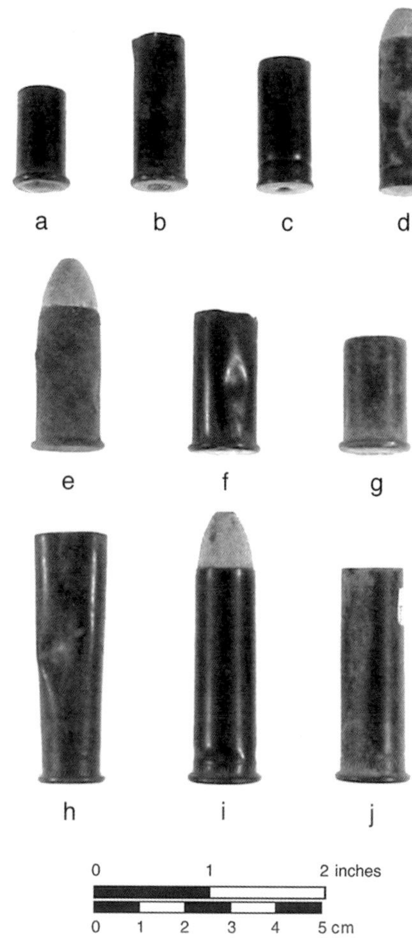

Fig. F.1. Fired and unfired cartridges from the battle site: a, fired .44-caliber Henry; b, fired .44/40; c, fired .45 Colt; d, unfired .45 Colt; e, unfired Spencer 56/50; f, fired Spencer 56/50; g, fired Spencer 56/56; h, fired .45 Springfield; i, unfired .50/70; j, fired .50/70.

.45-Caliber Colt Cartridge Cases

The collection contained three unfired and five fired .45 Colt Benét primed cartridges (fig. F.1c–d). The fired specimens are shorter cases that could be fired in either the Colt or the Smith & Wesson Scholfield. These Frankfort Arsenal–produced rounds represent two different Colt firearms that are associated with the army troops at the site.

.45/55 or .45/70-Caliber Cartridge Cases

A total of 174 .45/55 or .45/70-caliber cartridge cases were recovered from the battle site (fig. F.1h). All but six are Benét primed. The firing pin and extractor marks on the fired Benét primed cartridge cases indicate that all but one of the recovered specimens were fired in the Model 1873 Springfield carbine. The single exception is specimen 89, which was fired in a .50-caliber Sharps.

The six .45-caliber cartridges that are not Benét primed are specimens 147, 290, 340, 341, 372, and 373. Specimens 340 and 341 are brass Berdan primed cases fired in a Winchester, probably a Model 1886. Specimen 147 is a Berdan primed brass cartridge case with the head stamp C F 4 86, indicating that it is a government carbine case manufactured in April 1886. Specimen 290 is a Berdan primed case head-stamped R F 6 80, indicating a government rifle case manufactured in June 1880. This specimen was fired in the same firearm as specimens 372 and 373, both of which are Berdan primed brass Winchester-manufactured cases. These six Berdan primed cartridge cases postdate the battle and none of them matched to the Benét primed non-head-stamped cartridges. Analysis of the remaining .45-caliber cartridge cases revealed that a minimum of twenty-four Springfield Model 1873 firearms are represented in the collection (table F.1).

The presence of the .45/55 or .45/70 cartridges at the site is problematic. Even though the Springfield .45-caliber was the principle firearm adopted by the army in late 1873, no .45-caliber firearms are listed in the 1874 ordnance returns for companies of the 8th Cavalry that participated in the Red River War (appendix B). The only carbine listed for the companies of the 8th Cavalry that were at the Battle of Sweetwater Creek is the Sharps .50-caliber. According to a report from Capt. William Shoemaker, the army storekeeper in charge of the ordnance depot at Fort Union, the 8th Cavalry did receive the new .45-caliber Springfield carbines and .45-caliber Colt revolvers in 1874.[1] However, the ordnance returns for 1874 indicate that only Company M received the new carbines, and they did not participate in the campaign against the Indians.

Although it is possible that the .45-caliber Springfield cartridges from the site are associated with the Indians at the battle, this seems unlikely. These were some of the same Indians who had just left the battle with Lyman's supply train. At that battle site, none of the forty-one individual Springfield .45-caliber firearms identified from analyzed cartridges could be attributed to the Indian combatants. It is unlikely that the primary weapon of the Indians at the Battle of Sweetwater Creek site was the Springfield .45-caliber.

The six .45-caliber Springfield cartridges that clearly postdate the battle are undoubtedly associated with Fort Elliot, which was established in 1875 about 4 miles southwest of the battle site. Given the evidence currently on hand, we must assume that none of the .45-caliber Springfield cartridges on the battle site are related to the 1874 battle but are instead associated with activities of soldiers stationed at Fort Elliot.

Table F.1. Springfield .45/55 Cartridge Case Matches, Battle of Sweetwater Creek

Firearm	*Specimen Matches*
1	1, 2, 4, 5, 6, 7, 8, 138
2	3, 179.106
3	99, 124, 145, 146, 179.90
4	139, 161, 179.107
5	155, 179.3, 179.4, 179.8, 179.14, 179.19, 179.24, 179.27, 179.32, 179.40, 179.41, 179.42, 179.43, 179.71, 179.74, 179.76, 179.84, 179.98, 179.99, 179.101
6	178
7	179.6, 179.45, 179.57, 179.61, 179.87
8	179.7, 179.16, 179.17, 179.18, 179.22, 179.26, 179.28, 179.29, 179.33, 179.34, 179.38, 179.54, 179.68, 179.75, 179.82, 179.100
9	179.9, 179.10, 179.13, 179.31, 179.36, 179.37, 179.39, 179.109
10	179.95, 179.97
11	179.108
12	182
13	195, 202, 203, 204
14	196, 197, 198
15	199, 230, 297
16	200, 233
17	201
18	205, 231
19	206
20	212, 228
21	213
22	214
23	226
24	295

.50/70-Caliber Cartridge Cases

The collection includes 277 fired .50/70 cases and twelve unfired cartridges (fig. F.1i–j). Of the fired cases, ninety-one were too oxidized to analyze. The 186 fired cases that were analyzed were fired from twenty-six different firearms (table F.2). Of these, twenty-two firearms are associated with the 8th Cavalry soldiers at the battle, and the other four are associated with the Indian warriors. The majority of the cartridges were fired from .50-caliber Sharps rifles, but two cartridges were fired from a single Model 1866 Springfield rifle, and fifteen were fired from two separate Model 1868 or 1870 Springfield rifles. Most of the analyzed .50/70 cartridges are internally primed center-fire copper (Bloomfield Gilding Metal) cases, although three external Berdan primed brass cases (specimens 294, 322, and 359) are also present, as are two Remington Boxer primed cases (368 and 369), and one Martin folded-head case (291). These were commercially manufactured rounds made by Winchester and Remington. The Martin folded-head variety is a case made by Frankford Arsenal and used by the army for several years. The internally primed varieties include Benét cup and Martin bar primer types. The Martin bar primer was developed by the army at Frankford Arsenal and manufactured between October 1866 and March 1868 for use in the Model 1866 Springfield breechloading rifle, which is often referred to as the 2nd Allin Conversion.[2]

Spencer 56/50 and 56/56-Caliber Cartridges

The site collection contains forty-seven fired Spencer cases and sixty-five unfired cases associated with the Indian combatants (fig. F.1e–g). Of the unfired cases, fifty-six of them were recovered in a cluster, where they were apparently lost during the battle (fig. F.2). The recovered Spencer cases are of two calibers: .50-caliber (represented by eighty-two cases) and .56-caliber (represented by thirty cases). Twenty-five of the Spencer cartridges are impressed with the letters S.A.W., denoting manufacture by the Sage

Table F.2. .50/70 Cartridge Case Matches, Battle of Sweetwater Creek

Firearm[a]	*Specimen Matches*	*Comments*
1	10, 11, 13, 18, 19, 134, 219, 238, 239, 241, 243, 293, 325, 326, 342, 370, 483	
2	12, 14, 16, 17, 29, 44, 132, 266, 269, 278, 324, 540, 546, 547, 552, 554, 555, 556, 557, 559	
3	20, 21, 27, 28, 32, 35, 123, 220, 240, 244, 251,289, 497, 578	
4	24, 53, 245, 246, 265, 490, 500, 503, 505, 507, 516, 577	
5	25, 26, 34, 38, 40, 41, 50, 267, 268, 275, 284, 285,286, 287, 288, 475, 479, 533, 542, 543, 549	
6	30, 33, 45, 48	
7	31	Extraction problem
8	47	
9	52, 280	
10	54, 131, 133, 247, 478, 531, 532, 534, 535, 553, 568, 569, 579, 584, 589, 592, 599, 606	
11	81 (square firing pin), 85, 89 (.45-caliber), 95	
12	107, 108, 110, 113, 115, 137, 330, 481, 492, 495, 526	
13	130, 566, 574	
14	135	
15	148, 302	Model 1866 Springfield
16	157, 158, 159, 174, 175, 176, 177, 189, 190, 191, 192, 193	Model 1868 or 1870
17	208, 215, 216, 217, 218, 272, 291	291 Martin folded-head
18	221, 270, 271, 274, 477, 498, 502, 536, 576,583, 585, 601	
19	242, 264, 494, 496	
20	273, 343, 347	
21	277, 463, 564, 575	
22	294, 358, 368, 369	294 Berdan primed, Winchester-made case; 368 and 369 Remington-made cases
23	319, 321, 322	322 Berdan primed, Winchester-made case fired in Model 1868 or 1870
24	506, 514	
25	521	
26	527, 539, 587	

[a]Sharps firearm unless otherwise noted.

Ammunition Works, and eleven cases have the letter H, denoting manufacture by the New Haven Arms Company or the Winchester Company. Four cases are impressed with C.D.L., for C. D. Leet. There are sixty-nine specimens with no head stamp. The head is missing on three of the unfired cartridges.

Some non-head-stamped cartridge cases have marks on the head left by tool points of the power head used to hold the case during the bullet crimping process; others do not. There are two varieties of tool marks present. The most common consists of two vertical lines at the twelve o'clock and six o'clock positions on the case head. Several manufacturers used similar tool points, but this variety appears to be most consistent with that attributed to the U.S. Army's Frankford Arsenal.[3] The head-stamped cases with an H in a depressed circle also have tool point marks. There are three marks in a roughly triangular configuration on these cases, with one mark at the one o'clock position, one at the four o'clock position, and one at the seven o'clock position. The S.A.W. cases do not have tool point marks.

The Spencer cases represent nine different Spencer firearms and one Ballard rifle used at the battle (table F.3). In several instances, only a single cartridge case represents a firearm, but several have multiple matches. One case (specimen 58) has a single block firing pin imprint, indicating that it was fired in a Ballard firearm. One case (specimen 376) experienced extraction problems. Twenty-two of the Spencer cases were too oxidized for analysis.

Bullets

Fifty-two bullets and four pistol and rifle balls were recovered from the battle site (fig. F.3). The bullets were comparatively few relative to the number of cartridge cases recovered. The caliber of each bullet and ball as well as the weapon type from which it was fired if the bullet or ball was sufficiently intact to allow identification are shown in table F.4. Not surprisingly, most of the bullets are from cartridges

Table F.3. Spencer Cartridge Case Matches, Battle of Sweetwater Creek

Firearm	*Specimen Matches*	*Comment*
1	15, 67, 349, 363	
2	58	Ballard
3	60	
4	61, 88	
5	68	
6	71	
7	74, 77, 117, 345, 356, 361	
8	354, 365	
9	364, 371	
10	375, 376, 377	376 extraction problem

Fig. F.2. These fifty-six unfired Spencer cartridges were probably in a leather bag that was lost by one of the Indian warriors.

of the types recovered from the battle site. The bullets are five .44-caliber fired from Winchesters, one .44-caliber from a Colt Army Model 1860 pistol, six .45-caliber fired from Colt Model 1873 revolvers, twenty-five .45-caliber Springfields, four .50-caliber Springfields, three .50-caliber Sharps, one .50-caliber Spencer, five .50-caliber bullets that are too deformed to identify to weapon type, and two bullets that are too deformed and fragmented to identify to caliber or weapon type.

In addition to the bullets, four round balls were recovered that would have been fired from muzzle loader firearms. Two of the balls are .44- or .45-caliber from unidentified firearms, and two are .54-caliber from unidentified muzzle loaders. One of the .44- or .45-caliber balls (specimen 610) has a small indentation that appears to be from a ramrod.

Of the bullets and balls recovered, twelve are associated with the Indian combatants, seventeen are associated with the army combatants, and the twenty-five .45-caliber Springfield bullets—like the .45-caliber Springfield cartridges—apparently postdate the battle and are assumed to be associated with soldiers from Fort Elliot. The firearms represented by the Indian-associated bullets include muzzle loader rifles, .44-caliber Winchesters, .50-caliber Sharps, and .50-caliber Spencer rifles. The 8th Cavalry–associated bullets were fired from a .44-caliber Colt Army Model 1860 pistol, .45-caliber Colt Model 1873 revolver, .50-caliber Springfield carbines, and .50-caliber Sharps rifles.

Howitzer Canister and Lead Shot

Twenty-four fragments of howitzer canister, one canister end cap, and eighty-three lead balls or shot from the canister were recovered (fig. F.4). The howitzer canister was a cylindrical tin case with iron end caps (see fig. 5.8). The recovered end cap measures 11.5 cm in diameter. The canister would have contained forty-eight .69-caliber lead or iron balls arranged in four tiers and packed in sawdust. The canister was attached to a wood sabot, which in turn was attached to a flannel cartridge bag that contained the powder charge. The canister round was designed for use at ranges not exceeding 400 yards but was most effective at 100–200 yards.[4]

Friction Primer

One friction primer (fig. F.5c) was recovered from the battle site. The friction primer was the principal means of igniting the powder charge in cannons. It consisted of two copper tubes soldered together at right angles. The short tube was filled with a friction composition into which was inserted a wire serrated on the end. The other end of the wire was twisted to form a loop. Powder filled the long tube, which was sealed with a plug of wax.

To fire the cannon, the long tube of the friction primer was placed into the cannon vent. A long cord, or lanyard, with a hook was then attached to the wire loop on the friction primer and, at the appropriate time, was given a pull. The serrated wire pulled through the friction composition, igniting it and in turn the powder in the bore.[5]

Priming Wire

One priming wire was recovered (fig. F.5b) near the friction primer at the site. The priming wire was used for piercing the cartridge bag containing the powder charge before inserting the friction primer in the cannon vent.

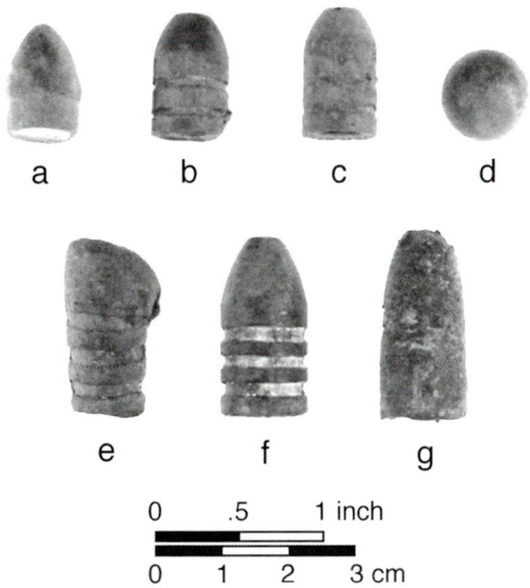

Fig. F.3. Miscellaneous bullets from the battle site: a, .44 Colt; b, .44 Winchester; c,.45 Colt; d, .44 or .45 ball; e, .45 Springfield; f, .50 Springfield; g, .50 Sharps.

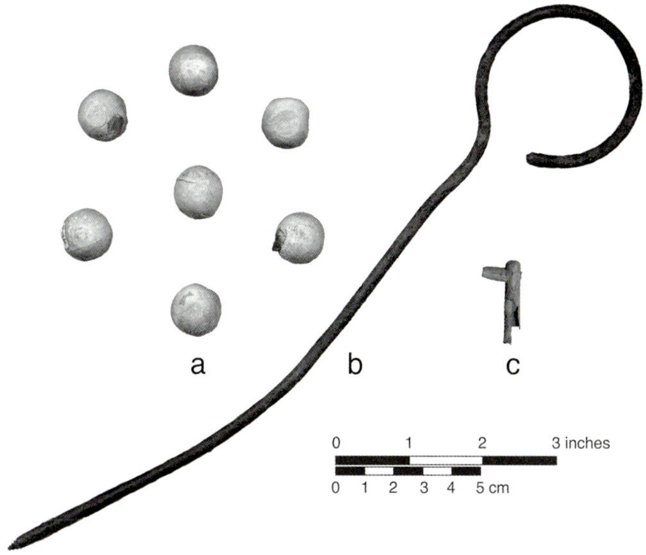

Fig. F.5. Artillery-associated artifacts: a, .69-caliber lead shot; b, priming wire; c, friction primer.

Fig. F.4. Recovered components of a 12-pounder howitzer canister round: a, .69-caliber lead shot; b, iron end cap; c, fragment of tin canister.

The recovered specimen is about 29 cm long and has a rounded or ring grip.

Benét Cup Primer

A single Benét cup cartridge primer was found on the battle site. This internal primer was used in .45- and .50-caliber cartridges. The primer was evidently dislodged from its cartridge case by the force of the explosion that fired the cartridge. The Benét primers have two holes in the body designed to transmit the flash of the primer charge to the black powder propellant.

Arrowpoints

Eight iron arrowpoints were recovered from the battlefield. The arrowpoints are of two manufacturing types: commercially produced and Indian made. The two commercially produced points (specimens 141 and 142, fig. F.6a–b) are similar in outline and more symmetrical than the Indian-made arrowpoints. They are also longer and have narrower blade widths than the Indian-made points (table F.5). Both commercially produced points have serrated tangs. The shoulders on specimen 141 angle down, forming short barbs, whereas those on specimen 142 are straight.

The six Indian-made specimens (329, 92, 249, 166, 91, 121; fig. F.6c–h) are more crudely formed and asymmetrical. They appear to have been made from a barrel hoop or similar metal stock and were cut from the stock with a chisel. On specimens 92 and 329 the stems are serrated. The serrations are not evenly spaced and not of uniform depth, suggesting that they were made with a metal file. The shoulders on all of the Indian-made points angle upward, though on specimen 91 they are nearly straight. The shoulders on specimen 121 are slightly rounded.

Non-Munitions Artifact

Button

A single army general service button (fig. F.7) was recovered from the site and was the only non-munitions artifact recovered. The button measures 19.5 mm in diameter. It does not have a backmark. This large button was worn on the jacket of the army uniform.

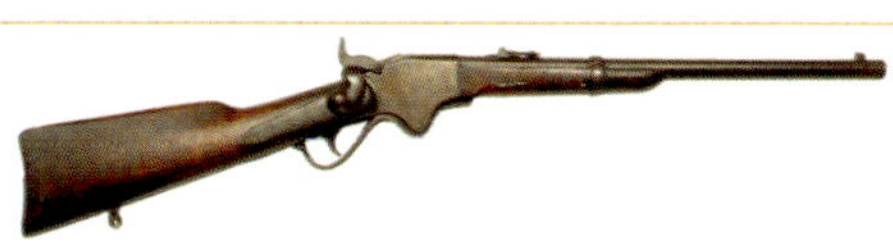

Table F.4. Identified Bullets and Associated Firearm Type, Battle of Sweetwater Creek

Specimen	*Caliber*	*Firearm Type*	*Comment*
39	.50	Unknown	Deformed
80	.45	Unknown	Deformed
93	.45	Springfield	
94	.50	Unknown	Deformed
101	.45	Springfield	
105	.45	Colt	
106	.50	Unknown	Deformed
119	.50	Unknown	Deformed
120	.50	Unknown	Deformed
122	.45	Colt	
129	.45	Springfield	
149	.45	Springfield	
150	.45	Springfield	
154	.45	Springfield	
156	.54	Unidentified muzzle loader	Ball
160	.45	Springfield	
167	.50	Unknown	Sharps
168	Unknown	Unknown	Fragment
169	.45	Springfield	
170	.45	Springfield	
171	.45	Springfield	
172	.45	Springfield	
173	.45	Springfield	
183	.45	Springfield	
184	.45	Springfield	
185	.45	Springfield	
186	.45	Springfield	
187	.45	Springfield	
188	.45	Springfield	
234	.45	Springfield	
248	.50	Springfield	
253	.45	Springfield	
254	.45	Colt	
255	.45	Springfield	
256	.44 or .45	Unknown	Ball
261	.50	Springfield	
306	.45	Springfield	
307	.45	Colt	
308	.44	Winchester	
309	.44	Winchester	
312	.44	Winchester	
315	.44	Winchester	
328	.50	Springfield	
415	.44	Colt	Model 1860 Army
426	.45	Colt	
570	.50	Springfield	
596	.50	Spencer	
608	.45	Colt	
609	.50	Sharps	
610	.44 or .45	Unknown	Ball with ramrod mark
613	.45	Springfield	
614	.45	Springfield	
615	Unknown	Unknown	Deformed
617	.54	Unidentified muzzle loader	Ball
618	.50	Sharps	
619	.44	Winchester	

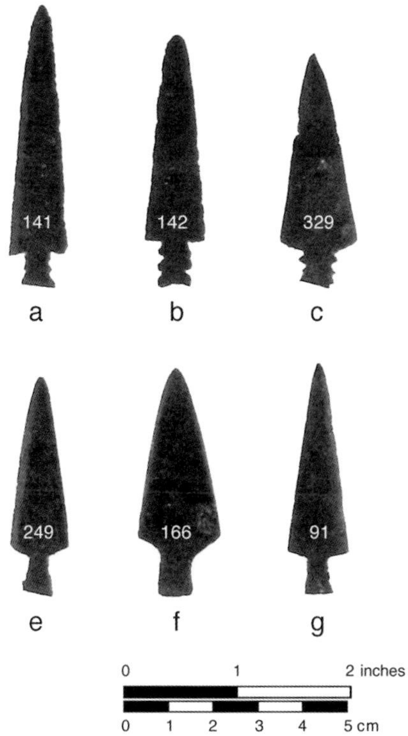

Fig. F.6. Metal arrowpoints recovered: a–b, commercially made and traded to the Indians; c–h, made by the Indians.

Table F.5. Arrowpoints, Battle of Sweetwater Creek

Specimen	*Length (cm)*	*Width (cm)*	*Thickness (cm)*
91	5.11	1.42	0.15
92	4.86	1.35	0.14
121	5.33	1.54	0.20
141	6.43	1.38	0.16
142	5.79	1.40	0.11
166	5.03	1.87	0.12
249	4.87	1.66	0.15
329	5.28	1.77	0.17
average	**5.34**	**1.55**	**0.15**

Fig. F.7. Army general service uniform button.

Appendix G

Descriptions and Analysis of Artifacts from the Battle of Palo Duro Canyon Site

Because only a relatively small portion of the Battle of Palo Duro Canyon site was investigated during the archeological survey and, as a result, so few cartridges and bullets were recovered from the site, none of the cartridge cases or bullets were subjected to detailed firearms analysis like those conducted for the other battle sites. The cartridges and bullets from this site were simply categorized and described as to type. The collection consists of 240 artifacts, which include 218 recovered during the 2002 archeological investigations and twenty-two recovered by personnel from the Panhandle-Plains Historical Museum during previous visits to the site. A total of 144 non-munitions-related artifacts were recovered. Of these, 141 are associated with the Indian occupants and three are associated with the 4th Cavalry troopers.

Arms and Ammunition

.44-Caliber Rimfire Cartridge Cases

Two .44-caliber rimfire cartridges were recovered from the battle site. Both were manufactured by the New Haven Arms Company (Winchester). Specimen 3-2 is a short case with no head stamp, and specimen 2-72 is a misfired long cartridge with an H head stamp. These Indian-associated cartridges were for the Henry rifle or Model 1866 Winchester.

.44-Caliber Smith & Wesson Cartridge Cases

Two center-fire .44-caliber cartridge cases (specimens 2-82 and 2-83) are consistent in dimensions with the .44-caliber Smith & Wesson American cartridge.[1] This cartridge was used in the Smith & Wesson single-action Model 3 revolver, known more generally as the 44 S&W American model. This model was in use in 1870 and may have been introduced in 1869. The U.S. Army used the revolver between 1871 and 1873, when the .45-caliber Colt was adopted as the standard sidearm. According to the 1874 ordnance returns (appendix B), the 4th Cavalry still had a few .44-caliber Smith & Wesson revolvers in use at the time of the battle in Palo Duro Canyon.

.45-Caliber Colt Cartridge Case

A single Colt Benét primed fired cartridge case (specimen 2-12) was recovered. The .45-caliber Colt cartridge was manufactured for use in the Colt Model 1873 revolver, which was the primary sidearm issued to cavalry troops beginning in 1874.

.45/55-Caliber Cartridge Cases

A total of forty-nine .45/55-caliber cartridge cases were recovered. All are Benét primed cases. Forty-two cartridges are associated with the army combatants and seven with the Indian combatants. The Indian-associated cartridges (specimens A670-2, 2-50, 2-51, 3-1, 3-7, 3-8, 3-12) were all fired in one or more .50-caliber Sharps carbines, as indicated by the firing pin drag marks visible on the heads of the cartridge cases. Firing pin drag marks are common to cartridges fired in Sharps carbines. In addition, all seven cartridges have split cases (fig. G.1). The cases apparently expanded and split lengthwise when they were fired in the larger .50-caliber chamber of the Sharps carbines. When the cases expanded it allowed the Benét primers to fall out of each of the cartridge cases. Seven Benét primers were also recovered—one near each of the split .45/55 cartridge cases.

.50/70-Caliber Cartridge Cases

Five .50/70-caliber cartridge cases were recovered from Indian-associated positions at the battle site. Firing pin drag marks on three of the cartridge cases suggests that they were fired in Sharps carbines. The other two cases appear to have been fired in Model 1868 or 1870 Springfield rifles. One of the Sharps-fired cartridges is Benét primed (specimen 2-2) and two are Martin primed (2-74 and A670-1). The Springfield-fired cartridges (2-67 and 3-3) are both Martin primed.

Spencer 56/50- and 56/56-Caliber Cartridge Cases

The site collection contains seven fired Spencer cases and one unfired case associated with the Indian combatants. Four of the eight are .50-caliber (1-3, 2-62, 2-79, and 2-80) and four (including the unfired case) are .56-caliber (2-5, 2-53, 2-70, and 2-107). Two of the .50-caliber cases are head-stamped with the letter H, denoting manufacture by the New Haven Arms Company or the Winchester Company. The others are not head-stamped.

Bullets

Eleven bullets or bullet fragments were recovered from the site: two .44-caliber Henry or Winchester, two .45-caliber Springfield, four .50-caliber, two unidentified fragments, and a .46-caliber rifle ball. One .50-caliber bullet is from a Spencer cartridge, one is from a Model 1868 or 1870 Springfield, and two are so impacted that identification to cartridge type is not possible.

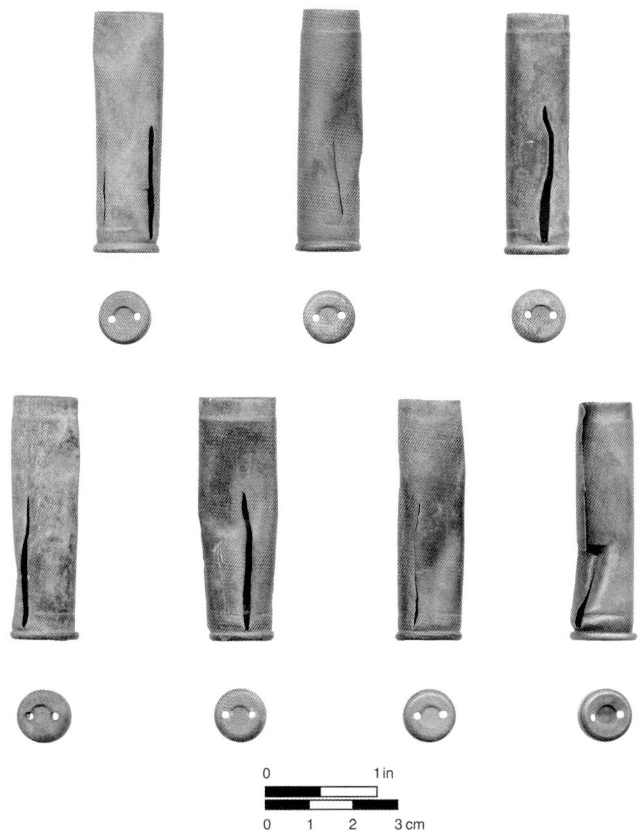

Fig. G.1. .45-caliber cartridge cases and Benét primers. These cases split when they were fired in .50-caliber Sharps guns.

Fig. G.2. Metal arrowpoints. Only specimen 2-15 has been finished. The others are roughly cut and unfinished.

Metal Arrowpoints

Nine iron arrowpoints were recovered during the investigations (fig. G.2). All nine were found at the same location along with three pieces of cut metal and several pieces of small wire. These items most likely were in a bag or other container that was lost during the battle. In fact, only specimen 2-15 appears to be a finished point; all the others are roughly cut and unfinished. Chisel cut marks are evident on all arrowpoints, indicating that they were made by an Indian.

The arrowpoints were made from one or several pieces of thin metal strap. The strap material has several small perforations, as evident on specimens 2-16, 2-19, 2-20, and 2-22. Perforations are also on two of the cut metal pieces (2-23 and 2-26), which apparently were being shaped for later use as arrowpoints. The arrowpoints (table G.1) range in length from 3.40 cm to 4.43 cm with an average length of 3.92 cm. They range in width from 1.30 cm to 1.76 cm with an average width of 1.46 cm. The arrowpoints show little variation in thickness, ranging from 1 mm to 1.1 mm.

Table G.1. Arrowpoints, Battle of Palo Duro Canyon

Specimen	*Length (cm)*	*Width (cm)*	*Thickness (cm)*
2-15	4.28	1.46	0.11
2-16	4.02	1.76	0.11
2-17	3.78	1.46	0.10
2-18	4.28	1.44	0.10
2-19	3.40	1.45	0.11
2-20	3.56	1.30	0.11
2-21	3.94	1.54	0.11
2-22	4.43	1.44	0.11
2-27	3.59	1.31	0.11
average	3.92	1.46	0.11

Gun Barrel

Specimen 2-134 is a 32.5 cm long portion of a U.S. Model 1841 "Mississippi" percussion rifle barrel (fig. G.3). The end of the barrel has been cut and broken off. Cut marks are also visible on the barrel near the rear sight notches. The rear sight is missing, as is the percussion nipple from the bolster. Below the nipple bolster on the bottom of the barrel is an identification mark, probably of the manufacturer's inspector. The mark consists of four small triangles whose tips all point in to form a stylized cross, as shown in fig. G.3. The breech plug of the barrel is broken and has been partially screwed out. The barrel measures 3.2 cm in diameter and has a bore diameter of 1.37 cm.

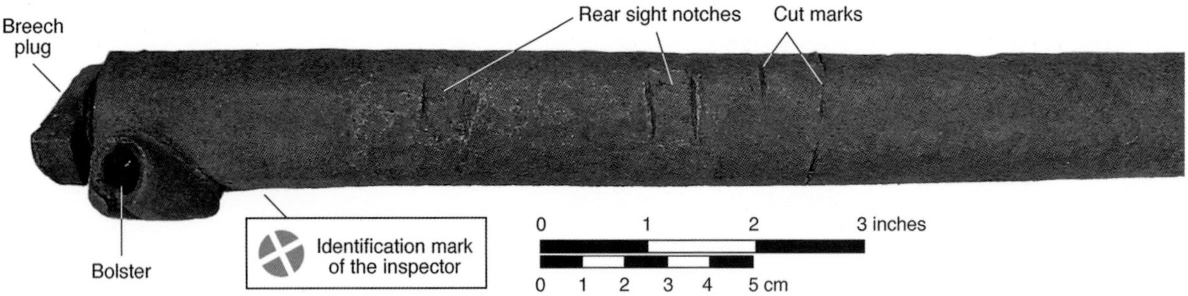

Fig. G.3. Portion of a U.S. Model 1841 "Mississippi" percussion rifle.

The "Mississippi rifle" owes its name to the successful use of this weapon by a Mississippi regiment under the command of Jefferson Davis during the Mexican War. The Harpers Ferry Armory manufactured a total of 25,296 of these rifles, and other contractors produced an additional 45,500 from about 1844 to 1855. The walnut stock of the rifle held a 33-inch-long round barrel. On the right side of the stock was a large brass patch box. The U.S. Model 1841 was the first regulation rifle made in the percussion ignition system at the national armories.[2]

Gun Screw or Pin

Specimen 2-71 is a gun screw or pin from an unidentified firearm. The specimen is brass and measures 2.25 cm in overall length. It has a smooth shank 1.5 cm long and then three threads just below a round, single-slot head. The smooth shank and short threads suggest that the specimen functioned as a pin rather than a screw. The specimen is similar to the hinge pin for a Springfield Model 1865 breechloading rifle.

Other Indian-Associated Artifacts

Ax Heads

Two iron ax heads were recovered (fig. G.4). Specimen 2-100, the larger of the two, is 17.3 cm long and 11.6 cm wide and weighs 1.47 kg. On one face of this specimen is a manufacturer's mark, but it is so worn that only a few letters are discernible. The letters that can be read are ICOLL, and below these letters appears the word STEEL. The ax form is a style that dates from about 1750 to 1850 or slightly later.[3] Specimen 2-100 was apparently used as an anvil, since both faces exhibit multiple cut marks from a cold chisel. The poll of the head also exhibits extensive battering from use as a hammer.

Specimen 2-108 measures 16.1 cm in overall length and 10.1 cm in width and weighs 0.91 kg. Though smaller, this ax form is the same as specimen 2-100. This specimen is marked D. SIMMONS & CO. COHOES—NY SUPERIOR CAST STEEL. On the opposite face is the letter G. This head does not exhibit the cold chisel marks seen on the head of specimen 2-100, and the poll also shows only slight battering.

Fig. G.4. Ax heads. Note the cold chisel cut marks on specimen 2-100, indicating use as an anvil.

Bead

A single small, blue glass seed bead (specimen 3-14) was found inside an iron tinkler recovered from the site when the tinkler was being cleaned in the laboratory. Glass beads were a common trade item to Native Americans from the time of the earliest contact with Europeans and through the late nineteenth century. Indians used beads to decorate clothing, bags, and an array of other items.

Bell

Specimen 2-4 is a brass bell with an iron clapper (fig. G.5a). The bell measures 3.58 cm wide at the base and is 2.75 cm tall. It is undecorated except for a single incised line around the periphery. Bells were often used to adorn clothing and were also commonly attached to horse trappings. A bell very similar to specimen 2-24 was recovered from the Battle of Red River site (see appendix D).

Bridle Bits

Specimen H27-14 from the Panhandle-Plains Historical Museum collection is a Spanish-style bridle snaffle bit (fig. G.6a). Snaffle bits are unlike the more familiar curb bits in that they are typically jointed in the middle and have no vertical side shanks. A snaffle bit allows a two- or three-year-old horse to be guided through training without undue pressure on the tongue, roof, or sensitive bars (gums) of the mouth. The most common snaffle bit has two arms that are jointed together, and each arm has an O-ring on its other end to which the reins are attached.

Specimen H27-14 has an overall length of 23.13 cm. One arm of the bit measures 9.24 cm with an O-ring of 2.87 cm diameter. The other arm measures 10.91 cm and has an O-ring of 3.46 cm diameter. Both O-rings are closed with a "butt" joint. The arms of the bit are joined with a "rattail" joint. These elements are common characteristics of Spanish-made eighteenth- and nineteenth-century bits.[4]

Specimen 2-1 appears to be an Indian-made version of a snaffle bit (fig. G.6b). The specimen consists of two pieces of heavy gauge wire linked together in the middle, with the ends of each piece bent into loops. The overall length of the specimen is 16.67 cm. One wire arm segment measures 8.67 cm long and the other is 8.90 cm. The thickness of the wire used to form the bit is 3.7 mm. Each of the looped ends of the arms has an inside diameter of approximately 8.9 mm. Both arms show evidence of teeth marks, which suggests that the artifact was in fact a snaffle bit.

Fig. G.5. Indian-associated domestic and personal items: a, brass bell and iron clapper; b, food grater; c, silver *naja;* d, pendant; e, spoon bowl.

Buckles

Four buckles were recovered from the site—three roller buckles and one D-shaped buckle. Two of the roller buckles (specimens 2-39 and 2-118) were for straps 1 inch wide and the other (specimen 2-63) for a strap 1.5 inches wide. The D-shaped buckle (specimen 2-133) fastened a strap about an inch wide and was probably used on a bridle.

Buttons and Waist Cinch Buckle

Three buttons and a waist cinch buckle are among the collections from the site. The buttons are all metal, four-hole buttons. These small, one-piece buttons each measure 14.5 mm in diameter. The waist cinch buckle (specimen 2-36) measures 28.5 mm long by 21.2 mm wide. The small size of this specimen suggests use on a woman's corset or other garment.

Concha

Specimen 1-1 is a saddle concha from the collection of the Panhandle-Plains Historical Museum. The tin concha has a diameter of 33.5 mm and is stamped with a floral wreath decoration on its face. Two rectangular cuts in the center of the concha allowed it to be attached to a leather tassel or thong. The concha may be associated with the Indian occupants or it may postdate the battle.

Cut Metal

Nine pieces of cut iron were recovered during the investigations. Three of these (specimens 2-23, 2-26, 2-117) were cut with a chisel, are triangular in shape, and appear

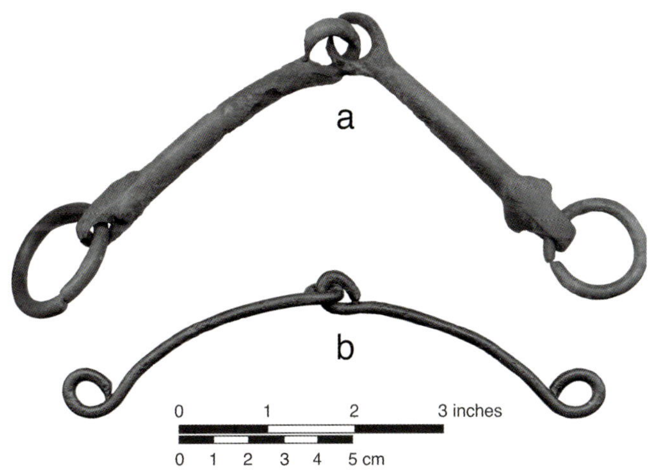

Fig. G.6. Spanish snaffle bit (a) and Indian-made snaffle bit (b).

to be preforms for arrowpoints. In fact, these three specimens were found in association with the nine recovered arrowpoints. Another arrowpoint preform is specimen 2-87, which is more diamond shaped in outline. The other five pieces of cut metal all appear to be fragments of barrel hoops that have been cut with a chisel but otherwise were not modified.

Edged Tools

Three specimens in the collection are classified as edged tools (fig. G.7). Specimen 2-40 is a rectangular piece of iron that measures 4.7 cm by 4.1 cm and is 3.5 mm thick. In profile the piece has a slight curve and one edge has been sharpened, apparently to allow the specimen to function as a scraping tool. Specimen 2-123 is similar to specimen 2-40 in that it is also a rectangular piece of iron; it measures 5.2 cm by 5.3 cm and is 1.3 mm thick. This specimen is also slightly curved in profile and one edge has been sharpened. Like specimen 2-40, specimen 2-123 probably functioned as a scraping tool.

Specimen A763-6, from the Panhandle-Plains Historical Museum collections, is the blade of a butcher knife. The tip of the knife has been broken. The cutting edge of the blade is concave and exhibits extensive use. Stamped on one side of the blade are the words LANDERS FRARY & CLARK, ETNA WORKS. The Landers, Frary, & Clark Company made a wide array of household items from the mid-1800s until 1965, when it went out of business.[5]

Fig. G.7. Indian-associated edged tools. Specimen A763-6 is a butcher knife blade.

File Fragment

Specimen 2-122 is an end fragment of a large bastard file. It measures 4.2 cm long, 2.9 cm wide, and 5 mm thick. Files were commonly traded to Native Americans, who used them in a variety of metalworking activities, particularly in the production and finishing of metal arrowpoints.

Food Graters

Two sheet iron fragments (specimens 2-54 and 2-114) may represent parts of food graters. They are both container body pieces perforated with numerous small holes (fig. G.5b). The specimens are probably parts of one or more small "radish" graters that could be found in many kitchens during the nineteenth century.

Frying Pan

Specimen 2-45 is a frying pan or skillet that is 25.4 cm in diameter and has a 33 cm long handle. The handle is attached to the pan by three rivets. The frying pan is typical of those manufactured during the latter half of the nineteenth century.

Harness Rings

Two iron harness rings (specimens 2-59 and 2-120) are in the collection. Specimen 2-59 has an inside diameter of 3.8 cm, and specimen 2-120 has an inside diameter of 4.5 cm. These rings could have been on a horse or mule harness.

Nails, Tacks, and Screws

A total of forty-four nails, tacks, and screws were recovered. Nails dominate the collection and include a single large, unused 18d square nail, a broken 8d square nail, three 4d square nails, and sixteen small saddletree nails.

In addition, ten unused horseshoe nails were found. The horseshoe nails are in three different lengths, and two head types are represented. Specimen 2-124 is a long nail that measures 6.87 cm and has a large beveled head. Seven nails, all in lot 2-56, measure 6.3 cm long and have small beveled heads. Another nail in lot 2-56 is 5.9 cm long and has a small beveled head. Finally, specimen 2-130 is the head only of a small bevel-headed nail. Though the horseshoe nails may have been lost by the soldiers during the battle, they were all recovered in areas where other Indian-associated artifacts were found and are probably items the Indians had secured from some unknown source.

Also recovered during the investigations were ten tacks: two small, round-headed tacks of the type commonly used by Indians to decorate gunstocks and other items, and eight larger tacks that were most likely used as decorations on saddles. These saddle tacks are of three varieties. One variety, of which there are two specimens (2-34.1 and 2-34.2), has a convex, plain, round, 1.57 cm diameter two-piece head. On the head is attached a square tapered shank that is 2.5 cm long. Another variety, of which there are three specimens (2-35.1, 2-35.2, 2-35.3), has a convex, plain, round,

1.90 cm diameter two-piece head with a square tapered shank that is approximately 1.3 cm long. The shanks on all three of these specimens have been bent and rolled into a tight curl. The last variety of saddle tack includes three specimens (2-29, 2-33, 2-42) that have convex, round, 2.25 cm diameter two-piece, cast brass heads with lead backings. Attached to the back of specimen 2-29 is a square tapered iron shank 3.0 cm long. The shanks are missing from the other two specimens. The faces of these tacks (fig. G.8) are decorated with a raised five-pointed star in the center surrounded by five raised dots and a floral wreath around the face edge. Items similar to these specimens have been described as "stickpins" made for Texas Confederate veterans.[6] The stickpins as described by Price, however, were made with the letters T E X A S around the points of the star on the face and the letters CS in the center of the star. Also, the shank of the stickpins measured 3.8 cm long. The lead backs on the specimens from the battle site suggest a measure of durability that would be warranted for a saddle tack but not for a stickpin.

In addition to the nails and tacks, three wood screws (specimens 2-32.1, 2-32.2, 2-32.3) were recovered from a single location. The screws measure 3.24 cm long and have flat, single-slot heads.

Naja

A silver *naja* (fig. G.5c) was recovered during the investigations. A *naja* (from the Navajo *najahe*, crescent) is a crescent-shaped pendant. It was adapted into Indian silverwork from Hispanic-Moorish sources, which had adapted the crescent from prehistoric Mediterranean sources. In the Hispanic culture of the sixteenth century, when the Southwestern and Plains Indians first saw the silver crescent suspended from the bridles of the conquistadores' horses, the *naja* was worn as a symbol to protect the rider from the "evil eye."[7] The *naja* from the battle site measures approximately 4.3 cm by 4.6 cm. Soldered to its back is a small hook used to fasten the *naja* to a necklace.

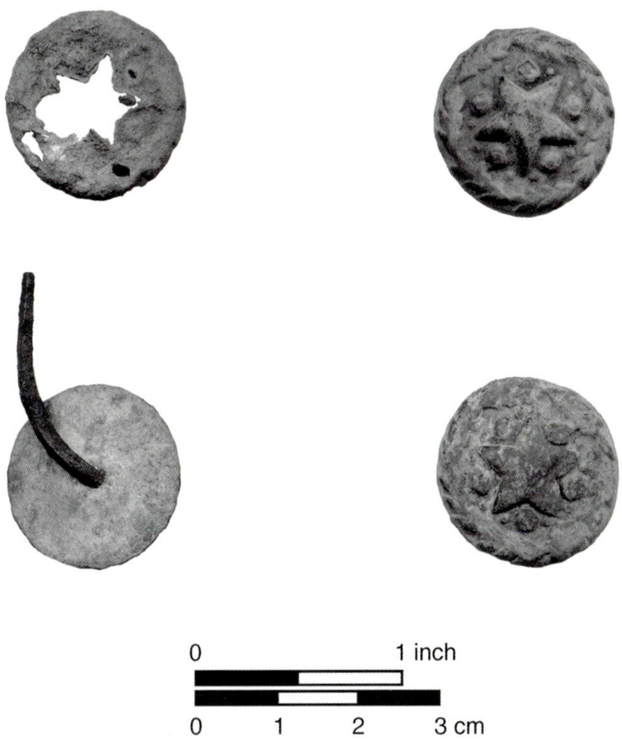

Fig. G.8. Large tacks used as decorations on a saddle.

Pendant

Specimen 2-105 is a circular brass token (fig. G.5d) that measures 2.35 cm across. Stamped in the center on one side are the letters J. B. A small hole has been drilled near the edge so that the token could be worn as a pendant. What the letters stand for and the artifact's original function are not known.

Picket Pin Fragments

Portions of four hand-made, wrought iron picket pins were recovered (fig. G.9). Three of the specimens are portions of the heads of separate pins. All three were manufactured by first thinning and then bending a single piece of iron over and onto itself to form a loop that functioned as the head of the pin. Specimens 2-60.1 and 2-60.2 are both broken just below the loop. Both of these specimens exhibit extensive battering on their heads. Specimen 2-61 is half of the looped head of a picket pin. All three pins were found in close proximity, perhaps indicating that they were all broken at the same time. Specimen 2-88 is a 47.5 cm long shank portion of a picket pin with a diameter of 1.6 cm.

Snap Hook

Specimen 2-136 is a snap hook (fig. G.9) for a halter chain. The snap hook is not army regulation and was apparently produced for the private sector. It was found in an area of the site where several Indian-associated artifacts were recovered and is assumed to be associated with the Indians at the site. Stamped into the back of the snap hook are the letters R. H. MORE . . . , followed by either the number 3 or 7.

Spoon Handle and Bowl

Pieces of two spoons were recovered during the investigations. Specimen 2-128 is a handle fragment, and specimen 2-127 is the bowl end of a large spoon. Though the two artifacts were found in close proximity, they are not parts of the same spoon. The bowl of specimen 2-127 has been bent to form a small spout at the end (fig. G.5e). It may be that this spoon was used to heat and melt pieces of bar lead to be poured into bullet molds.

Tinklers

Thirty-three rolled iron tinklers (lot 2-119) were recovered from a single location during the investigations. The tinklers (fig. G.10) vary in length from 1.36 cm to 2.10 cm

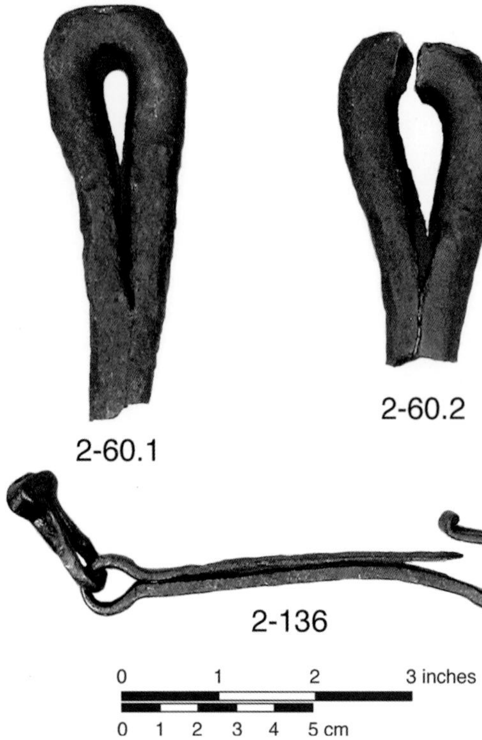

Fig. G.9. Head portions of hand-forged picket pins (specimens 2-60.1 and 2-60.2) and a snap hook (specimen 2-136) from a halter chain.

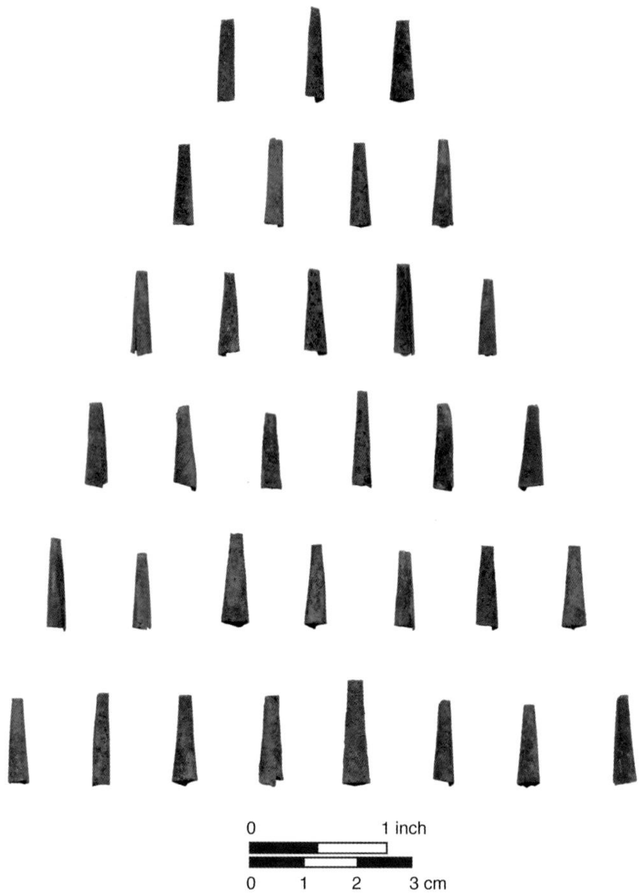

Fig. G.10. Thirty-three small tinklers recovered from a single location at the site. The tinklers were probably decorations on a leather pouch like the one shown in fig. G.11.

but average 1.56 cm (table G.2). Twenty-nine of the tinklers are rolled with a center curl, three have left curls, and one is right curled. A small, blue glass, seed bead was recovered from inside one of the tinklers. Because the tinklers were all found in one location, it is likely that they were attached as decorations to a small leather bag that was dropped by one of the Indian villagers. Tinklers and beads were often used to decorate leather bags like the one shown in fig. G.11.

Umbrella Glider Links

Eleven glider links from an umbrella were recovered (fig. G.12). All eleven specimens (2-9, 2-28.1, 2-28.2, 2-37, 2-38, 2-58, 2-76, 2-77, 2-78, 2-84, 2-86) appear to be from the same umbrella. Eight of the links are complete and three are fragments. The complete specimens measure 25.9 cm long. They have a square shank with a 2.5 cm long yoke on one end and a flat eyelet hole on the other. The yoke end would have attached to another link that was connected to the top of the umbrella's main rod, and the eyelet end would have attached to another link that probably had a finial end on it that was attached to the edge of the cloth of the umbrella. When the umbrella was opened, the three connected links formed one rib of the umbrella. All of the recovered umbrella links are unmodified except for specimen 2-86, on which the eyelet end has been sharpened to a point, apparently for use as an awl.

Wire

Nine pieces of wire were recovered from various locations on the battle site and may or may not be associated with the battle. Four small pieces (lot 2-24) were recovered in association with the cluster of unfinished metal arrowpoints. The function or intended purpose of the wire with the arrowpoints is not clear, but the association with the points was obvious.

Unidentified

One unidentified brass piece was recovered during the investigations. Specimen 2-116 is a thin piece of cut brass in the shape of a shield that measures approximately 5.91 cm long and 5.24 cm wide. Along the top edge of the "shield" are three small nail holes where the piece was attached to another object at some point, but the specimen has no other marks or lettering of any kind. The function of this artifact is not known.

Fig. G.11. Circa-1910 Kiowa leather bag decorated with iron tinklers and glass beads. From the collections of the Panhandle-Plains Historical Museum, accession no. 85/1.

Table G.2. Tinklers, Battle of Palo Duro Canyon

Specimen	*Length (cm)*	*Curl*
2-119.1	2.10	center
2-119.2	1.44	center
2-119.3	1.53	center
2-119.4	1.39	center
2-119.5	1.40	center
2-119.6	1.36	center
2-119.7	1.51	center
2-119.8	1.53	center
2-119.9	1.56	center
2-119.10	1.63	center
2-119.11	1.47	center
2-119.12	1.51	center
2-119.13	1.51	center
2-119.14	1.72	center
2-119.15	1.63	center
2-119.16	1.62	center
2-119.17	1.67	center
2-119.18	1.50	center
2-119.19	1.54	center
2-119.20	1.58	center
2-119.21	1.51	center
2-119.22	1.57	center
2-119.23	1.69	center
2-119.24	1.40	center
2-119.25	1.59	center
2-119.26	1.75	center
2-119.27	1.69	center
2-119.28	1.54	center
2-119.29	1.46	center
2-119.30	1.57	left
2-119.31	1.57	left
2-119.32	1.54	left
2-119.33	1.56	right
average	1.56	

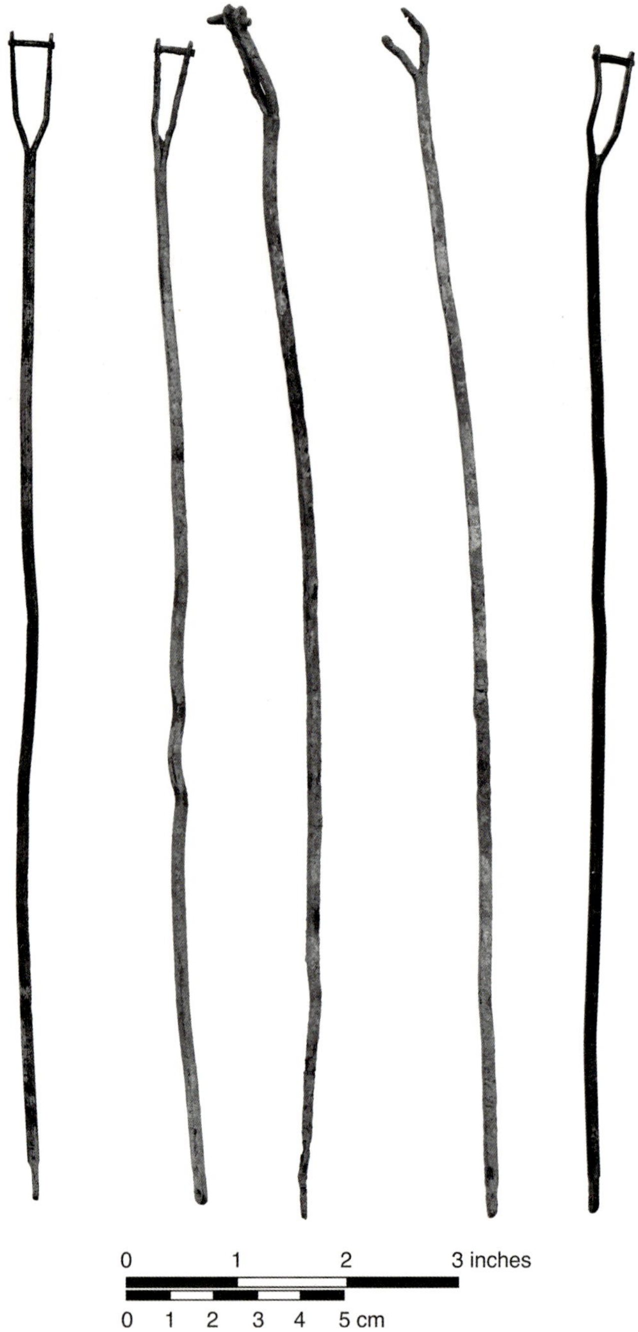

Fig. G.12. Umbrella glider links.

Other Army-Associated Artifacts

Horseshoes

Three horseshoes or horseshoe fragments were recovered. Specimens 2-8 and 2-10 are complete; specimen 2-44 is half a shoe. All three specimens are horseshoes of the Burden pattern, which was introduced just prior to the Civil War. Specimens 2-8 and 2-10 each have one nail still in the shoe, and specimen 2-44 has four nails in it. Specimen 2-8 is a left hind shoe with damage to the toe. Specimen 2-10 is a left front shoe with heel caulks. Specimen 2-44 also has a heel caulk.

Appendix H

Descriptions and Analysis of Artifacts from the Battle of Round Timber Creek Site and Grey Beard's Village Site

During the archeological investigations of the Battle of Round Timber Creek site, a total of 308 battle-related artifacts were recovered. Of these, 209 are associated with the army and ninety-nine with the Indians. A total of seventy-eight non-munitions artifacts were recovered at the battle site and Grey Beard's village site. Of these, twenty are associated with the 8th Cavalry troopers and fifty-eight with the Indians.

Arms and Ammunition

Preservation of the firearms artifacts from the Battle of Round Timber Creek site was excellent, with the vast majority of cartridge cases retaining clear and distinct firing pin impressions and clear extractor marks; many also had good preservation of breech face marks on the case head. Lead bullet preservation was good, with class characteristics preserved when impact deformation was not too extreme, though oxidation of the lead obscured some individual characteristics.

.40/70-Caliber Sharps Cartridge Cases

Three cartridge cases in .40/70-caliber (specimens 391, 392, 393) were noted in the collection (fig. H.1e). The cartridge cases are Berdan primed and, based on class and individual characteristics observed under microscopic examination, were fired in the same Sharps rifle. The .40/70-caliber straight-cased cartridge was introduced by Sharps about 1870 for the New Model 1868 Sharps carbine and continued in production with the Model 1874 rifle for many years afterward. These cartridge cases are typical of Sharps Company production runs.[1]

.44-Caliber Rimfire Cartridge Cases

The eight .44-caliber fired cartridge cases from the site are all of New Haven Arms Company (Winchester) manufacture in two lengths, short (fig. H.1a) and long (fig. H.1b). Case dimensions are consistent with Winchester-manufactured ammunition.[2] Microscopic examination of class characteristics on each cartridge case indicated that all eight cases (specimens 12 [long with H head stamp], 61 [short with no head stamp], 62 [long with H head stamp], 64 [short with H head stamp], 78 [long with H head stamp], 79 [long with H head stamp], 80 [long with H head stamp], 81 [long with H head stamp]) were fired in the same Henry rifle or Model 1866 Winchester. Both are lever-action magazine-fed repeating rifles based on the same breechblock system, the Model 1866 being a side-loading refinement of the Henry. Both could hold up to sixteen rounds in the magazine and chamber. Individual characteristics of the firing pins in the recovered Henry cartridge cases indicate that one Henry or Winchester Model 1866 fired these cases.

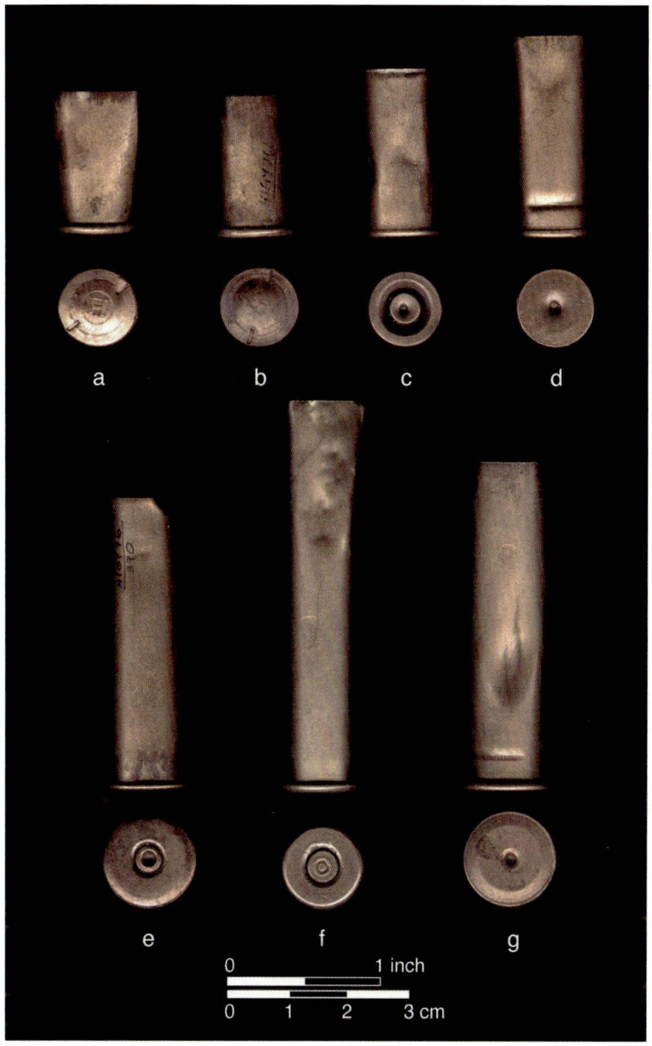

Fig. H.1. Miscellaneous cartridge cases and case heads: a, .44-caliber Henry short; b, .44-caliber Henry long; c, .44-caliber Smith and Wesson Russian Martin primed; d, .45-caliber Benét primed Colt; e, .40/70-caliber Winchester made by Remington; f, .40/60-caliber Berdan primed Sharps; g, .45-caliber Benét primed Springfield.

All but one fired .44-caliber case had two sets of firing pin imprints on the head. This indicates that, with the exception of specimen 79, the rounds fired in the gun required extra effort to lever open the breech block, remove and rotate the cartridge slightly, replace the cartridge in the chamber, then close the lever and fire the gun. The presence of multiple firing pin marks on seven cartridge cases indicates that the firearm was not functioning correctly. The firing pin on the rifle was either defective or dirty and was not traveling completely forward to strike the cartridge when the trigger was pulled. Whether the firearm was defective or dirty, the recovered cartridge cases suggest that only a half magazine was expended during the fight by this gun.

.44-Caliber Smith & Wesson Russian Cartridge Cases

Three Martin primed .44-caliber cartridge cases (specimens 295, 299, 304) are consistent in dimensions with the .44-caliber Smith & Wesson Russian cartridge (fig. H.1c). All three cartridges were fired in the same gun. Smith & Wesson introduced the caliber in 1870 for their Russian Military revolver. It was originally manufactured for the Imperial Russian government, but the U.S. Army purchased one thousand revolvers for issue to cavalry troops. No army Smith & Wesson revolvers were reported issued to men or officers of the 8th Cavalry. It is possible that one of the officers purchased a readily available civilian model or acquired one of the .44-caliber guns through army channels. It is also possible that the pistol is a lost army model or a civilian model that was in one of the warriors' hands.[3]

The three cartridge cases are consistent with the specifications for the 1870 second patent (Patent No. 111,856) of Edward Martin, an employee of the National Armory in Springfield, Massachusetts. This cartridge type was loaded only for a short period in 1871 at Frankford Arsenal.[4]

.45-Caliber Colt Cartridge Cases

The collection contained one fired .45-caliber Colt Benét primed cartridge case (specimen 384) (fig. H.1d) and four unfired cartridges. Frankford Arsenal produced this inside-primed center-fire cartridge beginning in 1873 for use in the Model 1873 Colt army revolver. The 8th Cavalry was not issued this model until June or July 1874.[5]

.45/70-Caliber Cartridge Cases

Two fired .45-caliber Benét primed cartridge cases were recovered at the battle site (specimens 315 and 390) (fig. H.1g), as was one unfired cartridge. The two fired cartridges were fired in separate guns. The first .45-caliber carbines were not received at the western cavalry posts until May 1874, but the 8th Cavalry was not armed with the Springfield Model 1873 until after September 1874.[6] These two .45-caliber guns may represent a post-battle deposition, although these early Benét primed cases suggest an early deposition, since the crimp holding the cup primer in place in the cartridge case was changed in 1877, and the two specimens definitely have the early so-called long primer crimp. It is equally possible these cartridge cases represent early unrecorded issues of the Model 1873 carbine to some members of the 8th Cavalry, perhaps new recruits sent from one of the training stations like Jefferson Barracks, Missouri, or perhaps these guns were procured by the officers before general issue to the enlisted men. We believe it is more likely, however, that they represent weapons captured by the Indian warriors from other army units.

.50/70-Caliber Cartridge Cases

The 191 fired .50/70-caliber cartridge cases from the site are mostly internally primed Benét cup center-fire copper (Bloomfield Gilding Metal) cases, although a few Remington-made Berdan externally primed brass raised-ring cases are also present (specimens 54, 55, 56, 57, 59, 124, 125, 126, 127, 128, 129).[7] All of the Remington raised-ring cartridge cases were fired in the same gun. Other cartridge case types represented are the Martin folded-head variety and the bar-primed type. Frankford Arsenal made the Martin folded-head cartridge case (specimens 16, 17, 203, 204, 220, 255) for several years, ceasing production around 1871. One other internally primed variety is the Martin bar-primed type (specimens 47, 294, 312, 314). The Martin bar primer was developed by the army at Frankford Arsenal and manufactured between October 1866 and March 1868 at that arsenal for use in the Model 1866 Springfield breechloading rifle, the so-called 2nd Allin Conversion.[8]

The .50/70 cartridge cases were fired in at least five different gun types (table H.1). These include Sharps carbines or rifles, the Model 1868 or 1870 Springfield rifle or carbine, and the experimental bolt action Ward-Burton carbine, and some cartridge cases had no clear marks but were likely fired in a Remington carbine, as suggested by the deep and nearly uniform firing pin impression; there is also an unidentified gun type (fig. H.2). This unidentified type is represented by cartridge cases fired in two different guns. The case heads have a long and wide scar offset from the firing pin imprint, suggesting some type of gun where the breechblock drops down into the receiver and some projection on the breech mechanism is responsible for the scarring (fig. H.3). Because two separate guns are represented, it is unlikely that the scarring is from a fault in the breech face.

Several of the Sharps-fired cases are of some interest. Some cases representing several different guns show misfires or multiple firing pin drag marks, indicating firing and extraction problems with these guns. Specimens 192, 378, and 380 all have three strikes and drag marks on the cartridge case head. Nine .50/70-caliber cartridge cases (specimens 5, 10, 11, 15, 20, 47, 49, 98, and 133) were too damaged to analyze. Ten unfired .50/70 cartridges were also recovered from the battle site.

The firing pin analysis of the .50/70 cartridge cases indicates that seventy-one individual weapons fired the cartridges: thirty-eight Sharps rifles or carbines (fig. H.4), five Remington-made guns, twelve Model 1868 or 1870 Springfield rifles or carbines, fourteen Ward-Burton carbines, and

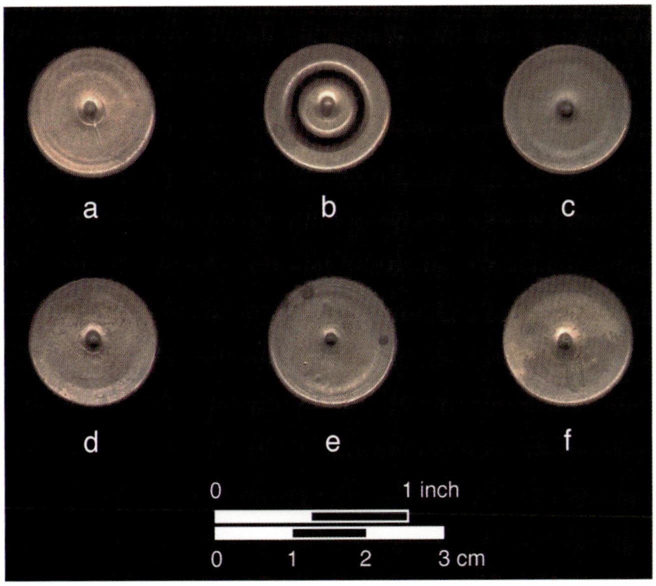

Fig. H.2. Head view of .50/70-caliber cartridge cases: a, Benét primed fired in a Sharps; b, Martin primed fired in a Sharps; c, Benét primed fired in a Remington; d, Benét primed fired in a Model 1868 or 1870 Springfield; e, Benét primed fired in a Ward-Burton; f, Benét primed fired in an unidentified gun type.

two unidentified guns (fig. H.5). On the basis of distribution of the recovered cartridges, a minimum of fifty-six guns are associated with the army scout patrol. This raises an interesting question. Why would a scout patrol of twenty-eight soldiers be carrying fifty-six carbines? The presence of the Sharps, Remington, Springfield, and Ward-Burton firearms is consistent with the known armament history of the 8th Cavalry in the early 1870s. Beginning in 1871, the army produced or procured several of these gun types to test and determine the best arm for cavalry service. The firearms were sent to various units, including the 8th Cavalry, for field trials about mid-year 1871. The 8th Cavalry retained its experimental guns until at least 1875. From the 1874 ordnance returns (appendix B) it is known that Farnsworth's Company H was issued mostly Sharps carbines, but it also had Ward-Burton, Springfield, and Remington carbines.

Though some of these .50/70-caliber firearms could have been in warrior hands, it is more likely that the represented Springfield, Remington, Ward-Burton, and most of the Sharps guns were experimental carbines in the hands of the 8th Cavalry. In that case, and for whatever reason, the only apparent explanation for the presence of fifty-six army-associated carbines at the site is that each trooper in the patrol was carrying and using two carbines. Perhaps the troopers were carrying two carbines each in case their experimental models failed or did not have adequate range. Since all of the carbines used the same .50-caliber ammunition, they would not have had to carry additional types of cartridges for the various gun models.[9]

Fig. H.3. Microscopic view of two .50/70-caliber cartridge cases fired in the same unidentified gun type. Note the long, wide breechface scar and the matching straie on specimens 355 (left) and 359 (right).

Spencer 56/50- and 56/56-Caliber Cartridge Cases

Spencer cases in two calibers, .50 and .56, were noted in the collection (fig. H.6). One variety, of which there are nineteen fired specimens, has no head stamp; one cartridge case (specimen 60) is head-stamped with the impressed letters S.A.W., denoting the Sage Ammunition Works; one (specimen 93) has the raised letter H, denoting the New Haven Arms Company or Winchester company; and two (speci-

Table H.1. .50/70 Cartridge Case Matches, Battle of Round Timber Creek

Firearm	Specimen Matches
Remington	
1	7
2	100
3	240, 265, 294
4	353
5	386
Sharps	
1	3, 46, 48, 87, 92, 94, 201, 202, 206, 231, 233
2	4, 6, 366
3	8, 16, 17, 23
4	9, 30, 51, 67, 88
5	13, 120, 132, 159, 210, 217, 382
6	14, 254
7	27, 135, 136, 137, 149
8	35, 69, 165, 167, 170, 253
9	42
10	54, 55, 56, 57, 59, 124, 125, 126, 127, 128, 129, 130
11	68
12	77, 169, 172, 223, 244, 381
13	91
14	96
15	97, 171, 177
16	131, 229, 257, 312
17	134, 191, 205, 209, 230, 246, 266
18	160, 388
19	162
20	180, 216, 218, 238, 250, 261, 262
21	192 (3 firing pin drag marks)
22	196, 212
23	203, 204, 220, 255, 258
24	211, 357, 380 (3 firing pin drag marks)
25	213, 387
26	219, 221, 222, 225, 227, 228
27	232
28	239
29	247
30	251, 256
31	264
32	267
33	314, 335
34	347
35	354, 358, 362, 367
36	356
37	365
38	378 (3 firing pin drag marks)
Springfield M1868 or 1870	
1	18, 186, 187, 193
2	22, 28, 50
3	31, 123, 179
4	45, 200
5	71, 259
6	86
7	121
8	122
9	183
10	207, 242, 260
11	208, 234, 235
12	214, 224, 226, 237, 241, 243, 245
Ward-Burton	
1	24
2	26
3	161, 188
4	163, 175
5	166
6	168, 173, 174, 176, 194
7	182, 199
8	185
9	189
10	195, 197, 198
11	236
12	252
13	268
14	396
Unidentified Gun Type	
1	355, 359
2	360, 361, 363

mens 306 and 320) are head-stamped with F.V.V.&Co, for Fitch, Van Vechten & Company.

There is another variety of non-head-stamped cartridge case, of which there are eleven fired specimens that have crimps on the upper body for holding the bullet in place and tool marks on the head left by tool points of the power head used to hold the case during the bullet crimping process. The tool point marks observed are two vertical lines at the twelve o'clock and six o'clock position on the case head. Several manufacturers used similar tool points, but this variety with the bullet crimp on the case body is consistent with Spencer ammunition manufactured by the U.S. Army's Frankford Arsenal.[10]

On the basis of microscopic individual characteristics, the examined Spencer cases from the site represent eight different Spencer firearms—three in 56/50-caliber and five in 56/56-caliber (table H.2). Two unfired Spencer cartridges were also recovered.

Bullets

There are twenty-seven battle-related lead bullets (fig. H.7) representing eight different gun types in the collection (table H.3). Seven bullets (specimens 19, 53, 75, 301, 302, 368, 369) are .50-caliber and range in weight from 327.2 to 351.1 grains. The bullets were all fired and have either a 6-right or 3-right land-and-groove rifling impressions. The

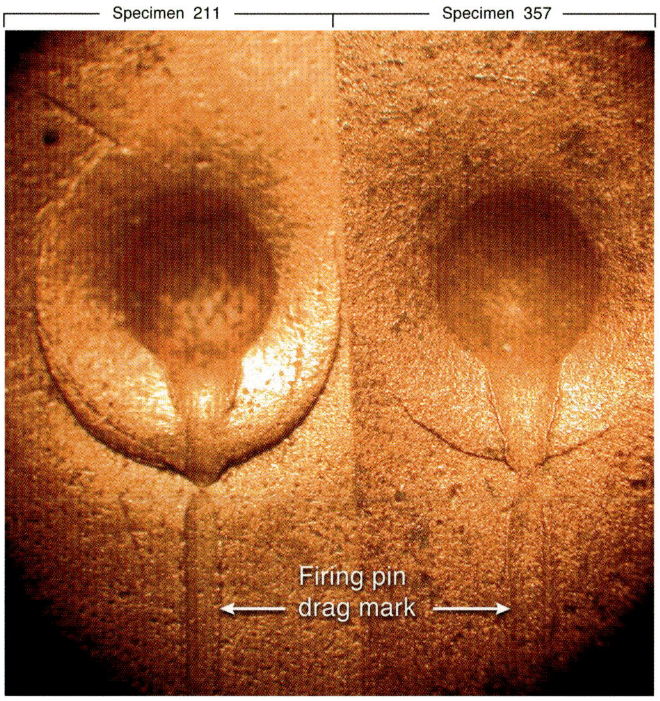

Fig. H.4. Microscopic view of two .50/70-caliber cartridge cases fired in a Sharps. Note the firing pin drag mark that is common to cartridges fired from a Sharps carbine.

shape of the bullets, their weight range, and rifling impressions are consistent with being fired in Spencer carbines or rifles. Ten other .50-caliber bullets (specimens 32, 33, 37, 102, 103, 105, 148, 248, 305, 376) all have 3-right land-and-groove rifling impressions and weigh between 425.4 and 452.4 grains. The weight, caliber, and rifling impressions are consistent with these rounds being fired from .50-caliber Springfield or other weapons rifled to government rifling specifications, such as the Sharps, Remington, and Ward-Burton carbines.

Four bullets are .44-caliber weighing between 195.4 and 244.1 grains (specimens 29, 107, 337, 383), and each has 6-right land-and-groove rifling impressions. This is consistent with being fired in a Henry Model 1866 or Model 1873 Winchester rifle.

Specimen 25 is a .45-caliber bullet that weighs 400 grains and has 3-right land-and-groove rifling, indicating firing in a Model 1873 Springfield rifle or carbine.

Four spherical lead balls are nominally .50-caliber, though each is slightly undersized: specimen 109 has a diameter of 0.46 inch and weighs 143 grains; specimen 277, 0.464 inch diameter, 151.3 grains; specimen 377, 0.48 inch diameter, 156.2 grains; and specimen 395, 0.48 inch diameter and 138.3 grains. Three of the balls were fired, have faint unidentified rifling impressions, and are impact damaged, with specimen 109 having sand and rock imbedded in its surface from impact. Specimen 277 was not fired, but it is an excellent example of a poorly cast bullet with voids on the surface resulting from hot lead being poured into an improperly heated or cold bullet mold. The casting sprue is still present. The bullet's overall poor casting and untrimmed sprue indicate that it was discarded as unusable. The other three bullets could have been fired in the same muzzle-loading .50-caliber gun. This large caliber was a very popular firearm type on the Plains prior to the introduction of self-contained cartridges in the mid-1860s. Specimen 377 has a ramrod impression on one side of the bullet that is consistent with a convex ramrod head, a common ramrod style on muzzle-loading guns of the nineteenth century. The rifling impressions are too light to identify class or individual characteristics to determine if one or more firearms are represented by these four bullets.

One bullet, specimen 34, is a .50-caliber hollow-base Minié ball. It has three rings or lubricating grooves around the base. It was fired from a gun with 8-right land-and-groove rifling. The bullet style is consistent in form with those used in the Civil War Gallager carbine, but the Gallager was not produced with 8-right rifling.[11] The only firearms known to have been manufactured with 8-right rifling are French and Swiss firearms. At present the source of the bullet remains unidentified, but it represents a single .50-caliber carbine or rifled musket.

Percussion Cap Tins

Two percussion cap tins (specimens 263 and 371) were recovered from Indian positions on the battle site. Both tins are round and have a diameter of approximately 4 cm. Specimen 263 is 1.45 cm tall; specimen 371 is 2 cm tall. Both were empty of percussion caps.

Table H.2. Spencer Cartridge Case Matches, Battle of Round Timber Creek

Firearm	*Specimen Matches*	*Comment*
56/50 Spencer		
1	1, 44	
2	306	F.V.V.&Co head stamp
3	307	
56/56 Spencer		
1	2, 63, 65, 389	Specimens 2 and 63 .50-caliber
2	52, 58, 60, 99, 139, 140, 141, 142, 143, 144, 145, 146, 147	Specimen 60 .50-caliber with S.A.W. head stamp
3	82	
4	93	H head stamp
5	274, 275, 313, 316, 319, 320, 339, 340, 342, 343, 375	Specimens 274–320 .50-caliber; Specimen 320 F.V.V.&Co head stamp

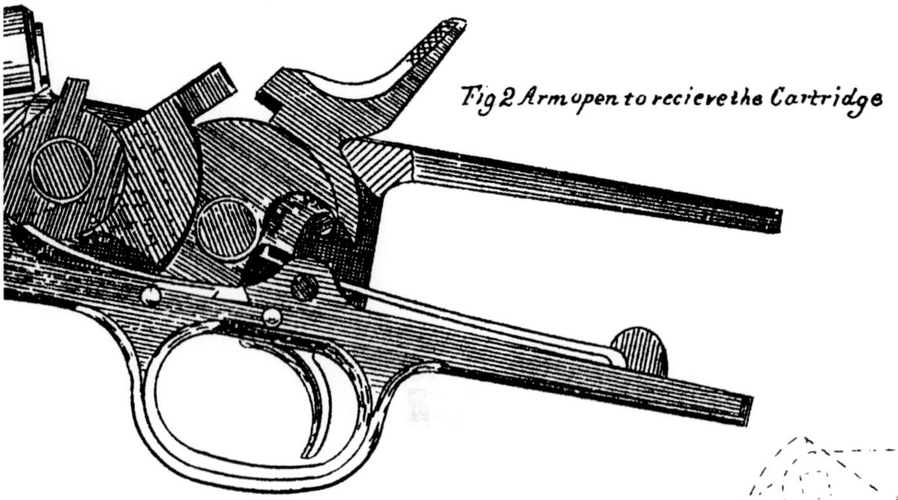

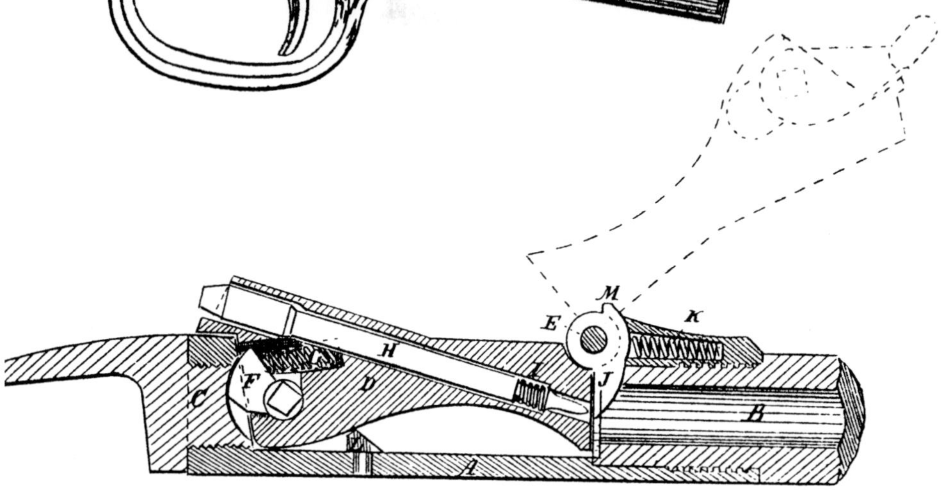

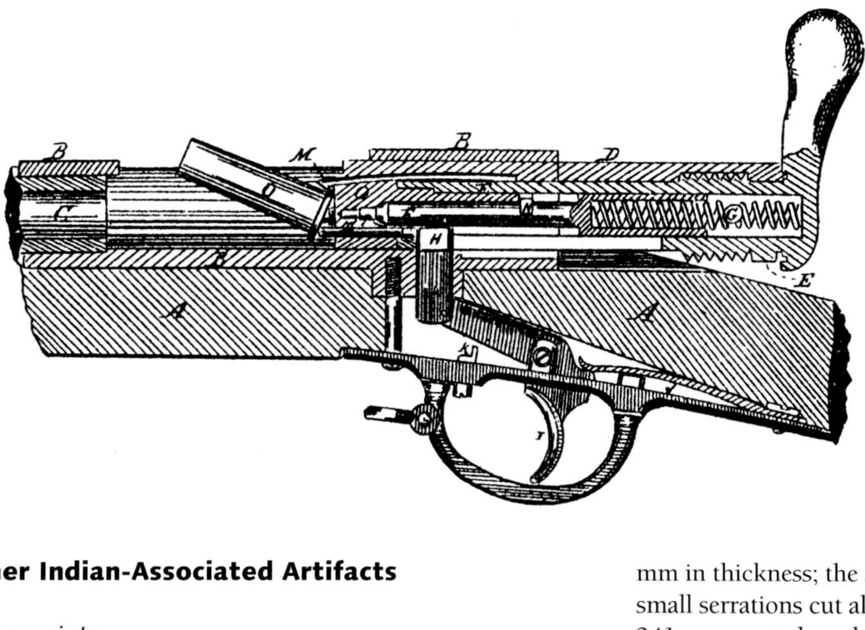

Fig. H.5. top, Remington carbine showing the breechblock and extractor arrangement; center, Model 1870 Springfield carbine showing breechblock (M), firing pin (H), and extractor (J) arrangement; bottom, Ward-Burton carbine showing the extraction process. From *Ordnance Memo 15*, 1874.

Other Indian-Associated Artifacts

Arrowpoints

Two iron arrowpoints were found at the Indian village site (fig. H.8). Both appear to have been Indian made, as indicated by chisel cut marks. Specimen 327 is 3.71 cm long, 1.60 cm wide, and 2.45 mm thick; the length of the stem on this specimen is 9.5 mm. Small serrations have been cut, probably with a file, along both edges of the stem. Specimen 341 measures 3.58 cm in length, 1.19 cm in width, and 1.92 mm in thickness; the stem length is 9.82 mm. It also has small serrations cut along both edges of the stem. Specimen 341 appears to have been fashioned from the tip of a small knife blade, since one of its edges is straight and the opposite edge is curved like that found near the tip of a knife.

Buckles

Six iron buckles were recovered from the Indian village site. Three are roller buckles (specimens 270, 326, 336), two are center-bar buckles (specimens 309 and 349), and

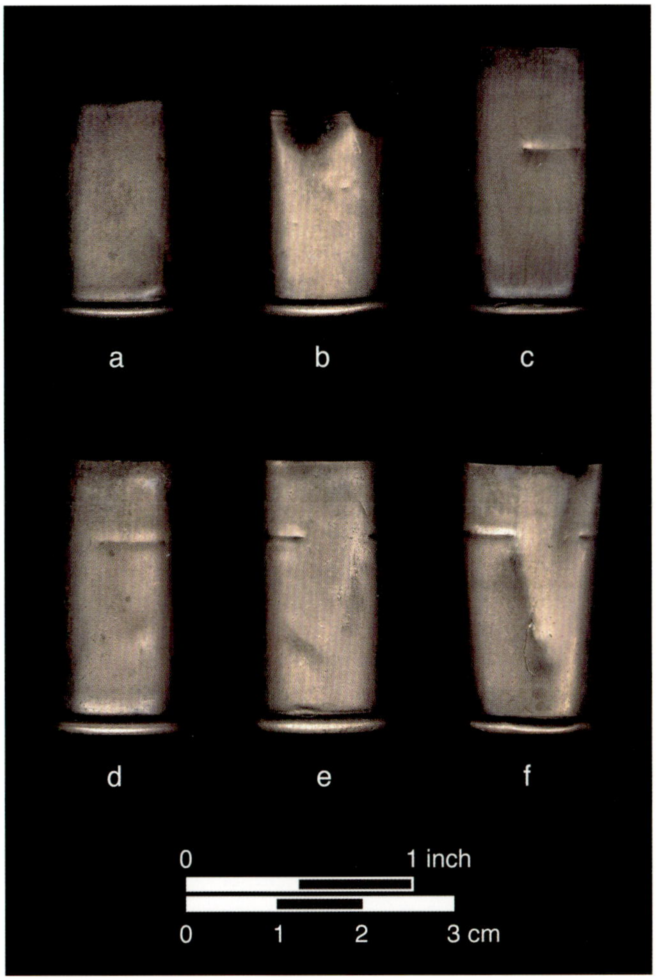

Fig. H.6. Spencer cartridge cases from the battle site: a-b, 56/56-caliber; c–d, 56/50-caliber; e, 56/50-caliber with rim crimp; f, 56/50-caliber without rim crimp.

Fig. H.7. Bullets from the battle site: a, .50-caliber Spencer-fired; b, .50-caliber with 3-right land-and-groove rifling; c, .44-caliber; d, .45-caliber Springfield; e, .50-caliber Minié ball; f, .50-caliber ball; g, unfired .50-caliber ball; h, .50-caliber ball with ramrod impression.

the other buckle is a D-shaped buckle (specimen 345). One of the roller buckles is large enough to accommodate a 2-inch-wide strap and was probably used on a packsaddle. The other roller buckles fastened straps of 0.75 and 1.25 inches and could have been used on a variety of leather straps on bridles or saddles. The two center-bar buckles fastened straps of 0.5 and 1 inch. Like the roller buckles, the center-bar buckles could have been used on a several bridle or saddle straps. The D-shaped buckle would have fastened a strap about an inch wide; it is probably from the throat latch on a bridle.

Buttons

Six military general service uniform coat buttons and one civilian style clothing button (fig. H.9) were recovered from the Indian village site. The six military buttons (specimens 278, 321, 322, 323, 324, 325) all measure approximately 19.4 mm in diameter. None of the military uniform buttons are backmarked. The six buttons were all recovered in close proximity on top of a sandy hill near the east side of the Indian village site. Most likely the buttons had been previously acquired by the Indian villagers rather than being from a garment lost by one of the soldiers during the battle, since no uniform cuff buttons were recovered.

The other button (specimen 290) is a 19 mm diameter flat brass button with a loop shank. This is a common clothing button of the early nineteenth century and was popular in the Indian trade for many years. This button had a manufacturing date ranging from 1800 to 1865.[12]

Cans

Two tin cans (specimens 279 and 300) were recovered at the Indian village site. They are hole-in-cap types with stamped ends and simple side-seam overlaps. The side seams were hand soldered. Specimen 279 is crushed and fragmentary but measures approximately 7.6 cm tall by 6.3 cm in diameter. Specimen 300 is 10.8 cm tall by 8.2 cm in diameter; the top of this can has been completely cut out.

Chisel

A cold chisel measuring 18.5 cm long and 3.6 cm wide was found at the Indian village site. The specimen (348) is

Table H.3. Bullets and Associated Firearm Type, Battle of Round Timber Creek

Specimen	*Caliber*	*Firearm Type*	*Comment*
19	.50	Spencer	
25	.45	Springfield M1873	
29	.44	Henry M1866 or Winchester M1873	
32	.50	Springfield, Sharps, Remington, or Ward-Burton	
33	.50	Springfield, Sharps, Remington, or Ward-Burton	
34	.50	Unidentified	Minié ball
37	.50	Springfield, Sharps, Remington, or Ward-Burton	
53	.50	Spencer	
75	.50	Spencer	
102	.50	Springfield, Sharps, Remington, or Ward-Burton	
103	.50	Springfield, Sharps, Remington, or Ward-Burton	
105	.50	Springfield, Sharps, Remington, or Ward-Burton	
107	.44	Henry M1866 or Winchester M1873	
109	.50	Muzzle loader	Ball
148	.50	Springfield, Sharps, Remington, or Ward-Burton	
248	.50	Springfield, Sharps, Remington, or Ward-Burton	
277	.50	Unfired	Ball with casting sprue
301	.50	Spencer	
302	.50	Spencer	
305	.50	Springfield, Sharps, Remington, or Ward-Burton	
337	.44	Henry M1866 or Winchester M1873	
368	.50	Spencer	
369	.50	Spencer	
376	.50	Springfield, Sharps, Remington, or Ward-Burton	
377	.50	Muzzle loader	Ball, ramrod impression
383	.44	Henry M1866 or Winchester M1873	
395	.50	Muzzle loader	

Fig. H.8. Iron arrowpoints from Grey Beard's village site.

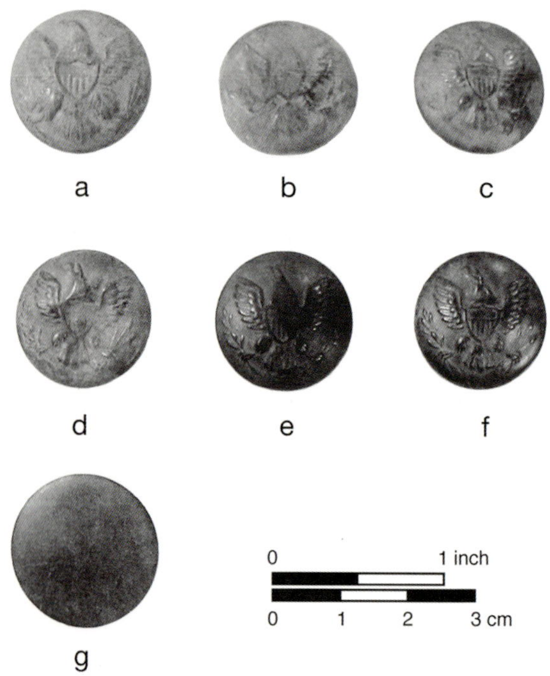

Fig. H.9. Buttons recovered from Grey Beard's village site: a–f, army uniform buttons; g, flat clothing button.

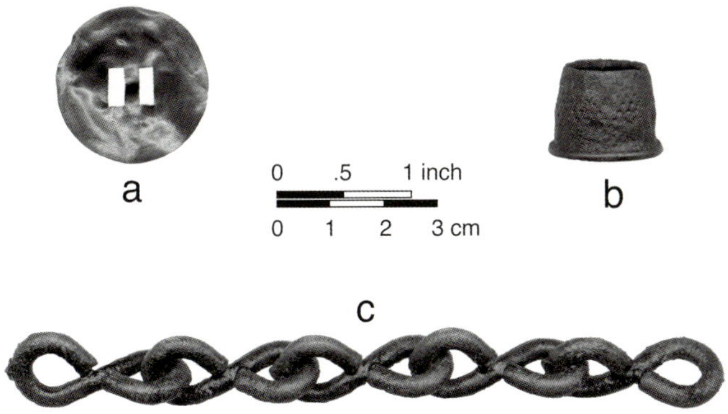

Fig. H.10. Indian-associated items from Grey Beard's village site: a, concha; b, thimble; c, curb chain.

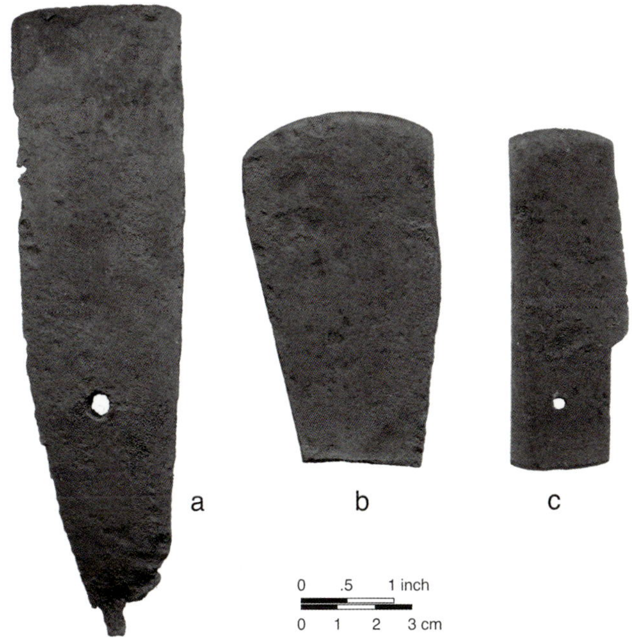

Fig. H.11. Indian-associated edged tools from Grey Beard's village site.

flat on each side and has twenty-two "notches" along both upper edges. The chisel head has been extensively hammered and flattened.

Concha

A concha (specimen 330) made of pressed tin was found at the village site. The undecorated circular concha (fig. H.10a) measures 29 mm in diameter. It has two rectangular slits cut near its center, which allowed it to be attached to a leather thong or strap. The concha was most likely used as a decorative element on a saddle.

Curb Chain

One bridle curb chain (specimen 298) was recovered. The chain (fig. H.10c) is composed of five links and has an overall length of 13.5 cm. This bridle curb chain is similar to Civil War–era styles.

Cut Iron and Brass

Four pieces of cut iron and one piece of cut brass were recovered from the Indian village site. Three of the iron pieces (specimens 283, 284, 288) are 1.9 cm wide straps of various lengths that have been cold-cut with a chisel. The straps may be barrel hoops for small kegs or casks. The other cut iron item (specimen 310) is a fragment of a flat metal piece that has been cut from a larger piece. It exhibits chisel cut marks around its entire edge. This piece may be from the bottom of a large frying pan or similar cast iron pot or pan.

Specimen 352 is a flat brass bar 7 cm long, 1.1 cm wide, and 3.5 mm thick. One end of the piece is broken and the other end is slightly rounded and beveled. What the brass piece is from has not been determined.

Edged Tools and Knives

Seven edged tools and three knives or knife blade fragments were found at the Indian village site. Six of the edged tools can be categorized as scraping tools. One of these, specimen 289 (fig. H.11a), is a fleshing iron. This is a curved iron bit that was meant to be mounted in a wood or bone handle and used to remove the flesh from animal hides. This artifact was cut from a piece of strap iron, and small serrations have been filed into the bit end.

Specimen 280 is a piece of strap iron that was altered by filing a series of small notches, creating a serrated edge. This piece could have been used for cutting or scraping. Specimen 344 (fig. H.11b) is a piece of flat iron, one edge of which has been filed to a bevel. Another edge on this artifact has been used as a hammer. Specimen 317 is a chisel-cut piece from the bottom of a frying pan or similar object, and one edge has been beveled by filing to create a scraping edge. Specimen 346 (fig. H.11c) is a fragment of a large knife blade of which both ends have been beveled for use as a scraping tool.

Specimens 276 and 334 are pieces of brass kettles that have been modified by filing and notching their edges to create a scraping tool (fig. H.12). The two artifacts are similar in size and shape, but they were made from two different kettles. Both specimens were cut from the upper portion of the kettle, but the container from which specimen 276 was cut was thicker and heavier than the kettle from which specimen 334 was made.

Two complete knives and a blade fragment of another knife were also recovered from the village site. One of the complete knives is a Sheffield Bowie knife with a bone handle and brass guard (specimen 271, fig. H.13). Overall

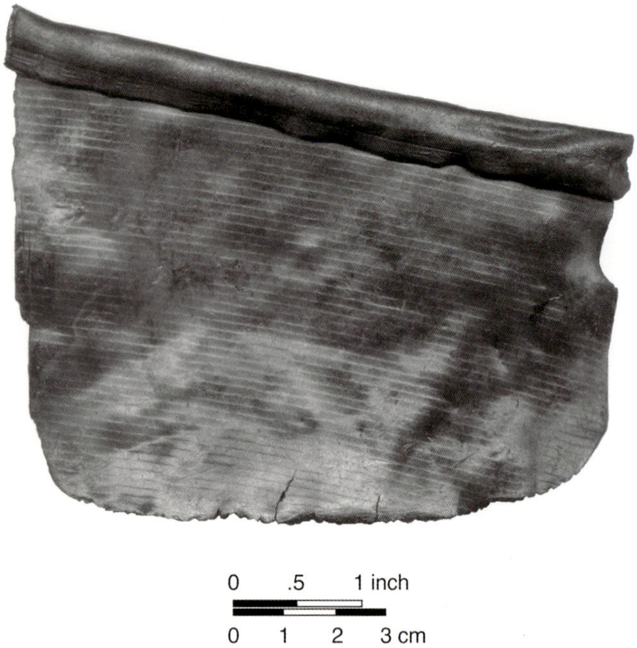

Fig. H.12. Piece of brass kettle utilized as a scraper. Note the filed serrations along the bottom edge of the piece.

length of this knife is 23.5 cm, and the blade length is 13.3 cm. This English-made knife was produced during the mid-1800s.[13] Specimen 374 is a complete butcher knife, though the wooden handle has deteriorated (fig. H.13). Three brass bolsters that held the wooden handle onto the knife are still in place. This knife also has a brass guard. Incised into both faces of the guard are diagonal and cross-hatched lines (fig. H.14). Apparently a sharp metal implement was used to incise the lines into the guard. The total length of the knife is 26.3 cm, and the blade length is 14.2 cm. Specimen 297 is a blade fragment from a large butcher knife. It measures 11.8 cm long by 3.1 cm wide.

File

Specimen 373 is a half-round bastard file (fig. H.15a) that measures 23.5 cm long and 1.75 cm wide. Files were a common and much sought-after trade item by the Indians. They were used in various metalworking tasks, from making projectile points to edging tools.

Food Graters

There are three pieces of sheet iron from the village site that may represent parts of food graters (specimens 281, 282, 329). These are container body pieces, each perforated with numerous small holes (fig. H.15b). The edges of the

▶ Fig. H.13. Sheffield Bowie knife (left, specimen 271) and butcher knife (right, specimen 374) from Grey Beard's village site.

Fig. H.14. Close-up view of the incised lines on the knife guard of specimen 374.

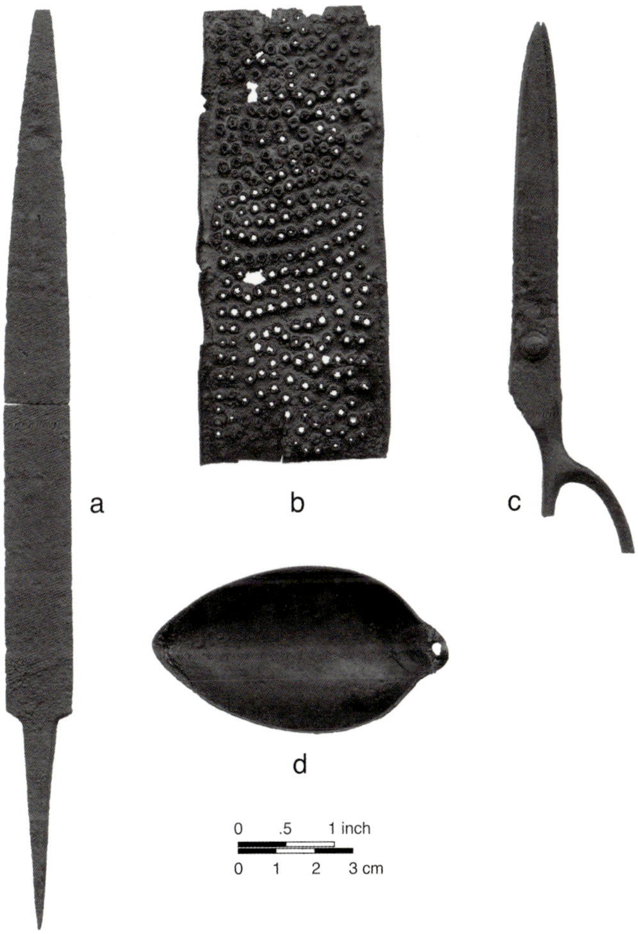

Fig. H.15. Metal tools from Grey Beard's village site: a, file; b, food grater; c, scissors; d, spoon bowl.

holes are raised to give a sharp edge. The fragments are probably parts of one or more "radish" graters that were common during the nineteenth century.

Horseshoe Nails

Seven unused horseshoe nails were recovered from an area of the Indian village site where several other village-related artifacts were found, suggesting that the nails are associated with the Indian villagers rather than with the army troopers. Though the nails are unused, the Indians often used nails as awls or other leatherworking tools.

Nails and Tacks

Five square nails and one square tack were recovered among the village-associated artifacts. The square nails are 4d in size and the tack is 2d. Like the horseshoe nails recovered from the site, none of the square nails or tack has been used or modified in any way. The nails and tack may have been stored in a bag or box and left when the villagers abandoned the site.

Saddle Ring

A single iron saddle ring (specimen 292) was recovered from the Indian village site. The ring is a skirt ring with an inside diameter of 4 cm.

Scissors

Specimen 350 is a fragment of a scissors (fig. H.15c). Both blades remain on the scissors, but the finger grips on the handles are broken. The lengths of the blades are approximately 8.5 cm, and the overall length of the scissors would have been about 15.25 cm.

Spoon

A single large spoon bowl (specimen 332) was collected at the village site. A perforation has been made at the juncture where the bowl would have connected to the spoon handle (fig. H.15d). The hole suggests that the spoon bowl was used as a decorative element suspended from a necklace.

Thimble

A thimble (specimen 235) was found at the village site. The thimble has an open top (fig. H.10b) and is a nineteenth-century tailor's sewing thimble.

Unidentified

Specimen 291 is a hand-forged, U-shaped link, possibly to a large chain or other type of fastener. The piece is not sufficiently complete for identification or determination of function.

Other Army-Associated Artifacts

Buckle

An iron roller buckle (specimen 104) was recovered from the battle site. The tongue of the buckle is broken off.

The buckle fastened a strap 2.5 cm wide and could have been used on various leather straps on a bridle or saddle.

Carbine Ring

A carbine ring (specimen 40) was recovered from the battle site. The ring (fig. H.16d) has a diameter of 1.9 cm. The ring would have attached to the stock of a carbine and allowed the carbine to attach to a carbine sling.

Carbine Sling Swivel and Snap Hook

Specimen 101 is a Civil War–era swivel-and-snap hook attachment (fig. H.16a) for a carbine sling. The carbine sling was made of black leather and was 56 inches long and 2.5 inches wide. The sling was attached to the swivel-and-snap hook, which clipped to a ring set into the stock of a cavalryman's carbine. The trooper wore the carbine sling over his shoulder so that if he had to move his position during a battle he could just drop the carbine and the gun would hang from his shoulder. The carbine sling was first introduced in this form in 1839 and remained in use relatively unchanged until a new model was introduced in 1885.[14]

Combination Screwdriver

A combination screwdriver for a Sharps conversion carbine (fig. H.16b) was recovered at the Indian village site and may have been lost there by one of the troopers. This screwdriver (specimen 308) was first used in 1868 when Sharps carbines began to be converted to fire .50-caliber metallic cartridges. The tool was made by modifying the Model 1863 combination tool. The modification consisted of removing the wrench from the Model 1863 tool and reshaping the blade so that it would fit into the head of the firing pin screw on the converted .50-caliber Sharps carbine. The modifications were done at Springfield Armory.[15] Specimen 308 has an overall length of 8 cm.

Dutch Oven

A cast iron dutch oven (specimen 95) was recovered from the battle site. The three-legged oven (fig. H.17) is 10 inches in diameter and has a capacity of one gallon. The steel bail handle is missing. Marked on the flanged lid of the oven is WESTERN FOUNDRY, N°. 2, LEAVENWORTH. KAS. The mark is for the Willson, Estes and Fairchild Western Foundry and Machine Shop, which was founded in 1858 in Leavenworth, Kansas. In 1869, the company changed its name to the Great Western Manufacturing Company.[16]

Frying Pan

Specimen 118 from the battle site is a 10-inch-diameter frying pan or skillet that is missing its handle. Three holes on the edge of the pan are where the handle would have been riveted onto the pan. The frying pan was recovered near the dutch oven.

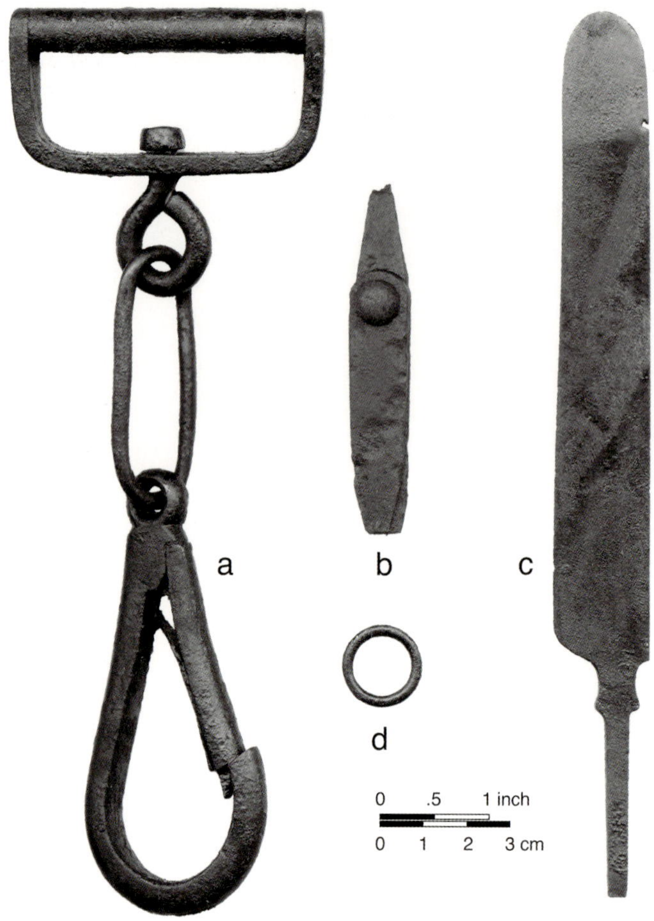

Fig. H.16. Army-associated artifacts from the battle site: a, carbine sling swivel and snap hook; b, combination screwdriver; c, mess knife; d, carbine ring

Horseshoes and Mule Shoes

There were nine complete horseshoes, one half of a horseshoe, and two complete mule shoes recovered at the battle site. All of the horseshoes are of the Burden pattern, which was developed prior to the Civil War and used extensively through the remainder of the nineteenth century. What is particularly interesting about this collection of shoes is that seven of the ten horseshoes still retain their complete set of eight nails. One other shoe retains seven nails, one has three nails, and the horseshoe half has one nail. The two mule shoes each retain six nails.

Because so many of the shoes retain most, if not all, of their nails, it appears that they were not thrown during the battle. Rather, it appears that the animals were killed during the battle, and the recovered shoes mark where they died. In fact, four of the horseshoes (specimens 70, 72, 73, 74) were recovered adjacent to one another near the south end of the high ridge, four other horseshoes (specimens 111, 112, 113, 114) were found clustered near the north end of

Fig. H.17. Dutch oven and lid recovered from the battle site. The oven was probably lost when the 8th Cavalry mules were killed during the battle.

the high ridge, and the two mule shoes (specimens 106 and 108) were next to each other in the central portion of the high ridge not far from where the dutch oven and frying pan were found. These locations undoubtedly mark where two of the cavalry horses and one pack mule were killed during the battle.

Knife

One Civil War–era "butter" knife blade (specimen 89) was recovered from the battle site. The knife (fig. H.16c) is typical of those included in army mess kits. The knife blade measures 14.7 cm, and it would have been set into a wooden handle.

Nails

Two nails are in the battle site collection. One (specimen 249) is a 4d square nail, and the other (specimen 85) is a small, round-headed tack 17.6 mm long. These items may be from one or more of the army supply or ration boxes.

Notes

Abbreviations

AGO	Adjutant General's Office
LC	Library of Congress
NA	National Archives
RG	Record Group

Chapter 1. Introduction

1. Scott et al., *Archaeological Perspectives;* Scott and Fox, *Archaeological Insights.*

2. See, e.g., *New York Tribune,* Oct. 7, 1874.

3. The Battle of Red River, fought on Aug. 30, 1874, in the lower reaches of Palo Duro Canyon, is often referred to as the First Battle of Palo Duro Canyon. Col. Ranald S. Mackenzie's battle of September 28, 1874, farther upstream in the canyon proper is often referred to as the Second Battle of Palo Duro Canyon.

4. In May 2005, TPWD acquired the portion of the Battle of Palo Duro Canyon site that was previously in private ownership.

Chapter 2. Historical Overview

1. Portions of this chapter were previously published as J. Brett Cruse, "Archeological Investigations at the Battle of Red River Site: New Perspectives on the 1874 Indian Campaign in the Texas Panhandle," *Southwestern Historical Quarterly* 106 (October 2002): 169–92.

2. Mayhall, *Kiowas,*15.

3. Ibid., 93. Comancheros were New Mexicans who traveled to the plains to trade with the Comanche. The term *Comanchero* first appeared in print in Josiah Gregg's *Commerce of the Prairies* in 1843, and it is likely that Gregg coined the term.

4. Secoy, *Changing Military Patterns,* 20–24.

5. The Plains Indians came to rely on the horse so heavily that it would prove to be to their own detriment. In *Man's Rise to Civilization,* Peter Farb presents a perceptive exposition of how the Plains Indians became trapped by this reliance and lost their ability to adapt.

6. Hoig, *Tribal Wars,* 214–15.

7. Fehrenbach, *Comanches,* 477.

8. Kappler, *Indian Laws and Treaties;* U. S. Bureau of Indian Affairs, "Medicine Lodge Peace Treaty 1869."

9. Fehrenbach, *Comanches,* 481.

10. Rogers, "Flint and Steel," 53–75.

11. Richard Irving Dodge, *The Plains of the Great West and Their Inhabitants,* quoted in Miles, *Personal Recollections,* 159.

12. Haley, *Buffalo War,* 24.

13. Sheridan to Adjutant General, October 13, 1881 (Sheridan Papers, Box 29, NA); John R. Cook, himself a buffalo hunter in the 1870s, left an account of an 1875 message from Sheridan to the Texas state legislature that expressed the military's attitude toward the destruction of the great buffalo herds. The legislature was considering a bill to protect the buffalo, which Sheridan protested. "Instead of outlawing the slaughter," declared Sheridan, "the legislature should strike a medal, with a dead buffalo pictured on one side and a discouraged Indian on the other, and bestow it upon the hunters." Cook, *Border and the Buffalo,* 163–64.

14. Rathjen, *Texas Panhandle Frontier,* 157; Baker and Harrison, *Adobe Walls,* 16–22.

15. Dixon, *Life of "Billy" Dixon,* 189–91.

16. Richardson, *Comanche Barrier;* Haley, *Buffalo War,* 56.

17. The estimates of the number of Indians who attacked the buffalo hunters at Adobe Walls vary widely, but according to original sources published shortly after the fight the figure was about two hundred Indians. Four days after the fight, for example, Fred Leonard wrote to his partner, A. C. Meyers, reporting that the post had been attacked by two hundred warriors (*Atchison Daily Champion,* July 10, 1874, 2). Lieutenant Baldwin repeated this figure in his contemporary diary (Diary Transcript for Aug. 19–20, 1874, in "Adobe Walls" vertical file, Boot Hill Museum, Dodge City, Kansas), and it was repeated by General Miles in his memoirs (Miles, *Personal Recollections,* 160) and by S. S. Van Sickel, who came into the trading post just after the fight (Van Sickel, *Story of Real Life,* 15). As the years passed and the stories were told and retold, the number of warriors increased in the memories of the participants, both white and Indian, but the contemporary evidence shows overwhelming that only about two hundred Indians were involved in the Adobe Walls battle.

18. The exact number of Indians killed during the battle is not known, but most estimates range from twelve to thirty. Nye, *Carbine and Lance,* 191; Miles, *Personal Recollections,* 160; West, "Battle of Adobe Walls," 36. Several days after the battle, some hide hunters who came in to Adobe Walls severed the heads from twelve of the dead Indians that were lying scattered around the compound and stuck them on the gate of the corral. Baker and Harrison, *Adobe Walls,* 97–98; Miles, *Personal Recollection,* 163.

19. Quoted in Carter, *On the Border with Mackenzie,* 525.

20. *Army and Navy Journal* 12 (July 25, 1874): 790; Leckie, *Military Conquest,* 198–99; *New York Herald,* July 22, 1874.

21. The brevet (Bvt.) rank was an honorary rank conferred on an officer by the U.S. Senate for "gallant and meritorious services," but this rank gave no additional right of command or extra pay. Officers were usually referred to by their brevet rank in military circles, in official correspondence, and by the press. Wilhelm, *Military Dictionary and Gazetteer.*

22. Sheridan to Sherman, September 5, 1874, in Taylor, *Indian Campaign,* 17–18.

23. Wallace and Hoebel imply in *Comanches,* 327, that Quanah was the leader of the Kwahada band, whereas Sturm states that Isatai was the leader in "Notes of Travel in Search of the Quah-di-ru Band of Comanches" (RG 98, Military Department of the Missouri, Letters Received, 1875-S248/2, NA).

24. John Davidson to J. M. Haworth, Jan. 9, 1875, cited in Kavanagh, *Comanches,* 449; Haley, *Buffalo War,* 212–13.

25. Richard H. Pratt to Spencer F. Baird, Feb. 9, 1878, List of Indians: Notes on the Preceding List, in Baird, "Catalogue of Casts," 201–13.

26. R. H. Pratt, May, 1875, Report of Indian Prisoners Confined in Ft. Marion, San Augustine, Florida, during the month of May, 1875 (Central Superintendency, Letters Received by the Office of Indian Affairs, Microcopy No. 234, Roll 66, Frames 831–32, Oklahoma Historical Society).

27. Pratt to Adjutant General, July 24, 1875, in Taylor, *Indian Campaign,* 304.

28. Robinson, *Satanta,* 194.

Chapter 3. Field and Laboratory Methods

1. See Scott et al., *Archaeological Perspectives.*

2. Gunther and Gunther, *Identification of Firearms;* Harris, "Sherlock Holmes Would Be Impressed," 36–39, 82; Hatcher, *Textbook of Firearms Investigation;* Hatcher et al., *Firearms Investigation, Identification, and Evidence.*

Chapter 4. Historiography and Archival Research

1. George W. Baird, "Papers: Excerpts from the Diary of Lieut. Frank D. Baldwin" (Kansas State Historical Society, Topeka); W. C. Brown, "Baldwin Indian Territory Expedition, From His Own Diaries" (W. C. Brown Papers, Western Historical Collection, University of Colorado, Boulder; cited hereafter as Baldwin I. T. Expedition); Col. Charles A. P. Hatfield, "The Comanche, Kiowa and Cheyenne Campaign in Northwest Texas and Mackenzie's Fight in the Palo Duro Canon, September 26 [*sic*], 1874" (Panhandle-Plains Historical Museum, Canyon, Texas); General Ranald S. Mackenzie, "Letterbook" (Thomas Gilcrease Institute of American History and Art, Tulsa, Oklahoma); McFadden, "Thompson McFadden's Diary," 198–232.

2. Miles, *Personal Recollections,* 167–70, 172–74.

3. Baldwin, *Memoirs;* Dixon, *Life and Adventures of Billy Dixon.*

4. Carter, *Old Sergeant's Story;* Carter, *On the Border;* Marshall, *Miles Expedition.*

5. Richardson, *Comanche Barrier;* Richardson, *Frontier of Northwest Texas;* Haley, *Fort Concho;* Nye, *Carbine and Lance;* Rister, *Fort Griffin.*

6. Taylor, *Indian Campaign,* 2–3.

7. Nye, *Plains Indian Raiders,* 180.

8. Leckie, *Military Conquest,* 169–71. Leckie and other historians placed the battle on McClellan Creek. Mackenzie's own report, however, placed it on the North Fork of the Red River. Wallace, *Ranald S. Mackenzie's Official Correspondence,* 142.

9. Leckie, *Military Conquest,* 226–27.

10. Utley, *Frontier Regulars,* 219–20, 225, 231. Utley seems to contradict himself on the issue of oversight, characterizing the effort as a decentralized one at the beginning of the chapter (219) and then pointing to Sheridan's close involvement in October 1874 and Pope's "closer supervision [of] his subordinates" during the campaign (231).

11. Hutton, *Phil Sheridan,* 416–19; Wooster, *Nelson A. Miles,* 68, 292–97.

12. Haley, *Buffalo War,* 261–62.

13. Augur to Mackenzie, Aug. 28, 1874 (M-1495, Roll 8, frames 414–20, NA).

14. Miles to the Assistant Adjutant General, Department of the Missouri, Dec. 24, 1874 (RG 393, Part I, E-2927, p. 272, NA).

15. Court-martial of William R. Price (RG 393, PP-4678, Exhibit R, NA; cited hereafter as Price Court-martial).

16. Ruffner to the Assistant Adjutant General, Department of the Missouri, June 15, 1875 (RG 77, Entry 52, Box 18, NA).

17. Price Court-martial, 559–60. The court-martial file does not include those records or any indication that the judge advocate returned them to the office of the chief engineer of the Department of the Missouri at the close of Price's trial.

18. Ibid., 84–85, 99, 139, 248–49, 457, 527–28.

19. "Papers in the case of Major W. R. Price, 8th Cavalry" (RG 393, Part I, E-2601, Box No. 40, NA).

20. Price to Williams, October 19, 1874, and Farnsworth to Price, Nov. 6, 1874 (RG 393, Part I, E-2601, Box No. 40, NA). Baldwin to Baird, Nov. 9, 1874 (RG 393, Part I, E-2601, Box No. 41, NA).

21. Baird, map of area between the Canadian and Washita rivers (RG 393, Part I, E-2601, Box No. 41, NA).

22. Taylor, *Indian Campaign,* 21–24; Miles to Assistant Adjutant General, Department of the Missouri, Sept. 1, 1874 (M-1495, Roll 8, frames 509–515); Miles to "Dear General," Sept. 2, 1874 (RG393, Part I, E-2601, NA).

23. Haley, *Buffalo War,* 190–91; Leckie, *Military Conquest,* 224; Buell to Generals Sheridan or Augur, Oct. 12, 1874 (M-1495, Roll 8, frames 920–22, NA); Buell to Assistant Adjutant General, Department of Texas, Feb. 24, 1875 (M-1495, Roll 9, frames 168–217, NA).

24. White Horse, Oct. 21, 1874 (M-1495, Roll 8, frames 594–98, NA); Neill to the Assistant Adjutant General, Headquarters Military Division of the Missouri, Oct. 22, 1874 (M-1495, Roll 8, frames 935–36, NA); Augur to "Dear General Sheridan," Dec. 3, 1874 (M-1495, Roll 8, frames 1248–51); Covington to Maxon, Fort Sill, Jan. 19, 1875 (M-1495, Roll 9, frames 63–64, NA); Drum to General Augur, San Antonio, Nov. 10, 1874 (RG393, Part I, E-4875, NA); Neill to the Assistant Adjutant General, Headquarters Department of the Missouri, Nov. 14, 1874 (M-1495, Roll 8, frames 1079–81, NA); Augur to Drum, Nov. 16, 1874 (M-1495, Roll 8, frames 987–89, NA); Baird to Hartwell, Nov. 28, 1874 (RG393, Part I, E-2927, 225–26, NA); Augur to "Dear General Sheridan," Dec. 3, 1874 (M-1495, Roll 8, frames 1248–51, NA); Pratt to General [Davidson], Jan. 11, 1875 (RG393, Part I, E-4875, NA); Davidson, January 12, 1875 (RG393, Part I, E-4875, NA).

25. Haley, *Buffalo War,* 181–3; Mackenzie to Taylor, Sept. 19, 1874 (RG393, Part I, E-4875, NA); Baird to Compton, Camp on Canadian near Oasis Creek, Sept. 21, 1874 (RG393, Part I, E-2927, NA); [Miles] to Davidson, McLellan [*sic*] Creek, Sept. 21, 1874 (RG393, Part I, E-2927, 90–91, NA); Mackenzie to Assistant Adjutant General, Department of Texas, Oct. 1, 1874 (RG393, Part I, E-4875, NA); Miles, Special Orders No. 40, Oct. 9, 1874 (RG393, Part I, E-2929, NA); Pope to Sheridan, Chicago, Illinois, 1874 (M-1495, Roll 8, frames 969–72, NA); [Miles] to Lewis, Camp Supply, I.T., Nov. 23, 1874 (RG393, Part I, E-2927, p. 218, NA); [Miles] to Assistant Adjutant General, Department of the Missouri, Nov. 27, 1874 (RG393, Part I, E-2927, 223–24, NA); [Miles] to Compton, Jan. 11, 1875 (RG393, Part I, E-2927, 289–90, NA). The cited documents represent only a fraction of the hundreds of missives Miles, in particular, directed to Davidson, Price, Bristol, Compton, Farnsworth, Heutig, Biddle, Abbott, Baldwin, Pratt, Mackenzie, and others as he directed and coordinated their actions.

26. Price to Williams, Department of the Missouri, Nov. 11, 1874 (RG393, Part I, E-2601, NA).

27. Miles to Assistant Adjutant General, Department of the Missouri, Sept. 17, 1874 (RG393, Part I, E-2601, NA).

28. Ibid.

29. Baird to Commanding Officer, Nov. 26, 1874 (RG 393,

Part I, E-2927, 220, NA); Miles to the Assistant Adjutant General, Dec. 24, 1874 (RG 393, Part I, E-2927, 272, NA); Price Court-martial, Exhibit R.

Chapter 5. Army and Indian Strategies, Tactics, and Weapons

1. Chun, *US Army,* 5; Utley, *Frontier Regulars,* 15.
2. Quoted in Urwin, *United States Cavalry,* 144.
3. For detailed discussions of U.S. Army Indian policies and military tactics employed after the Civil War, see Wooster, *Military and United States Indian Policy;* Utley, *Frontier Regulars;* Jamieson, *Crossing the Deadly Ground;* and McChristian, *U.S. Army in the West.*
4. Sherman to Grant, Dec. 28, 1866, Senate Executive Document, No. 15, 39th Congress, 2d session, II, 1867, serial 1277, 4.
5. Hutton, *Phil Sheridan,* 53; Wooster, *Military and United States Indian Policy,* 28.
6. Chun, *US Army,* 18; Hoig, *Tribal Wars,* 256–58.
7. Utley, "Chained Dog," 22.
8. Miles to the Assistant Adjutant General, Nov. 12, 1874 (RG 393, Part I, E-2927, 199–200, NA).
9. Davidson to the Assistant Adjutant General, Nov. 28, 1874 (RG 393, M-1495, Roll 8, Frames 1158–69, NA).
10. Diary of Lieutenant Frank Baldwin, Microfilm Roll #DIAZO, Henry E. Huntington Library, San Marino, California (hereafter cited as Baldwin Diary).
11. Upton, *Cavalry Tactics.*
12. Hoig, *Tribal Wars;* Newcomb, "Re-examination of the Causes."
13. Berthrong, *Southern Cheyennes,* 42–43.
14. Wooster, *Military and United States Indian Policy,* 37–38.
15. Mishkin, *Rank and Warfare,* 61–63; Carter, *On the Border,* 58.
16. Rodenbough, *Sabre and Bayonet,* 291–92.
17. Humfreville, *Twenty Years,* 53.
18. Carter, *On the Border,* 289–90.
19. War Department, "Comparison of 'Lined' with 'Wad' Carbine Cartridges," Ordnance Notes 43 (1875).
20. Garavaglia and Worman, *Firearms of the American West,* 32–34.
21. Ibid., 83.
22. Gluckman, *United States Martial Pistols,* 213–17, 233–36; Hutchins, "Boots and Saddles."
23. See Colonel Merritt, *Army and Navy Journal* 14 (Aug. 26, 1878): 48.
24. Hazlett et al., *Field Artillery Weapons;* Coggins, *Arms and Equipment.*
25. Melton and Pawl, *Guide to Civil War Artillery Projectiles.*
26. Hazlett et al., *Field Artillery Weapons;* Coggins, *Arms and Equipment.*
27. Melton and Pawl, *Guide To Civil War Artillery Projectiles.*
28. Berk, *Gatling Gun;* Wahl and Toppel, *Gatling Gun;* Jacobsen, *1886 Machine Gun Manual.*
29. Miles, *Personal Recollections,* 272–73.
30. Haley, *Buffalo War,* 217; Leckie, "Red River War," 98–99; Chalfant, *Cheyennes at Dark Water Creek.*
31. Miles to Sherman, July 8, 1876 (Sherman Papers, Vol. 44, LC).
32. Rickey, *Forty Miles a Day,* 219; Whitman, *Troopers,* 185–86.
33. Kenner, *Comanchero Frontier,* 85.
34. Bates et al., *Cheyenne/Arapaho Ledger Book,* 85.
35. Ibid.; Report of the Secretary of the Navy, 1864, House Executive Document 1, 38th Congress, 2nd Session, Series No. 1221.
36. Barnes, *Cartridges of the World,* 6th ed., 281; Gluckman, *Identifying Old U.S. Muskets,* 388.
37. Coates and Thomas, *Introduction to Civil War Small Arms* 48.
38. Garavaglia and Worman, *Firearms of the American West,* 125–26.
39. Hook and Pegler, *To Live and Die,* 86.
40. Humfreville, *Twenty Years,* 52; Hook and Pegler, *To Live and Die,* 86–87.

Chapter 6. The War Begins

1. Several previous researchers have indicated that Miles took a mountain howitzer with him on his campaign, but this is incorrect. Miles tested the howitzer at Fort Dodge but found its range to be inadequate, stating, "I judge after careful trial that the mountain howitzers would be of little use, as they have too short a range, the extreme range being not above 1100 or 1200 yards, and at that range their fire is very inaccurate, so that they could be easily silenced by rifles of the present improved pattern." Miles goes on to state, "I took from Fort Dodge, at which place the howitzers were left, a three-inch Parrott gun with ammunition." Miles to the Assistant Adjutant General, Aug. 19, 1874 (RG 393, M-1495, Roll 8, 338–39, NA); Miles to the Assistant Adjutant General, Sept. 1, 1874 (RG 94, AGO, Military Correspondence, File 2815–1874, NA); *Army and Navy Journal* 12 (Aug. 8, 1874): 820; Marshall, *Miles Expedition,* 11.
2. Miles to Pope, Aug. 3, 1874 (RG 393, Part I, Entry 2927, NA); Special Order No. 6, Aug. 5, 1874, and Special Order No. 7, Aug. 6, 1874 (RG 393, Part I, Entry 2929, NA).
3. Baldwin I. T. Expedition.
4. Miles to the Assistant Adjutant General, Aug. 25, 1874 (RG 94, AGO, Military Correspondence, File 2815–1874, NA).
5. Marshall, *Miles Expedition,* 3; report by Lieutenant R. H. Pratt titled "Information," Sept. 21, 1874 (RG 393, Part I, Entry 4875, Box 2, NA); *New York Herald,* Sept. 26, 1874.
6. Miles to Pope, March 4, 1875 (2750 AGO 1875, filed with RG 94, AGO, Military Correspondence, 2815–1874, NA). This Palo Duro Creek is a tributary of the Beaver River and should not be confused with Palo Duro Canyon of the Red River.
7. Steinbach, *Long March,* 69; *Army and Navy Journal* 12 (Sept. 5, 1874): 52.
8. Miles to Pope, March 4, 1875 (see note 6); Miles, *Personal Recollections,* 166–67; *Army and Navy Journal* 12 (Aug. 22, 1874): 21.
9. Miles to Pope, Sept. 1, 1874 (3852 AGO, Military Correspondence, filed with RG 94, AGO, Military Correspondence, 2815 1874, NA).
10. Baldwin I. T. Expedition.
11. McFadden, "Thomas McFadden's Diary," 203; Rogers, "To the Canyon of the Tule," 282–83.
12. Miles to Pope, Sept. 1, 1874 (see note 9). This report places the August 29 camp on the Salt Fork of the Red River, but collation of reported distances from recognizable points shows it to have been on Mulberry Creek. The error is understandable, since Mulberry Creek is considerably larger than the upper portion of the Salt Fork.
13. According to Baldwin there were seventy-five to one

hundred Indians, but Miles states that two hundred Indians attacked Baldwin and the scouts. Baldwin I. T. Expedition; Miles to the Assistant Adjutant General, Sept. 1, 1874 (RG 393, M-1495, Roll 8, 509–515, NA).

14. Miles to the Assistant Adjutant General, Sept. 1, 1874 (see note 13); Miles, *Personal Recollections,*168.

15. Miles to the Assistant Adjutant General, Sept. 1, 1874 (see note 13); Miles to Pope, Sept. 1, 1874 (see note 9); *New York Herald,* Sept. 26, 1874; *Army and Navy Journal* 12 (Sept. 17, 1874): 70.

16. Miles initially reported three Indians killed during the battle but later revised that figure, stating, "I find that my report of the number of dead upon the field was much too small: there have been reported to me Seventeen dead bodies on the battle field, or hid in cañons on this side of the river. . . . from all the reports and information received, I am now satisfied that the loss was not less than twenty-five killed and a much larger number wounded." Miles to Pope, September 5, 1874, in Taylor, *Indian Campaign,* 26–28.

17. McFadden, "Thomas McFadden's Diary," 205; Baldwin Diary.

18. Miles, *Personal Recollections,* 170; Lieutenant G. M. Baird to Captain W. Lyman, Sept. 1, 1874 (RG 393, Part I, Entry 2927, 47–48, NA); Baldwin I. T. Expedition.

19. Record of Colonel J. W. Pope, A. Q. M. General, United States Army, (RG 94, Appointments, Commission, and Promotion Papers 5401–1871, NA), 6: "(1) In the engagement of August 3 [*sic*], 1874, the Gatling guns under Colonel Pope were used for the first time on record on the firing line and said guns charged the hostile Indians with the Squadron of Major James Biddle." Wahl and Toppel, *Gatling Gun.*

20. Miles states that the battle "extended over at least twelve miles from their [the Indian's] first attack to their last position." Scout Thomas McFadden writes in his diary that the running battle "brought us to the banks of Red River about ten miles from where the first attack was made." Miles to the Assistant Adjutant General, Sept. 1, 1874 (see note 13); McFadden, "Thomas McFadden's Diary," 205.

21. On the basis of artifact distribution, the site encompasses approximately 22,238 acres, or about 34.75 square miles.

22. Miles, *Personal Recollections,* 168.

23. These sources include Haley, *Buffalo War;* Rathjen, *Texas Panhandle Frontier;* and Rogers, "To the Canyon."

24. T. C. Fowler of Silverton, Texas, showed us two Gatling gun cartridges he had found on the Griffin Hills. Also, Henry W. Taylor states that, when he observed the rifle pits on the Griffin Hills in 1882, "there were as many as a half bushel of rifle shells in each of these pits." Burton, *History of the J A Ranch,* 12.

25. Frasca and Hill, *.45–70 Springfield.*

26. Baldwin I. T. Expedition; McFadden, "Thomas McFadden's Diary," 204.

27. Miles to the Assistant Adjutant General, Sept. 1, 1874 (see note 13); Baldwin Diary.

28. Miles to the Assistant Adjutant General, Sept. 1, 1874 (see note 13).

29. Baldwin Diary.

30. J. W. McKinley, "J. W. McKinley's Narrative." n.d. 10 lvs. (J. W. McKinley Papers, Panhandle-Plains Historical Museum Archives).

31. Hazlett et al., *Field Artillery Weapons;* Coggins, *Arms and Equipment.*

32. Baldwin I. T. Expedition.

33. Ibid.

34. Miles to the Assistant Adjutant General, Sept. 1, 1874 (see note 13).

35. Baldwin Diary, see entries for August 30 and September 6; Baldwin I. T. Expedition.

36. For a discussion of Historic Indian sites on the Southern Plains, including Site 41BI544, see Cruse, "Detecting Historic Indian Sites."

37. Miles to Assistant Adjutant General, Aug. 25, 1874, and Miles to Pope, Sept. 5, 1874 (RG 94, AGO, Military Correspondence, File 2815–1874, NA).

38. Miles to the Assistant Adjutant General, Sept. 1, 1874 (see note 13).

39. Ibid.

40. Burton, *History of the J A Ranch,* 12.

Chapter 7. The Indians Take the Offensive

1. Although the agreed rendezvous was Oasis Creek, Lyman grew tired of waiting and sent Lieutenant West to find the other train. Lyman then moved his train to meet the other, and the exchange of supplies took place at Commission Creek. Lyman, "Fight with the Comanches and Kiowas"; Carriker, *Fort Supply Indian Territory,* 95.

2. W. H. Lewis to the Assistant Adjutant General, Sept. 12, 1874 (RG 94, AGO, Military Correspondence, File 2815–1874, NA); Archambeau, "Battle of Lyman's Wagon Train."

3. The scouts with Baldwin were Lem Wilson, William Schmalsle, and Ira Wing. The men had had their own desperate encounter with Indians after leaving the camp on Battle Creek, having fought off a group of twenty warriors in a running engagement that lasted some five hours until the Indians finally abandoned the pursuit. Baldwin I. T. Expedition.

4. This battle is sometimes referred to as the Battle of the Upper Washita; see Archambeau, "Battle of Lyman's Wagon Train." For what is probably the most detailed and accurate accounts of both the Lyman's Wagon Train and Buffalo Wallow battles, see Neal, *Valor across the Lone Star.*

5. Some confusion exists as to how many teamsters were mortally wounded. Lyman initially states, "The Assistant Wagoner McCoy is mortally wounded, I fear." Lyman to Commanding Officer, Camp Supply, Sept. 10, 1874 (AGO, Letters Received, file 3941, filed with RG 94, AGO, Military Correspondence, 2815–1874, NA). Lyman later writes, "Assistant Wagonmaster Sandford was dangerously wounded (stomach) while getting ammunition for this front, where he was actively engaged." Lyman, "Fight with the Comanches and Kiowas." Neal believes that both men were wounded at the battle, that the first man was James McCoy, who died of his wound the next day and was buried alongside Sergeant DeArmond, and that the second teamster was James L. Stanford, who later died of his wounds at the Camp Supply post hospital. Neal, *Valor across the Lone Star,* 385–86, nn. 18, 24. Marshall also states that James L. Standford died in the hospital at Camp Supply on November 27. Marshall, *Miles Expedition,* 45.

6. Rodenbough, *Sabre and Bayonet,* 303.

7. Nye, *Carbine and Lance,* 215–18; Miles to Pope, Sept. 17, 1874 (RG 393, M-1495, Roll 8, 559–62, NA).

8. Lyman, "Fight with the Comanches and Kiowas."

9. Report by Lieutenant R. H. Pratt titled "Information,"

Sept. 21, 1874 (RG 393, Part I, Entry 4875, Box 2, NA); Lyman, "Fight with the Comanches and Kiowas."

10. Nye, *Carbine and Lance,* 217–19. Nye, *Bad Medicine and Good,* 192–94.

11. Lyman, "Fight with the Comanches and Kiowas"; Taylor, *Indian Campaign,* 226.

12. *Army and Navy Journal* 12 (October 3, 1874): 117; Rodenbough, *Sabre and Bayonet,* 304.

13. Lyman, "Fight with the Comanches and Kiowas."

14. Ibid.

15. Miles to the Assistant Adjutant General, Sept. 17, 1874 (RG 393, Part I, Entry 2601, NA). In 1865, Erskine S. Allin patented his method of converting the army's muzzle loaders to breechloaders. This first-model conversion, now called the Model 1865 Springfield but known to ordnance men as "Allin's Alteration," also acquired the widely used nickname "needle gun," because of the long, slender firing pin that extended diagonally through the entire length of the breechblock. Garavaglia and Worman, *Firearms of the American West,* 9–10.

16. Lyman, "Fight with the Comanches and Kiowas."

17. Miles to Pope, Sept. 17, 1874 (see note 7); Miles to the Assistant Adjutant General, March 4, 1875 (RG 94, AGO, Military Correspondence, 2815–1874, NA).

Chapter 8. Outnumbered Twenty-Five to One

1. One of the most detailed accounts of this battle can be found in Neal, *Valor across the Lone Star,* 155–69.

2. Dixon, *Life of "Billy" Dixon,* 201.

3. Miles, *Personal Recollections,* 173; Dixon, *Life of "Billy" Dixon,* 202–3; Haley, *Buffalo War,* 160.

4. Bard, *Life and Adventures of "Billy" Dixon;* Dixon, *Life of "Billy" Dixon,* 206.

5. Haley, *Buffalo War,* 165.

6. Miles to the Assistant Adjutant General, Sept. 17, 1874 (RG 393, Part I, Entry 2601, NA); Dixon, *Life of "Billy" Dixon,* 214; Miles to Charles G. Smith, Dec. 25, 1874 (AGO, Letters Received, file 5519, filed with RG 94, AGO, Military Correspondence, File 2815–1874, NA).

7. *Canadian Record,* Sept. 20, 1927.

Chapter 9. The Indians Elude the 8th Cavalry

1. The historical accounts in this section are taken from Price to Williams, Sept. 23, 1874 (RG 94, AGO, Military Correspondence, File 2815–1874, NA), and Nye, "Excitement on the Sweetwater," 241–49, except as otherwise noted.

2. Farnsworth to Field Adjutant, Sept. 23, 1874, in Taylor, *Indian Campaign,* 61.

3. Haley, *Buffalo War,* 162; see also Rogers, "Luck, Logistics and Major Price," 31.

4. Price to Williams, Sept. 23, 1874 (RG 94, AGO, Military Correspondence, File 2815–1874, NA).

5. Thomas, *Cannons,* 32.

6. Price to Mahnken, Feb. 12, 1875 (RG 393, Part I, E–2601, NA). Price states in this correspondence that this howitzer was later lost in quicksand while crossing the Canadian River and "was never recovered."

Chapter 10. The Turning Point of the War

1. Mackenzie to Auger, Dec. 2, 1874 (RG 94, AGO, Military Correspondence, File 2815–1874, NA); Knox, "Battle of Palo Duro."

2. Wallace, *Ranald S. Mackenzie,* 130–31.

3. Carter, *On the Border,* 485–88; Leckie, *Military Conquest,* 220–21.

4. Wallace, *Ranald S. Mackenzie,* 136–37; Hatfield, "Comanche, Kiowa and Cheyenne Campaign," 131; Haley, *Buffalo War,* 178; Nye, *Carbine and Lance,* 221.

5. K'ya-been was killed during the battle in Palo Duro Canyon. In 1901, an Indian burial believed to be that of K'ya-been was found in a rock-covered crevice in Palo Duro Canyon. Burgan, "Proposal."

6. Wallace, *Ranald S. Mackenzie,* 138–45.

7. Mackenzie to Auger, Dec. 2, 1874 (see note 1); Pierce, *Most Promising Young Officer,* 149–53.

8. TPWD acquired this property in May 2005.

9. Carter, *On the Border,* 493.

Chapter 11. A Most Desperate Fight

1. Farnsworth does not mention the Comanchero guide, but his name appears on the list of those who lost certain equipment during the battle. Farnsworth to the Adjutant General, Nov. 27, 1874, in Taylor, *Indian Campaign,* 109–10.

2. Farnsworth's orders to lead the scout patrol are Special Orders No. 36, Price to Farnsworth, Nov. 2, 1874 (RG 393, Part I, Entry 2601, NA). There is a great deal of confusion regarding the Indian whom Farnsworth apparently took with him. Major Price states after the Indian was captured that, "this Indian was shot." Price to the Assistant Adjutant General, Nov. 7, 1874 (RG 393, Part I, Entry 2601, NA). Lieutenant Farnsworth, however, states, "I did not derive, nor did I attempt to obtain any information from the captured Indian taken with me, who claimed to be a Kiowa. He was killed I am informed and believe, during the fight." Farnsworth to the Battalion Adjutant, Nov. 12, 1874 (RG 393, Part I, Entry 2601, NA). George Bent says that the Indian who accompanied Farnsworth was a Cheyenne guide named Brown Blackbird and that he was captured, but not killed, by the Cheyenne warriors during the battle. Hyde, *Life of George Bent,* 362–63. J. T. Marshall states that the Indian with Farnsworth was an Arapaho guide. Marshall, *Miles Expedition,* 39.

3. Farnsworth to the Field Adjutant, Nov. 7, 1874 (RG 393, Part I, Entry 2601, NA).

4. Ibid.

5. Farnsworth to the Battalion Adjutant, Nov. 12, 1874 (RG 393, Part I, Entry 2601, NA).

6. Baldwin Diary. The two older sisters, Sophia and Catherine, were recovered from Stone Calf's band shortly before its formal surrender early in March 1875.

7. Price to the Assistant Adjutant General, Nov. 7, 1874 (see note 1).

8. Hyde, *Life of George Bent,* 362; Marshall, *Miles Expedition,* 39.

9. The National Archives file containing the court-martial proceedings is RG 393, PP-4678, 1–757 and exhibits. On November 12, 1874, Col. Nelson A. Miles had Major Price arrested, and charges were preferred against him. Price was charged with disobeying an order from his commanding officer (see note 11), conduct unbecoming an officer, neglect of duty, and conduct to the prejudice of good order and military discipline. Major Price was ordered to Camp Supply, and in June 1875 his court-martial was convened at Fort Lyon, Colorado Territory. The court found Major Price guilty and he was sentenced "to be reduced in rank so

that his name shall appear in the list of Majors of Cavalry next below the name of James Biddle." On December 12, 1876, President Grant remitted the sentence and Price was restored to his former relative rank of major.

10. J. T. Marshall writes that the bodies of William Densham and Rufus Hibbard were both "horribly mutilated, entrails taken out, faces and limbs cut into pieces, scalped and everything done that savage ferocity could invent." Marshall, *Miles Expedition,* 39. The editor of Marshall's correspondence, Lonnie J. White, indicates that the scalps from the two soldiers were found by Baldwin and his troops at the Battle of McClellan Creek on November 8. However, Capt. Richard Pratt, who commanded the scouts for Colonel Davidson's command, writes, "We found the bodies of the two soldiers, and as I had command of about eighty scouts and held the advance of our troops, I was the first to enter the vacated camps. The two soldiers had been scalped, and near the centre of the camp, on high ground, I found a pole about 10 feet high, on the top of which was the fresh scalp of one of the soldiers, while the sod around the pole, for a distance of twenty feet or more, was all worn out by the dancing of the Indians. I found out afterwards that their women and children had danced all night around that scalp." Pratt is clearly referring to the vacated camp found near the North Fork of the Red River after Farnsworth's battle and not the Indian village attacked by Baldwin on McClellan Creek. Beecher, "Capt. Pratt's Views on the Indian Question." See also Pratt, *Battlefield and Classroom,* 75.

11. In a letter to the assistant adjutant general at Fort Leavenworth, Colonel Miles writes, "As Major Price failed to carry out his instructions contained in order enclosed with my report of November 9th 1874, and marched his command *away from, and in an opposite direction* from the sound of the fight; and as he has, in my opinion, persistently and designedly disobeyed, disregarded and misconstrued nearly every order he has received; I have ordered him in arrest, and shall prefer charges against him." Miles to the Assistant Adjutant General, Nov. 12, 1874 (RG 393, Part I, E-2927, 198–99, NA).

12. Davidson to the Assistant Adjutant General, Nov. 28, 1874 (RG 393, M-1495, Roll 8, Frames 1158–59, NA).

13. Baldwin Diary.

14. Ibid.

15. Price to the Assistant Adjutant General, Nov. 7, 1874 (see note 1) .

16. Farnsworth to the Field Adjutant, Nov. 7, 1874 (see note 3); Marshall, *Miles Expedition,* 39; Private Hechner writes that there were twenty-five men in the patrol, but Lieutenant Farnsworth states that the patrol had twenty-eight men. Rea, "Red River War Diary," 29.

17. Farnsworth to the Battalion Adjutant, Nov. 12, 1874 (see note 1).

18. *Army and Navy Journal* 22 (Sept. 26, 1885).

19. Rea, "Red River War Diary," 30.

20. General A. B. Dyer to Springfield Armory, Nov. 18, 1871 (RG 156, Vol. 38, Entry 7, NA).

21. Neal, *Valor across the Lone Star,* 130–32.

22. Wallace, *Ranald S. Mackenzie's Official Correspondence,* 142.

Chapter 12. Conclusions and Legacy

1. Scott et al., *Archaeological Perspectives,* 118–19.

2. Baldwin Diary; Miles to the Assistant Adjutant General, Nov. 9, 1874 (RG 393, M-1495, Roll 8, frames 1054–60, NA).

3. Carter, *On the Border,* 481–84; Wallace, *Ranald S. Mackenzie,* 136–37; Mackenzie, "Memorandum of March of the 1st Column from Camp of Fresh Fork of the Brazos" (RG 393, M-1495, Roll 8, frames 709–13, NA).

4. Wallace, *Ranald S. Mackenzie,* 155–56.

5. Sheridan to Sherman, Oct. 24, 1874, and Buell to Miles, Oct. 18, 1874 (RG 94, AGO, Military Correspondence, File 2815–1874, NA).

6. Miles to Assistant Adjutant General, March 4, 1875 (ibid.).

7. Miles to Assistant Adjutant General, Dec. 5, 1874 (ibid.).

8. Ibid.; Miles to Lewis and Biddle, Dec. 5, 1874 (RG 393, Part I, E-2927, 243–44); Miles to the Adjutant General, Dec. 26, 1874 (ibid., 276–77).

9. Miles to Bristol, Sept. 15, 1874 (ibid., 70).

10. Report by Lieutenant R. H. Pratt titled "Information," Sept. 21, 1874 (RG 393, Part I, Entry 4875, Box 2, NA).

11. Oswald, "History of Fort Elliott," 3–8.

Appendix D. Descriptions and Analysis of Artifacts from the Battle of Red River Site and the Indian Village Site (41BI544) in Tule Canyon

1. Scott et al., *Archaeological Perspectives,* 162.

2. Kinzer, "Invention of the Extractor."

3. McDowell, *Development of the Henry Cartridge,* 35–36.

4. Hoyem, *Historical Development of Small Arms Ammunition,* 129; McDowell, *Development of the Henry Cartridge,* 63–64.

5. Madis, *Winchester Book,* 79, 97.

6. Frasca and Hill, *.45–70 Springfield;* Frasca, *.45–70 Springfield, Book II.*

7. Logan, *Cartridges;* Sellers, *Sharps Firearms,* 181–82.

8. Berk, *Gatling Gun,* 15–17.

9. Marcot, *Spencer Repeating Firearms,* 81.

10. Ibid., 201.

11. Barber, *Rim Fire Cartridge,* 9–10, 34–35.

12. Ibid., 187.

13. At the time the Gatling gun was examined in February 1999 by Douglas D. Scott, it was on loan from the Smithsonian Institution National Museum of American History.

14. Hamilton and Emery, *Eighteenth-Century Gunflints,* 21.

15. Witthoft, "History of Gunflints," 36.

16. Melton and Pawl, *Introduction to Field Artillery Ordnance;* Jones, *Artillery Fuses,* 96.

17. Coggins, *Arms and Equipment;* Melton and Pawl, *Guide to Civil War Artillery Projectiles.*

18. Hanson, "Upper Missouri Arrow Points." Russell, *Firearms, Traps, and Tools.*

19. Taylor, "Preliminary Study of Metal Arrow Points," 27.

20. Baldwin Diary.

21. Shaffer et al., *Gun Tools,* 284.

22. Di Peso, *Sobaipuri Indians.*

23. Steffen, *Horse Soldier;* Scott et al., *Archaeological Perspectives,* 205.

24. Gillio et al., "Some Common Artifacts."

25. Adams et al., *Dark Canyon Rancheria,* 62.

26. Rock, "Cans in the Countryside."

27. Steffen, *Horse Soldier;* Sylvia and O'Donnell, *Civil War Canteens.*

28. Steffen, *Horse Soldier,* 183.

29. Scott et al., *Archaeological Perspectives,* 208.

30. Steffen, *Horse Soldier*, 178, 183.
31. Anonymous, "Ammunition Boxes."
32. Reedstrom, *Bugles, Banners and War Bonnets*, 233.

Appendix E. Descriptions and Analysis of Artifacts from the Battle of Lyman's Wagon Train Site

1. Scott et al., *Archaeological Perspectives*, 113–15.
2. Burnside, "Internally Primed 50–70 Cartridges"; Logan, *Cartridges*, 79, 92; Barnes, *Cartridges of the World*, 6th ed.
3. Barber, *Rim Fire Cartridge*, 33.
4. Marcot, *Spencer Repeating Firearms*, 200; Barber, *Rim Fire Cartridge*, 3, 34–35.
5. Barber, *Rim Fire Cartridge*, 187.
6. Scott et al., *Archaeological Perspectives*, 196.
7. Dixie Gun Works, "Black Powder Guns," 238.
8. Quartermaster, "U.S. Army Wagon Harness."
9. Fike, *Bottle Book*.

Appendix F. Descriptions and Analysis of Artifacts from the Battle of Sweetwater Creek Site

1. William R. Shoemaker to Chief of Ordnance, Jan. 6 and July 2 (& endorsements), and Report of Operations at Fort Union Arsenal, June 30, 1874 (RG 156, Letters Received, Ordnance Dept., NA), cited in Oliva, *Fort Union*, 593.
2. Barnes, *Cartridges of the World*, 6th ed.; Burnside, "Internally Primed 50–70 Cartridges"; Logan, *Cartridges*, 79.
3. Barber, *Rim Fire Cartridge*, 187.
4. Lord, *Civil War Collector's Encyclopedia*.
5. Ibid.; Thomas, *Cannons*.

Appendix G. Descriptions and Analysis of Artifacts from the Battle of Palo Duro Canyon Site

1. Barnes, *Cartridges of the World*, 6th ed., 264.
2. Coates and Thomas, *Introduction to Civil War Small Arms*.
3. Russell, *Firearms, Traps, and Tools*.
4. Di Peso, *Sobaipuri Indians*, 192–96.
5. Lifshey, "Saga of Landers, Frary & Clark."
6. Tice, *Uniform Buttons of the United States*, 473.
7. Dempsey, "Naja."

Appendix H. Descriptions and Analysis of Artifacts from the Battle of Round Timber Creek Site and Grey Beard's Village Site

1. Sellers, *Sharps Firearms*, 208–17.
2. Barnes, *Cartridges of the World*, 10th ed., 517.
3. Ibid., 290; Gluckman, *United States Martial Pistols*, 254; Pate, "Original Nickel Plated Cavalry Revolver," 15.
4. Treadwell, *Metallic Cartridge*, plates 19–23.
5. Kopec, *Study of the Colt Single Action Army Revolver*, 305–6; Kopec and Fenn, *Colt Cavalry and Artillery Revolvers*, 237.
6. Frasca, *.45–70 Springfield, Book II*, 156; McAulay, *Carbines of the U.S. Cavalry*, 101.
7. Hoovestol, *E. Remington & Sons Cartridges*.
8. Logan, *Cartridges*, 79, 92.
9. McAulay, *Carbines of the U.S. Cavalry;* Ordnance Memorandum 15, "1874 Report of the Board of Officers Selecting a Breech-System for the Muskets and Carbines of the Military Service, Together with Their Report upon the Subject of Trowel Bayonets." Report of the Secretary of War, Chief of Ordnance Report, House Executive Documents, 1st Session, 43d Congress, Washington, D.C.
10. Barber, *Rim Fire Cartridge*, 187.
11. Thomas and Thomas, *Handbook of Civil War Bullets*, 17.
12. Hunt, "Fort Union," 17–20.
13. Shaffer et al., *Gun Tools*, 91.
14. Steffen, *Horse Soldier*.
15. Phillips, *Excavated Artifacts*, plate 102.
16. *Leavenworth Times*, January 12, 1968.

Bibliography

Articles, Books, and Manuscripts

Adams, Christopher D., Diane E. White, and David M. Johnson. *Dark Canyon Rancheria Apache/Military Battle Site, Lincoln National Forest New Mexico.* Alamogordo, New Mexico: United States Department of Agriculture, 2000.

Anonymous. "Ammunition Boxes." *Haversack* 1, no. 4 (1979).

Archambeau, Ernest R. (ed.). "The Battle of Lyman's Wagon Train." *Panhandle–Plains Historical Review* 36 (1964): 89–101.

Baird, Spencer F. "Catalogue of Casts Taken by Clark Mills, Esq., of the Heads of Sixty-Four Indian Prisoners of Various Western Tribes, and Held at Fort Marion, Saint Augustine, Fla., in Charge of Capt. R. H. Pratt, U.S.A.," *Proceedings of the United States National Museum* 1 (1878): 201–13.

Baker, T. Lindsay, and Billy R. Harrison. *Adobe Walls: The History and Archeology of the 1874 Trading Post.* College Station: Texas A&M University Press, 1986.

Baldwin, Alice B. *Memoirs of the Late Frank D. Baldwin, Major General, United States Army.* Los Angeles: Wetzel Publishing, 1929.

Barber, John L. *The Rim Fire Cartridge in the United States and Canada 1857–1984.* Tacoma, Washington: Armory Press, 1987.

Bard, Frederick S. *Life and Adventures of "Billy" Dixon of Adobe Walls, Panhandle, Texas.* Guthrie, Oklahoma: Cooperative Publishing, 1914.

Barnes, Frank C. *Cartridges of the World.* 6th ed. Northfield, Illinois: DBI Books, 1989.

———. *Cartridges of the World.* 10th ed. Iola, Wisconsin: Krause Publishing, 2003.

Bates, Craig, Bonnie Kahn, and Benson Landford. *The Cheyenne/Arapaho Ledger Book from the Pamplin Collection.* Portland, Oregon: Robert B. Pamplin Jr., 2003.

Beecher, Henry Ward. "Capt. Pratt's Views on the Indian Question after Twenty-Four Years' Experience." *Red Man Magazine,* December 1890–January 1891.

Berk, Joseph. *The Gatling Gun: 19th Century Machine Gun to 21st Century Vulcan.* Boulder: Paladin Press, 1991.

Berthrong, Donald J. *The Southern Cheyennes.* Norman: University of Oklahoma Press, 1963.

Burgan, Scott. "A Proposal for the Identification of an Historic Indian Burial Found in Palo Duro Canyon." *Transactions of the 28th Southwest Federation of Archeological Societies,* 1992, 3–15.

Burnside, Graham. "Internally Primed 50–70 Cartridges." *Texas Gun Collector* 60 (1955): 24–27.

Burton, Harley True. *A History of the J A Ranch.* Austin, Texas: Press of Von Boeckmann-Jones Company, 1928.

Carriker, Robert C. *Fort Supply Indian Territory, Frontier Outpost on the Plains.* Norman: University of Oklahoma Press, 1970.

Carter, Robert G. *The Old Sergeant's Story: Winning the West from the Indians and Bad Men in 1870 to 1876.* New York: Frederick B. Hitchcock, 1926.

———. *On the Border with Mackenzie: Or, Winning West Texas from the Comanches.* Washington, D.C.: Eynon Printing, 1935.

Chalfant, William. *Cheyennes at Dark Water Creek: The Last Fight of the Red River War.* Norman: University of Oklahoma Press, 1997.

Chun, Clayton K. S. *US Army in the Plains Indian Wars, 1865–91.* Oxford, United Kingdom: Osprey Publishing, 2004.

Coates, Earl J., and Dean S. Thomas. *An Introduction to Civil War Small Arms.* Gettysburg, Pennsylvania: Thomas Publications, 1990.

Coggins, Jack. *Arms and Equipment of the Civil War.* Garden City, New York: Doubleday, 1962.

Cook, John R. *The Border and the Buffalo: An Untold Story of the Southwest Plains.* Topeka, Kansas: Crane, 1907.

Cruse, J. Brett. "Archeological Investigations at the Battle of Red River Site: New Perspectives on the 1874 Indian Campaign in the Texas Panhandle." *Southwestern Historical Quarterly* 106, no. 2 (2002): 169–92.

———. "Detecting Historic Indian Sites: The Case for Metal Detecting as an Archeological Strategy." *Bulletin of the Texas Archeological Society* 74 (2003): 103–30.

Dempsey, Maggie. "Naja." *Relics,* August 1977, 8–9.

Di Peso, Charles C. *The Sobaipuri Indians of the Upper San Pedro River Valley.* Dragoon, Arizona: Amerind Foundation, 1953.

Dixie Gun Works. "Black Powder Guns, Shooting Supplies, and Antique Gun Parts." Catalogue 145. Union City, Tennessee, 1966.

Dixon, Billy D. *The Life and Adventures of Billy Dixon of Adobe Walls.* Guthrie, Oklahoma: Cooperative Publishing, 1914.

Dixon, Olive K. *Life of "Billy" Dixon.* Reprint, Austin: State House Press, 1987.

Farb, Peter. *Man's Rise to Civilization: The Cultural Ascent of the Indians of North America.* 2d ed. New York: Dutton, 1978.

Fehrenbach, T. R. *Comanches: The Destruction of a People.* Reprint. New York: Da Capo Press, 1994.

Fike, Richard E. *The Bottle Book: A Comprehensive Guide to Historic Embossed Medicine Bottles.* Salt Lake City: Peregrine Smith Books, 1987.

Frasca, Albert J. *The .45–70 Springfield, Book II.* Springfield, Ohio: Frasca Publishing, 1997.

Frasca, Albert J., and Robert H. Hill. *The .45–70 Springfield.* Northridge, California: Springfield Publishing, 1980.

Garavaglia, Louis A., and Charles G. Worman. *Firearms of the American West, 1866–1894.* Niwot: University Press of Colorado, 1997.

Gillio, David, Frances Levine, and Douglas Scott. "Some Common Artifacts Found at Historical Sites." *Cultural Resources Report* 31. Albuquerque: U.S. Forest Service, Southwestern Region, 1980.

Gluckman, Arcadi. *United States Martial Pistols and Revolvers.* New York: Bonanza Books, 1956.

———. *Identifying Old U.S. Muskets, Rifles, and Carbines.* New York: Bonanza Books, 1965.

Gregg, Josiah. *Commerce of the Prairies.* Edited by Max Moorhead. Norman: University of Oklahoma Press, 1954.

Gunther, Jack D., and Charles O. Gunther. *The Identification of Firearms.* London: John Wiley and Sons, 1935.

Haley, J. Evetts. *Fort Concho and the Texas Frontier.* San Angelo, Texas: San Angelo Standard Times, 1952.

Haley, James L. *The Buffalo War: The History of the Red River Indian Uprising of 1874.* Norman: University of Oklahoma Press, 1976.

Hamilton, T. M., and K. O. Emery. *Eighteenth-Century Gunflints from Fort Michilimackinac and Other Colonial Sites.* Mackinac Island, Michigan: Mackinac Island State Park Commission, 1988.

Hanson, James. "Upper Missouri Arrow Points." *Museum of the Fur Trade Quarterly* 8 (4): 2–8.

Harris, C. E. "Sherlock Holmes Would Be Impressed." *American Rifleman* 128 (5): 36–39, 82.

Hatcher, Julian S. *Textbook of Firearms Investigation, Identification, and Evidence Together with Textbook of Pistols and Revolvers.* Plantersville, South Carolina: Small-Arms Technical Publishing, 1943.

Hatcher, Julian S., Frank J. Jury, and Jac Weller. *Firearms Investigation, Identification, and Evidence.* Harrisburg, Pennsylvania: Stackpole Books, 1977.

Hatfield, Col. Charles A. P. "The Comanche, Kiowa and Cheyenne Campaign in Northwest Texas and Mackenzie's Fight in the Palo Duro Canyon, September 26 [*sic*], 1874." *West Texas Historical Association Year Book* 5 (June 1929): 128–33.

Hazlett, James C., Edwin Olmstead, and M. Hume Parks. *Field Artillery Weapons of the Civil War.* Newark: University of Delaware Press, 1983.

Hoig, Stan. *Tribal Wars of the Southern Plains.* Norman: University of Oklahoma Press, 1993.

Hook, Jason, and Martin Pegler. *To Live and Die in the West: The American Indian Wars.* Oxford, United Kingdom: Osprey Publishing, 1999.

Hoovestol, Howard. *E. Remington & Sons Cartridges.* Bismark: Privately published by the author, 2000.

Hoyem, George A. *Historical Development of Small Arms Ammunition.* Vol. 1. Tacoma, Washington: Armory Publications, 1981.

Humfreville, J. Lee. *Twenty Years among Our Hostile Indians.* Reprint. Mechanicsburg, Pennsylvania: Stackpole Books, 2002.

Hunt, William J., Jr. "Fort Union Trading Post National Historic Site, 32WI17, Material Culture Reports Part V: Buttons as Closures, Buttons as Decorations: A Nineteenth Century Example from Fort Union." Lincoln, Nebraska: Midwest Archeological Center, National Park Service, 1986.

Hutchins, James S. "Boots and Saddles on the Frontier." *Westerners Brand Book.* Chicago: 12, 1966.

Hutton, Paul A. *Phil Sheridan and His Army.* Lincoln: University of Nebraska Press, 1985.

Hyde, George E. *The Life of George Bent, Written from His Letters.* Edited by Savoie Lottinville. Norman: University of Oklahoma Press, 1968.

Jacobsen, Jacques N., Jr. *The 1886 Machine Gun Manual.* Reprint. Fort Sill, Oklahoma: U.S. Army Field Artillery School, 1989.

Jamieson, Perry D. *Crossing the Deadly Ground: United States Army Tactics.* Tuscaloosa: University of Alabama Press, 1994.

Jauken, Arlene F. *The Moccasin Speaks: Living as Captives of the Dog Soldier Warriors.* Lincoln, Nebraska: Dageforde Publishing, 1998.

Johnson, Virginia W. *The Unregimented General: A Biography of Nelson A. Miles.* Boston: Houghton Mifflin, 1962.

Jones, Charles H. *Artillery Fuses of the Civil War.* Alexandria, Virginia: O'Donnell Publications, 2001.

Kappler, Charles J. *Indian Laws and Treaties.* Reprint. New York: Interland Publishing, 1979.

Kavanagh, Thomas W. *The Comanches, A History, 1706–1875.* Lincoln: University of Nebraska Press, 1996.

Kenner, Charles L. *The Comanchero Frontier: A History of New Mexican–Plains Indian Relations.* Norman: University of Oklahoma Press, 1969.

Kinzer, James B. "The Invention of the Extractor: The Successful Winchester Repeating Rifle." *Gun Report* 28, no. 8 (1983): 34–38.

Knox, Bill. "Battle of Palo Duro." *Southwest Heritage* 1, no. 4 (1967): 16–24.

Kopec, John A. *A Study of the Colt Single Action Army Revolver.* Whitmore, California: John A. Kopec, 1992.

Kopec, John A., and H. Sterling Fenn. *Colt Cavalry and Artillery Revolvers: A Continuing Study.* Newport Beach, California: Graphic Publishers, 1994.

Leckie, William H. *The Military Conquest of the Southern Plains.* Norman: University of Oklahoma Press, 1963.

———. "The Red River War of 1874–1875." *Panhandle-Plains Historical Review* 29 (1956): 78–100.

Lifshey, Earl. "The Saga of Landers, Frary & Clark." Available at http://www.toaster.org/landers.html. Accessed October 1, 2005.

Logan, Herschal C. *Cartridges.* New York: Bonanza Books, 1959.

Lord, Francis A. *Civil War Collector's Encyclopedia: Arms, Uniforms, and Equipment of the Union and Confederacy.* Harrisburg, Pennsylvania: Stackpole Press, 1963.

Lyman, Wyllys. "A Fight with the Comanches and Kiowas," *Army and Navy Journal* 12 (Oct. 31, 1874): 186–87.

Madis, George. *The Winchester Book.* Brownsboro, Texas: Art and Reference House, 1979.

Marcot, Roy M. *Spencer Repeating Firearms.* Irvine, California: Northwood Heritage Press, 1983.

Marshall, J. T. *The Miles Expedition of 1874–1875: An Eyewitness Account of the Red River War.* Edited by Lonnie J. White. Austin, Texas: Encino Press, 1971.

Mayhall, Mildred P. *The Kiowas.* Norman: University of Oklahoma Press, 1971.

McAulay, John D. *Carbines of the U.S. Cavalry, 1861–1905.* Lincoln, Rhode Island: Andrew Mowbray, 1996.

McChristian, Douglas C. *The U.S. Army in the West, 1870–1880.* Norman: University of Oklahoma Press, 1995.

McDowell, R. Bruce. *Development of the Henry Cartridge.* Metuchen, New Jersey: A.M.B., 1984.

McFadden, Thomas. "Thomas McFadden's Diary of an Indian Campaign, 1874." Edited by Robert C. Carriker. *Southwestern Historical Quarterly* 75, no. 2 (1971): 198–232.

Melton, Jack W., Jr., and Lawrence E. Pawl. *Introduction to Field Artillery Ordnance, 1861–1865.* Kennesaw, Georgia: Kennesaw Mountain Press, 1994.

———. *Guide to Civil War Artillery Projectiles.* Kennesaw, Georgia: Kennesaw Mountain Press, 1996.

Miles, Nelson A. *Personal Recollections and Observations.* Chicago: Werner, 1896.

Mishkin, Bernard. *Rank and Warfare among the Plains Indians.* New York: J. J. Augustin, 1940.

Neal, Charles M., Jr. *Valor across the Lone Star.* Austin: Texas State Historical Association, 2002.

Newcomb, W. W., Jr. "A Re-examination of the Causes of Plains Warfare." *American Anthropologist* 52, no. 3 (1950): 317–30.

Nye, Wilbur S. *Carbine and Lance: The Story of Old Fort Sill.* Norman, University of Oklahoma Press, 1937.

———. "Excitement on the Sweetwater." *Chronicles of Oklahoma* 16, no. 2 (1938): 241–49.

———. *Bad Medicine and Good.* Norman: University of Oklahoma Press, 1962.

———. *Plains Indian Raiders: The Final Phases of Warfare from the Arkansas to the Red River.* Norman: University of Oklahoma Press, 1968.

Oliva, Leo E. *Fort Union and the Frontier Army in the Southwest.* Santa Fe, New Mexico: Southwest Cultural Resources Center, National Park Service, 1993.

Oswald, James M. "History of Fort Elliott." *Panhandle-Plains Historical Review* 32 (1959): 3–8.

Pate, Charles W. "The Original Nickel Plated Cavalry Revolver, The S&W Model 3." *Man at Arms* 2, no. 1 (1980): 10–15.

Phillips, Stanley S. *Excavated Artifacts from Battlefields and Campsites of the Civil War, 1861–1865.* Chelsea, Michigan: BookCrafters, 1974.

Pierce, Michael. *The Most Promising Young Officer: A Life of Ranald Slidell Mackenzie.* Norman: University of Oklahoma Press, 1993.

Pratt, Richard H. *Battlefield and Classroom: Four Decades with the American Indian, 1867–1904.* New Haven, Connecticut: Yale University Press, 1964.

Public Information Division, U.S. Army. *The Medal of Honor of the United States Army.* Washington, D.C.: Government Printing Office, 1948.

Quartermaster. "U.S. Army Wagon Harness, (Horse and Mule)." Washington, D.C.: Government Printing Office, 1877.

Rathjen, Frederick W. *The Texas Panhandle Frontier.* Austin: University of Texas Press, 1973.

Rea, Bob (ed.). "The Red River War Diary of Private John Hechner." *Panhandle-Plains Historical Review* 71 (1998): 24–38.

Reedstrom, Ernest L. *Bugles, Banners and War Bonnets.* New York: Bonanza Books, 1977.

Richardson, Rupert N. *The Comanche Barrier to South Plains Settlement.* Glendale, California: Arthur H. Clark, 1933.

———. *The Frontier of Northwest Texas, 1846–1876.* Glendale, California: Arthur H. Clark, 1963.

Rickey, Don, Jr. *Forty Miles a Day on Beans and Hay: The Enlisted Soldier Fighting the Indian Wars.* Norman: University of Oklahoma Press, 1963.

Rister, Carl C. *Fort Griffin on the Texas Frontier.* Norman: University of Oklahoma Press, 1956.

Robinson, Charles M., III. *Satanta: The Life and Death of a War Chief.* Austin, Texas: State House Press, 1997.

Rock, James T. "Cans in the Countryside." *Historical Archaeology* 18 (2): 97–111.

Rodenbough, Theophilus. *Sabre and Bayonet: Stories of Heroism and Military Adventure.* New York: G. W. Dillingham, 1897.

Rogers, Jerry L. "To the Canyon of the Tule: Colonel Nelson A. Miles and the Indian Territory Expedition, 1874." *Texas Military History* 7, no. 3 (1968): 267–94.

———. "The Flint and Steel: Background of the Red River Way of 1874–1875." *Texas Military History* 7, no. 4 (1969): 153–75.

———. "Luck, Logistics and Major Price: Problems of the Indian Territory Expedition, Autumn 1874." *Texas Military History* 8, no. 1 (1970): 27–53.

Russell, Carl P. *Firearms, Traps, and Tools of the Mountain Men.* Albuquerque: University of New Mexico Press, 1977.

Scott, Douglas D., and Richard A. Fox Jr. *Archaeological Insights into the Custer Battle: An Assessment of the 1984 Field Season.* Norman: University of Oklahoma Press, 1987.

Scott, Douglas D., Richard A. Fox Jr., Melissa A. Connor, and Dick Harmon. *Archaeological Perspectives on the Battle of the Little Bighorn.* Norman: University of Oklahoma Press, 1989.

Secoy, Frank. *Changing Military Patterns of the Great Plains Indians.* Reprint. Lincoln: University of Nebraska Press, 1992.

Sellers, Frank. *Sharps Firearms.* North Hollywood, California: Beinfield Publishing, 1978.

Shaffer, James B., Lee A. Rutledge, and R. Stephen Dorsey. *Gun Tools: Their History and Identification.* Eugene, Oregon: Collectors' Library, 1992.

Simmons, Marc, and Frank Turley. *Southwestern Colonial Ironwork: The Spanish Blacksmithing Tradition from Texas to California.* Santa Fe: Museum of New Mexico Press, 1980.

Steffen, Randy. *The Horse Soldier,* Vol. 2: *The Frontier, the Mexican War, the Civil War, the Indian Wars, 1851–1880.* Norman: University of Oklahoma Press, 1978.

Steinbach, Robert H. *A Long March: The Lives of Frank and Alice Baldwin.* Austin: University of Texas Press, 1989.

Sylvia, Stephen W., and Michael O'Donnell. *Civil War Canteens.* Orange, Virginia: Moss Publications, 1983.

Taylor, Anna Jean. "A Preliminary Study of Metal Arrow Points." Unpublished manuscript on file at the Texas Historical Commission, Austin.

Taylor, Joe. F. (ed.). *The Indian Campaign on the Staked Plains, 1874–1875: Military Correspondence from War Department Adjutant General's Office, File 2815–1874.* Canyon, Texas: Panhandle-Plains Historical Society, 1962.

Thomas, Dean S. *Cannons: An Introduction to Civil War Artillery.* Gettysburg, Pennsylvania: Thomas Publications, 1985.

Thomas, James E., and Dean S. Thomas. *A Handbook of Civil War Bullets and Cartridges.* Gettysburg, Pennsylvania: Thomas Publications, 1996.

Tice, Warren K. *Uniform Buttons of the United States, 1776–1865.* Gettysburg, Pennsylvania: Thomas Publications, 1997.

Treadwell, T. J. *Metallic Cartridges (Regulation and Experimental) as Manufactured and Tested at the Frankford Arsenal, Philadelphia, Pennsylvania.* Reprint. Washington, D.C.: Government Printing Office, 1873.

Upton, Emory. *Cavalry Tactics, United States Army.* New York: Appleton and Company, 1874.

Urwin, Gregory J. W. *The United States Cavalry: An Illustrated History.* Poole, Dorset, United Kingdom: Blandford Press, 1983.

Utley, Robert M. *Frontier Regulars: The United States Army and the Indian, 1866–1891.* New York: Macmillan, 1973.

———. "A Chained Dog: The Indian Fighting Army." *American West* 10, no. 4 (1973): 18–24, 61.

Van Sickle, S. S. *A Story of Real Life on the Plains.* Cedar Rapids, Iowa: Metcalf, 1895.

Wahl, Paul, and Donald R. Toppel. *The Gatling Gun.* New York: Arco Publishing, 1965.

Wallace, Ernest. *Ranald S. Mackenzie's Official Correspondence*

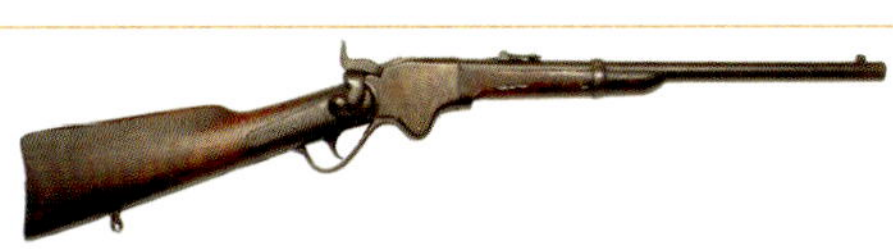

Relating to Texas, 1871–1875. Lubbock: West Texas Museum Association, 1967.

———. *Ranald S. Mackenzie on the Texas Frontier.* Reprint. College Station: Texas A&M University Press, 1993.

Wallace, Ernest, and Adamson Hoebel. *The Comanches: Lords of the South Plains*. Norman: University of Oklahoma Press, 1952.

West, Derek G. "The Battle of Adobe Walls (1874)." *Panhandle–Plains Historical Review* 36 (1963).

Whitman, S. E. *The Troopers: An Informal History of the Plains Cavalry.* New York: Hastings House, 1962.

Wilhelm, Thomas. *Military Dictionary and Gazetteer.* Rev. ed. Philadelphia: L. R. Hamersley and Company, 1881.

Witthoft, John. "A History of Gunflints." *Pennsylvania Archaeologist* 36, nos. 1 and 2 (1966).

Wooster, Robert. *The Military and United States Indian Policy, 1865–1903*. New Haven, Connecticut: Yale University Press, 1988.

———. *Nelson A. Miles and the Twilight of the Frontier Army.* Lincoln: University of Nebraska Press, 1993.

Government Documents

U.S. Bureau of Indian Affairs. Medicine Lodge Peace Treaty 1869. Washington, D.C.: Copy on file at the Panhandle-Plains Historical Museum Archives, Canyon, Texas.

U.S. Congress, House. Executive Document 1, Report of the Secretary of the Navy. 38th Congress, 2d sess., 1864, series no. 1221.

U.S. Congress, House. Executive Documents. Report of the Secretary of War, Chief of Ordnance Report. Ordnance Memorandum 15, "1874 Report of the Board of Officers Selecting a Breech-System for the Muskets and Carbines of the Military Service, Together with Their Report upon the Subject of Trowel Bayonets." 43d Congress, 1st sess.

U.S. Congress, Senate. Executive Document No. 15. 39th Congress, 2d sess., II 1867, serial 1277, 4.

U.S. War Department. Comparison of "Lined" with "Wad" Carbine Cartridges. Ordnance Notes, No. 43, Washington, D.C., 1875.

Federal Records Groups, National Archives

Record Group 77

Entry 52, Box 18

Record Group 94

AGO, Military Correspondence, File 2815–1874

Appointments, Commission, and Promotion Papers, File 5401–1871

Microfilm 1495, Rolls 8, 9

Record Group 98

Military Department of the Missouri, Letters Received

Record Group 156

Letters Received, Ordnance Department

Record Group 393

Part I, Entry 2601, Boxes 40, 41

Part I, Entry 2927

Part I, Entry 2929

Part I, Entry 4875, Box 2

PP-4678, 1–757, and exhibits

Personal Collections

Boot Hill Museum, Dodge City, Kansas

Frank Baldwin Diary Transcript for Aug. 19–20, 1874, in "Adobe Walls" vertical file

Henry E. Huntington Library, San Marino, California

Diary of Lieutenant Frank Baldwin, Microfilm Roll #DIAZO

Kansas State Historical Society, Topeka, Kansas

George W. Baird Papers, 1874–1891

Library of Congress, Washington, D.C.

William T. Sherman Papers, Vol. 44.

Oklahoma Historical Society, Oklahoma City, Oklahoma

Central Superintendency, Letters Received by the Office of Indian Affairs, Microcopy No. 234, Roll 66

Panhandle-Plains Historical Museum and Archives, Canyon, Texas

J. W. McKinley Narrative

Thomas Gilcrease Institute of American History and Art, Tulsa, Oklahoma

General Ranald S. Mackenzie, Letterbook

University of Colorado Library, Boulder, Colorado

W. C. Brown Papers. Western Historical Collection, Lt. Frank Baldwin, "Baldwin Indian Territory Expedition, from His Own Diaries"

Newspapers

Army and Navy Journal

Vol. 12, July 25, 1874; Aug. 8, 1874; Aug. 22, 1874; Sept. 5, 1874; Sept. 17, 1874; Oct. 3, 1874; Oct. 31, 1874

Vol. 14, Aug. 26, 1878

Vol. 22, Sept. 26, 1885

Atchison Daily Champion, July 10, 1874

Canadian Record, Sept. 20, 1927

Leavenworth Times, Jan. 12, 1968

New York Herald, July 22, 1874; Sept. 26, 1874

New York Tribune, Oct. 7, 1874

Maps

"Part of Campaign Map of the Indian Territory and Texas," Map Files, Department Engineer, Southern Department, Fort Sam Houston, Texas, File No. 396.

"Map of Area between the Canadian and Washita Rivers," RG 393, Part I, E-2601, Box No. 41, NA.

Index

Figures and tables are indicated with *f* and *t*. All entries that begin with numerals, e.g., ".45-caliber," are found at the spelled-out form. "Cartridges" refers to fired and unfired ammunition.